Oedipus and the Devil

Early modern people drew the boundaries between body and soul differently. They had a lively sense of the interaction between supernatural power and the natural world. What did masculinity and femininity mean in a mental universe dominated by magic? What was the cultural impact of the Reformation and Counter-Reformation on this magical world and its images of gender? How were the boundaries between the rational and irrational drawn, and how did this affect the psychic life of men and women?

Oedipus and the Devil explores the psychological dimension of popular culture in early modern Europe. Based on detailed historical case studies, and using a combination of feminist theory and psychological analysis, the book explores sexual attitudes, masculinity and femininity, magic, concepts of excess, exorcism and witchcraft. Marking a shift away from the view that gender is a product of cultural and linguistic practice, the author argues that sexual difference has its own psychological and physiological reality, which is part of the very stuff of culture and must influence the way we write history.

This bold and imaginative book transforms our view of the relations between men and women, and marks out a new route towards understanding the body and its relationship to culture and subjectivity.

Lyndal Roper is Reader in History at Royal Holloway, University of London. Her last book was *The Holy Household: Women and morals in Reformation Augsburg* (1989). She was co-editor, with Jim Obelkevich and Raphael Samuel, of *Disciplines of Faith, Studies in Religion, Politics and Patriarchy* (1987).

Oedipus and the Devil

Witchcraft, sexuality and religion
in early modern Europe

Lyndal Roper

London and New York

First published 1994
by Routledge
11 New Fetter Lane, London EC4P 4EE

Simultaneously published in the USA and Canada
by Routledge
29 West 35th Street, New York, NY 10001

Reprinted 1995

© 1994 Lyndal Roper

Typeset in Palatino by
Intype, London
Printed and bound in Great Britain by
TJ Press (Padstow) Ltd, Padstow, Cornwall

British Library Cataloguing in Publication Data
A catalogue record for this book is available from the British Library

Library of Congress Cataloguing in Publication Data
A catalogue record for this book is available from the Library of Congress

ISBN 0-415-08894-1 (hbk)   ISBN 0-415-10581-1 (pbk)

Contents

Plates

Preface

I'm one of those people for whom writing can never be the result of solitary labours. Writing, for me, always comes out of conversation. I want to begin with an acknowledgement of all the many friends who have argued, talked, written letters, commented on papers, helped me to think and supported me. They have shaped this book.

The essays contained here were written between 1988 and 1992, in Germany and Britain. They were written with both a German- and an English-speaking audience in mind, and they arose out of the experiences and debates I lived through in both places. As an Australian, I come from a migrant culture. The tension between these two languages and different cultures has not always been comfortable, but it has constantly forced me to rethink, to question the point from which I start. And it has also brought me the pleasure of being at home in more than one place. I would like to acknowledge here especially the warmth, hospitality and openness which I have received from my German friends: they have given me more than I can say.

Institutions have generously supported my research. In particular, a year at the Wissenschaftskolleg in Berlin in 1991–2 allowed me the free space and time to try out ideas and explore themes I would not otherwise have had the courage to attempt. I should especially like to thank Etienne François, historian of Augsburg and much more, Amos Hetz, dancer and philosopher of movement, and Patrizia Pinotti, who taught me about so many things. Among others, Horst Bredekamp, Hinderk Emrich, Menachem Fisch, Ingrid Gilcher-Holtey, Michael Lackner, Larissa Lomnitz, Sigrid Metken, Lolle Nauta, Claudia Schmölders and Gabi Warburg at the Wissenschaftskolleg all changed the way I thought. The Deutscher Akademischer Austauschdienst financed a research trip in 1991, and the British Academy awarded me research grants which made it possible to carry out archival work. The History Department at Royal Holloway College, University of London, has been generous in supporting my research, not only in granting me leave of absence and sabbaticals, but in providing an intellectual environment which makes working life fun.

I should like to thank the librarians at the Wissenschaftskolleg in Berlin who were extraordinarily helpful, finding books and articles from the vaguest information, Herr Dr Wolfram Baer and the staff of the Stadtarchiv Augsburg, the staff of the Staats- und Stadtbibliothek Augsburg, the staff of the Staatsbibliothek München and especially Liselotte Renner, the staff of the Handschriftenabteilung in the Staatsbibliothek Berlin, Erika Kartschoke and the Berlin project 'Love and Marriage in the Sixteenth Century' at the Freie Universität Berlin and the staff of the British Library.

I should also like to thank Sally Alexander, Hans-Jürgen Bachorski, Ingrid Bátori, Judith Bennett, Willem de Blécourt, Guy Boanas, Wendy Bracewell, Roland Bracewell-Shoemaker, Alan Bray, Philip Broadhead, Alison Brown, Susanna Burghartz, Stuart Clark, Trish Crawford, Leonore Davidoff, Natalie Zemon Davis, Cyril Edwards, Hella Ehlers, Liz Fidlon, Laura Gowing, Annabel Gregory, Barbara Hahn, Karin Hausen, the *History Workshop Journal* Collective, Pia Holenstein, Olwen Hufton, Eva Hund, Michael Hunter, Lisa Jardine, Mark Jenner, Ludmilla Jordanova, Rolf Kiessling, Eva Labouvie, Yasmin Lakhi, Elisabeth Lintelo, Nils Minkmar, Maria E. Müller, Jinty Nelson, Alex Potts, the editors of *Radical History Review*, Jörg Rasche, Gareth Roberts, Bernd Roeck, Jörg Rogge, Ailsa Roper, Cath Roper, Stan Roper, Hans-Christoph Rublack, Ulinka Rublack, Raphael Samuel, Peter Schöttler, Regine Schulte, Beate Schuster, Peter Schuster, Gerd Schwerhoff, Bob Scribner, Pam Selwyn, Kathy Stuart, Anne Summers, Rosalind Thomas, Ann Tlusty, John Tosh, J.B. Trapp, Hans Wilhelm, Lore Wilhelm and Charles Zika.

In Germany, I should especially like to thank Michael Schröter, who drank vast numbers of cups of coffee with me and made me think, Peter Morgan, from whom I learnt so much about Germany now, Wolfgang Behringer, who is always finding witches for me, Heide Wunder, who has done so much to create feminist history in Germany, and Norbert Schindler, whose generous faith in the project helped make it possible for me to finish it. Natalie Zemon Davis read the book and is an inspiration. In Britain, Nick Stargardt proof-read the entire manuscript while telling me about the history of children, Lorna Hutson worked through the introduction and taught me to read early modern texts, Ruth Harris tirelessly commented on drafts and even pre-drafts – my intellectual debt to her is immense, Alison Light read everything and had the courage to tell me when it would not do (the test of real friendship), my brother Mike Roper cheerfully heard and read endless raves and papers – his work on masculinity has been a very great influence – and Barbara Taylor has acted as 'editor', giving me the confidence not only to keep going until I got it right, but to know when it was okay not to go further. Without her, without all of them, no book.

Acknowledgements

The author and publishers would like to thank the copyright holders below for their kind permission to reproduce the following material:

'Was there a crisis in gender relations in sixteenth-century Germany?', in Monika Hagenmaier and Sabine Holtz (eds), *Krisenbewusstsein und Krisenbewältigung in der Frühen Neuzeit. Festschrift für Hans-Christoph Rublack (Crisis in Early Modern Europe)*, Peter Lang 1992.

'Will and honour: sex, words and power in Reformation Augsburg', *Radical History Review*, 43, 1989, pp. 45–71.

'Sexual utopianism in the German Reformation', *Journal of Ecclesiastical History*, 42, no. 3, Cambridge University Press 1991, pp. 1–25.

'Blood and codpieces: masculinity in the early modern German town': an earlier version of this essay was published as 'Männlichkeit und männliche Ehre im 16. Jahrhundert', in Heide Wunder and Karin Hausen (eds), *Frauengeschichte-Geschlechtergeschichte*, Campus Verlag 1992.

'Magic and the theology of the body: exorcism in sixteenth-century Augsburg', was published in Charles Zika (ed.), *No Gods Except Me: Orthodoxy and religious practice in Europe 1200–1700*, The History Department, University of Melbourne.

'Witchcraft and fantasy in early modern Germany', *History Workshop Journal*, autumn 1991, by permission of Oxford University Press.

'Oedipus and the Devil': a German version of this essay was published in Andreas Blauert and Gerd Schwerhoff (eds), *Mit den Waffen der Justiz. Beiträge zur Kriminalitätsgeschichte des Spätmittelalters und der Frühen Neuzeit*, Frankfurt 1993.

1 Introduction

I

In 1686, Appolonia Mayr, a jilted servantwoman, confessed that she had murdered her newborn baby. The Devil had promised that if she killed her child, her lover would marry her. She had strangled the infant at a little hill beyond the Lech bridge, just before the small town of Friedberg. She still knew the place and could find it. There was a tree not far away and she had walked into the fields, and it was midday that it happened.[1] Describing the birth and murder, she said 'The Evil Spirit left her no peace. It was only a moment, the Devil touched it [the child] as if he were a midwife, it happened quite quickly that the child came out. She strangled it immediately with the hand, and she felt no pain in the delivery.'[2] Then Appolonia walked on: 'She left it lying quite naked, uncovered, and unburied. . . . The Devil did not go with her, but remained staying by the child, and she did not look back.'[3]

What do we make of such a cultural fragment? Here a woman is apparently committing infanticide as a kind of love magic, in a crazed and hopeless attempt to force her lover to marry her. Alone on the path between the fields and the village, she has walked beyond human habitation – the sole tree which marks the spot is the only distinguishing mark of the landscape. She bears the child without female assistance. The Devil acts as midwife, and it is he who remains standing over the child. Appolonia herself hardly acts at all – she barely strains to give birth, she leaves the child uncovered in the bushes and keeps on walking. All the more stark is her single deed: the strangling of her newborn child with her hand. Appolonia Mayr was burnt as a witch. She lived in a world in which the Devil was a character one might meet on any lonely pathway, who might whisper whom to kill, how to control others.

How does one understand such a world? There has been a long line of attempts to do so, from the judges who first interrogated such criminals, to the publishers of broadsheets who turned such horrible cases into entertainment, to the nineteenth-century practitioners of cultural history,[4] to historians of our own day. Then as now, much of this interest is animated by fascination with a foreign, yet familiar world. Such cases pose puzzles about our own identity, teasing us to specify in what the historical consists. They present us with a time which was apparently innocent of our notion of the person, when moral categories had a different shape, when the relation between the natural and supernatural was differently conceived. To analyse such a world, we have borrowed many tools. We have learnt from anthropology and from literary criticism to read our texts with an eye for symbol and ritual, to decipher kinship structures and, above all, to stress the otherness of early modern society.[5] Such an approach has enabled us to measure the distance which separates us from that other world, to make it 'historical' by reconstructing the collective nature of early modern society, viewing subjectivity itself as culturally constructed.

How will historical approaches based on these assumptions help us interpret Appolonia Mayr's story? One might see her as an exemplar of mid-Counter-Reformation womanhood, tormented by the sexual guilt imposed on her through Catholic re-education and social discipline. Her story about the Devil might be read as the hackneyed script which Baroque culture required women guilty of any female sin to recite. Like a good seventeenth-century Catholic, conscious – as historians would lead us to expect – of her religious confessional identity, Appolonia describes how she searched for 'Catholic people' in Augsburg at whose inn she might give birth.

But there is something which is deeper and more disturbing in her behaviour. When Appolonia returned to the city of Augsburg some months later, it was her demand to the Franciscan friars that they give her the baptismal certificate for her dead baby which set the whole case in train. In her first interrogation, Appolonia hotly denied having killed her baby, telling how 'nearly one hour after the birth she desired to see her child', only to be informed that it was already dead after having been taken to the Franciscans for baptism. The lost record of the infant's baptism – proof that it had eternal life – comes to stand for the loss of the child itself. As Appolonia put it, 'she just wanted to see her child again; she could not live thus any more'.[6] There is a suicidal desperation in her attempts to obtain the piece of paper: her search for it ensnared her in the web of bureaucracy which would inevitably uncover her crime and expose her tissue of lies about its death. This speaks not so much of confessional identity and sexual guilt – Appolonia made no secret of her pregnancy – as of the sheer agony of the loss of her baby, pain which is not the product of Counter-Reformation religiosity. The various, indeed inconsistent, accounts she offered of where and how she gave birth make the historian (and her interrogators) despair of ever uncovering the 'truth', but they may tell us other things.

Appolonia's fantasies about the Devil have little to do with ritual. They are so tangibly located and speak of such individual misery that it is inadequate to speak of collective beliefs and symbols. The process by which Appolonia came to describe her pain through talking about the Devil is far more complex than a mere recapitulation of cultural stereotypes. It is certainly true that the plausibility of her testimony to both her interrogators and herself depended on a shared belief in the powers of the Devil, but Appolonia created her own story about motherhood and guilt. And it was a story with its own sacrilegious, Marian inflection: as she told it first, she spoke of how, as a stranger, she asked to be taken in at an inn, and how she gave birth in a lonely room with a bed of straw.

It was stories such as that of Appolonia Mayr which first began to make me uneasy with the way I had been constructing the relationship between individual subjectivity and culture. In this book, I want to argue against an excessive emphasis on the cultural creation of subjectivity, and to argue that witchcraft and exorcism, those most alien of early modern social phenomena, or courtship and ritual, those seemingly irreducibly collective early modern social events, cannot be understood without reference to their psychic dimension. My claim is that early modern people had individual subjectivities, characterized by conflicts which are not entirely unfamiliar. I am not claiming that there is no historical gulf between our time and the early modern period: that would be absurd. But I want to suggest that the supposed gap between ourselves and the past, which we use to justify a particular way of dealing with that past world, is less complete than we sometimes suppose, and that the assumption of difference is not always a useful heuristic tool. Indeed, I think it has hampered our understanding of the complexity of early modern people as individuals.

This book has three implicit preoccupations: first, the importance of the irrational and the unconscious in history; second, the importance of the body; and third, the relation of these two to sexual difference. The subjects with which it deals are the nature of masculinity and femininity, the cultural impact of the Reformation and Counter-Reformation and the central role of magic and witchcraft in the psychic and emotional world of the early modern period and in what we take to be 'rationality'. These chapters document a shift on my part away from the conviction that gender is a product of cultural and linguistic practice, towards the view that sexual difference has its own physiological and psychological reality, and that recognition of this must affect the way we write history. The task with which I have been engaged is how to write a cultural history of early modern Germany in which sexual difference will not just be added on as an afterthought, a further variable, but will be genuinely incorporated. This means that courtship, the history of motherhood, witchcraft, possession and masculinity – all fields in which gender is at issue, and where the relation of psyche and body are at stake – are central cultural areas. It means that, far from being an incidental matter, sexual difference, both as physiological and psychological fact and as social construction, is part of the very stuff of culture. This consequence is still only haltingly acknowledged in early modern cultural history, which largely continues to treat the issue of gender as if it were a question of women's participation – or lack of it – in popular and élite culture.

Yet, central as I believe sexual difference is to conceiving of culture, I found I could no longer simply apply the tools which I had acquired from feminist history to the study of early modern Europe. As I shall go on to argue, along with other feminists writing now, I have come to think that feminist history, as I and others used to practise it, rested on a denial of the body. These chapters represent an attempt – often not fully articulated – to think out a different route towards understanding the body, culture and subjectivity.

II

For historians, the problem of subjectivity in the past has primarily presented itself as a question of explaining how large movements of historical transformation (the rise of capitalism, the Reformation, the development of the state) altered individuals' self-perceptions. Here, the work of the sociologists Max Weber and, later, Norbert Elias has been deeply influential, particularly among those who study Europe in the period 1500 to 1800. Weber's *The Protestant Ethic and the Spirit of Capitalism*[7] still shapes the way we see the early modern period, even as historians dispute its empirical detail. We owe to Weber the vision that the changes connected with the rise of Protestantism were linked with the origins of capitalism because these transformations valued new qualities in lay people, promoting the rational, calculating, disciplined individual, a kind of person who could cope with the regimen of the market. Luther's doctrine of the 'calling' was new because of its 'valuation of the fulfilment of duty in worldly affairs as the highest form which the moral activity of the individual could assume', giving 'everyday worldly activity a religious significance'.[8] 'Rational conduct on the basis of the idea of the calling'[9] was thus born of Protestant asceticism. Norbert Elias's work offers the prospect of linking psychoanalytic insight with historically informed sociology.[10] As his ideas have been taken up by historians of the early modern period, they have tried to show how such abstract, general historical transitions as the Reformation and Counter-Reformation, or the growth of bureaucracy and the state, had effects not only on politics but on those much less tangible dimensions of human history, the constitution of human subjects themselves, their emotions, perceptions, behaviour and even their gestures. And recently, in a powerful philosophical synthesis, Charles Taylor has argued that the origins of the modern western sense of individualism and identity are to be located in the rise of what he terms 'inwardness' in the wake of the Protestant Reformation. This was accompanied by a move away from an older, magical world-view in which the boundaries between oneself and the natural world were essentially permeable. As he puts it, 'Disenchantment was driven by and connected with a new moral/spiritual stance to the world. . . . It was connected to a new piety, and what we see emerging is a new notion of freedom and inwardness, which this piety fostered.' By contrast:

> The decline of the world-view underlying magic was the obverse of the rise of the new sense of freedom and self-possession. From the viewpoint of this new sense of self, the world of magic seems to entail a thraldom, an imprisoning of the self in uncanny external forces, even a ravishing or loss of self. It threatens a possession which is the very opposite of self-possession.[11]

Such syntheses have the merit of opening up new areas of human experience to historical investigation. However, illuminating as these accounts of the relation between historical change and psychology are, I want to argue that they are based on a problematic account of subjectivity, and that when historians draw upon Elias or Weber, we run the risk of schematizing the experience of historical subjects. Following Weber, the early modern period is often held to see the birth of the ideal of the rational, economic man, or, as Taylor might put it, of the rise of a new sense of 'self-possession', of individual identity. But, as the challenge of psychoanalysis to models of rational behaviour might suggest, human behaviour is not solely determined by conscious consideration, and identity is not a secure possession but a piecemeal process of identifications and separations. So far from ushering in the birth of the rational ascetic individual, the early modern period saw a renewed interest in magic and the irrational, and this is a central component of the subjectivity which we now like to view as 'rational' or 'modern'. Magic and the irrational are integral to it, and not mere teething problems concomitant with a 'crisis arising in the transition between identities'.[12] Our own attachment to the story of the rise of individualism and rationality is, I think, part of the reason that we so often associate the witch-craze with the intolerance and so-called irrationality of the middle ages, even while we know that witch-hunting was an early modern, not a medieval phenomenon.[13] As such, its history belongs to our own era.

Elias's narrative of the rise of civilization seems at first to offer greater respect to the irrational and to those areas of human experience which elude the familiar categorizations of historical narrative. And his work has indeed been enormously fruitful for historians of early modern Europe.[14] Elias presents an account of the rise of *civilité*, the progressive disciplining of the unruly body, a curbing of natural human drives, and shows how these processes are linked to social and political change. The human being learns to control the natural functions through the fabric of manners, while 'society is gradually beginning to suppress the positive pleasure component in certain functions more and more strongly by the arousal of anxiety'.[15] During the sixteenth century, Elias argues, people of the aristocracy gradually acquired a new set of manners and began to hedge their natural drives about with social taboos and inner discipline, a process which was mimicked by their social inferiors. The court society of Louis XIV saw the culmination of this discipline of the body, which was a crucial component of the development of absolutism:

> During the stage of the court aristocracy, the restraint imposed on inclinations and emotions is based primarily on consideration and respect due to others and above all to social superiors. In the subsequent stage, renunciation and restraint of impulses is compelled far less by particular persons; expressed provisionally and approximately, it is now, more directly than before, the less visible and more impersonal compulsions of social interdependence, the division of labour, the market, and competition that impose restraint and control on the impulses and emotions.[16]

This is a conception of human psychology strongly influenced by early Freudianism, with its emphasis on the power of the drives.[17]

Elias's debt to psychoanalysis, however, has taken a particular form. In his work, the psychic is seen to be socially variable and historically contingent, since there is a 'connection between social structure and personality structure'.[18] The organization and balance of the different elements within the psyche is not held to be universal nor ahistorical. Thus Elias claims that in the later middle ages control over the drives was less assured: it was a world in which 'people gave way to drives and feelings incomparably more easily, quickly, spontaneously, and openly than today, in which the emotions were less restrained and, as a consequence, less evenly regulated and more liable to oscillate more violently between extremes', so that their 'drive controls' 'were not of the same degree as in later periods, and they did not take the form of a constant, even almost automatic self-control'.[19] Indeed, 'because emotions are here expressed in a manner that in our own world is generally observed only in children, we call these expressions and forms of behaviour "childish" '.[20] Throughout his work, civilization is counterposed to instinct, and the body is conceived as an anarchic collection of drives which civilization, even in its most 'advanced' form, keeps under tenuous control. In much historical writing influenced by Elias, this view of the period before the rise of the bourgeois, disciplined individual finds its counterpart in a picture of the free, undisciplined culture of pre-

Reformation carnival, a vision which owes much to the work of the Russian cultural theorist Bakhtin on the writings of Rabelais.[21]

As a result, it becomes possible for historians to employ theory which historicizes the unconscious while at the same time paradoxically evading the challenge that psychoanalysis poses to a traditional historical perspective. (Similarly, when historians write about the history of gesture, clothing or cleaning, they appear to be writing about the body but are actually often writing about discourse about the body; an important subject in itself, but, as I shall argue below, one whose formulation as discourse precisely takes the sting out of the problem of subjectivity as both a corporeal and psychic phenomenon.) Despite its radical potential, this psychoanalytic incorporation of the irrational, derived as it is from Elias and others, is essentially Weberian in form: it harnesses the rise of the modern subject to the rise of the rational, the 'adult', tying subjectivity to the rise of the modern. For Charles Taylor, it is also the 'disenchantment of the world', the loss of the magical world-view, which is the precondition for the rise of the sense of self as we know it in the modern world.[22]

In the historical common sense which has developed around this issue, there is a simple transparency about the move from a rowdy, carnival, Bakhtinian culture to a modest organization of the disciplined person: historical transformations occur, and individual subjectivity follows suit. But it is far from clear that this is the appropriate way to conceive of how social change interacts with individual subjectivity. When, for instance, we can identify a movement of moral reform or a project of disciplining, this does not tell us what its effects may be on the psyche or the body it is meant to historicize. As the French theorist Michel Foucault has taught us, such movements may undermine rather than bolster the values they uphold. A different deployment of psychoanalysis would enable us to see the dynamic between repression and libido as crucial to the modest comportment of the bourgeois citizen. At the same time, the licence of the Bakhtinian subject has its own superego formations. The Rabelaisian literature which, translated by the Calvinist Johann Fischart, became such an important part of sixteenth-century German writing, cannot be understood as pure carnival. It is a product of Latinate, literate, moralist culture. The carnivalesque is not a survival of an older, more libidinous, rustic era, caught in Fischart's writing like a fly in amber. Or, as Horst Bredekamp has shown, when fifteenth-century Florentine followers of Savonarola burnt images on the carnival bonfire of vanities, repudiating a society they believed to be a political tyranny, their own moralist destruction of art itself took on the character of a fetish.[23]

This becomes particularly apparent if we think about repression itself, the notion so fundamental to historical work based loosely on Elias's psychological theory. It would be possible to view discipline ordinances as a gigantic project of repression, and, indeed, this is largely how they have been viewed. Protestants, so this line of argument might run, became 'confessionalized' as prostitution was banned, dancing cleaned up, rowdy behaviour brought under control and the family learnt to pray together. Sexual modesty increased and sexual behaviour became more subject to restraint. Making rules, however, does not guarantee conformity. Behavioural prohibitions, as Foucault has stressed, can create, even in their advocates, their own compulsions and transgressive possibilities. When Protestant divines preached vigorously against the evil of dancing and fulminated against the erotic temptations of touch in dance, their ornate rhetoric also helped to sexualize what they termed 'venereal dancing'. Instead of seeing repression as a simple imposition of control, we need to see it as an active part of the formation of sexual identities. The unconscious is not a kind of inefficient psychic sewer for negative urges, which eventually fills up and starts to pollute the clean upper reaches of the mind. We need rather to employ a dynamic model of the unconscious – the vision which can also be found in Freud's mature work – so that we can see the constant interaction between desire and prohibition.[24]

The underlying difficulty here is that neither Weber nor Elias offers a satisfactory explanation of the way social change affects individual psyche. Indeed, we still lack such a theory. In the meantime, as historians, we often write as if social change impinges directly and uniformly upon the individual's mental structure, as if the psyche were a kind of blank sheet for social processes to write upon. This is partly why sexual, racial or class differences are not the key dialectic in Elias's work – changes tend to trickle down from the upper to the lower classes and popular culture lacks dynamic – and why the state shoulders such a weight in historical explanations influenced by Elias's ideas. Changes in the structure of the state become the explanatory black box, the reasons for changes in manners, social comportment, even perception. Ironically, such history restores the primacy of the political to historical explanation, precisely at the moment when social and cultural history are seeking to establish their independent legitimacy.[25] And the political history on which it draws is often based on the old abstractions such as 'absolutism' which current revisionist historians are increasingly jettisoning. At the same time, historical work which attempts to deal with subjectivity finds it hard to allow space for the irrational or for fantasy in the subject: if for no other reason, the illogic of the unconscious offends against our own sense of what makes for rationally persuasive, satisfying explanation. A rationalist account of subjectivity can only be partial; yet the imperative of historical synthesis pushes us to simplify, to present the conscious rationalizations of the subject, or to produce a clear, sketch-map psychology in which the logic of political change provides the contours of narrative.[26]

The dilemma is not Elias's alone. Any use of a psychoanalytically-influenced theory faces the difficulty of how to apply to an entire society a model which is designed to uncover the unconscious mental processes of an individual. This is why psychoanalytic insights have fared better in biography.[27] Whereas psychoanalysis can show the infinitely varied, imaginative use individuals can make of the materials of their predicaments, creating their own symbolic language and symptoms,[28] psychogenetics of the Elias type proposes a historical, but identikit kind of psychology in which individual psychic creativity has little place. A historically useful application of psychoanalysis, however, must allow for individual agency and the possibility that individuals can think and feel against the social grain – a goal that is easier to specify than to achieve.

III

So far, we have considered how approaches influenced by Elias and Weber have dominated the way subjectivity is conceptualized for the early modern period. But there are other traditions which have also dealt with the issue of the historical formation of subjectivity, taking their cue from post-structuralist discussion of the death of the subject. The work of the French thinker Michel Foucault, with its emphasis on the power of language and the importance of discourse in the constitution of the individual subject, has proved enormously influential.[29] It has enabled us to explore the construction of sexual desire through language, broadly interpreted, and it has opened the way to a far more sophisticated and varied understanding of the body and sexuality.[30] For historians of the sixteenth and seventeenth centuries, however, Foucault's work places them in something of a quandary. Foucault, whose project was a pessimistic re-evaluation of the rationalist legacy of the Enlightenment, locates the major historical transitions in the eighteenth century.[31] But the ambivalent effects of sexual regulation about which Foucault wrote so persuasively can be dated well back before the eighteenth century. As a result, writers who are influenced by Foucault but whose period is the early modern era use methods adopted from Foucault while frequently resting their narrative on a historical scheme which is borrowed from Elias.

Even among approaches which attempt to question theories of the subject based loosely on Weber or Elias, however, and which turn instead to a creatively eclectic use of anthropology or to discourse theory, the concept of subjectivity with which we are presented is often a determinedly collective one. This collective subjectivity is then inscribed on the individual. Consequently, the dimension of the psychic is missing here, as, indeed, it is in the work of Foucault. Some of the appeal of, for instance, Natalie Zemon Davis's *The Return of Martin*

Guerre is the way it teases us with the possibility that the imposter Arnaud du Tilh might indeed have succeeded in passing himself off as Martin Guerre had not the 'real Martin' unexpectedly returned from the wars: in what more, then, does identity consist than in the sum of the collective testimonies and expectations of the villagers?[32] Or in Robert Darnton's *The Great Cat Massacre*, where it is the world of the journeymen we are asked to enter, their consciousness is a group product; strangely enough, one which can be read, not from what they say, but from a literary product of one of their number. As Harold Mah has argued, the semi-fictionalized autobiography of Nicolas Contat on which Darnton draws for his description of symbolic life in the printers' workshop is a highly literary production, structured around neat narrative reversals.[33]

In a similar vein, I think the current fascination with the history of perception – of time, of the senses, of the materiality of daily life – both further strengthens us in the conviction of the absolute otherness of the past, and allows us, when we think about the consciousness of early modern people, to substitute the level of immediate sensory perception for that of the psyche. It is as if, once we grasp that early modern people heard and smelt things differently, or inhabited a 'visual culture' (as we do not?), we know what makes them different from ourselves. There is a host of current German syntheses of early modern 'daily life', a genre which is almost totally absent from Anglo-American historiography, in which the culture of the 'little people' is presented by means of analysis of popular ritual and festival.[34] These constitute attempts to restore the common people to history, and to burst the bounds of what we term culture: to write about weddings and carnival, gossip and slander, attitudes to time and the calendar instead of the 'high' culture of the élite alone. This has immeasurably enhanced our understanding of early modern culture and has helped us imaginatively to recreate the sensory as well as the discursive, and to think about the detail of early modern life, the objects people used, the habits of their daily lives.[35] But so far as people's psychic lives are concerned, there is a danger that such studies may present a cast of rustic characters whose simple mental lives are all the same, a history where the sensory substitutes for the psychic and, with it, a history which, despite its ambition, sometimes serves to reinvoke the historical condescension towards *das Volk*, the common people.

In much of the writing influenced by Foucault, by contrast, which does claim an interest in the individual and the atypical, psychoanalysis is viewed as yet another regulatory narrative, a discourse produced by a particular concatenation of late nineteenth-century developments which constituted yet another deployment of power through a new fascination with sex. The conviction that psychoanalysis could not therefore have anything to say about a pre-Freudian world has been very strong in

early modern history.[36] Even when psychoanalysis is drawn upon
to dredge the murkier waters of Renaissance writing, a post-
structuralist-tinged conviction of the death of the subject is used to
guarantee historicity. So, subjectivity, in Stephen Greenblatt's work, rests
on articulation. In Greenblatt's view, language is not the medium of the
self but is its fabric, and language's permeability to convention and
power is the prism of the way in which the self can never be free.[37] In
a brilliant article, Greenblatt argues that psychoanalysis proposes at
some level a notion of the self which is simply foreign to Renaissance
culture, and, in consequence, psychoanalysis itself testifies to the distance which separates us from early modern understandings of the
self.[38] In other words, we know that we are dealing with early modern,
historical subjects because they do not evince a concept of the individual
– this is what their historical distance consists of – and yet it is the post-
structuralist critique of the subject and of psychoanalysis which is drawn
upon to read our evidence in this manner.

Indeed, this is the supposed location of the early modern world's
otherness: its characteristic cultural collectivity and the absence of the
concept of the individual self. Symbols, rituals, collective corporations
– these are the early modern historian's stock in trade. The use of
anthropology, which allows us to stress the exoticism of this society,
enables us, oddly enough, both rationally to grasp the otherness of this
world, while furnishing us with a written guarantee of the modernity
of our own time. There is of course a circular argument here. The means
we use to interpret the society also allow us to shunt off all that puzzles
us about early modern society into the realm of the 'pre-modern'
while using the very concept of the peculiarity of the early modern
to deny the usefulness of psychic categories. As a result, early
modern people can threaten to become dancing marionettes, tricked out
in ruffs and codpieces, whose subjectivities can neither surprise nor
unsettle.

At the same time, the literary turn creates particular problems for
cultural history. It is striking that Greenblatt in *Renaissance Self-
Fashioning*, one of the roundest portraits we have of early modern subjectivity, should find it possible to write only about men – a strategy into
which he is forced by his understanding of self-identity as consisting of
what can be expressed in one's own written words. But early modern
Europe was still an oral culture, a culture which, as the work of Norbert
Schindler shows, offered peasants, beggars and vagabonds a host of
complex forms of expression and cultural creativity. In an extraordinary
essay on nicknames, Schindler is able to bring to life the merciless
inventiveness of oral culture's creation of public personae; in a reconstruction of the mental world of Salzburg boy beggars accused of witchcraft, he shows how the impossible longings of one boy were expressed

in his fantasies of a *Zauberer-Jackl* who would fulfil his deepest wishes, teaching him to read, write and shoot.[39]

The literary, moreover, was predominantly a male culture. Even when, for instance, we try to reconstruct the mental world of the peasant woman Bertrande de Rols, wife of Martin Guerre, we are actually reliant upon the text of the male lawyer Jean de Coras who chose to write about the case. It is his wry, sophisticated reflections on certainty and the nature of wifely fidelity which ultimately prove more riveting and more nuanced than the subjectivity of the inscrutable Bertrande. Despite all our intentions, the feminine is once again of interest in so far as it illumines what men thought about it.[40]

Considerations about the distinctively collective nature of early modern culture, and the foreignness to it of our notion of the person, go some way, I think, towards explaining the particular reluctance early modern historians have expressed towards using psychoanalysis more directly. Psychoanalysis, it is often argued, is a product of the nineteenth century, a world characterized by the nuclear family of the Viennese upper middle class. But the claim is stronger than simply the recent origins of the theory: it is that 'family' as we now know it, the unconscious and individuality are so radically different that this precludes the use of psychoanalytic categories altogether. Consequently, the claim that psychoanalysis cannot be used to study early modern societies reaches to the very heart of what makes the study of early modern Europe distinctive. It touches the constitution of our field itself. It concerns the extent of historical change, the concept of the subject, the role of religion and ritual; in short, the justification for our rejection of terms such as 'family' and 'individual' to apply to the early modern world. In these essays, by contrast, these are precisely the terms I have found myself drawn to use in order to approach an understanding of early modern people which does more than treat them as colourful pyschic primitives from a carnival world; which takes individual subjectivity seriously enough to be able to pose the difficult question of what, precisely, is historical in subjectivity.

In this sense, the project of this book is somewhat different from the ways in which psychoanalysis has more often been used. Where psychoanalysis is deployed in discursive analyses within history, the relationship is more often a flirtation than a marriage. Linguistic analysis is combined with psychoanalytic insight to support a view of human personality as intrinsically contingent, changing as language changes. The problem with this account is that there is no compelling explanation in psychological terms as to why these contingent changes should take the form they do: the explanatory claims of psychoanalysis are simply set aside. By contrast, from the moment of its own original self-understanding as a science, psychoanalysis claimed to offer a universal account of human psychological functioning. It thus seems inimical to any historical account of subjectivity.

Let me summarize the dilemma which seems to confront us. On the one hand, psychoanalysis is itself an antique, a historical creation of the nineteenth century. On the other, psychoanalysis makes universalist claims about human psychological functioning which seem irreconcilable with the study of history. However, I think we simply need to refuse this apparent dilemma. All theories have their histories, and psychoanalysis, like Marxism, another child of the nineteenth century, is constantly changing. It does not endanger the status of the historical to concede that there are aspects of human nature which are enduring, just as there are aspects of human physiology which are constitutional.[41] The hard part – as much a subject of debate within psychoanalysis itself – is to specify what precisely is historical about subjectivity. What I want to avoid is a developmental account of collective subjectivities which turns individuals into mere exemplars of a narrative of collective historical progression. What sets this project apart from many of the uses which have been made of psychoanalysis is that I want to take the explanatory claims of psychoanalysis seriously, so that it provides a way of accounting for meaningful behaviour and individual subjectivity in particular historical circumstances.

IV

For many historians, feminists and non-feminists alike, 'gender' was the category through which it looked as if women's history might have the potential not only to enter history as a respectable historical field, but to reshape the historical narratives themselves. The axiom that gender identity was not a biological given but a historical creation was immensely liberating: the historian's task was to lay bare the precise historical meaning of masculinity and femininity in the past, thus relativizing the content of these constructs in the present. We were able to show, for instance, that early modern men delighted in fashion and clothes, that medieval women were to be found working in practically all sectors of the economy, that motherhood, when infants were sent to wet-nurses, must have constituted a different bond from the relationship we know today.

At the same time, the anthropology of early modern societies cried out for some incorporation of a female perspective. One only has to turn to a classic text such as Clifford Geertz's analysis of the Balinese cockfight to be confronted with the absence of women from the cultural theatre.[42] Partly because discourse theory, psychoanalytic ideas about masculinity and anthropology are woven together into an apparently seamless whole, women's restriction to walk-on parts gives us more of a jolt. Most accounts of popular culture are actually about men's culture, often about courtship ritual in another guise. The rage to which this kind of exclusion gives rise – the worse because it is a true mirror of the society which produced this culture – has led to some powerful feminist work of reconstruction. It has also enabled feminists to insist on a cultural anthropology which will include women. But how is this to be done?

The problem here is very deep and its origins lie within cultural history itself. Because cultural history traditionally sought to create a unified object of study for itself, it naturally inclined to see culture as uniform within a particular bounded group and as shared. This is as true of Sebastian Franck's wonderful sixteenth-century ethnography of regional identity[43] as it is of the work of the great nineteenth-century cultural historians and sociologists. It is no accident that *Gemeinschaft*, that hardly translatable term of shared cultural and communal identity, should have been such a crucial term for German nineteenth-century attempts to grasp pre-modern societies, just as the equally elusive sixteenth-century term, *Gemeinde*, ambiguous between church congregation, communal unit and group of subjects, was to prove such a powerful mobilizing term in the Peasants' War.[44] But nearly always, the leading ideas of this shared culture are those of men. The terms on which women have access to this culture are either as a cultural resource or else as creators of a separate, female culture. This latter view, however, undermines the idea of culture – or indeed of language – as a unified whole, and challenges the terms on which the project of cultural history might be possible.

When the so-called new cultural history broke with the idea of linear narratives, disrupting the unity of culture, it seemed to offer a new space for feminist history. If our cultural heritage was necessarily fragmented, if the fiction of a unified culture could be surrendered, then women were guaranteed a voice in the story. (Paradoxically, in fact, some of even the new cultural history does rely in the end on a unity of culture, based on the shared nature of language: a solution which simply replicates the problem of women's relation to culture at another, more intractable level.)[45] For feminist historians, the lure of cultural anthropology and discourse theory was its organizing power. If gender was created through discourse, or through social behaviour and interaction, the substance of sexual difference was historical – and therefore, it was something we could change. Gender as a concept consequently seemed to offer a way of giving feminists access both to anthropological history and to discourse history. Joan Scott's 1985 article resoundingly affirmed not only that gender *was* a historical category but that it was a category of historical analysis.[46] Deconstruction allowed feminists to juggle with the reversals and inversions, hidden meanings and endless contradictions of sexual difference – as if sexual difference were no longer a prison from which one could not escape but an ethereal substance, an endless play of light and shadow in which the intellect could delight.

Applied historically, however, deconstruction has the tendency to reproduce its own tricks and paradoxes. The contradictions of femininity in sixteenth-century Germany bear an uncanny resemblance to those of twentieth-century Britain. Indeed, Scott herself remains tantalizingly vague about the sense in which gender *is* a historical category. For while we have learnt to discern the effects of gender in politics, war and business history – all the historical territories which historians once used to believe to be the preserve of real male history – what remains less clear is how gender itself effects historical change. Instead, we borrow from the state- and class-based narratives of historical transformation, leaving it vague what causal difference gender makes. Gender appears more often to be a matter of key, transposing the old familiar historical songs into soprano or bass registers: the tunes, however, remain the same.

If gender is to be a category of social explanation, it must bridge the gap between discourse, social formation and the individual sexed subject.[47] Just as cultural anthropological approaches and discourse theory seemed, in the end, to offer a somewhat flat account of subjectivity, so also, feminist history, because of its symbiotic critical relationship with these intellectual developments, remained caught in the limitations of the terms it criticized. In the final analysis, gender, for all its splendid play of discursive variegation, remains a category whose content proves elusive, and whose causal claims are a cypher.

Recently, feminist writers, too, have rejected the comfortable orthodoxy of the distinction between sex and gender.[48] Judith Butler has pointed out that the sex/gender distinction naturalizes sex, itself the product of culture, while reinstating the very binary distinction between nature and culture which we need to question.[49] This move robs historians of the sociological tools we once used to present sexual identity as a historical and social product. It turns out that the part of sexual identity which could once be neatly isolated as social creation, distinct from the 'givenness' of biological sex, reveals itself to be no more a creation than sex itself. 'Gender' as a sociological category is an illusion created by the terms of its own delimitation.

Yet history has not been done out of a job by post-modernism. Ironically, history and historians are very important to post-structuralist sceptics. For if sex, the person and sexual identities are contingent creations, not just at the level of detail, but as ontological categories, then it becomes crucial that there be 'other worlds' in which these categories did not organize experience. History seems to offer both such other possible worlds and an account of how we came by the categories with which we now live. Butler's demolition of 'sex' and 'person' proceeds by demonstrating the contingency of those very categories and their embeddedness in the binary divisions they seek to critique. But it is an irony of her position that she introduces the very same pattern at the historical level, as she aims to 'expose the contingent acts that create the appearance of a naturalistic necessity'.[50] There is an implicit historical 'before' and 'after', defined by the presence or absence of the binary oppositions her argument reifies; the moment *before* 'the category of "women", the subject of feminism, is produced and restrained by the very structures of power through which emancipation is sought'.[51] Historians, who are equally complicit in the search for grand moments of transformation around which to create narrative suspense – how, after all, do you organize a gripping history of emotion if you have no historical epochs around which to group your chapters? – then often reach for the chestnuts: it must be the Renaissance, the Reformation or Absolutism which explains change. The problem with this kind of work is that too much is made to follow from the historical. That a distinction looks different in different historical periods does not show that it is entirely contingent. History itself plays too great and yet too little a role in this kind of work: too much, because an overemphasis is placed on the degree to which human beings change; too little, because the stress on discursive creation oversimplifies subjectivities and foreshortens the range and complexity of historical determinants.

Surrendering the distinction between sex and gender has certainly brought gains. There have been explorations of the history of biological sex itself. Thomas Laqueur has argued that until the eighteenth century, a one-sex model of the body predominated in which sexual difference was a matter of degree, not of two distinct sexes.[52] This is a powerful synthesis, which challenges our most basic assumptions about the naturalness of sexual distinction. Yet what Laqueur is actually describing is the discourse of medical theory. It is not apparent that it was by means of such theory that early modern people understood their bodies. Rather, their culture rested on a very deep apprehension of sexual difference as an organizing principle of culture – in religion, work, magic and ritual. It is a far easier task to investigate literate discourse on sexual difference than it is to get at the way early modern people actually conceived of sexual difference, because such structures are not fully conscious, and cannot be articulated with the same transparency as medical theory. Randolph Trumbach has argued for the rapidly shifting nature of the relation between the categories of sex and gender: eighteenth-century Londoners, he claims, had a model of three sexes – man, woman, hermaphrodite – and three genders, the third 'illegitimate gender' being 'the adult passive transvestite effeminate male or molly who was supposed to desire men exclusively'. By the late nineteenth century there were two sexes and four gender roles, 'man, woman, homosexual man, and lesbian woman'.[53] In much of this writing, sexual identity becomes a kind of masquerade for which the early modern period is the theatre; as if to have a sexual identity in early modern Europe was to participate in a permanent cross-dressing party. Indeed, by a curious sleight of hand, cross-dressers and transsexuals are often the examples to which historians turn when they consider the problem of individual subjectivity in general in early modern Europe.[54]

The challenge of the history of the body to discourse theory is that it confronts discursive creationism with the physical, with a reality that is only in part a matter of words. So, for instance, while Londa Schiebinger's fascinating account of the development of the science of anatomy in the eighteenth century is able to show how gendered notions became written into perceptions of skeletal difference, one wonders naggingly whether there may not actually be differences between the skeletons of the two sexes which are not a creation of eighteenth-century science.[55] It is of course true that we experience the body through mediations of various kinds, and, because we want to emphasize the way notions of the body are constructed, the temptation is to write as if there were nothing *but* a historically constructed body. Our own terminology does not help: 'the body', after all, is itself an irritatingly non-physical abstraction.

Sexual difference is not purely discursive nor merely social. It is also physical. The cost of the flight from the body and from sexual difference is evident in what much feminist historical writing has found it impossible to speak about; or indeed, in the passionate tone of the theoretical work which most insists on the radically constructed nature of sexual difference. In my own work, this gap is most evident in the oldest of these essays, on will and honour. It is an essay about the social construction of gender through language and social practice – but its sources tell another story about the pain and pleasure of love. At its heart there is an absence: bodies. How indeed can there be a history of sex which is purely about language and which omits bodies?

I do not think I was untypical in seeking to escape femininity by a flight from the body and a retreat to the rational reaches of discourse. The pain, the frustration and the rage of belonging to the sex which does not even yet have its own history, and which is so often in the role of outsider in any intellectual context, make it tempting to deny sexual difference altogether – or to attempt to design one's sexual identity in any way one chooses. This is a wild utopianism. As Barbara Taylor has shown, it has its roots in the very beginnings of feminism, in the passionately ambivalent, even misogynist rhetoric of Mary Wollstonecraft, for example, about the failings of 'systematically voluptuous' women.[56] It is also a deeply creative force. It has enabled both men and women to envisage new ways of organizing relations between the sexes, and new fields of action for women and for men. Yet when utopianism becomes intellectual, and loses its imaginative relation to the givenness of bodies, it does so at great cost. We need an understanding of sexual difference which will incorporate, not fight against, the corporeal.

V

These concerns are preoccupations of our own time; indeed, of a very particular moment in the history of feminism when we have had to part with some illusions about what can be made anew. But they are also issues with which early modern people were passionately engaged. The Reformation, as I have argued elsewhere, drew much of its strength from its moralizing redeployment of an older, household-based utopianism, which had clearly defined roles for men and women, old and young.[57] By allowing and encouraging clergy to marry and form their own households, Protestants put the issue of the body firmly on the agenda. Was holiness incompatible with sexual expression? If the body were God's creation, what sin attached to sex within marriage? What were the distinct offices of men and women?

The first generation of reformers faced the question of the difference between the sexes in their daily lives, with little help from their libraries to make sense of what it was to be a married priest. It was not that clerics had not lived with women or were not infamous as womanizers, quite the reverse. But marriage meant that the first generation of Protestant clergy had to reach a conscious, articulated accommodation with sexual difference, shaped no longer by the ideal of a single-sex monastic community. Consequently, sexual difference emerged as an explicit theme in their conversation and writing, and sometimes in a disarmingly concrete sense of the disturbance that living with the opposite sex entails, as when Luther describes the shock of seeing a pair of plaits in bed beside him.[58] Sexual difference was, of course, anything but a new intellectual theme, but Protestant clergy had to develop a literature about marriage and womanhood which did more than align women with Eve and sexual temptation. The public estate of matrimony necessitated an accommodation with sexual difference – difficult as the monastic heritage of sexual suspicion was to overcome, and much as it still cast its shadow over what they wrote.

In what did sexual difference consist? It would be tempting to dismiss Luther's views on women as little more than the rantings of a particularly rabid patriarch, and regard Protestantism as the heir of his rigid sexual conservatism. But this would be to miss the peculiar tone of early Protestant understandings of sexual difference and the body, and to fail to catch its utopianism. For Luther, whose earthy rhetoric still has the power to take one's breath away, sexual difference was material, the stuff of the body itself. So he says, in a passage which earns its place in every anthology of misogyny, that

Men have broad shoulders and narrow hips, and accordingly they possess intelligence. Women ought to stay at home; the way they were created indicates this, for they have broad hips and a wide fundament to sit upon, keep house and bear and raise children.[59]

Sexual difference is natural fact, God's creation, and it dictates female fate: one follows from the other so directly that there is no intervening symbolic realm. Woman and house belong together not as metaphor but as fact. For Luther, the substance of womanhood was maternity, an equation so powerful that as early as 1520 he proposed that a woman whose husband could not give her children should have the right to sleep with another.[60] The same collapsing of femaleness and maternity is evident in his homily that women who die in childbirth are saved: 'Let them bear children to death; they are created for that.'[61] What Luther is doing here is reclaiming the process of birth from the realm of the powers of darkness and evil, arguing against the idea that women giving birth were under the power of the Devil and that if they died giving birth, should not be buried in consecrated ground.[62] By pulling all aspects of female existence into the light of the Protestant idea of the calling, Luther linked fate, corporeal difference and creation to form a powerful, materialist vision of sexual difference.

This is important because Luther and other sixteenth-century thinkers, radicals and orthodox, were working within a different intellectual framework while dealing with issues which are still very much our own concerns. We may be able to think these through differently if we allow ourselves to be surprised by what Luther, Catholic exorcists or radical Anabaptists – who all understood the relation between body and soul differently – had to say. Recovering sixteenth-century thought should not consist in castigating Luther for his misogynist errors. The heritages which after all have shaped us deserve more than correction and dismissal, for to do so would be to fail to take our own past sufficiently seriously.

But a history which analysed Luther's thought alone – or indeed, that of the first generation of reformers – would be far from providing a gendered cultural map of early modern Germany. One of the heuristic axioms that feminist history has made part of our methodology is always to ask: how did women see this? But when we pose this question in an oral culture, where the written sources we have are nearly always by men, we draw a blank. If we work only with these sources, gender history threatens to become a reinterpretation of the thought of powerful thinkers, a history of ideas read against the grain, to be sure, but a history that reinstates the old canon and denies individuals' capacities to make their own meanings.

Here it seems to me that witch-trials offer an opening. Witches were not always mere consumers of male discourse, providing witchcraft fantasy on order. They used the elements of their culture to create narratives which made sense of their lives: of their unbearable hatreds, agonies, jealousies. These came from the Devil, an explanation which did not rob women of agency – for they listened to the Devil's voice. Witchcraft confessions have often been understood as the projections of a male-dominated society. But this is to ignore the creative work which the witch herself carried out, translating her own life experiences into the language of the diabolic, performing her own diabolic theatre. The fantasies she wove, though often forced from her through torture, were her own condensations of shared cultural preoccupations – like the Host one witch swept neatly together having trampled it on the floor, a rite of dishonouring the Host as old as the ritual murder trials against Jews, and yet as mundanely her own as her broom; or like the vision of the Devil which Appolonia Mayr evokes, standing over the child's corpse, localized on a precise path and field, with a tree behind in the background, yet resonant with fantasies about the Devil as child-stealer. Their judges and scribes noted all this with fascinated attention. And in this way witches themselves carried out cultural work, creating the narrative of the witch anew, making sense of emotions and cultural process. Willing or not, witchcraft trials are one context in which women 'speak' at greater length and receive more attention than perhaps any other.[63] In the European west, women could be evil: always more than nature, they were not just projections of male fantasies of evil but active embodiments of it.

VI

I have been arguing that both social constructionism and linguistic constructionism short-circuited the realm between language and subjectivity, as if there were no space here to be bridged. Language, by means of its social character, simply impressed a social construction of gender upon the wax of the individual psyche. Or, in the social constructionist version of this theory, collective rituals, performances, habits of work or sociability are seen to imprint themselves upon the individual psyche. When the variable of gender is added, the effect is barely more than to inflect the kind of subjectivity the group mediates: masculinity and femininity themselves are both collectively created. Theories of these kinds link individual and collective psychology. They supply an account of subjectivity which is inherently, though superficially, historical; for as social conditions change, so also will individual consciousness. And as discourses become transformed, so too must the linguistic expressions of the individual be transformed.

But one further consequence of this vision of the subject and the social is to reinstate the division between the mental and the corporeal. For the early modern period this ought to make us pause, for this was the period *before* our familiar vision of the division between between mind and body – our Cartesian heritage – was articulated. An engagement with pre-modern society, with its magical world-view and its belief in the demonic, with its assumption that emotions can cause harm in others or its conviction that sanctity can be seen and felt in the uncorrupted body of the saint itself, offers us the chance of rethinking our own habitual classifications of mental and corporeal. Our nineteenth-century heritage is a conception of the rational which banishes witchcraft, spells, the demonic and the popular to the margins of society, the underworld or the rural. Or, as one might caricature this, it was as we grew enlightened that the world became disenchanted.[64] But looking at the early modern world can allow us to suspend the distinction between the rational and the irrational, thus helping us to understand our own intuition of the mind-body relation in new ways. As these essays argue, magic, exorcisms and sexual utopianism, so far from being exotic manifestations of the pre-modern, were central to early modern society – and, as Eva Labouvie has demonstrated in a suggestive reconstruction of the logic of early modern peasant sorcery, to rationality itself.[65] It is in the arena of the magical, the irrational, in witch-trials that – paradoxically enough – the individual subject of the early modern period unfolds.

Bodies have materiality, and this too must have its place in history. The capacity of the body to suffer pain, illness, the process of giving birth, the effects on the body of certain kinds of exercise such as hunting or riding – all these are bodily experiences which belong to the history of the body and are more than discourse. We are familiar with the idea that culture shapes how we experience bodily events, and we have learnt from Norbert Elias how social structure impacts on bodily comportment – we are less ready to admit, or to explore historically, how particular patterns of movement, clothes, illnesses in turn influence culture and subjectivity.

Bodies are not merely the creations of discourse. What we have is a history of discourses about the body; what we need is a history that can problematize the relation between the psychic and the physical. Indeed, the beginnings of psychoanalysis lie in the fascination with the juncture between the physical and the psychic. In Freud's essay on *Senatspräsident* Dr Daniel Paul Schreber, it is the physical dimension of Schreber's paranoid illness which captures Freud's attention: Schreber's retention of his faeces or his belief that his body was turning into that of a woman.[66] Psychic disturbance takes physical form; distorted body-images are among the most important features of the illness and offer the clues to its healing. In part because of its interest in sexuality, the paradigmatic area where imagination and physiology coincide, psychoanalysis has offered a powerful way of understanding how bodily experience must of necessity be connected with mental life. One might argue that there can be no experience of the body which is not also psychic, no way of grasping the body without the mediation of mental representations and, therefore, no 'body' which is not historically constructed. But this is only half the story.

What we lack is a fully developed theoretical account of how the physical flows back into the psychic. In Freud, the physical is supplied through a partially biologistic understanding of the drives, but this is about physical functioning rather than bodies themselves. In the work of the psychoanalyst Melanie Klein, bodies dissolve into body images, as if there is nothing that holds together the disembodied breasts, penises and corporeal interiors which populate the psychic imagination.[67] Because of the importance of articulation in psychoanalysis, the so-called 'talking cure', psychoanalysis can sometimes seem to be itself a kind of drama involving the production of a certain kind of text, so that the connection between psyche and body can seem to be just discourse. But this would be to leave out the interconnection between the psychic and the somatic, the problematic which animates so much of Freud's writing and which was the source of many of the theoretical breakthroughs as well as many of the splits within the psychoanalytic movement in its early years. Indeed, it still today remains a vexed area.

The body as we experience it is more than the sum of tactile and kinetic impressions. Our experience of the body is organized by body images. These are in part culturally created, and to that extent they have a collective history. We gain access to these only partially through language, and it is misleading, I think, to equate them with discourse or language.[68] In searching for the body images of the sixteenth century, I am looking for something more than the ways the body was talked about; I want to delineate the only partially conscious images of the body which lie below the surface of language. Body images, bodily malfunction or even what the psychoanalyst Joyce McDougall calls somatic expression, can be a kind of mute communication, a prelinguistic resource to which we resort when language dries up in inexpressible psychic pain.[69] The body rears its head, so to speak, often only when we are ill, or in agony – a restriction of bodily expression to the pathological. But bodily expression can also be integrated in positive experience, for example, in the pleasure of dance or in sexual delight. And since we are our bodies (more so than we like to admit), bodily symbolism belongs to the deepest religious tools we have.[70] It can convey what we find impossible to put into words.

This was particularly so in the sixteenth century. It is no accident that it should have been the issue of communion which so inflamed passions and divided early modern people. Communion, after all, is far more than a metaphor. Taking communion is a physical process, and the ingestion of the Host, the drinking of the wine, was a physical act through which community and the relationship with God was consummated. Theologically, the issue for reformers was how to understand Christ's incarnation, for the ritual posed the question of the relationship between the divine and the human. The issue around which battle was joined was not only how one should understand the corporeality of the divine, but how this ritual should be carried out: should both elements or only one be received? Should one receive the elements from the hands of the priest? Could one touch the Host? That is, the question of the body, and the boundaries between human and divine, lay at the very heart of the Reformation.[71]

How did early modern Germans visualize the body? What conscious and unconscious imagery lies beneath their language? Although I did not realize it, the preoccupation with this question is what relates this series of essays to one another. Early modern German culture furnishes a variety of ways of grasping the body. In the literature of excess, the body is imagined as a container for a series of processes: defecation, sexual pollution, vomiting. Fluids course about within the body, erupting out of it, leaving their mark on the world outside. The body is not so much a collection of joints and limbs, or a skeletal structure, as a container of fluids, bursting out in every direction to impact on the environment.[72] This vision of the body as a container of evil fluids is reminiscent of what the psychoanalyst Melanie Klein has to say about the child's conceptualization of the mother's body as a vessel containing evil and dangerous substances,[73] or what the French theorist Julia Kristeva describes as 'abjection', a state which is also related to the tie with the maternal body.[74] But what is different is that the accent is not so much on the badness of the fluids contained in the body as in the pleasure of release. What in Klein and Kristeva is viewed as a negative, pathological imagination – to be sure, part of the psychic heritage we all share – is in this writing a source of pleasure. This is a particular way of eroticizing bodily openings – mouth, anus, penis – as if the operation of the muscles could be simply enjoyed, as if there could be a world where no inhibitions operated to curb the free exchange of fluids between inner and outer, as if the enjoyment of simple release, simple expulsion, is the transgression – a conception which derives its imaginative pull from the literature of repression, of muscular control. This is a world which recalls that of the infant who does not have to control his or her defecation or excretion. And it is also a state in which the boundaries between the self and others, the bounded self and the fluids which spill into the surrounding world, have become melted, as if one could approach the state in which there is no longer distinction between self and world, mother and baby. Yet the literature of excess is anything but a regression *tout court*. Its preoccupations were highly literate, framed within a Latinate, written culture, and it constituted a linguistically sophisticated, controlled cultural creation.[75]

The matching half of this imagistic set is to be found in the literature of discipline: the sets of ordinances, proclamations and mandates which secular authorities promulgated with increasing elaboration from the late fifteenth century, reaching a first full expression in the years of the Reformation, and continuing well into the seventeenth century. This is a literature which crosses the Catholic/Protestant divide. And it was accompanied by a moralist literature, reaching its high point in the Devil books of the mid-sixteenth century. This, too, conceives of vices as a kind of inner fluid, constantly threatening to burst the bounds of discipline. It is as if the individual is a shapeless collection of active sins constantly threatening to burst through the musculature of morals. Discipline is a kind of 'fence', to use the metaphor of the Augsburg councillors, which has but little strength against the untameable brute force of the lusts within.[76] This literature cannot best be understood, I think, on the repression/release model, for once again, the body is conceived of as a kind of vessel barely able to contain the forces inside it, all of which are imagined in highly active terms as physical activities: gluttony, fighting, fornicating, blaspheming. Even the house, the basic unit of social organization, is conceived of as a skin so thin that it can hardly hold its murderous denizens together: the master patriarch, most likely to fall prey to every kind of vice, the mistress, only too ready to surrender herself to concupiscence, the children, servants and apprentices, naturally inclined to disorder and disrespect for parental authority. A vision of the house, then, which conceives of *disorganization*, anarchy rather than articulation as the natural state.

Another corporeal map, this time a Catholic one, is evident in exorcism, a practice which enjoyed a renewed vogue in the second half of the sixteenth century as Catholics aimed to prove the superiority of their religion over Protestants.[77] Here again, the *insides* of the body are of crucial importance, for it is in the bodily interior that the demons are housed. The demon must be brought out of the body and into the light, expelled from the bodily cavity, if the sufferer is to be cured. This time, however, the expulsion is an unmistakably good thing, while the passage of demons out of the body is painful not pleasurable, producing bodily writhings and contortions. The openings of the body take on especial significance: the devils often leave via the mouth, and bodily orifices such as the ears and nose play an important role. Unpleasant sensual experience plays a powerful role in exorcism: the audience smell a foul, diabolic sulphurous stench, as if we are not very far from the man of excess, the audience are riveted by sounds, by the utterances of the hidden devils speaking from within the body of the possessed woman, sometimes with a man's voice, the hum of prayer and invocation which, like repeated formulae, comforts through sensual rather than linguistic means, through touch, as the audience hold the possessed woman in their laps, grasp her and can feel for themselves the strength of the diabolic forces which thrust her about.

There is certainly a sexual undertow in this imagination. It is no coincidence that exorcisms took place on beds, nor that the spectacle involved the woman rolling about on the ground, her dress askew and her shame uncovered. Nor was it an accident that exorcisms also demonstrated the honour due to Mary, who is at once both mother and virgin. If we ask what map of the body Mary might represent on this grid, then we can speculate that although as a mother, she might potentially be a container of all these terrifying and dangerous substances that inhabit maternal bodies, sexually she is a sealed body, pierced only by the Holy Ghost. She might thus represent a femininity which is safe and impossible. In terms of bodily imagery, it may be that, imaginatively, Mary offers a counter-resolution to the spectacle of possessed femininity as the exorcist frees the victim with her aid. But it is a resolution which provokes the repetition of the drama, precisely because the resolution is impossible.[78]

The sexual fantasies of witchcraft draw on similar visions of a body which can lose its organization, and in which liquids within the body become poisonous, killing instead of nourishing. The most common form such fantasies took was apparently to cluster around the ideas of feeding and nourishment of babies in the first six weeks of life. Sexual fantasies to which witches give voice often also display a similar vision of a disorganized body: in English witch fantasies, teats appear not confined to the breast, but all over the body as the Devil's mark; they are often to be found near the anus or vagina, as if the bodily orifices had become interchangeable.[79] Sexual activity, when it takes place at the witches' sabbath, is imagined as an orgy in which 'sodomy', that medieval catch-all, becomes an imprecise term for every kind of unorthodox sexual coupling, imprecise because what it refers to cannot quite be named or imagined. That is to say, I do not think that sexual intercourse at the witches' sabbath is just a 'reversal' of normal sexual behaviour, an inversion which 'turns the world upside down' for a moment, but which leaves its categories intact.[80] Rather, what we encounter here is a disordered imagination in which anal and oral sex *don't* reinstate the heterosexual norm of which they are the inverse, but dissolve the categories of the discrete, functioning body altogether. Something much more primary is at work here, fantasies to do with sex and death, with non-reproductive intercourse, sexual union as an engulfment which destroys the identity, and behind this, the horror of sex with the mother herself, the return to the death of the womb. In this sense, I think the fantasies of witchcraft are heir to these earlier visions of the body, but now their maternal content becomes much more manifest. They, too, give voice to very primitive kinds of mental distress, to the moment when distinctions between oneself and others seem to elide, when the shape of the body seems to blur and utter helplessness and terror result.

It is easier to delineate the kinds of semi-conscious imaginings of the body that are at work here than it is to explain, historically, why they should have proved particularly compelling at certain historical moments. If I were to hazard a chronological chain of imaginative connection, I would speculate that the image of the excessive body which constantly breaks out of its own boundaries – the preoccupation with the processes of excreting – and the fascination with muscular control acted in vortex fashion, pulling some kinds of imagination back towards earlier scenes from childhood. The transition from a vision of the body which was primarily of a male body, but which could also be applied to female bodies (the grotesque excessive comic figure Grobian had his female equivalent Grobiana[81]), to a concentration on the female body alone, which we find in images of witchcraft, is important.[82] Fascination with boundaries, control and the substances within the body allowed one to imagine and indeed experience the loss of boundaries altogether, the filling of the body with evil substances and the elision of the gap between one's own body and the maternal body. These terrifying spectres nourished the corporeal imagination of the witch-craze. Why and how these spectres seized the minds of individuals and groups of people at some times and some places will require a detailed compilation of social factors, and an exploration of the relation between judicial process and political power – an explanation which it is beyond the scope of this book to give. But I am claiming that part of the answer must lie in the psychic and corporeal realms, and that we neglect these at our peril.

VII

I have been advocating an approach to early modern subjectivities which will recognize the collective elements of culture without trivializing individual subjectivity. I have been arguing that gender cannot be under-stood as the social acquisition of an unproblematic sexual identity. Sexual difference has a bodily dimension. Sexual identity can never be satisfactorily understood if we conceive it as a set of discourses about masculinity or femininity. Nor can the individual subject be adequately understood as a container of discourse – a conception which evacuates subjectivity of psychology. We are very far from knowing how such discourses relate to people's own sexual identities, which nearly always lack the coherence – or even the comforting contradictions – of discourse. Understood as a discursive creation alone, gender is not a category of historical analysis because, lacking an account of the connections between social and psychic, it cannot adequately conceptualize change.

It is far easier to insist on the need for a history of early modern culture which will incorporate the subjective, the psychic and the corporeal than it is to show how that history will look. This volume records my own movement towards this position, and it is thus inevitable that the book represents a journey, not an arrival. But I am convinced that unless history and cultural anthropology – and we ourselves – can learn to admit the psychic and the corporeal, we shall never truly encounter the past.

NOTES

1 Stadtarchiv Augsburg (hereafter cited as StadtAA), Urgichtensammlung (hereafter cited as Urg.), 1686, 23 March 1686, Appolonia Mayr; and see on infanticide in general in this period, Richard van Dülmen, *Frauen vor Gericht. Kindsmord in der Frühen Neuzeit*, Frankfurt am Main 1991; Otto Ulbricht, *Kindsmord und Aufklärung in Deutschland*, Munich 1990; Alfons Felber, *Unzucht und Kindsmord in der Rechtsprechung der freien Reichsstadt Nördlingen vom 15, bis 19, Jahrhundert*, Bonn 1961.

2 StadtAA, Urg., 13 May 1686, Appolonia Mayr, qu. 150:

> der böse habe Ihr kein frid gelassen. es seie nur ein Augenblick gewesen, der Teuffel habs angeruhrt, als wan Er ein hebam were, seie gar bald geschehen. das dz kind heraus gewesen. Sie habs auch gleich ertrosselt mit der hand, vnd sie habe im bringen kein schmerzen gespuhrt.

3 'Ja sie habs also gantz nackent ligen lassen, vnbedeckt, vnd unbegraben.' StadtAA, Urg., 4 April 1686, qu. 113; 'der Teuffel seie nicht mit Ihr gegangen, sondern beym kind stehen bliben, sie habe weitter nicht vmbgesehen' (qu. 114).

4 Most famously, Jules Michelet, *La Sorcière*, Paris 1862; or see also J. Janssen, *Geschichte des deutschen Volkes seit dem Ausgang des Mittelalters*, vol. 8, ed. and rev. Ludwig Pastor, Freiburg im Breisgau 1894, for example pp. 459–62 on criminality, and part 3 chs 7 and 8 on witchcraft as part of the volumes on culture; Gustav Freytag, *Bilder aus der deutschen Vergangenheit*, vol. 2, part 2, 7th edn, Leipzig 1873, pp. 358–74, extensive discussion of a possession case from Frankfurt as part of cultural history.

5 The last few years have seen a quantum leap in the sophistication with which such approaches have been applied to early modern Europe, especially in German historiography. See, in particular, the pioneering use of anthropology in Bob Scribner, *Popular Culture and Popular Movements in Reformation Germany*, London 1987; David Sabean, *Power in the Blood. Popular culture and village discourse in early modern Germany*, Cambridge 1984; and Norbert Schindler, *Widerspenstige Leute. Studien zur Volkskultur in der frühen Neuzeit*, Frankfurt am Main 1992. Excellent examples of the historical–anthropological approach are collected in the ongoing series edited by Richard van Dülmen, *Studien zur historischen Kulturforschung*.

6 'Fast Ein stund nach der geburth habe sie begert Jhr kind zu sehen', 'Sie wolle halt ihr kind wieder sehen, kenne also nicht mehr leben', StadtAA, Urg., 1685, 16 Nov. 1685, Appolonia Mayr.

7 Max Weber, *The Protestant Ethic and the Spirit of Capitalism*, trans. Talcott Parsons, New York 1958.

8 ibid., p. 80.

9 ibid., p. 180.

10 Norbert Elias, *The Civilizing Process: Sociogenetic and psychogenetic investigations*, trans. Edmund Jephcott, 2 vols, Oxford 1978, 1982 (first published Basle 1939): vol. 1, *The History of Manners*; vol. 2, *State Formation and*

Civilization; idem, The Court Society, trans. Edmund Jephcott, Oxford 1983 (first published Darmstadt and Neuwied 1969).

11 Charles Taylor, *Sources of the Self. The making of the modern identity,* Cambridge 1989, p. 192.

12 ibid., p. 192.

13 The modernity of its techniques, too, and, in particular, the importance of printing in the witch-craze, has been pointed out by Walter Rummel, 'Gutenberg, der Teufel und die Muttergottes von Eberhardsklausen. Erste Verfolgung im Trierer Land', in Andreas Blauert (ed.), *Ketzer, Zauberer, Hexen. Die Anfänge der europäischen Hexenverfolgungen,* Frankfurt am Main 1990.

14 Among the many examples see Günther Pallaver, *Die Verdrängung der Sexualität in der frühen Neuzeit am Beispiel Tirols,* Vienna 1987, which regards the Catholic church as having been instrumental in the process of 'disciplining' through its use of the confessional in the period after the Reformation and explicitly draws on Elias; Heinrich Richard Schmidt, 'Die Christianisierung des Sozialverhaltens als permanente Reformation. Aus der Praxis reformierter Sittengerichte in der Schweiz während der frühen Neuzeit', *Zeitschrift für historische Forschung,* Beiheft 9, 1989, pp. 113–63; Roger Chartier (ed.), *Passions of the Renaissance* (= G. Duby, *A History of Private Life,* vol. 3), trans. Arthur Goldhammer, Cambridge, Mass. 1989; Georges Vigarello, *Concepts of Cleanliness. Changing attitudes in France since the Middle Ages,* trans. Jean Birrell, Cambridge 1988; for a textbook on early modern European history inspired by Elias, see Pieter Spierenburg, *The Broken Spell. A cultural and anthropological history of preindustrial Europe,* London 1991; for a history of health and the body influenced by Weber and Elias, Alfons Labisch, *Homo hygienicus: Gesundheit und Medizin in der Neuzeit,* Frankfurt am Main 1992; for an interesting use of some of his themes in Martin Dinges, 'Der "feine Unterschied". Die soziale Funktion der Kleidung in der höfischen Gesellschaft', *Zeitschrift für historische Forschung,* 19, 1992, pp. 49–76; and Stephen Mennell, *All Manners of Food: Eating and taste in England and France from the Middle Ages to the present,* Oxford 1985; and for a thoughtful, thoroughgoing application of Elias's ideas by a scholar influenced by both psychoanalysis and sociology, see Michael Schröter's work, including *"Wo zwei zusammenkommen in rechter Ehe". Sozio- und psychogenetische Studien über die Eheschliessungsvorgänge vom 12. bis 15. Jahrhundert,* Frankfurt am Main 1985, and 'Zur Intimisierung der Hochzeitsnacht im 16. Jahrhundert', in Hans-Jürgen Bachorski (ed.), *Ordnung und Lust. Bilder von Liebe, Ehe und Sexualität in Spätmittelalter und Früher Neuzeit,* Trier 1991. For a critique of Elias, see Hans Peter Duerr, *Der Mythos vom Zivilisationsprozess,* 3 vols, Frankfurt am Main 1988, 1989, 1992: vol. 1, *Nacktheit und Scham;* vol. 2, *Intimität;* vol. 3, *Obszönität und Gewalt.*

15 Elias, *A History of Manners,* p. 142.

16 ibid., p. 152; and his brilliant account of court rituals in *The Court Society.*

17 Elias trained in England as a group therapist. See Michael Schröter (ed.), *Norbert Elias über sich selbst,* Frankfurt am Main 1990, pp. 81–4 where, in interview, Elias mentions his own orthodox Freudian analysis and his work with group analysis; Karl-Siegbert Rehberg, 'Form und Prozess. Zu den katalysatorischen Wirkungschancen einer Soziologie aus dem Exil: Norbert Elias', in Peter Gleichmann, Johann Goudsblom, Hermann Korte (eds), *Materialien zu Norbert Elias' Zivilisationstheorie,* Frankfurt am Main 1977, p. 105; and note Elias's comment in a letter: 'I think that probably Freud's ideas had a greater influence on my thinking than those of any theoretical sociologist', in J. Goudsblom, 'Responses to Norbert Elias's Work in England, Germany, the Netherlands and France', in P. Gleichmann, J. Goudsblom and

H. Korte (eds), *Human Figurations. Essays for Norbert Elias*, Amsterdam 1977, p. 78.

18 Elias, *A History of Manners*, p. 201.

19 ibid., pp. 214, 215.

20 ibid., pp. 200–1.

21 Mikhail Bakhtin, *Rabelais and His World*, trans. Hélène Iswolsky, Cambridge, Mass. 1968; and see also Norbert Schindler, 'Karneval, Kirche und verkehrte Welt. Zur Funktion der Lachkultur im 16. Jahrhundert', in *idem, Widerspenstige Leute*.

22 Taylor, *Sources of the Self*, pp. 185–98.

23 Horst Bredekamp, 'Renaissancekultur als "Hölle": Savonarolas Verbrennungen der Eitelkeiten', in Martin Warnke (ed.), *Bildersturm. Die Zerstörung des Kunstwerks*, Munich 1973.

24 See Peter Stallybrass and Allon White, *The Politics and Poetics of Transgression*, London 1986, pp. 5, 22, for a slightly different statement of this point. However, in the end, their reliance on the Elias model of historical change does, I think, commit them to a similar model of historical progression of the psyche.

25 Chartier (ed.), *Passions of the Renaissance*, esp. pp. 15–17, and 'Introduction' to the volume by Philippe Ariès, pp. 4, 9.

26 For a critique of this interest in the symbolic and the irrational, a feature of much of the new cultural history, see Raphael Samuel, 'Reading the Signs', *History Workshop Journal*, 32, 1991, pp. 88–109.

27 See, for example, the excellent psychoanalytic biography of Louis XIII by Elizabeth W. Marvick, *Louis XIII: The making of a king*, London 1986; and *idem, The Young Richelieu: A psychoanalytic approach to leadership*, Chicago, Ill. 1983; Elizabeth Young-Breuhl, *Anna Freud: A biography*, New York 1988; the classic Erik H. Erikson, *Young Man Luther. A study in psychoanalysis in history*, London 1959; or the looser use of psychoanalysis in Ray Monk, *Ludwig Wittgenstein: The duty of genius*, London 1990.

28 See Joyce McDougall, *Plea for a Measure of Abnormality*, Paris 1978, New York 1980, London 1990; *idem, Theatres of the Mind: Illusion and truth on the psychoanalytic stage*, New York 1985; *idem, Theatres of the Body. A psychoanalytic approach to psychosomatic illness*, London 1989.

29 Among historians the most influential works of Foucault include: Michel Foucault, *Discipline and Punish. The birth of the prison*, trans. Alan Sheridan, Harmondsworth 1977; *idem, Madness and Civilisation. A history of insanity in the Age of Reason*, London 1967; *idem, The History of Sexuality*: vol. 1, *An Introduction*, London 1979; vol. 2, *The Use of Pleasure*, New York 1985.

30 On the late reception of Foucault's work in Germany, see Peter Schöttler, 'Historians and Discourse Analysis', *History Workshop Journal*, 27, 1989, pp. 37–65, first published in Jürgen Fohrman and Harro Müller (eds), *Diskurstheorien und Literaturwissenschaft*, Frankfurt am Main 1988. For excellent recent work on the history of the body see, among others, Barbara Duden, *Geschichte unter der Haut. Ein Eisenacher Arzt und seine Patientinnen*, Stuttgart 1987; *idem, Der Frauenleib als öffentlicher Ort. Vom Missbrauch des Begriffs Leben*, Hamburg 1991; Esther Fischer-Homberger, *Medizin vor Gericht. Zur Sozialgeschichte der Gerichtsmedizin*, Darmstadt 1988; Ludmilla Jordanova, *Sexual Visions. Images of gender in science and medicine between the eighteenth and twentieth centuries*, Hemel Hempstead 1989; Roy Porter and G. S. Rousseau (eds), *Sexual Underworlds of the Enlightenment*, Manchester 1987; Edward Shorter, *A History of Women's Bodies*, New York 1982; Francis Barker, *The Tremulous Private Body*, London and New York 1984; Arthur E. Imhof (ed.), *Leib und Leben in der Geschichte der Neuzeit* (Berliner historische Studien 9), Berlin 1983; Ilsebill

Barta-Fliedl and Christoph Geissmar (eds), *Die Beredsamkeit des Leibes. Zur Körpersprache in der Kunst*, Salzburg 1992; August Nitschke, *Körper in Bewegung. Gesten, Tänze und Räume im Wandel der Geschichte*, Stuttgart 1989; Kathleen Adler and Marcia Pointon (eds), *The Body Imaged. The human form and visual culture since the Renaissance*, Cambridge 1993; Michael Feher, Ramona Naddaff and Nadia Tazi (eds), *Fragments for a History of the Human Body*, Cambridge, Mass. 1989.

31 Foucault, *The History of Sexuality*, vol. 1.

32 Natalie Zemon Davis, *The Return of Martin Guerre*, Cambridge, Mass. 1983; Robert Finlay, 'The Refashioning of Martin Guerre', *American Historical Review*, 1988, pp. 552–71; Natalie Zemon Davis, 'On the Lame', *American Historical Review*, 1988, pp. 572–603. Davis herself proposes a much more complex, nuanced notion of the self in early modern Europe and places stress on the role of memory as a guarantee of selfhood: ibid., p. 602. And see also Natalie Zemon Davis, 'Boundaries and the Sense of Self in Sixteenth-Century France', in Thomas C. Heller, Morton Sosna and David E. Wellbery (eds), *Reconstructing Individualism. Autonomy, individuality, and the self in western thought*, Stanford, Calif. 1986.

33 Robert Darnton, 'The Great Cat Massacre of the Rue Saint-Severin', in *idem*, *The Great Cat Massacre and other Episodes in French Cultural History*, London 1984; Roger Chartier, 'Texts, Symbols, and Frenchness', *Journal of Modern History*, 57, 1985, pp. 682–95; Robert Darnton, 'The Symbolic Element in History', *Journal of Modern History*, 58, 1986, pp. 218–34; Dominick LaCapra, 'Chartier, Darnton and the Great Symbol Massacre', *Journal of Modern History*, 60, 1988, pp. 95–112; James Fernandez, 'Historians Tell Tales: Of Cartesian cats and Gallic cockfights', *Journal of Modern History*, 60, 1988, pp. 113–27; Harold Mah, 'Suppressing the Text: The Metaphysics of ethnographic history in Darnton's Great Cat Massacre', *History Workshop Journal*, 31, 1991, pp. 1–20.

34 See Anna Davin, 'Women, the Everyday and History', forthcoming in Heide Dieckwisch, *Alltagsgeschichte*, who points out that a similar tradition of the history of everyday life did exist in 'amateur' Anglo-American historiography of the 1930s and 1950s.

35 For some excellent examples of this approach, see Bernd Roeck, *Lebenswelt und Kultur des Bürgertums in der frühen Neuzeit (Enzyklopädie deutscher Geschichte*, ed. Lothar Gall with Peter Blickle, vol. 9), Munich 1991; Richard van Dülmen, *Kultur und Alltag in der frühen Neuzeit. 16. bis 18. Jahrhundert*, 3 vols: vol. 1, *Das Haus und seine Menschen*, Munich 1990; vol. 2, *Dorf und Stadt. 16–18. Jahrhundert*, Munich 1992; Paul Münch, *Lebensformen in der frühen Neuzeit*, Berlin 1992.

36 There are, however, some notable exceptions: Marvick, *Louis XIII*; Lynn Hunt, *The Family Romance of the French Revolution*, London 1992; John Demos, *Entertaining Satan. Witchcraft and the culture of early New England*, Oxford 1982; Michel de Certeau, *The Writing of History*, trans. Tom Conley, New York 1988; and *idem*, *The Mystic Fable: vol. 1, The Sixteenth and Seventeenth Centuries*, trans. Michael B. Smith, Chicago, Ill. 1992.

37 See, esp., Stephen Greenblatt, *Renaissance Self-Fashioning*, Chicago, Ill. 1980.

38 Stephen Greenblatt, 'Psychoanalysis and Renaissance Culture', in *idem*, *Learning to Curse: Essays in early modern culture*, London 1990.

39 Schindler, 'Die Welt der Spitznamen. Zur Logik der populären Nomenklatur', and 'Die Entstehung der Unbarmherzigkeit. Zur Kultur und Lebensweise der Salzburger Bettler am Ende des 17. Jahrhunderts', both in *idem*, *Widerspenstige Leute*, p. 301.

40 But see Davis, 'Boundaries and the Sense of Self'.

41 As Sally Alexander has put it, 'The subjectivity of psychoanalysis does

not . . . imply a universal, human nature, it suggests that some forms of mental functioning – the unconscious, phantasy, memory, etc. – seem to be so.' Sally Alexander, 'Women Class and Sexual Differences in the 1830s and 1840s. Some reflections on the writing of feminist history', *History Workshop Journal*, 17, 1984, pp. 125–49; and also *idem*, 'Feminist History and Psychoanalysis', *History Workshop Journal*, 32, 1991, pp. 128–33. See also here the fascinating article by Norbert Elias on the emotions: 'On Human Beings and Their Emotions: A process–sociological essay', *Theory, Culture and Society*, 4, 1987, pp. 339–61.

42 Clifford Geertz, 'Deep Play: Notes on the Balinese cockfight', in *idem, The Interpretation of Culture*, London 1975.

43 Sebastian Franck, *Weltbuch, speigel vnd bildtniss des gantzen erdtbodens*, Tübingen, V. Morhart 1534.

44 See, on the resonance of *Gemeinde*, the work of Peter Blickle, *The Revolution of 1525: The German Peasants' War from a new perspective*, trans. Thomas Brady and Erik Midelfort, Baltimore, Md 1981: *idem, Gemeindereformation: Die Menschen des 16. Jahrhunderts auf dem Weg zum Heil*, Munich 1985; Sabean, *Power in the Blood*; and Lyndal Roper, 'The Common Man, the Common Good, Common Women: Gender and language in the German Reformation commune', *Social History*, 12, 1987, pp. 1–22; John Theibault, 'Community and Herrschaft in the Seventeenth-Century German Village', *Journal of Modern History*, 64, no. 1. 1992, pp. 1–21.

45 See, for instance, David Sabean's path-breaking *Power in the Blood*.

46 Joan W. Scott, 'Gender: A useful category of historical analysis', reprinted in *idem, Gender and the Politics of History*, New York 1988.

47 Here see Sally Alexander's important exploration of this point in 'Women, Class and Sexual Differences'.

48 See, in particular, Denise Riley, *'Am I that Name?' Feminism and the category of 'Women' in history*, London 1988.

49 Judith Butler, *Gender Trouble. Feminism and the subversion of identity*, New York and London 1990.

50 ibid., p. 33.

51 ibid., p. 2.

52 Thomas Laqueur, *Making Sex. Body and gender from the Greeks to Freud*, Cambridge, Mass. 1990; and for different views, see Evelyne Berriot-Salvadore, 'The Discourse of Medicine and Science', in Natalie Zemon Davis and Arlette Farge (eds), *A History of Women in the West*, vol. 3, *Renaissance and Enlightenment Paradoxes*, Cambridge, Mass. 1993; and Gianna Pomata 'Uomini mestruanti: somiglianze e differenze fra i Sessi in Europa in età moderna', *Quaderni Storici*, 79, 1992, pp. 51–103.

53 Randolph Trumbach, 'London's Sapphists: From three sexes to four genders in the making of modern culture', in Julia Epstein and Kristina Straub (eds), *Body Guards. The cultural politics of gender ambiguity*, New York and London 1991, pp. 112, 113; 'Sex, Gender and Sexual Identity in Modern Culture: Male sodomy and female prostitution in Enlightenment London', in John C. Fout (ed.), *Forbidden History: The state, society, and the regulation of sexuality in modern Europe. Essays from the Journal of the History of Sexuality*, Chicago, Ill. 1992.

54 Rudolf Dekker and Lotte C. van de Pol, *The Tradition of Female Transvestism in Early Modern Europe*, trans. Judy Marcure and Lotte C. van de Pol, Basingstoke 1989.

55 Londa Schiebinger, 'Skeletons in the Closet: The first illustrations of the female skeleton in eighteenth-century anatomy', in Catherine Gallagher and Thomas Laqueur (eds), *The Making of the Modern Body. Sexuality and society*

in the nineteenth century, Berkeley, Calif. 1987. I am grateful to Peter Lake for pointing this out.

56 Mary Wollstonecraft, *A Vindication of the Rights of Woman*, London 1992, introduction by Barbara Taylor, p. xxiv.

57 *The Holy Household. Women and morals in Reformation Augsburg*, Oxford 1989. On the origins of sixteenth-century humanist ideals of the household in Xenophon's *Oeconomicus* see Lorna Hutson, *The Usurer's Daughter*, London forthcoming 1994.

58 'Primus annus coniugii macht eim seltzame gedancken. Sedens enim in mensa cogitat: Ante solus eram, nu bin ich selbs ander; in lecto expergiscens sihet er ein par zopffe neben yhm liegen, quas prius non vidit', *D. Martin Luthers Werke: Kritische Gesamtausgabe. Werke*, 60 vols, Weimar 1883–1983, *Tischreden*, vol. 3, p. 211, no. 3178 a.

59 'Männer haben eine breite Brust und kleine Hüften, darum haben sie auch mehr Verstandes denn die Weiber, welche enge Brüste haben und breite Hüfter und Gesäss, dass sie sollen daheim bleiben, in Hause still sitzen, Kinder tragen und ziehen', *D. Martin Luthers Werke* (Weimar edition), WA *Tischreden* vol. 1, p. 19, no. 55 (1531), and see also *Luthers Werke*, WA TR, vol. 2, p. 285, no. 1975 where Luther makes the comparison cruder: in women, the place where the dung comes out is larger and so they have a lot of shit and little sense. Quoted in Julia O'Faolain and Lauro Martines (eds), *Not in God's Image. Women in history*, New York 1973, p. 209.

60 Luther, *De captivitate Babylonica ecclesiae praeludium*, 1520, *D. Martin Luthers Werke*, vol. 6, pp. 558–9.

61 *Luthers Werke*, WA, 10, part II, p. 275, Vom ehelichen leben (1522) p. 296: instead of praying to St Margaret in childbirth, the woman is exhorted thus: 'Gib dir das kind her und thu darzu mit aller macht, stirbstu drober, sso far hyn, wol dyr, Denn du stirbist eygentlich ym edlen werck und gehorssam gottis.' Quoted in Merry Wiesner, 'Women's Response to the Reformation', in R. Po-Chia Hsia (ed.), *The German People and the Reformation*, Ithaca, NY and London 1988, p. 151.

62 See, on the effects of the Reformation on churching, Susan C. Karant-Nunn, 'A Women's Rite: Churching and the Lutheran Reformation', in R. Po-Chia Hsia and B. Scribner (eds), *History and Anthropology in Early Modern Europe. Papers from the Wolfenbüttel conference 1991*, forthcoming; and on women and Protestantism, Heide Wunder, *Er ist die Sonn', sie ist der Mond. Frauen in der Frühen Neuzeit*, Munich 1992, esp. pp. 65ff.

63 The opposite view is maintained by Claudia Honegger, 'Hexenprozesse und "Heimlichkeiten der Frauenzimmer": Geschlechtsspezifische Aspekte von Fremd- und Selbstthematisierung', in Alois Hahn and Volker Kapp (eds), *Selbstthematisierung und Selbstzeugnis: Bekenntnis und Geständnis*, Frankfurt am Main 1987: she claims that the (misogynist) assumptions of the interrogators make it impossible for women to speak as anything other than mere instantiations of their sex. This seems to me, however, to overstate the extent to which interrogators influence what they wish to hear, a constraint which is after all shared to some degree by every conversation.

64 For a powerful critique of this view, see Bob Scribner, 'The Reformation, Popular Magic and the "Disenchantment of the World" ', *Journal of Interdisciplinary History*, 23, 1993, pp. 475–94.

65 Eva Labouvie, *Zauberei und Hexenwerk. Ländlicher Hexenglaube in der frühen Neuzeit*, Frankfurt am Main 1991; *idem, Verbotene Künste. Volksmagie und ländlicher Aberglaube in den Dorfgemeinden des Saarraumes (16.–19. Jahrhundert)*, St Ingbert 1992.

66 Sigmund Freud, 'Psychoanalytische Bemerkungen über einen autobiographi-

sch beschriebenen Fall von Paranoia (Dementia paranoides)', *Sigmund Freud. Studienausgabe*, Frankfurt am Main 1969–75, vol. 7, pp. 133–203.

67 Melanie Klein, *Love, Guilt and Reparation and Other Works 1921–45*, new edn, London 1988; idem, *Envy and Gratitude and Other Works 1949–63*, new edn, London 1988; idem, *Narrative of a Child Analysis*, new edn, London 1989; idem, *The Psychoanalysis of Children*, London 1989.

68 Compare, here, Barbara Maria Stafford, *Body Criticism. Imaging the unseen in Enlightenment art and medicine*, Cambridge, Mass. and London 1991, on what she terms 'nondiscursive articulations' in the eighteenth century (p. 6), and see Sharon Fermor, 'Movement and Gender in Sixteenth-Century Italian Painting', in Adler and Pointon (eds), *The Body Imaged*.

69 McDougall, *Theatres of the Body.*

70 See Caroline Walker Bynum, *Fragmentation and Redemption. Essays on gender and the human body in medieval religion*, New York 1992, esp. the introductory essay, 'History in the Comic Mode'.

71 Miri Rubin, *Corpus Christi. The Eucharist in late medieval culture*, Cambridge 1991; de Certeau, *The Mystic Fable*, pp. 79ff.; Natalie Zemon Davis, 'Missed Connections: *Religion and Regime*', *Journal of Interdisciplinary History*, 1, 1971, pp. 381–94; and Guy Swanson, 'Systems of Descent and Interpreting the Reformation', *Journal of Interdisciplinary History*, 1, 1971, pp. 419–46.

72 On the 'bodiliness' of early modern culture, see Norbert Schindler, 'Karneval, Kirche und verkehrte Welt. Zur Funktion der Lachkultur im 16. Jahrhundert', in idem, *Widerspenstige Leute*, esp. pp. 159–67.

73 Melanie Klein, *The Psychoanalysis of Children*, trans. Alix Strachey, rev. edn, London 1989 (originally published 1975).

74 See, for example, Julia Kristeva, *Powers of Horror. An essay on abjection*, trans. Leon S. Roudiez, New York 1982; idem, *Desire in Language. A semiotic approach to literature and art*, ed. Leon S. Roudiez, trans. Thomas Gora, Alice Jardine and Leon S. Roudiez, London 1980.

75 Michael Screech, *Rabelais*, London 1979; Erich Auerbach, *Mimesis. The representation of reality in western literature*, trans. Willard Trask, Princeton, NJ 1953, pp. 262–84; see also Maria E. Müller, 'Naturwesen Mann. Zur Dialektik von Herrschaft und Knechtschaft in Ehelehren der Frühen Neuzeit', in Heide Wunder and Christina Vanja (eds), *Wandel der Geschlechterbeziehungen zu Beginn der Neuzeit*, Frankfurt am Main 1991; Pia Holenstein, *Der Ehediskurs der Renaissance in Fischarts Geschichtklitterung. Kritische Lektüre des fünften Kapitels* (Deutsche Literatur von den Anfängen bis 1700, 10), Berne, Frankfurt am Main, New York and Paris 1991.

76 Roper, *The Holy Household*, pp. 57ff.

77 See H.C. Erik Midelfort, 'Sin, Melancholy, Obsession: Insanity and culture in 16th century Germany', in S.L. Kaplan (ed.), *Understanding Popular Culture*, Berlin 1984; and on Protestant understandings, Stuart Clark, 'Protestant Demonology: Sin, superstition, and society (*c.* 1520–*c.* 1630)', in Bengt Ankarloo and Gustav Henningsen (eds), *Early Modern European Witchcraft. Centres and peripheries*, Oxford 1990.

78 Marina Warner, *Alone of all Her Sex: The myth and cult of the Virgin Mary*, London 1976.

79 See Jim Sharpe, 'Witchcraft and Women in Seventeenth-Century England: Some northern evidence', *Continuity and Change*, 6, 1991, pp. 179–200; and Marianne Hester, *Lewd Women and Wicked Witches. A study of the dynamics of male domination*, London 1992, esp. pp. 161–97.

80 On inversion in witchcraft, see the classic article by Stuart Clark, 'Inversion, Misrule and the Meaning of Witchcraft', *Past and Present*, 87, 1980, pp. 98–127.

81 Friedrich Dedekind, *Grobianus und Grobiana*, trans. C. Scheidt, Frankfurt 1567.

82 Exorcism is interesting here, since both men and women may be possessed. Midelfort shows that women predominated in the possession stories contained in Martin Delrio's *Disquisitionum Magicarum Libri Sex* (1599–1600), as well as in Weyer's *De Praestigiis Daemonum* (1583) (Midelfort, 'Sin, Melancholy, Obsession', pp. 139–40), when possession cases first grasped confessional imaginations. However, by the last two decades of the sixteenth century, there were approaching as many men as women individual possessions and more male than female cases in the first half of the seventeenth century. Midelfort, 'The Devil and the German People: Reflections on the popularity of demon possession in sixteenth-century Germany', in Steven Ozment (ed.), *Religion and Culture in the Renaissance and Reformation* (Sixteenth-Century Essays and Studies, 11), Kirksville, Mo. 1989, p. 110.

Part I

2 Was there a crisis in gender relations in sixteenth-century Germany?

I

Judith Bennett has recently urged that the most important task currently confronting feminist historians is to think more clearly about the analysis of historical change. We need, she argues, to develop historical narratives of short- and long-term transformation of gender relations; we need to think about the extent of the impact of shifts in the meanings of masculinity and femininity on the ongoing system of gender relations: in short, gender needs to become a category of historical analysis.[1] This is not as easy as it sounds. Vast historical changes may barely disturb the relations of power between men and women. On the other hand, concepts of gender may display extraordinary volatility at certain moments, such as the French Enlightenment or the German Reformation. They may even, as, for instance, in the propagandist attacks on Marie-Antoinette in the French Revolution as a lesbian and prostitute and her husband Louis XVI as an impotent cuckold, become the currency of political debate itself[2] – yet little may actually change in the relations between the sexes.

Where, then, do we place the Reformation in the history of gender relations? Did the movement we term the Reformation actually constitute such a crisis? There seems currently to be a consensus emerging among historians of the Reformation that the first half of the sixteenth century did indeed witness a crisis in gender relations. Out of this period of disruption there emerged, in both Catholic and Protestant Europe, a more securely patriarchal ordering of relations between the sexes which was to dominate *ancien régime* Europe until the eighteenth century.

In this chapter, I want both to review the evidence that there was a crisis in gender relations in Reformation Germany, and to suggest that the model of historical change which it proposes is misconceived. There was certainly a period of intense flux in gender relations in sixteenth-century Europe: indeed, I think we have underestimated its extent. By focusing on the problem of 'woman', we have been blinded to the way masculinity also underwent its own crisis in the sixteenth century. After all, a movement which changes the sexual status of its clergy, turning models of chastity into exemplars of matrimonial harmony, clearly transforms the meaning of manhood. But the crisis of the Reformation years was not followed by a period of stability in gender relations. Far from it: there was no 'golden era' of patriarchal relations. The 'crisis' was never resolved.

But first, we need to consider the concept of crisis. Drawn as it is from the pathology of the body, it is a metaphor at once compelling and suspicious for historians of gender. The medical moment of crisis is the point at which the body either rallies from illness or succumbs.[3] But gender, so feminist theorists have argued, is a matter of social construction, not physical constitution. This is what confers historical status upon the concept, making the interplay between the sexes a matter of historical record. Inoculated against trust in the 'natural', feminist historians have reason to be chary of deriving gendered truths from facts about the body. In this chapter I want to commit a certain kind of heresy, by claiming that it is precisely the physicality of the concept of crisis, anchoring gender relations in the flesh, which makes the notion useful to feminist historians. There is, I want to argue, an inherent complementarity in gender relations which makes it inevitable that changes in the notion of 'woman' should change the meaning of 'man'. The tragedy of the body – in which we are all imprisoned, more or less happily – is that sexual difference is insurmountable for most of us. The psychological aspects of gender and the tough persistence of sexual difference, however varied its meanings, in the end undermine, I think, any attempt to provide a straight narrative line for the history of patriarchy.

II

Currently, most historians appear to agree that the Reformation seems to mark some kind of transition towards a newly resurgent patriarchalism in society. Thomas Robisheaux, for example, shows how in German rural communities like Hohenlohe, the gradual adoption of Lutheranism and, above all, Lutheran marriage practices, worked ultimately to shore up the power of village peasant patriarchs, who could choose their sons-in-law, control their parcels of land and direct inheritance even from beyond the grave.[4] For England, Patrick Collinson concludes that, despite its contradictory effects, the Reformation was the cradle of a family that is recognizably 'modern'.[5] Steven Ozment sees the German Reformation as resulting in a restoration of the sanctity of marriage which, by removing the multiple sexual destinies possible in the later medieval church, made marriage the single ideal for all, and removed the option of life among a brotherhood or sisterhood.[6] Merry Wiesner has argued that employment opportunities for women were declining through the sixteenth century, so that economic change further served to undermine female independence.[7] From the work of Gerald Strauss and Susan Karant-Nunn we have learnt of the rigours of Lutheran education, and the firm hand of the patriarchs in disciplining unruly young boys.[8] The history of the political fortunes of the civic communes in the years of the Reformation and beyond reveals how communitarian principles of government gradually yielded to a vision of my lords of the council as fatherly rulers, not so different from their cousins, the rulers of small nascent absolutist states.[9] In marriage, education, politics and religion, the sixteenth century does indeed seem to be the crucible of an emerging stable patriarchal society.

The evidence from Catholic areas presents some striking similarities. In seventeenth-century France, Robin Briggs has found Catholic clerics administering doleful marriage guidance that reinforced male authority – though priests tended to remain half-hearted advocates, at best, of the joys of matrimony. The confessional, it seems, became a means not only of naturalizing male headship in the household, sanctifying its order by engaging women in rigorous self-policing, especially of their sensuality, but it also aimed to further the interests of the state, for whom household order was crucial to domestic peace.[10] As Sarah Hanley has shown, in sixteenth-century France one can find a politics of marriage as thoroughgoing as anything Reformation Germany had to offer: parental control of marriage was underwritten by royal statute in contradiction of the decrees of Trent, and women who bore illegitimate children faced stiff penalties.[11] Despite the growth of new female orders during the early years of the Counter-Reformation, enclosure became required of convent women, and ideals of female sanctity seem to have shifted so that a saint was more likely to be contained within her convent, her spirituality domesticated and enclosed, not roaming perversely through the streets. Hence the moves by the church against *beatas* documented by, among others, Elizabeth Rapley for France and Mary Perry for Spain: these powerful women offering authoritative prophecies and spiritual counsel did not suit the new, more sharply segregated patriarchal society of reformed Catholicism.[12] Perhaps it was this clearer division of male and female roles which permitted a new wave of Marian devotion to develop in Counter-Reformation Europe, sponsored, among others, by the Jesuits. The cult of an idealized woman, Marianism flourished particularly among all-male groups – as Louis Châtellier has reminded us, early Marian sodalities were at first brotherhoods only, where the threat of the real feminine had, at least temporarily, been removed.[13]

III

What was the substance of this transformation of gender relations in the case of Reformation Germany? So far as its effects on women are concerned, the broad outlines are by now fairly clear. The key areas of change concerned marriage, the regulation of sexuality and the abolition of convents. By advocating marriage for all, whether of lay or clerical estate, the reformers precipitated a reconsideration of the place of sexuality: now, bachelorhood was no longer the precondition of a clerical career, and sexual renunciation was no longer associated with holiness. Marriage was the calling appropriate for almost everybody, and it was understood as a relation of hierarchy. Like other sanctified relations of authority and submission, marriage was conceived in bilateral terms: the governance of the husband was counterposed to the subordination of the wife, who ought to 'obey him as her head'. This paradigm of the relations between the sexes so saturated Reformation thinking that the discourse of wifehood began to displace that of womanhood altogether. There is almost no rhetoric of motherhood in the early years of the Reformation.[14]

Morals were the second major area of change. Taking over the old concerns of the pre-Reformation morals ordinances, reformed authorities clothed them in a religious garb: the vices of drunkenness, gorging, adultery and whoredom became sins, their chastisement entrusted to new, far more effective courts (sometimes exclusively lay, sometimes a mixture of church and secular) which, together with the new church, undertook the implementation of a 'brotherly discipline'. Familiar as the sentiments of the Discipline Ordinances may have been to their sixteenth-century hearers' ears, this time they meant business. In place of the confessional or the spasmodic punishment, the miscreant now confronted the combined forces of church and secular authority which – despite their differences in emphasis on what counted as sin – generally worked closely enough together in practice to amount to a much more efficient moral policing system, sometimes even a dual system of church and secular control.[15] The creation of the godly city seemed to be assured when discipline was implemented: the introduction of the Discipline Ordinance forms the culmination of the city clerk Jörg Vögeli's epic narrative of the Reformation in Constance, and he reproduces it as the climax of his text.[16] Sin, however, was gendered, and so were its wages. Though the ordinances seem to use gender-neutral language, they often betray their assumption that, for instance, drinking and gambling were male sins by adducing the damage they cause 'wife and child';[17] while the passages on fighting and drawing weapons generally presume that it is men who are more likely to be the subjects of discipline (in Augsburg, for instance, women's fines for fighting are half men's).[18] Paragraphs on adultery and concubinage are clearly attempts to redraw the ground-rules of sexual relations, and they introduce the idea that women might lead men astray.

Here the role of the prostitute is of importance, not so much because the closure of brothels was an exclusive Protestant concern – it was not: Catholic towns, too, closed brothels and tried to expel prostitutes.[19] But, having closed brothels and set about banishing prostitutes, evangelical councillors denied there was a category of prostitutes as such. Rather, there were women who engaged in illicit sexual relations. Whether the crime was adultery or fornication turned on the marital status of the participants; prostitutes were thus more 'sinful' than their clients because their 'misbehaviour' was simply more frequent. Consequently, they faced exile while their clients usually escaped with fines. The effect was to blur the distinction between prostitutes – no longer seen as a separate, dishonourable group – and 'honourable' women. And it also resulted in a slippage of the rhetoric of whoredom, which could now easily be applied to women who, though they did not engage in sex for money, could be viewed as 'wanton': women who had sex with men before securing public promises of marriage, women who committed adultery. Thus, although the intention of the rhetoric against fornication and adultery was to penalize men and women equally, in practice it often served to excuse the man. All women, not just prostitutes, might practise the arts of seduction. The procedure in criminal cases merely served to demonstrate the point: in Augsburg, as in Basel, as Susanna Burghartz's researches are showing, a man's best strategy when accused of fornication or sued for paternity was to claim that 'she' had led him on, had incited him, that she 'ran after him more than he her'. Because she took the sexual initiative, she could be classed as a whore, thus minimizing male culpability. 'Lust' could thereby be displaced on to woman.[20]

The third key area of change concerns convents. The reformers' hostility to convent women often makes explicit its deep antagonism to women who were not wives. Bernhart Rem weighed the work of the Christian wife and mother in the scales against the prayers of the unmarried nun, sunk in the toils of a burning lust which had no outlet. He left his readers in no doubt as to which version of femininity God found pleasing.[21] The strategies which convent women devised to protect themselves and their institutions against hostile civic authorities were caught in similar antinomies about the nature of womanhood. Nuns turned to their order, to the Pope, to outside authorities for protection against secular authority, but these appeals merely strengthened suspicions that they plotted treason and did not recognize the authority of secular rulers.[22] Or, like the abbess Caritas Pirckheimer in Nuremberg, they attempted to invoke sisterly authority against family authority. Having failed to protect her convent through deals with civic councillors, Pirckheimer dramatized the forced departure to their homes of some nuns from her convent in the most public way she could devise, staging a tearful farewell, ceremoniously taking off their veils, belts and white habit and dressing them in 'worldly' clothes. The nuns awaited the 'grim wolves' – the council's henchmen – to drive them away as if they were going to execution, making it apparent that the young convent women did not wish to return to the bosom of their Protestant families, and exploiting the publicity their route into town offered by mobilizing the sympathy of the women selling fruit at the market they passed on the way.[23] The abbess's authority over her nuns, her spiritual daughters, was at loggerheads with the authority of the biological father and mother, as Pirckheimer makes evident by supplying a series of dramatized exchanges between the 'sheep' daughters and their 'grim wolf' mothers. Katerina Ebner retorts to her mother, 'you a mother of my flesh, but not of my spirit, because you did not give me my soul, therefore I am not obliged to obey you in matters which are against my soul'.[24] To evangelicals, this was further proof that convent influence undermined the sanctity of the household.

In the sphere of sexual relations, then, the Reformation drew its strength from the crisis that was felt to exist in the nature of womanhood, a crisis which it helped to foment. This crisis was enacted in the symbolic realm as well: whereas Catholicism's spiritual universe had both a feminine and a masculine register, with saints of both genders and a powerful role for Mary, reformed religion proclaimed gender to be irrelevant. Mary was not the Queen of Heaven but a model of humility for all Christians, male and female, to imitate; the religious rhetoric of motherhood and nursing which was such a powerful symbolism in late medieval Catholicism was assumed only with caution in early Protestantism for pedagogical, rather than mystical ends, as Jane Dempsey Douglass has pointed out.[25] For early evangelicals, the body was, in a sense, another of those 'indifferent matters', neither a vehicle of divine healing miracles nor closer to God if kept chaste and virginal. By contrast, Counter-Reformation Catholicism reawoke Marian devotion, particularly in relation to exorcism: significantly, the point at which the conjunction between physical and spiritual torment was at its most riveting. Exorcism, after all, involved the battle of spiritual forces in the theatre of the body itself.[26]

We might say, then, that the Reformation proceeded partly by mobilizing sexual anxiety and invoking the Eden of an ordered household. Moral reform would bring about a godly, reformed community; convents had no place in the sanctified republic of households. Its rhetoric at once fended off and nursed a powerful sense of sexual crisis. But disturbance in the meaning of womanhood inevitably necessitates ructions in the meaning of its complement, manhood. This dimension has hitherto received considerably less attention.[27]

IV

If the Reformation's exemplar of evil womanhood was the prostitute, her male counterpart was the Catholic cleric. In Reformation polemic he was variously accused of many of the sins of excessive manhood: he carries weapons, drinks to excess, is a secret whorer and a creature of lust who may even debauch young boys. He is cast as a sexual competitor, stealing wives and naïve daughters who, however, are so deeply mired in the sin of Eve as to be eager to yield to his seductive arts. In one of the most vivid of these lampoons, a married woman praises the cleric who has shriven her as no cleric ever did before.[28] Monks are twitted by lascivious women in many of the early sixteenth-century woodcuts. Such a figure of hatred is the priest that even on his deathbed the pious Protestant pastor must rally himself for a final spit at the Catholic clergy, renouncing not so much Catholic doctrine as the individual who embodies all that is held to be wrong with the old church, the priest.[29]

Theological difference took anthropomorphic form. Protestants, especially Protestant clergy, tended to cast the Catholic cleric as a particular kind of man because the doctrinal battle engaged two different kinds of manliness, rather as it set the pious married woman against the lusting nun. The Catholic cleric became the repository of a set of fears about manhood. These anxieties, of course, were most familiar to Protestant clergy: after all, the first generation of Protestant clerics often had to resolve their own sexual status in a new way. For many of them, joining the evangelical movement was to entail leaving the all-male living environment of the monastery and entering the estate of matrimony, where manhood had to be proven in companionship with the opposite sex. The pre-Reformation clergy enjoyed a distinctive sexual status: in principle they were virgins, men who had not acquired manhood by mastering a woman through sexual intercourse, men who were in a sense castrated. Yet they were also imagined as enjoying a special intimacy with women, and reputed to be sexual libertines, even if many a parish priest was in reality living in prosaic stable concubinage.[30] When Protestant clergy joined the ranks of the other heads of household, becoming men like them, it is not surprising that the figure of the hated Catholic priest took on a kind of psychic necessity for evangelicals, as he began to represent aspects they wished to obliterate from their own masculine identity. Time and again evangelicals termed the Catholic monks whores of the Devil, painting the Pope as the arch-whore. Monks and priests were thus women of the most lustful kind, beings who were to be excoriated partly because they stood for the clergy's own too recent past.

In Reformation polemic, theological dispute, too, could become a tussle of titans, a clash of male personalities as much as of doctrine.

This element of doctrinal debate is evident to us in the intemperate invective of much propagandist writing. Modern commentators have been embarrassed by the stream of insult which marks much of Luther's combative writing. Its pulse, however, has the genuine rhythm of evangelicalism. This point could be illustrated with numerous examples, but Luther's *Wider Hans Wurst* will suffice here. In this tract, Luther abuses Catholic clergy as hellish prostitutes and brides of the Devil. In wonderfully energetic invective he sets them against the true Brides of Christ as whores who do not obey, 'an apostate, erring, married whore, a house-whore, a bed-whore, a key-whore', metaphors which convey how their sexual promiscuity undermines household order. The Catholic church is even a kind of anus, for:

> We too were formerly stuck in the behind of this hellish whore, this new church of the pope. We supported it in all earnestness, so that we regret having spent so much time and energy in that vile hole. But God be praised and thanked that he rescued us from the scarlet whore.[31]

Here the Catholic clergy are represented as women and as sodomitical partners: by implication their Protestant peers, who take the active position, are real men. The tract concludes by impugning its target, Heinrich of Wolfenbüttel, as a coward barely able to guard even women and not in control of his own bodily functions. He is not a man but a timid creature, all sound and fury, but like Pharaoh's followers when they chased the Israelites to the Red Sea, one glance from God is enough to make him 'do it in his shoes' with panic.[32]

The structure of the Reformation's early advance often enhanced the tendency to demonize one's opponents. The Reformation proceeded by means of highly personal preaching battles between individual clergy, each with their own congregational audience who might later be moved to mob the opponent.[33] The true Christian preacher could come to represent the Word, so that attacks on him could be read as part of salvationist history: Paulus Speratus, preaching in hostile Würzburg, spoke of how 'in me the word of God has been persecuted'.[34] The targets of evangelical attack were seldom restricted to false belief but concerned one's opponents, and the currency of abuse was often sexual. So, for example, the preacher Paul Lindenau attacked the Burgomaster at Zwickau Herman Mühlpfort from the pulpit, as much for his moral failings as his lack of evangelical fervour, couching these in sexually coloured language. Lindenau reputedly accused him of having 'erected a shrine to Venus' when he held an elaborate wedding for his son.

> You whore, you lout, you proud wretch, you haughty boob, you highfalutin donkey. . . . You hold council against me, you brought me

here and want to drive me out again because I won't condone your
airs, misdeeds, knavery, shitting around, thievery, and whoring![35]

But the evangelical movement drew on a positive rhetoric of masculinity
as well. As Hans-Christoph Rublack has pointed out, early evangelical
rhetoric made much of the concept of brotherly love.[36] The resonance
of this phrase lay in the world of male collectivities such as guilds,
peasant assemblies and militias, and it invoked models of collective
action among men. Brotherly love, as Rublack has shown, was a fundamental norm of town society and it was this world of secular male
brotherhood which evangelical clergy joined when they married and
sought citizenship and admission to guilds. Some swapped clerical life
altogether for the civic life: Jakob Vogt transferred his state

> because at this time God our lord has revealed to me and to many
> others, how our presumed service to God and our imagined holiness
> were worth nothing before God, but were a most damnable mislead-
> ing, so that, for the honour of God and the sake of my soul and with
> certainty of conscience I have left for a better life, taken off my
> cassock and joined a life of work, and I have learned a trade and
> joined the marital estate[37]

– a eulogy of marriage and honest craft toil which might have made
the bosom of the humblest craftsman swell with pride. The ideal of
brotherhood could speak both to the poor craftsman hostile to the unfair
division of resources in his town and hating the 'big jacks' who got it
all, and to the élite, who invoked 'brotherly love' to describe the basis
on which they held power. For a brief moment in the Peasants' War,
the revolutionary movement itself was symbolized by a male figure, a
peasant who, with his flail, confident pose and rough boots, had all the
attributes of robust masculinity.[38] If the ideal of brotherly love was
ultimately to become an authoritarian, paternalist vision, and if the
power of the civic authority to punish was the interpretation of
'brotherly love' which was eventually to win the day, its success must
be explained in part by the power of that rhetoric of masculine bonding
itself and its shared appeal to master craftsman, merchant, apprentice
and day-labourer alike.

Brotherhood meant bonds between men. It was not a vision of community which could incorporate women. The extent to which the evangelical rhetoric of brotherhood drew its strength from its single-sex
vision of equality is betrayed in the strikingly similar structure of the
taunts made by women accused of involvement in early Reformation
disturbances. Anna Fasnacht was said to have shouted in Augsburg in
1524 that if men did not take action to introduce the Reformation, then
'we women must and shall take action'; Hans Husel's wife in
Nördlingen called out that if the men were not prepared to hand over

the canon to the peasants, then the women would do so.[39] Women's action was invoked as the ultimate threat should the impetus of the men's brotherhood seem to slacken. If women were to act, this would represent an admission by the men of their own unmanning.[40]

In the towns, the effect of evangelical advocacy of marriage and insistence on sexual discipline was to propose a vision of masculinity which was as unitary as its ideal of femininity. The real man was a household head, a little patriarch ruling over wife, children, servants, journeymen and apprentices. Like the city fathers on the council, he was vested with the power to chastise; like them his good governance consisted in careful stewardship of the household's limited resources. What gave one access to the world of brothers was one's mastery of a woman which guaranteed one's sexual status. This was a very old lay ideal: marriage had long been the precondition of mastership and full membership of the guild. But now this ideal was to apply to all men. The closure of brothels, formerly the pleasure-ground of unmarried men, thus resulted in an even sharper theoretical alignment of heterosexual experience with masterhood.[41] As a result, the unmarried young man might come to seem not securely male. The literature of the 'Trousers Devil', for instance, mocks the exhibitionist clothing of young men. But as writers like Gregorius Wagner thunder against the excesses of youth attire, they are drawn to condemn extravagant clothing because it draws attention to the codpiece 'as if there was sweet honeycomb inside'.[42] Their own rhetoric proposes these youths as objects of sexual desire.

The gap between ideal and reality was, however, wider in the case of husbands than of wives. As the economy contracted and guilds made entry more difficult, masterhood was a status which ever fewer sixteenth-century craftsmen could attain. And councils themselves knew that town patriarchs were not the wise governors they ought to be: men were guilty of the sins of drunkenness and gambling; they were lazy, godless good-for-nothings who did not exercise their disciplining duties with paternal mildness but punched, beat, kicked and bit their wives. Ironically, the council's power to punish led it to intervene in the domestic sphere – often at the wife's insistence – thus undermining the master's household rule which it claimed to uphold.[43]

V

So far, I have argued that the Reformation articulated deep anxieties about masculinity and femininity, that part of the vigour of its rhetoric came from its mobilization of these fears, and that it propounded the reordering of sexual relations as part of the means of averting God's wrath from his sinful people. The evangelical movement garnered support in part because that rhetoric spoke to fears in the late medieval society about the instability of the household, its economic decline and the attendant breakup of the political ideal of the brotherly commune. But did the Reformation, once institutionalized, resolve the crisis in gender relations it helped to foment?

To this question the resounding answer must be 'no'. Evangelicals certainly advocated godly households, but they were frankly uncertain what to do – beyond issuing fruitless admonitions – when confronted with real life, drunken, lazy, godless patriarchs. They proved unable to abolish prostitution or root out the evils of adultery. Manliness did not become stable: the Devil Books of the mid-sixteenth century delight in the sins of manhood they excoriate, and trade at times on a sexual ambiguity as troubling to any unified vision of masculinity as it was doubtless titillating to its readers. The Protestant pastor's household created new opportunities for scandal: in Nördlingen, the preacher Kaspar Kantz was separated from his wife and refusing to take her back; pastoral visitors unearthed several cases of immorality among reformed clergy in the Saxon diocese of Grimma in 1529; and, as Luise Schorn-Schütte's work on the clergy is showing, Protestant pastors' claim to the right to discipline their flock proved to be tinder for conflict between church and council for generations to come.[44] Even the theology of marriage, so often taken to be the lodestone of Reformation morals, lacked the crystal clarity one might expect: leading theologians found themselves advising Philip of Hesse to commit bigamy secretly; and as late as the seventeenth century, it was possible for Protestant pastors to argue that, in some circumstances, princes might take a second wife.[45]

These complexities must give us pause if we wish to characterize the late sixteenth and seventeenth centuries as the golden age of patriarchy, ushered in by the crisis of the Reformation and Counter-Reformation. The witch-craze, which reaches its peak during these years, cannot, I suggest, be read as an index of the extent of patriarchal authority. As I have argued elsewhere, it may have as much to do with taking women's fears seriously (whose denunciations of suspected witches often helped to spark the trials), and its existence may do more to document the instabilities of sexual identities – the ills for which women's love magic might offer a cure, for instance – than it does to prove the effectiveness of fatherly rule.

The history of gender relations will certainly need to chart changes in the two sexes' access to property, resources and political power. But it will do well to remember that the meaning of sexual difference is relative, that shifts in the meaning of femininity will occasion realignments in the meaning of manhood. One of the most sobering reflections that the history of gender relations offers is the sheer tenacity of sexual division: the campaigns against prostitution in sixteenth-century German towns bear more than a passing resemblance to the struggles around the Contagious Diseases Act in nineteenth-century Britain; the evangelical moralism of the sixteenth-century German town seems not totally dissimilar to that of twentieth-century evangelical North America. Much of the tissue of the relations between the sexes and many of the points of conflict are perennial. Issues like motherhood, the control of sexuality, the division of labour have a disconcerting habit of turning up on the pages of histories of more than one century. Sexual divisions are more than simple assignments of social place, and this is why deep change is difficult while lability, at least, seems to be a fairly permanent feature of sexual identities, past and present. Between the fixities of gender roles and the glittering profusion of sexual identities which historians discern in discourse lies the realm of the psychic. Without a theory of subjectivity, I believe, we shall be unable either to account for the tenacious hold of sexual stereotypes in the present or the past, or to explain the attraction of particular rhetorics of gender at particular historical moments. But the concept of the psyche assumes that body and mind, emotion and history are interrelated, and that sexual identities, while they may have a history, are not mere social constructions.[46] To a far greater extent than the divisions of race and class, sexual differences are ingrained in the body, and difference, if not its meanings, seems to be an irreducible fact of life. Historians do indeed need to provide narratives of the history of gender relations, but these stories may proceed in a series of twin spirals rather than in straight lines.

NOTES

1 Judith M. Bennett, 'Feminism and History', *Gender and History*, 1, 1989, pp. 251–72; Joan W. Scott, 'Gender: A useful category of historical analysis', *American Historical Review*, 91, no. 5, 1986, and in her *Gender and the Politics of History*, New York 1988.

2 Simon Schama, *Citizens. A chronicle of the French Revolution*, New York and London 1989, pp. 203–27; Elizabeth Colwill, 'Just Another *Citoyenne*? Marie-Antoinette on trial, 1790–1793', *History Workshop Journal*, 28, 1989, pp. 63–87; and see Joan Wallach Scott, 'French Feminists and the Rights of "Man": Olympe de Gouge's declarations', *History Workshop Journal*, 28, 1989, pp. 1–21.

3 Jürgen Habermas, *Legitimation Crisis*, trans. Thomas McCarthy, London 1976 (first published in German 1973), pp. 1–2; and on crisis as merely the outcome of long-term causes, Emmanuel Le Roy Ladurie, 'The Crisis and the Historian', in *idem, The Mind and Method of the Historian*, trans. Sian Reynolds and Ben Reynolds, London 1981 (first published in French 1978).

4 Thomas Robisheaux, *Rural Society and the Search for Order in Early Modern Germany*, Cambridge 1989.

5 Patrick Collinson, 'The Protestant Family', in *idem, The Birthpangs of Protestant England. Religion and cultural change in the sixteenth and seventeenth centuries*, London 1988, p. 93.

6 Steven Ozment, *When Fathers Ruled. Family life in Reformation Europe*, Cambridge, Mass. and London 1983.

7 Merry E. Wiesner, *Working Women in Renaissance Germany*, New Brunswick, NJ 1987.

8 Gerald Strauss, *Luther's House of Learning. Indoctrination of the young in the German Reformation*, Baltimore, Md and London 1978; Susan Karant-Nunn, 'The Reality of Early Lutheran Education: The Electoral District of Saxony, a case study', forthcoming.

9 See, for example, Thomas A. Brady, 'In Search of the Godly City: The domestication of religion in the German urban Reformation', in R. Po-Chia Hsia (ed.), *The German People and the Reformation*, Ithaca, NY and London 1988: Thomas A. Brady, *Ruling Class, Regime and Reformation at Strasbourg 1520–55* (Studies in Medieval and Reformation Thought 22), Leiden 1978; Hans-Christoph Rublack, 'Is There a "New History" of the Urban Reformation?', in T. Scott and E.I. Kouri (eds), *Politics and Society in Reformation Europe. Essays for Sir Geoffrey Elton on his sixty-fifth birthday*, New York 1987; Hans-Christoph Rublack, 'The Song of Contz Anahans: Communication and revolt in Nördlingen, 1525', in Hsia (ed.), *The German People*; Kaspar von Greyerz, 'Stadt und Reformation. Stand und Aufgaben der Forschung', *Archiv für Reformationsgeschichte*, 76, 1985, pp. 6–63; Lyndal Roper, *The Holy Household. Women and morals in Reformation Augsburg*, Oxford 1989.

10 Robin Briggs, *Communities of Belief. Cultural and social tensions in early modern France*, Oxford 1989.

11 Sarah Hanley, 'Engendering the State: Family formation and state building in early modern France', *French Historical Studies*, 16, 1989, pp. 4–27.

12 Elizabeth Rapley, *The Devotes. Women and church in seventeenth-century France*, Montreal and London 1990; Mary E. Perry, *Gender and Disorder in Early Modern Seville*, Princeton, NJ 1990, Jodi Bilinkoff, *The Avila of Saint Teresa: Religious reform in a sixteenth-century city*, Ithaca, NY and London 1989.

13 Louis Chatellier, *The Europe of the Devout*, Cambridge 1989; R. Po-Chia Hsia, *Society and Religion in Münster 1535–1618*, New Haven, Conn. and London 1984, esp. pp. 65–7.

14 Roper, *The Holy Household*, esp. pp. 59–60.

15 The standard work on these courts in the reformed areas remains Walter Köhler, *Zürcher Ehegericht und Genfer Konsistorium*, 2 vols (Quellen und Abhandlungen zur schweizerischen Reformationsgeschichte 7, 10), Leipzig 1932, 1942. See also Heinz Schilling, ' "History of Crime" or "History of Sin"? Some reflections on the social history of early modern church discipline', in Scott and Kouri (eds), *Politics and Society*; and Paul Münch, *Zucht und Ordnung. Reformierte Kirchenverfassungen im 16. und 17. Jahrhundert (Nassau-Dillenburg, Kurpfalz, Hessen-Kassel)*, Stuttgart 1978. As recent work is showing, interest in discipline was not peculiar to reformed Protestantism: Robisheaux, *Rural Society*; William J. Wright, *Capitalism, the State, and the Lutheran Reformation: Sixteenth-century Hesse*, Athens, Ohio 1988; R. Po-Chia Hsia, *Social Discipline in the Reformation: Central Europe 1550–1750*, London and New York 1989.

16 Jörg Vögeli, *Schriften zur Reformation in Konstanz, 1519–1538* (Schriften zur Kirchen- und Rechtsgeschichte 39, 40, 41) 2 vols, Tübingen 1972–3, vol. 1, pp. 442–65. See, on the Constance ordinance, Fritz Hauss, 'Blarers Zuchtordnungen', in Bernd Moeller (ed.), *Der Konstanzer Reformator Ambrosius Blarer 1492–1564. Gedenkschrift zu seinem 400. Todestag*, Constance and Stuttgart 1964; and Hans-Christoph Rublack, *Die Einführung der Reformation in Konstanz von den Anfängen bis zum Abschluss 1531* (Quellen und Forschungen zur Reformationsgeschichte 40), Gütersloh 1971, pp. 87–93.

17 For example, *Ains Erbern Rats/ der Stat Augspurg/ Zucht vnd Pollicey Ordnung*, Augsburg 1537, fo. a v (r).

18 *Ains Erbern Rats/ der Stat Augspurg/ Zucht vnd Pollicey Ordnung*, Augsburg 1537, fo. b v (r–v).

19 Merry Wiesner, 'Paternalism in Practice: The control of servants and prostitutes in early modern German cities', in Phillip N. Bebb and Sherrin Marshall (eds), *The Process of Change in Early Modern Europe. Essays in honor of Miriam Usher Chrisman*, Athens, Ohio 1988; Lyndal Roper, 'Mothers of Debauchery: Procuresses in sixteenth-century Augsburg', *German History*, 6, 1988, pp. 1–19; Roper, *The Holy Household*; Beata Schuster, 'Frauenhandel und Frauenhäuser im 15. und 16. Jahrhundert', *Vierteljahrsschrift für Sozial- und Wirtschaftsgeschichte*, 78, 1991, pp. 172–89; Peter Schuster, *Das Frauenhaus. Städtische Bordelle in Deutschland 1350 bis 1600*, Paderborn 1992; Iwan Bloch, *Die Prostitution*, 2 vols, Berlin 1912–25; Brigitte Rath, 'Prostitution und spätmittelalterliche Gesellschaft im österreichisch-süddeutschen Raum', in H. Kühnel (ed.), *Frau und spätmittelalterlicher Alltag* (Veröffentlichungen des Instituts für mittelalterliche Realienkunde Österreichs 9), Vienna 1986; Franz Irsigler and Arnold Lassotta, *Bettler und Gaukler, Dirnen und Henker. Aussenseiter in einer mittelalterlichen Stadt. Köln 1300–1600*, Cologne 1984 (in Cologne, the brothel was closed in 1591 under the influence of the Counter-Reformation: pp. 192–3).

20 Roper, *The Holy Household*; Susanna Burghartz, 'Rechte Jungfrauen oder unverschämte Töchter? Zur weiblichen Ehre im 16. Jahrhundert', in Karin Hausen and Heide Wunder (eds), *Frauengeschichte – Geschlechtergeschichte*, Frankfurt am Main 1992; and Susanna Burghartz, 'Jungfräulichkeit oder Reinheit? Zur Änderung von Argumentationsmustern vor den Basler Ehegericht im 16. und 17. Jahrhundert' in Richard van Dülmen, (ed.), *Dynamik der Tradition*, Frankfurt am Main 1992; for comparable English material, Laura Gowing, 'Gender and the Language of Insult in Early Modern London', *History Workshop Journal*, 35, 1993, pp. 1–21; *idem*, 'Women, Sex and Honour: The London Church Courts 1572–1640', PhD. diss. University of London 1993; and note, for example, the Constance Discipline Ordinance which explicitly states that men need pay neither compensation for loss of virginity nor childbed expenses 'if she ran after him': Vögeli, *Reformation in Konstanz*, p. 457.

21 Bernhart Rem, *Ain Christlich schreiben/ so ain Euangelischer brüder seiner schwestern/ ainer closter iunckfrawen zugeschickt*, Augsburg n.d.; *idem, Ain Sendtbrieff an ettlich Closterfrawen zu sant katherina vnd zu sant niclas in Augsburg* [Augsburg, P. Ulhart] 1523; and see *Antwurt zwayer Closter frauwen im Katheriner Closter zu Augspurg/ an Bernhart Remen/ Vnd hernach seyn gegen Antwurt* [Augsburg, P. Ulhart 1523].

22 Roper, *The Holy Household*, pp. 206–44.

23 Merry Wiesner, 'Women's Response to the Reformation', in Hsia (ed.), *The German People*, esp. p. 158; *Die "Denkwürdigkeiten" der Caritas Pirckheimer (aus den Jahren 1524–1528)*, ed. Josef Pfanner (Caritas Pirckheimer – Quellensammlung 2), Landshut 1962, pp. 79–84.

24 'Du pist ein mutter meins flaysch, aber nit meins geist, dann du hast mir mein sel nit geben, darumb pin ich dir nit schuldig gehorsam zu sein in den dingen, die wider mein sel sind': Pirckheimer, *Denkwürdigkeiten*, p. 81.

25 Jane Dempsey Douglass, 'Calvin's Use of Metaphorical Language for God: God as enemy and God as mother', *Archiv für Reformationsgeschichte*, 77, 1986, pp. 126–40; and see Caroline Walker Bynum, *Jesus as Mother: Studies in the spirituality of the high middle ages*, Berkeley, Calif. and London 1982; and by the same author, *Holy Feast and Holy Fast: The religious significance of food to medieval women*, Berkeley, Calif. and London 1987; and see Natalie Zemon Davis, 'City Women and Religious Change', in her *Society and Culture in Early Modern France*, London 1975.

26 H.C. Erik Midelfort, 'The Devil and the German People: Reflections on the popularity of demon possession in sixteenth-century Germany', in Steven Ozment (ed.), *Religion and Culture in the Renaissance and Reformation,* Kirksville, Mo. 1989.

27 See Merry Wiesner, 'Guilds, Male Bonding and Women's Work in Early Modern Europe', *Gender and History,* 1, 1989, pp. 125–37. For path-breaking work on the history of masculinity see Michael Roper, 'Masculinity and the Evolution of Management Cultures in British Industry 1945–85', PhD. diss., University of Essex 1989; Alan Bray, 'Homosexuality and the Signs of Male Friendship in Elizabethan England', *History Workshop Journal,* 29, 1990, pp. 1–19; Lynne Segal, *Slow Motion,* London 1990.

28 Steven Ozment, *The Reformation in the Cities: The appeal of Protestantism to sixteenth century Germany and Switzerland,* New Haven, Conn. and London 1975, pp. 53–4; R.W. Scribner, *Popular Culture and Popular Movements in Reformation Germany,* London 1987, pp. 246ff.

29 Pamela Biel, 'Heinrich Bullinger's Death and *Testament*: A well-planned departure', *Sixteenth-Century Journal,* 22, 1991, pp. 3–14, esp. p. 7.

30 Scribner, *Popular Culture and Popular Movements,* pp. 246–56; and see Chapter 4.

31 'eine abtrunnige verlauffene ehehure, eine haushure, eine betthure, ein schlusselhure';

> Denn wir sind weiland auch der hellischen huren des Bapsts newen kirchen ym hindern gesteckt mit gantzem ernst, Das vns leid ist, so viel zeit vnd muhe ynn dem loche schendlich zu bracht, Aber Gott lob und danck der vns von der roten lester huren erloset hat
> (*D. Martin Luthers Werke,* 60 vols, Weimar 1883–1983 (hereafter cited as *WA*), vol. 51, pp. 503, 498–9, translation of Eric W. Gritsch, *Luthers Works,*
> vol. 41, Philadelphia 1966, pp. 208, 206)

32 *WA*, 51, pp. 569–70.

33 There are numerous examples of this. In Zwickau there was a public preaching feud between Johannes Egranus and Thomas Müntzer which led to public disorder on several occasions, and bitter controversy between clergy of different persuasions continued after the departure of both: Susan Karant-Nunn, *Zwickau in Transition 1500–1547: The Reformation as an agent of change,* Columbus, Ohio 1987, pp. 92–136; and her 'What was Preached in German Cities in the Early Years of the Reformation? *Wildwuchs* versus Lutheran unity', in Bebb and Marshall (eds), *The Process of Change.* Bernd Moeller, in 'Was wurde in der Frühzeit der Reformation in den deutschen Städten gepredigt?', *Archiv für Reformationsgeschichte,* 75, 1984, pp. 176–93, also notes the strong element of criticism of the clergy and clerical immorality in evangelical preaching.

34 'wie . . . in mir das work ist verfolget worden', Hans-Christoph Rublack, *Gescheiterte Reformation. Frühreformatorische und protestantische Bewegungen in süd- und westdeutschen geistlichen Residenzen* (Spätmittelalter und Frühe Neuzeit. Tübinger Beiträge zur Geschichtsforschung 4), Stuttgart 1978, p. 11, n. 24.

35 Karant-Nunn, *Zwickau in Transition,* p. 160.

36 Hans-Christoph Rublack, *Eine bürgerliche Reformation: Nördlingen* (Quellen und Forschungen zur Reformationsgeschichte 51), Gütersloh 1982, pp. 46–7; Hans-Christoph Rublack, 'Political and Social Norms in Urban Communities in the Holy Roman Empire', in Kaspar von Greyerz (ed.), *Religion, Politics and Social Protest. Three studies on early modern Germany,* London 1984.

37
> Dweyl aber Zu disser Zyt gott vnsser Herr mir mit sampt andern vilen

eröffnet hat, wie das vnnsser vermeinter Gotts dienst vnnd verwenete geistlicheyt vor gott nit gelt, sonnder ein hohe verdamliche gleissnerische verfürung sihe, hab ich mich vmb der eeren Gottes vnnd meines heils willen mit sicherm gewissen eines bessern daruon gethon, die kutten hingelegt vnnd in ein arbevtssam leben gethann, ein handtwerck gelernet vnnd ehelichen stadt an mich genomen.

(Rublack, *Eine bürgerliche Reformation*, pp. 191–2)

38 Lyndal Roper, ' "The Common Man", "the Common Good", "Common Women": Gender and meaning in the German Reformation commune', *Social History*, 12, 1987, pp. 1–21.
39 ibid.; Rublack, 'The Song of Contz Anahans', pp. 114–15.
40 In an important article, Marion Kobelt-Groch has demonstrated that women were indeed involved in the Peasants' War. But though it was not impossible for women to act with men as part of a community, nevertheless, as Kobelt-Groch shows, their actions were often separately noted. Frequently they acted in concert as a group of women, and their activities were viewed as deeply disruptive: 'Von "armen frouwen" und "bösen wibern" – Frauen im Bauernkrieg zwischen Anpassung und Auflehnung', *Archiv für Reformationsgeschichte*, 79, 1988, pp. 103–37; and on the meanings of feminine insubordination, see Claudia Ulbrich, 'Unartige Weiber. Präsenz und Renitenz von Frauen im frühneuzeitlichen Deutschland', in Richard van Dülmen (ed.), *Arbeit, Frömmigkeit und Eigensinn*, Frankfurt am Main 1990.
41 Roper, *The Holy Household*; and see Heide Wunder, 'Überlegungen zum Wandel der Geschlechterbeziehungen im 15. und 16. Jahrhundert aus sozialgeschichtlicher Sicht', in Heide Wunder and Christina Vanja (eds), *Wandel der Geschlechterbeziehungen zu Beginn der Neuzeit*, Frankfurt am Main 1991.
42 Andreas Musculus, *Vom Hosen Teuffel. Anno MDLV*, prefatory poem by Gregorius Wagner, in Ria Stambaugh (ed.), *Teufelbücher in Auswahl*, 5 vols, Berlin and New York 1970–80, vol. 4, p. 5.
43 Roper, *The Holy Household*, pp. 165–205.
44 Rublack, *Eine bürgerliche Reformation*, p. 208; Scribner, *Popular Culture and Popular Movements*, p. 252; Luise Schorn-Schütte, 'Protestantische Pfarrer in der frühen Neuzeit', paper given at conference on 'Problems in the Historical Anthropology of Religion in Early Modern Europe' at the Herzog August Bibliothek Wolfenbüttel, June 1991, in R. Po-Chia Hsia and B. Scribner (eds), *History and Anthropology in Early Modern Europe. Papers from the Wolfenbüttel conference 1991*, forthcoming.
45 See Chapter 4; Paula Sutter Fichtner, *Protestantism and Primogeniture in Early Modern Germany*, New Haven, Conn. and London 1989, p. 77.
46 Here I part company with Denise Riley's stimulating *'Am I that Name?' Feminism and the Category of 'Women' in History*, London 1988.

3 Will and honour: sex, words and power in Augsburg criminal trials

INTRODUCTION

When we write about relations between men and women, it can be tempting to see heterosexual relations as the most fundamental site of oppression: here, it would seem, is the key to both patriarchial power and women's attraction to it.[1] Perhaps, in some not always explicitly theorized way, this may account for the turn feminist history has taken towards a particular interest in prostitution, rape and sex crimes. Analysing the historical forms of oppression in heterosexual relations promises to make gender a primary historical category. Instead of the history of prostitution or rape being historical byways, they are shown to be central routes to understanding past societies. So, for instance, Anna Clark's book takes rape as a paradigmatic way of investigating the oppression of women by men in the eighteenth century;[2] or Judith Walkowitz's history of nineteenth-century English prostitution uses that issue to get to the heart of relations between men and women and explore nineteenth-century feminism.[3]

Important as it is to make these topics central to historical understanding, however, I think there may be a danger here. By treating heterosexuality as the key to understanding past patriarchies we have already transported our own notion of what is sexual into past societies whose delineation of the field of the sexual may be different. Even more importantly, while we need to relate sexual subordination to other kinds of social oppression, the patterns we chart will inevitably be complex. We cannot do justice to women's erotic feelings and desires if we see heterosexuality as a social construct with fixed terms and immovable parameters, one that imposed itself on women so that they, like sexual automata, acted out a script of male domination. On the other hand, to write in terms of women's 'consent' to sexual relations with men is surely inadequate to the task. Grounded as the notion of 'consent' is in a liberal notion of the individual, deciding actor, it distorts early modern people's own language.

My project in this chapter is to examine the way men and women

Der Nasen tantz zu Gümpelsbrunn bis Sonntag:

Plate 3.1 Hans Sebald Beham, *The Dance of Noses at Gimpelsbrunn*

Source: W. Strauss, *The German Single Leaf Woodcut, 1500–1550*, New York, Hacker Art
  Books 1974.

Note: This woodcut is crammed with phallic imagery: cock, breeches, etc., with the
  wreath/vagina speared triumphantly below the nose/penis.

talked about heterosexual relations at a moment in the European past
when the social and political context of sexual behaviour was changing
and when the meaning of sexuality itself – its definition and the rules
governing it – were in flux. By studying this language, I do not expect
to gain a sure understanding of what these people's sexual life was like,
nor do I hope to offer a new model for comprehending the place of
heterosexuality in gender and social relations. As Ludmilla Jordanova
has remarked, 'language is not transparent but opaque; and . . . to see
through, or rather into it, is thus an act of interpretation'[4] – a caution
which is particularly relevant when we first look at words that seem
familiar, or think that we recognize desire, jealousy or anger in our
sources. But I do hope to reveal the historical instability of both sexual
meaning and its social place and, perhaps, to suggest some of the routes
that brought us to our own sense of what heterosexuality means.

The moment I am studying is the sixteenth century, during the Reformation when secular authority was replacing the church as the prime

interrogator of people about their sexual behaviour. The place is Augsburg, one of the period's most important centres of craft and commerce. The sources I shall be using are not the high discourses of Reformation polemic or legal tracts, but interrogation records from the criminal court of the town, generated when townspeople – most often artisans and labourers – who had committed sexual crimes were called to account.

CRIMINAL INTERROGATIONS AS SOURCE

Carried out under the threat of torture, in council territory, the language men and women use in criminal trials is clearly forced discourse. In other contexts, men and women would have spoken differently about sexuality. Indeed, the selfsame members of the council who carried out the interrogation on a rotation basis would not all have employed the lofty language of sinful work, marital exercises and so forth in their own sexual relations (which, in any case, did not always conform to the reformed ideals they tried to police). What was said was recorded by a male scribe, in German, so that we have a formal list of numbered questions drawn up before the interrogation and a record of responses in the third person, corresponding to or at times departing from the list, and sometimes in 'summary'. Our sources are manifestly not a sort of early modern version of the oral history interview – conducted by a rather less sympathetic interrogator equipped with thumbscrews instead of a tape recorder. They are the constructed record of a conversation where the differences of power are highly visible, and the distance of the record from 'memory' cannot be overlooked. It is thus a peculiarly distanced form of reporting. Unlike the 'pardon tales' which early modern French people might tell to secure a royal pardon for a capital offence, and which Natalie Davis has used to open windows on to early modern mental life, these narratives were not shaped freely by their authors.[5] They are better seen as a triangular dialogue between council, man and woman.

Yet the language of those interrogated reveals much about class and gender in these people's world. Indeed, the difficulties of our sources – which do not faithfully record people's experience – can be turned to advantage, because they require us to look at how men and women construct their 'experience' within a dialectic of power.[6]

THE ECONOMY OF MARRIAGE

To understand what those interrogated were saying about sexual relations, we need first to consider the meaning of marriage. In sixteenth-century urban society, sexual categories were central to social organization. Production was organized in household-based units, each headed by a married master skilled in the mysteries of the craft. He directed the labour of unmarried apprentices and journeymen and his wife and children owed him loving deference. In an individual's life cycle, the stages of sexual and work life were supposed to synchronize: a man got married when he became a master, took on citizenship and gave up the right to visit the brothel; a woman attained a mature womanhood through marriage, which secured her social and sexual position, making her mistress of a small household.[7] For both women and men, social status in the craft world had to be sealed by marriage. Marriage was the axis of early modern identity, personal and social. Consequently, adultery ruptured a productive as well as sexual union, so that adulterous lovers literally destroyed their social existence. Frequently such couples ended up in voluntary exile because they could not accommodate sexual desire and economic existence within one household. They had destroyed the one possible public form of economically viable existence. In trying to understand what sixteenth-century townsfolk said about sexuality, therefore, we have always to bear in mind that in talking about sex they are inevitably speaking about position, class and honour.

SINFUL WORK: THE LANGUAGE OF THE COUNCIL

The changes associated with the Reformation had enormous influence on the control of sexual behaviour in Augsburg.[8] Fired by a new evangelical moralism, the Augsburg town councils of the 1530s, 1540s and 1550s sought to root out prostitution and reform society. The two new courts, the Discipline Lords and the Marriage Court, were established in 1537 to deal with many of the moral offences which had previously been the concern of church authorities. At the same time, the criminal court, which had always been staffed by Small Council members, meeting in rota, began increasingly to subject sexual sinners to criminal interrogation and framed more precise questions.[9] Who was the first? How many times had unmarital acts been committed? With whom, when and where?

The Discipline Ordinance of 1537 which established the morals court and gave guidance to the new marriage court was a key document of Augsburg's moral Reformation. It furnished a justification of the council's power of intervention to discipline not only the 'public' sins such as swearing or adultery, which had always lain within its purview, but to take over the entire field of sexual regulation from the church. Permeated with religious language, the ordinance describes each 'vice' (*Laster*) by reference to godly law and specifies the appropriate penalty. Adultery is a 'godless evil', and in addition to unmarital concubinage, there is 'flagrant public whoredom and sinful fleshly works'.[10] Indeed, in the homilies which the councils of the late 1530s and 1540s routinely delivered with punishments, fornication and adultery became 'sinful work' or 'unmarital deeds'; while the term 'prostitution' (transformed in the extract above to a biblical state of sexual anarchy rather than a profession) disappeared, dissolved into the categories of 'sinful work' and 'adultery'. It had become a moral state, not a designation of work.[11]

Hand in hand with this defence of the council's moral authority went an exposition of its political power. The preface to the ordinance announces that the council

> being reminded of its office and authority commended to it by God, finding also, that in no way must it be suffered or endured, that unchristian, punishable deeds and life should be allowed; therefore and to prevent all vice and disorder . . . an honourable Council has, by God's grace and with careful consideration, drawn up this following ordinance.[12]

Like God the almightly Father, the council 'admonish[es]' its subjects 'in a fatherly and faithful manner' to lead a better life, a divine parallel which also hinted at the council's (desired) omnipotence.[13] The council must punish sinners or else God's punishment will be visited on the entire city. In such rhetoric, there is a clear shift to a paradigm of authority as paternal instead of consensual. The alternative, older view of council authority saw it as derived from the collective brotherhood of the guilds and patriciate, expressing the will of the 'common city'. Vestiges of this old communitarian rhetoric continued to hover in the council's language, and the shift in the perspective of power as deriving from below to descending from above was not to be completed until later in the century.[14] What is striking here is that it should have been the issue of moral power – the council's right to discipline its subjects' bodily comportment – that was crucial to its transformation of political metaphor.

The new moralism and the new understanding of authority certainly left their imprint in the language recorded from those interrogated. Yet the changes wrought were gradual, and other features of sexual language endured. In what follows, it will chiefly be to these more idiomatic turns of speech and story strategy that I will refer, taking material from throughout the first half of the sixteenth century.

SILENCE

Perhaps what is most striking in the language of the men and women interrogated is their determined reticence about sexual acts. The more the council demanded precise information, insisting that men and women state exactly where, how often, with whom and when sexual acts occurred, the more the mass of circumstantial information seems

Plate 3.2 Hans Springinklee, *Women's Bath*

Source: W. Strauss, *The German Single Leaf Woodcut, 1500–1550*, New York, Hacker Art
     Books 1974.

only to highlight their silence about what occurred as 'she did his will'
(an expression to which we shall return). Here we may be dealing with
the scribe's standard bowdlerizations, but there are a few exceptions
to the rule of inexplicitness where men admit to 'put[ting] it in four or
five times',[15] to 'never com[ing] in there',[16] or, in the more languid
language of one schoolteacher, 'he forgot himself with her this night'.[17]
In any case we still need to account for a form of interrogation which
required full circumstantial details but did not frame precise questions
about sexual acts. Whether by conscious effort of those interrogated or
by council censoring, a screen of silence and privacy was created in
this context. Silence could even come to signify sex. So important was
calculated silence as a means of insinuating that someone had a sexual
relationship that those who wished to impugn another's sexual reputation had merely to state to the council that, for instance, a woman

had gone to a priest's house and 'what they did there was not known to him';[18] or 'many women of ill repute go in and out there, and what they did there he had no knowledge'.[19]

But very often, our records stop short, referring to 'doings', 'arrangements' or 'dealing' that subsequently occurred.[20] Much recent historiography has argued that early modern people engaged in sexual *acts* without understanding themselves as having sexual identities: the homosexual, so it is argued, was an invention of the nineteenth century.[21] Interestingly enough, however, our sources are here stubbornly inexplicit about what 'acts' occurred. It is we who reconstrue this language to mean 'penetration'. Their language – 'doing his will', 'he did with her according to his will with her for up to an hour'[22] – need not necessarily prioritize one act, but may rather suggest that a sexual experience was completed in a series of stages. Marriage itself, after all, was a process involving a series of steps – from engagement through signing of a property contract, public wedding procession, bridal mass, to the 'bedding down' of the couple before witnesses – not a transition accomplished in a single ritual moment.[23]

The speakers' refusal to describe or name these acts is paralleled by the indirect language they employ in describing their genitals. Sexual organs are usually not directly referred to, but spoken of – in gender identical fashion – as his or her 'shame'.[24] 'Shame' here is not, I think, the opposite of 'honour'; it refers to parts of the body which are sexual, important, taboo and to be touched with respect, but are not necessarily polluting or dishonourable. To be sure, their conception of the sexual differs from ours and from that of the nineteenth century in subtle ways, but rather than implying an *absence* of sexual identity, it points to these people's keen sense of their sexuality. The language used to describe genitalia could also sharply distinguish male sexuality from female. Unlike 'shames', which apparently were not gender-identified, men's genitals could sometimes be imagined as separate beings, and are referred to as 'it', a mechanism which yet further distances the speaker from the body and leaves it grammatically vague what noun precisely 'it' is standing in for. We might see a parallel usage here in the unattached penises of the French fabliaux described by Sara Melhado White, or in the imagery of carnival time, where penises parade as rampantly independent objects.[25] The devotional imagery of the Incarnation which Steinberg describes can remind us, too, of the visibility of the penis in this phallic culture.[26] Women's genitals, by contrast, did not have a clear, publicly recognizable representation. In the criminal interrogations and in council pronouncements, the rare references are to 'a secret place of her body', 'the secret place', stressing hiddenness and mystery.[27]

THE WILL

Two themes in particular stand out in the language men and women use during interrogation; that of honour, and that of will. When women spoke of a sexual encounter, their routine euphemism was 'to do his will'. Men similarly would speak of 'having his will with her', 'she should follow his will'. Admirably suited to a criminal context, this language made the issue of intentionality central. Judges could construct a calculus of responsibility and punish accordingly. But it was also a language which confounded the distinctions it tried to insist upon. An asymmetrical form of words, only a *man's* will could be 'done': a man could not submit to or do a woman's will. Thus it constructed sex as a submission to a man's will, so that heterosexual sex seems to reinforce men's social superiority and their supposed greater intellect and will.

At its extreme, this language could become welded to the language of possession, so that a man might say, as Anna Peutinger alleged Wolf Rechlsperger did, 'But since she was his, that she should be of his will.' Peutinger immediately continues the narrative, 'and so she was robbed of her virginity'.[28] Making no linguistic distinction between reported speech and event, and allowing no pause for her response, her sentence collapses the two in a unity of cause and effect in which she cannot be held to blame for her 'dishonour'. Similarly, by focusing on the male will, men could employ such turns of phrase to legitimate the effacement of the female will altogether, so that a woman's agreement might be construed from her lack of objection. As one man argued, 'if it was not her will she could well have screamed'.[29] Even the blunt 'she was of ill repute' might be used as proof that she must have consented.[30] Both sexes could employ the language of men's will to obliterate the woman's attitude – sometimes, to female advantage, to conceal a woman's own complicity; sometimes as a means to deny that intercourse had been forced by the man.

In order, therefore, to shift blame to the woman, a man had to argue that 'she incited him', or 'was willing', or that 'it was her will' that he could 'have his will' with her. At times the contradictory logic of assigning 'will', as it was understood in its masculine sense, to women, threatened to turn the men's statements into farce. So Franz Riem stated that a woman had 'necked him, tried to undo the button on his codpiece', and that all had happened 'on her incitement and movement', so that finally, 'as he noticed this, he did his will with her'.[31] Much as he laboured to transfer all motive and action to her, intercourse itself remained stubbornly constructed as a male activity. The preliminaries may be a matter of acquiescence or even of willing agreement on the woman's part, but sexual encounters, in this language, necessarily involve submitting to 'his will'.

We can expand this point negatively by looking at an interrogation where the man's account was not confirmed by the council. Hans Karrer, who had formerly been accused of Anabaptism, was summoned before the council on a charge of wife-beating. He recounted his marital unhappiness in a litany which reiterated the verb *leiden*, to suffer, perhaps a term he had taken over from Anabaptist theologies of suffering and passivity. He told the council that his wife would punch him and kick him away if from time to time he 'desired ... bodily work' of her – but all this he would 'suffer' if only she would 'give him good greeting' and keep him at least as well as a servant.[32] In this case, council authority was not used to shore up Karrer's flagging patriarchal position, but rather to undermine his right to discipline: he was put in irons, read a homily and told to behave himself.[33] This was a far more partisan punishment than usual in such a marital quarrel, partly because Karrer, a subversive Anabaptist, had already proved a religiously unreliable household head. But Karrer's use of the language of endurance, subservience and passivity in place of the active masculine language of will and desire surely also undermined his authority with the council, placing him outside the patriarchal order they ordinarily upheld. Hence, he was denied their support.

Yet the language of will was also volatile. The 1537 ordinance marked a recategorization of the crime of rape, which was incorporated into the sections of the ordinance dealing with fornication instead of being classified (as in the 1276 civic code) with crimes of violence. According to the ancient statute, a woman might herself engage in trial by combat with her rapist, and the penalty for rape was death.[34] The new ordinance retained the punishment 'on body or life'. But the altered context was highly significant. Immediately following the rape clause is a paragraph concerning 'anyone who, by work or deed, persuades a virgin or widow to his will'. This latter crime merited only a four-week term of imprisonment, eight days of which had to be served while the rest could be commuted to a fine.[35] The effect of this modification was to align rape and seduction more closely to one another, so that a man's best defence against a charge of rape was now to argue that the woman had in some sense been 'persuaded' to his will. Previously, cases tended to concentrate on both the completion of intercourse and the fact of the woman's injury rather than primarily on the question of female consent. The consequence of the change was to link both rape and seduction more closely with normative male heterosexual behaviour, which was understood as getting a woman to do one's will. The instability of acceptable male sexual behaviour entailed by this simultaneous downgrading of the seriousness of rape and widening of the scope of wrongful seduction meant more scrutiny both of the man's 'will' and the precise nature of the woman's attitude.

A proper understanding of the resonances of the term 'will' and the sources of its persuasiveness requires a look at its theological underpinnings. Human beings' wills were more inclined to evil than to good, according to the dominant notion that emerged from medieval teachings; and this was how the men who sat on the myriad of local town councils all over Germany saw human nature. The will, therefore, needed to be directed towards good, and it was the job of Christian magistrates to hedge it about with rules so as to encourage it along the right path.[36] Reformation theology, by contrast, with its emphasis on salvation through faith alone, argued that good deeds could never earn God's grace. Concerned as evangelicals were to stress the absolute nature of divine omnipotence, they tended to minimize the capacity of the human will to achieve good. Evangelicalism was thus potentially at odds with some fundamental tenets of sixteenth-century common sense. When early modern people and reformed councils used the language of will, they therefore invoked terminology resonant with the themes of salvation, grace and merit. But they also straddled an uneasy paradox, for the 'will' might both be capable of positive good and be irredeemably mired in sin.

It was a paradox essential not only to legal discourse, as we have seen, but to masculinity itself. The male sexual will was allied with mastery, so that sexual intercourse irreducibly meant 'doing his will' and was embedded in patriarchal relations of subordination. Yet, at the same time, to be a man was to be more rational and less subject to the force of lust than a woman. The fear that 'having her' might actually entail submission to the unbridled, dominating lust of the woman was never far from the surface of male imagination.[37] Woodcuts depict men confined in cages, while luxuriously clothed women twit them, or show the prostitute's lover as fool. She should not 'lead me about on a fool's rope', complained one man, both angry that the rich young woman who titillated him would not allow him to have his way, and fearful that she had succeeded in enslaving him to lust.[38]

In the modern west, sex has persistently been viewed as a male appetite, so that intercourse often becomes defined in terms of men's desires and pleasures. Feminists have argued that such a language invariably makes it difficult if not impossible for women to voice active sexual desires or to seek their own pleasure.[39] While much of our evidence seems to confirm such a pattern, sixteenth-century European society will not entirely fit into this model. This was a society which retained a cosmology placing women in the world of the irrational, the bodily, the sensual and hence the sexual. It saw women's sexual passions as a strong force, and had a robust language of women's physical pleasure. 'Come and let yourself be rubbed up', one man called to a woman in the street he did not even know – a jibe which took women's pleasure into account and did not equate it with penetration.[40] Such language is clearly linked to male fears and fantasies about female sexuality, but it also recognizes female pleasure.

Plate 3.3 Niklas Stoer, *Lovers' Birdhouse*

Note: This image of women snaring men reflects the fear, never far from the male
   imagination, of being enslaved to women.

While apparently incompatible with a language of will, which saw
men as the desiring subjects, this notion of female lustiness could
occasionally allow women to use the language of will to describe their
own desire. Indeed, the council's own concern with the adjudication of
responsibility contributed to this, for it increasingly focused on the
extent of the woman's agreement to a sexual encounter. As Deborah
Cameron has pointed out in an important critique of Dale Spender's
theory of language, linguistic forms do not completely prescribe what
we can say, and women too can use 'male language'.[41] Agnes Axt,
married to a tavern-keeper, ate and drank with the male clientele (itself
immodest behaviour) and had an affair with a *Knecht*, a social subordi-
nate. Questioned by the council, she did not confine herself modestly
to accounts of her doings but made counter-accusations, saying that her
husband and brother-in-law kept her meanly and beat her, as if their
maltreatment of her could be weighed in the balance against her infi-
delity. Asked whether she had had any involvement with the notorious

libertine patrician, Anthoni Paumgartner, she stated that 'Although Anthoni Paumgartner had approached her several times about dishonour, this [dishonour] she did not want to give place to.'[42] But she then admitted that if they had not been disturbed, 'she *may* have had unmarital work with Paumgartner, as was her will.'[43] Having coaxed this confession from her, however, the council's prescription for Axt's path to redemption lay in renouncing this kind of active desire and embracing the rhetoric of subordination. In two letters which accompany the record of the interrogation, Agnes acknowledges in a regular hand which was almost certainly not her own, and in a language that is far removed from her angry tones in interrogation, that

> I, poor imprisoned female have sinned against God, your Graces as a just authority, my pious husband, my old father and mother and the whole kinship, out of stupidity and departure from the grace of God, and have unfortunately forgotten myself against female respectability.

She pleads that in the future she will behave 'with all fair and responsible respectability, as is fitting for a pious honourable woman' even though 'I have forfeited honour and mercy of my husband and his kin'.[44] At least in order to secure the pardon of the council, Agnes had to annihilate her will and become a penitent wife. Somewhat perplexedly, her husband (who had been sent a copy of this petition for comment) declared that the council, which could better adjudicate such matters, should determine whether or not she could be released from prison. Well might he have been baffled by this rapid and implausible transformation.[45]

HONOUR

The concept of will, allied as it was to male power, was inherently problematic for women as a means of organizing their sexuality. Instead, women who appear in interrogations more readily employed the concept of honour. Like a kind of material possession, honour was something which women might barter with men. Indeed, the legal framework insisted that it had a price, so that a woman whose virginity was 'taken' by a man could claim damages. However, unlike the fairly uniform amounts paid for childbed expenses or costs of raising a child, the damages were not a fixed tariff but a sum which the woman herself set, depending on her social status and, less clearly, on the means of her seducer. To claim it thus involved the woman in asserting her injury and insisting on her worth in a direct calculus of honour and money. She had arithmetically to estimate and then defend her relative social position.

But the link between honour and money was not a shame-free one.

One woman recounted proudly how she had said that 'her honour was dearer than money, again and again as much money as that'[46] as her master tried to seduce her, laying down 8 gulden before her on the table – more than her annual wages would have totalled, and enough to constitute a more than respectable dowry. The fairy-tale language of her account is heightened when it becomes clear in the interrogation that she had an illegitimate child already. To the council, who held that a woman who was no longer a virgin had forfeited her honour and would be sure to agree to any sort of sexual encounter, such a state-ment would have been incomprehensible except as pretence. For her, the meaning may have been that she would not engage in sex for money. The fabulous sum offered thus restored her honour, for she could present herself as having chosen not to be a prostitute. As she describes her eventual seduction, she is at pains to make it clear that she 'received nothing' and does not initially seem to have claimed even her childbed expenses from her erstwhile master. Here, honour is not so much a thing as a self-description to which women might lay claim by devising their own stories.

Just as the concept of will associated with men could also have a female, less powerful and somewhat contradictory register, so too the concept of honour, primarily a term which organized women's sexual experience, had a male sexual analogue. Men's honour, too, might be at stake in sexual encounters. One man joked with another that he should have intercourse with a woman 'to save men's honour',[47] another was rumoured to be no man, either at bed or table.[48]

Honour for men, however, was centrally an economic and social term, and seems to have derived its sexual import from its social meaning. Men's honour was established competitively and corporately through the guilds. The 'dishonourable' professions like that of hangman or knacker isolated their practitioners from respectable society, while the guild insignia and guild houses provided a sense of lineage and dignity for craftsmen. At the same time, this collective honour was also related to sexual behaviour, but in a different way from that of women. Guilds, who, like the goldsmiths, wanted to accentuate their honour still further, might claim that none of their young men visited prostitutes. If unmar-ried masters and married workers began to enter the trade in large numbers, overturning the boundaries of marital status, the dignity of the trade was put at risk.[49]

For women, by contrast, honour was paradigmatically personal, dependent to a far greater degree on her sexual comportment alone.[50] Honour was also asymmetrical, for while a man could take a woman's honour, intercourse with a woman did not normally imperil a man's honour. As slander cases show, the most direct way to assault a woman's honour, married or not, was to call her a whore. Indeed the insult was so tiresomely frequent that the council used its own shorthand verb, 'to be-whore someone', to classify the cases.[51] By contrast, a man might be called a thief or traitor, insults which classed him with the dishonourable criminals whose trades undermined the property rights and political integrity of the whole commune.

JEALOUSY

Honour and will conspired to create the framework of sexual loyalty which made it very difficult for women to express sexual jealousy directly.[52] Cuckolded men could take their opponent to court, or express their anger overtly by challenging their woman's seducer to a fight (and with less danger to themselves, they could also assault their wives). But the cuckolded woman was a non-concept. Indeed, she hardly ever appears to testify or accuse her husband. Unlike that of her husband, her honour was not held to be injured by her husband's or suitor's infidelities. Whereas a wife's agreement 'to do the will' of someone apart from her husband transgressed the subordination of wife to husband, the husband who seduced another woman only indirectly infringed the chain of subordination of another couple. Women's revenge therefore had to be oblique, and men interrogated frequently describe their womenfolk's reactions in terms of secret retaliation. So, Matheis Dietl, involved in a relationship with his servant which pre-dated his marriage, had the servant kitted out with a coat and dowried with 17 gulden. The affair continued and eventually the scandal reached court. Under interrogation, he accused his wife of having tried to encourage the woman's husband to beat her and drag her about by the hair, an accusation which the council did not dismiss out of hand. He produced a series of cases in which, he said, his wife had treated the servant badly. She was no innocent victim of his adultery but a scheming, jealous harridan: this, rather than outright denial of the affair, was his strategy to mitigate punishment.[53] The persuasive force of his narrative depended on the notion, shared by council and subjects alike, that jealous women were devious, dangerous and cruel.

If proven, allegations of female vengefulness could elicit a stern response from the council. In a notorious case in 1533, Barbara Hegk asked Michel Scherpfstain to avenge the slight to her honour which had occurred when a gunsmith had promised her marriage 'several times' but had not kept his vow. She paid Scherpfstain to stab him, and he wounded the gunsmith in the arm. This was no mere contract job: Scherpfstain was her friend, and he described their relationship as one where they 'were dear to each other and sought good trust together'.[54] The council's judgement on the pair was a grisly death sentence: she was to be bricked up alive, he executed by the Perlach tower, quartered and each quarter hung at a main city gate.

The punishment seems incommensurate with the offence, given the routine street woundings among young men in brawls. Its severity can be explained partly by the inequalities of social position. The wronged woman was only a cook in another's household, while the young gunsmith, whose wife she had so desperately wanted to become, was a man with a future as a master in one of the most prestigious crafts and a member of an established craft family. Her friend was a mere servant (though to a patrician) and a foreigner. To the council, it might seem that such violence could be used to obliterate the class differences so central to the system of sexual dalliance of the upper guild strata and patriciate from which its own members came. No man might be safe from the machinations of powerless and vindictive women.

The case also dramatized the fragility of masculinity. Barbara Hegk had effectively used taunts to make Scherpfstain act, mocking him in words which burned deeply enough for him to recount them to the council, as 'a hairless, slanderous man'. This insult at once couples the imputation of lack of beard (and therefore of developed penis) with the accusation that Scherpfstain was a liar, one who does not keep his word and cannot be an authoritative male speaker. Worse, the assassin had infringed the rules of honour relating to bodily comportment on the streets, for he had not warned the gunsmith or given him time to turn and draw his weapon. Stabbing immediately and secretly, he had wounded in an underhand, feminine manner.[55]

But the underlying import of the case concerned female jealousy. The disruptive threat of the woman's jealousy, here acted out successfully (or nearly so), seemed to exemplify the untrammelled feminine anger which could not be assuaged by paying for Hegk's honour, but which called out for blood. Even under interrogation, she stated that 'she ordered Michel to chop off the gunsmith's arm, and brand him so that he be branded'. She explicitly employed the word *rechen*, to avenge, recalling her words to Scherpfstain as 'she wanted very much to avenge herself'. The council would have been highly sensitive to this unauthorized appropriation of two of its juridical techniques: maiming the limb which perjured and branding criminals. She transported this not into a cry for formal justice, but an elemental, almost biblical cry for public revenge, a coupling which may have touched on a certain uneasiness about the nature of the council's own disciplining role. This was the transitional period before the development of the 1537 legislation and the full elaboration of a fatherly rather than brotherly authority; an authority which was to be expressed in lengthy interrogations, admonitions and the use of fines and imprisonment for criminals in preference to judicial maiming.

LANGUAGE OF THE BODY

To this point I have been using the three-way dialogue of council, man and woman, reading it to explore the concepts relating to sex in the craft milieu in Augsburg. For historians who deal largely with written sources it is tempting to see the past as a series of words. I am painfully conscious that this approach runs the danger of making sex seem like a language game which has little at all to do with the body. So in this last section I want to explore the bodily language of men and women, as it emerges in the interrogations.[56]

As men described them, sexual encounters were structured to begin with games and joking (*gayseln, scherzen*) or direct sexual touchings, often with tickling: an interesting counter-example to Maria Valverde's generalization that the erotic and the comic are incompatible.[57] So one man in a rape case described how he had pulled the woman's hair.[58] This detail was included because he needed to insist that a period of sexual teasing had taken place which would imply her agreement. Whether or not it 'really happened', the rough, jocular hair-pulling was a recognized kind of courtship preliminary. Another described how he had 'joked' with the woman he was accused of raping, and she with him.[59] The concept of female consent, too, was acted out physically, as the men saw it: to agree to penetration was to 'open her legs'; to object was to 'clap one leg over the other', or 'position herself strangely'.[60]

In many accounts, nakedness is an important moment. Nearly always it is the woman who is more naked, while the man is partly or even fully dressed. Nakedness, however, is often a matter of the unclothing of particular parts of the body: thus one man was 'naked in his shirt'.[61] The description of female 'nakedness' seems to indicate a greater sexualization of the woman's body as an object of erotic arousal for the man. She does not have the same power of visual mastery over him, and while she incites him by her nakedness her own sexual desires seem to lack a bodily language of objectification.[62] For the man, the woman's nakedness usually indicated a measure of agreement, at least as this is described in interrogation; but the accounts are also scrupulous not to confuse nakedness with consent, so that there is usually a brief reported dialogue which, like an authorial device, makes the state of play quite clear. This emerges especially clearly in an interrogation of Lienhart Numenbeck and Waltpurg Frosch, where both parties to the adultery include portions of a dialogue held in bed, but there is no agreement on its content.

> Numenbeck claimed Frosch joked with him, offered him food which they ate in bed, and 'he said what did he want with her in her petticoat?; she should undress for he would not bite her. Upon which he turned to her, so they cuddled each other; then he acted as if he wanted to get on top of her, and she said but you said that you

would do nothing to me, I will not do your will. To which he said, truly I will not force you. Then he turned away from her and lay still, and in a little while she said, he should turn again to her and have power over her body and goods, after which he turned and did bodily work with her'.[63]

Frosch strenuously denied that she had surrendered her body and goods to him. Her narrative has him combining threats with black-mail: Numenbeck said he would do nothing to her, and she had told him 'I am no good for wicked things.' Refusing to leave her house, he had threatened, 'If you will not be quiet I will make such a noise in the house that you'd rather be quiet.' He had said so many good words to her that she had lain down beside him, dressed, though he was naked. 'She did not want to undress, to which he said she should undress or he would rip her clothes from her neck, whereupon she let herself be persuaded to undress, thus [he] wanted to come on her, but she did not want to do it.' He then works on her pity by feigning illness until she eventually yields.[64]

Here we see familiar themes: Frosch tries to efface her agency in the affair as far as possible and her narrative proceeds in hesitant fits and starts. Numenbeck acknowledges his active part in the affair but insists on Frosch's total submission: for his version, the crucial point is her surrender of all power over body and goods, and her provision of food at the beginning prefigures this offering. Both see Frosch's undressing as a turning point in the story, while Numenbeck is somehow naked before either comments.

One interrogation has survived which makes the language of the body and its stages far more explicit; and I shall close with an extended discussion of this case because it can tell us a great deal about the body and illuminate how sexual relations always had to be negotiated with marriage and craft-workshop realities in view. Hans Hieber and a maid Margaret worked together as apprentice and servant for the same master and mistress. Hieber asked her to marry him and she, after some hesi-tation, agreed. But the following night, she begged him to 'count her free' of the promise and she 'would take it upon her soul'. This, Hieber says, he readily did. But according to his account, she later asked him for a pedlars' wares, and he bought them, saying 'if someone peddles goods from him she must earn it by him'.[65] Then began a series of night encounters where, as he puts it, he would snooze while the rest of the household slept and she plaited wool. When her work was finished, they would both go up to her room and he would 'warm himself by her'.

Their descriptions mark out careful stages of bodily contact and regions of the body. As part of the bargain, she was always 'naked': Hieber was sometimes fully 'naked', at times partially clothed – that is, he was sometimes 'in his shirt', sometimes 'in his clothes'. But before he got into bed (he took care to inform the council interrogators) 'he always took his shoes off first'[66] – a detail which seems to be incorporated because he was at pains to present the encounter as a respectful one, not a subjection to lust. Hieber's account is an almost mathematical delineation of respect and boundaries. In bed they would play with each other: he touched her on her breast and on her 'shame', but she would tickle him and never touched him on his 'shame', a fact which Hieber views as exemplifying her modesty. Similarly, Hieber carefully states that though he kissed her, she did not kiss him, concluding, 'If he said this of her he would do her an injustice.'[67] Her sexual exploring is playful, comic, but does not extend to direct touching of his genitals: his is more confidently sexualizing and objectifying of her body for which he has jestingly paid to 'warm himself by'. By not engaging in direct genital exploration she preserves her intact, modest and honourable femininity.

On one occasion, however, 'he came over to her and had to do with her which she suffered. Thus he thought he had taken her virginity although he could not completely win her or come in to her'.[68] There is a great tension in the narrative over this moment, and despite what could be interpreted as the total loss of her honour and virginity, Hieber is careful to surround the narrative both before and after this section with descriptions of the limits and modesty of her deportment.

Throughout the interrogation runs the subtext of the need for man and woman to marry at the right time to the right person, thus achieving social status in the craft world of Augsburg. For Margaret, a foreign servant, it was essential to find a husband who had or could acquire guild and citizenship rights so that he could set up a workshop of which she could be the mistress. For Hieber, it was important to time marriage so that it coincided with his becoming a master.[69] But, as Hieber describes exactly what occurred at this point of transition, his testimony becomes terse and confused, in contrast to the voluble specificity of his description of the nightly courtship. On the day that he performed his masterpiece in the home of a neighbouring master, his father had been sent for by his own master and mistress who approved the match with Margaret. That is, their summons must have been a mechanism for gaining parental approval for his marriage. But his father was not at home, Hieber enigmatically says, and breaks off to describe a conversation with Margaret whom he met as he left the house. She told him that a certain 'Matheus', perhaps a rival for her affections, 'was after him'.

The conjunction of these two pieces of narrative only makes sense in terms of the expectations surrounding marriage. Here, at the point when masterhood was within his grasp, should have been the moment to gain his father's approval and ask publicly for Margaret's hand in marriage.

Plate 3.4 Erhard Schoen, *Cage of Fools*

Source: W. Strauss, *The German Single Leaf Woodcut, 1500–1550*, New York, Hacker Art Books 1974.

Note: Prostitutes capturing men, fleecing them, and making fools of them.

But the absence of his father is Hieber's shorthand way of indicating that this conjunction did not result. The threat from Matheus was thus a portent of revenge because Margaret, now presumably renowned in gossip as the object of Hieber's affections, had received no proposal of marriage, imperilling her honour. Hieber resumes the story with a dialogue with another of his mates about the dangerous Matheus, in which, his narrative implies, Hieber denied his relationship with Margaret. She, however, overhears this discussion, calling out – as he puts it – 'he [Hieber] lied as a scoundrel for he had lain with her a good hundred times'. Thereupon, Hieber recounts, 'he became enraged, she lied as a whore for he had made her into a whore'.[70]

This exchange is the nub of Hieber's story. By a painful paradox of the language of honour, she can justly accuse Hieber of lying about their relationship, but his retort caps hers, because a whore is by nature a liar. His words also sadly take responsibility for making her into a whore, in contrast to his studied respect of her as he describes their physical relationship to the council. He thus publicly destroys her honour as she truly insists on her rights. The language of sex can only construct her as a whore who submitted to his will. His honour is not impaired, but he can be seen to have acted badly, so he acknowledges anxiety about what Matheus, her defender and vehicle of revenge, may do to him. For Margaret, by contrast, the way to restore her honour was to institute proceedings against Hieber for slander – a course of action, however, which risked exposure of the truth and ignominy for her. Though early modern European culture recognized women's desire, their 'honour' was far more perilously exposed in sexual relations than men's honour, and their bodies were more fully 'sexualized' than were the men's, who gazed at and even touched their 'shames'. Within the bodily language of a culture which allowed expression of both men's and women's sexual desires, therefore, were enshrined modes of different male and female behaviour and different 'bodilinesses', just as each sex had a different relation to the linguistic modes of will and honour.

A decade later, a similar case came before the council which indicates how concepts of will and honour had been transformed by the Reformation. Hans Dempf and Anna Has, who had been employed with the same master, had a sexual liaison, though neither had guild or citizenship rights in the town.[71] But in this case neither master nor mistress would admit that they had known of or tolerated the affair, since this would have amounted to 'housing people for sin', an offence which was punishable and involved participating in the sin of the fornicators. The couple's master thus made a point of insisting in his narrative of events that as soon as he had discovered Has's relationship, he had dismissed her. It was clear from other testimony, however, that he had encouraged Dempf, saying that he should sleep with her 'in order to save male honour'. In the language of moral rebuke, the council told Dempf that 'he had once promised Has marriage; and so brought her to fall',[72] a manner of speaking which was far removed from the male banter of Dempf and his master. Though Dempf insisted that he had offered to marry Has only if she became pregnant, a mode of proceeding which fully accorded with rural courtship rituals, this was adjudged by the council to be, 'a most punishable matter'. What remained constant was the determination of such relationships by the demands of guild and citizenship needs. As one witness described the relationship, 'Has did as a daughter who wanted to have a husband very much, and since Dempf was a fine young man, who could weave well, he pleased her better than others including this witness.'[73] To the men involved, Has's sexually active behaviour could be perceived as dishonourable, and as a potential challenge to the sexual prowess and honour of men. At the same time, Dempf and his master's imputation of sexual forwardness to Has was clearly a strategy to undermine her case to the council, by presenting her as an immodest woman.

We could interpret this paradox of honour as proof of the universal, unavoidable subordination of women to men in this asymmetrical sexual system. However, I want to resist such a conclusion, for it would mean that all heterosexual relations, even in this pre-nineteenth-century world which acknowledged women's sexual power, were irredeemably subordinating. Nor do I think that a liberal notion of 'what women consented to' will help us here to delineate non-oppressive sex, because this leaves the construction of 'sex' unexamined, obliterates the way terms such as 'will' and 'consent' shift in historical meaning and ignores how language could be used differently by women and men.

In sixteenth-century Augsburg, women and men negotiated a social and sexual terrain in which power was, to be sure, unequally dispersed, but in which male control of the female body was not a given. Women could be made subject to men's 'will' and men's 'honour', but they could also lay claim to honour, desire and even will. For men and women alike, these terms had social and economic meaning as well as sexual import, but their significance differed for each sex, and their meaning could change with the context of the telling.

Sixteenth-century Augsburg represents a transitional moment in European history, when secular control of sexual behaviour was replacing ecclesiastical and when new rules to govern sexual behaviour were being implemented. The confrontation of the new and the old accounts for much of the ambiguity and illogic of the categories the people who appeared in these sources used to conceptualize their sexuality. But these very confusions can help us historicize sexual meaning, sexual subordination and the social place of heterosexuality. Sexuality in Reformation Augsburg had profound significance for gender and social relations, and so it was understood by city patricians and artisans alike. But it was different from what went before, and different from ours. To appreciate that difference and to render it with adequate subtlety is an essential step in the feminist project of deconstructing patriarchy.

NOTES

1 The view of heterosexuality as an institution, imposed rather than innate, which is at the core of patriarchy, has been explicitly developed by Adrienne Rich in 'Compulsory Heterosexuality and Lesbian Existence', *Signs*, 5, 1980, reprinted in Ann Snitow, Christine Stansell and Sharon Thompson (eds), *Desire: The politics of sexuality*, London 1984.

2 Anna Clark, *Women's Silence, Men's Violence: Sexual assault in England, 1770–1845*, London 1987.

3 Judith Walkowitz, *Prostitution and Victorian Society: Women, class and the state*, Cambridge 1980.

4 Ludmilla Jordanova, 'The Interpretation of Nature: A review of Keith Thomas' *Man and the Natural World*', *Comparative Studies in Society and History*, 29, no. 1, 1987, p. 196.

5 Natalie Zemon Davis, *Fiction in the Archives: Pardon tales and their tellers in sixteenth-century France*, London 1988.

6 See A. Portelli, 'The Peculiarities of Oral History', *History Workshop Journal*, 12, 1981, pp. 96–107; L. Passerini, 'Work Ideology and Consciousness Under Italian Fascism', *History Workshop Journal*, 8, 1979, pp. 82–108.

7 See Lyndal Roper, 'Going to Church and Street: Weddings in Reformation Augsburg', *Past and Present*, 106, 1985, pp. 62–101.

8 On the Reformation in Augsburg, see F.W. Roth, *Augsburgs Reformationsgeschichte*, 4 vols, Munich 1901–11; K. Sieh-Burens, *Oligarchie, Konfession und Politik im 16. Jahrhundert. Zur sozialen Verflechtung der Augsburger Bürgermeister und*

Stadtpfleger 1518–1618, Munich, 1986; P. Broadhead, 'Popular Pressure for Reform in Augsburg', in W. Mommsen and R. Scribner (eds), *Stadtbürgertum und Adel*, Stuttgart 1979; and Lyndal Roper, *The Holy Household. Women and morals in Reformation Augsburg*, Oxford 1989.

9 Here the impulse may also have derived from the provisions of Charles V's imperial law code, the *Carolina*, which dealt with judicial procedure.

10 *Ains Erbern Ratss/ der Stat Augspurg/ Zucht und Pollicey Ordnung. MDXXXVII*, Augsburg 1537, fo.b i(v).

11 Lyndal Roper, 'Discipline and Respectability: Prostitution and the Reformation in Augsburg', *History Workshop Journal*, 19, 1985, pp. 3–28.

12

> darumb erinnert sich an Erber Rat jres von Got befohlen Ampts vnd Oberkait/ Befindt auch/ das sich kains wegs leiden noch fügen wölle/ den Vnchristlichen/ sträfflichen wercken vnd leben raum vnd stat zelassen/ ... Hat ain Erber Rat/ auss Gottes gnaden/ vnd mit guter vorbetrachtung/ nachfolgende Ordnung begreiffen vnnd verfassen lassen
>
> (*Ainss Erbern Rats/ der Stat Augspurg/ Zucht vnd Pollicey Ordnung*, Augsburg 1537, fo. a ii r)

13 See Jonathan Goldberg's fascinating 'Fatherly Authority: The politics of Stuart family images', in Margaret W. Ferguson, Maureen Quilligan and Nancy J. Vickers (eds), *Rewriting the Renaissance: The discourses of sexual difference in early modern Europe*, Chicago, Ill. 1986.

14 See my ' "The Common Man", "the Common Good", "Common Women": Gender and meaning in the German Reformation commune', *Social History*, 12, 1987, pp. 1–21.

15 'Vnnd hab Im. In darein gethan, bey vier oder funff maln', Stadtarchiv Augsburg (hereafter cited as StadtAA), Urgichtensammlung (hereafter cited as Urg.), 11 Oct. 1496, Hans Rotklinger.

16 'er Im nye darein komen sey', StadtAA, Urg., 12 Oct. 1496, Conrad Scheyfelin.

17 'Er habe sich dise nacht mit Jr vergessen', StadtAA, Urg., 7 March 1541, Johannes Gebhart. This phrase was also employed by the council in the 1537 ordinance but is otherwise rarely used by those interrogated.

18 StadtAA, Urg., 21 June 1524, Narcis Bichler, 'was sie ausgericht Jme nit wissenn were': the story is an attempt to extricate himself from an accusation of paternity.

19 'es geen Eytl vnnuz weybs personen aus vnnd ein, vnnd ... was sy außgericht Jme vnbewisst', StadtAA, Urg., 3 Nov. 1542, Appolonia Sailer, testimony of Hans Hillpranndt. Sailer was suspected of brothel-keeping.

20 See, for example, 'zuschaffen haben': StadtAA, Urg., 21 June 1524, Narcis Bichler; 16 Nov. 1529, Wolf Keck. 'mit ein Ander ... gehandlit': Urg., 3 March 1534, Lienhart Numenbeck; 13 March 1531, Stoffel Burckhart. 'leipliches Werck': Urg., 8 Oct. 1539, Anthoni Geiger; 26 April 1541, Hans Eckenperger; 3 March 1534, Lienhart Numenbeck. 'Bei Ime gelegen': Urg., 16 March 1536, Hans Landsperger; 17 Jan. 1541, Anna Peutinger.

21 For cogent arguments for this view, see Jeffrey Weeks, *Sex, Politics and Society: The regulation of sexuality since 1800*, London 1981; and his *Sexuality and Its Discontents: Meanings, myths and modern sexualities*, London 1985; Judith Brown, *Immodest Acts: The life of a lesbian nun in Renaissance Italy*, Oxford 1986, esp. n. 54, pp. 171–2.

22 StadtAA, Urg., 4 Dec. 1533, Anna Paur: 'Mit Jr seins willens biß ongefarlich Auf ein stund gehandlt.' Compare Thomas Laqueur, 'Orgasm, Generation and the Politics of Reproductive Biology', in C. Gallagher and T. Laqueur

(eds), *The Making of the Modern Body: Sexuality and society in the nineteenth century*, Berkeley, Calif. 1987, on the diffusion of sexual feeling.

23 See Beatrice Gottlieb, 'Getting Married in Pre-Reformation Europe: The doctrine of clandestine marriage and court cases in fifteenth-century Champagne', Ph.D. thesis, Columbia University; Roper, 'Going to Church and Street'; Michael Schröter, 'Wo zwei zusammenkommen in rechter Ehe . . . ', *Sozio- und Psychogenetische Studien über Eheschliessungsvorgänge vom 12. bis 15. Jahrhundert*, Frankfurt am Main 1985, esp. pp. 381–5; James A. Brundage, *Law, Sex and Christian Society in Medieval Europe*, Chicago, Ill. 1987, pp. 494–505.

24 There are very occasional direct references to male genitals. See, for example, *privet* (privy parts): StadtAA, Urg., 5 Oct. 1528, Simon Westbach; *Scwanz* (tail, prick): Urg. 1 May 1532, Christoff Schmid, priest. This latter was an unusual case because Schmid was accused of sodomy. In a later case, a distinction is made between *Manlichen glid* (male organ) and *schamb* (shame): StadtAA, Urg., 1560a, 8 April 1560, Jörg Haffner, Michael Gastel. They were accused of love sorcery.

25 Sara Melhado White, 'Sexual Language and Human Conflict in Old French Fabliaux', *Comparative Studies in History and Society*, 24, 1982, pp. 185–210.

26 Leo Steinberg, *The Sexuality of Christ in Renaissance Art and in Modern Oblivion*, London 1984. See also Caroline Walker Bynum, 'The Body of Christ in the Later Middle Ages: A reply to Leo Steinberg', *Renaissance Quarterly*, 39, 1986, pp. 399–439; Rona Goffen, 'Renaissance Dreams', *Renaissance Quarterly*, 50, 1987, pp. 682–706, pp. 703–4.

27 'ain[em] haimblichen ort, Jrs leibs': StadtAA, Urg., 30 Jan. 1527, Michel Faiser, sentence of condemnation by the council; 'haimlichen ortenn': Urg., 3 Feb. 1535, Margaret Spilman, who healed the 'haimlicen ortenn' of women. Circumlocutions are also used: for instance, 'hab Im aber die Eer nit genomen, dann er Im nye darein komen scy': Urg., 12 Oct. 1496, Conrad Scheyfelin; 'also vermeint Er hab Jr die Junckfrauschaft genomen Wie wol er dan mocht sie nit gar gewynnen noch zu Jr einkommen mogen', 12 Nov. 1533, Hans Hieber.

28 StadtAA, Urg., 17 Jan. 1541, Anna Peutinger. 'dieweil Si doch sein were, das Si seins willenns sein sollt vnnd Si allso Jrer Junnckfrauschafft beraubt'. She represents this exchange as 'threatening' (*betroelichenn worttenn*).

29 StadtAA, Literalien, 16 March 1536, Hans Landsperger (actually an Urgicht: Urg. for these years are missing), 'het wol megen schreienn vmb hilff wan es Ir will nit gewesen were'. See also Urg., 11 Oct. 1496, Hans Rotklinger, 'Er habs nit genöt, dann es hab sich nit geweret, Er wiss auch nit on es sein will gewesen sey oder nit.' This is a clear case of rape, so that his agnosticism on whether or not it was her will can only be read as wishful thinking. Interesting is his attempt to argue that it was not rape because 'es hab sich nit geweret'.

30 StadtAA, Literalien, 16 March 1536, Hans Landsperger, 'vnd seie hieuor auch beschrait gewesen'.

31 StadtAA, Urg., 11 May 1527, Franz Riem, 'solhs auff Jr anraitzen vnnd bewegen', 'gehalst, vnd nochmalln den nestel am laz wellen auffthun, als er solhs vermerckt, hette Er seins willens mit Jr gehenndelt'.

32 StadtAA, Urg., 12 June 1533, Hans Karrer, 'Sein weib hab Jne auch offter malen mit fauschten geschlagenn Wann er leipliche werck mit Jr ye zu zeiten zepflegen begert mit fuessen von Jr gestossen Das alles hab er Guotlich geliten wolt es noch gern leydenn', 'Wann sie Jne hielt wie ein knecht vnd gebe Jm guotenn gruess wolt er es geren leiden Aber sie sey Jres munds nit maister.'

33 StadtAA, Strafbuch des Rats, 17 June 1533, fo. 2 v.
34 C. Meyer, (ed.), *Das Stadtbuch von Augsburg*, Augsburg 1872, pp. 88–9, art. XXXI.
35 *Zucht und Pollicey Ordnung*, Augsburg 1537, fo. b (r).
36 See Gerald Strauss, *Luther's House of Learning: Indoctrination of the young in the German Reformation*, Baltimore, Md. 1978; and *idem*, 'Success and Failure in the Lutheran Reformation', *Past and Present*, 67, 1975 pp. 30–63.
37 'hat sie gehabt,' StadtAA, Urg., 12 Oct. 1496, Conrad Scheyfelin.
38 'sie Jne also am narrensail vmgefurt', StadtAA, Urg., 29 Dec. 1559, Matheus Sondau.
39 See, for example, Mariana Valverde, *Sex, Power and Pleasure*, Toronto 1985, pp. 166ff.
40 StadtAA, Urg., 26 Oct. 1506, Simon Hiller, 'sie soll sich aufreiben lassen'.
41 Deborah Cameron, *Feminism and Linguistic Theory*, London 1985.
42 StadtAA, Urg., 26 May 1542, Agnes Axt, 'Wieuol Anthoni Paumgartner Sy etlich mal vneern halb angesprochen, dem ahb Sy aber nit stat thun wöllen.'
43 'mocht Sy mit Jme Paumgartner wie Sy willens gewest, vneeliche werckh triben haben'.
44
    Ich Arms gefanngens weibspild wider Gott, Eure gnadenn, als ain gerechte Oberkhait, Meinen frumen Haußwirth, vnd Allte Vatter vnnd Muetter, vnnd ain gannze fraindschafft, aus blödigkhait vnnd verlassung der gnaden Gottes mich laider wider die Weiplich Erberkhait vergeßen vnd gesündet hab. . . .

    'mich aller pillichenn vnnd schuldigenn Erberkhait, wie ainer fromen Erlichen Frawen zusteet zuhallten, vnnd befleissenn', 'das Jch Jnn den hass vnnd straff E. G. Mainß haußwirths, vnnd der freündschafft durch vergessenhait auss schwachhait gefallen'.
45 Compare the bail bond of a man who had served a prison term of four years on account, as he acknowledged, of his 'gaming, excessive drinking, squandering of his father's goods and property, and in particular, with disobedience, and actually physically attacking my dear father', StadtAA, Urfehdensammlung, 18 Dec. 1538, Jeronimus Langenmantel (patrician). In his bail bond, he recognizes the paternal authority of both his father and the council, and states that he 'gratefully' accepts the 'paternal punishment' meted out to him. (The function of the bail bond was to protect the council from retaliation for its punishments.) But unlike the female letter of apology, his is a far more self-confident statement. He compares himself to the 'prodigal son' of the parable and describes himself as 'born anew'. Aside from the requisite submission to paternal authority, the letter does not show the kind of total self-abnegation required of Agnes Axt.
46 StadtAA, Urg., 4 Dec. 1533, Anna Paur, 'Sie Wolle des gellt nit Jr Eer seie Jr lieber dan souil gellt Aber vnd Aber souil.'
47 'so sollt Er mannseer retten', StadtAA, Urg., 29 Jan. 1544, Hans Dempff.
48 StadtAA, Urg., 5 Sept. 1532, Margaret Becz.
49 See Klaus Joachim Lorenzen-Schmidt, 'Beleidigungen in Schleswig-Holsteinischen Städten im 16. Jahrhundert: Städtische Normen und soziale Kontrolle in Städtegesellschaften', *Kieler Blätter zur Volkskunde*, 10, 1978, pp. 5–20; F. Glenzdorf and H. Treichel, *Henker, Schinder und arme Sünder*, 2 vols, Bad Münster 1970.
50 Rainer Beck, 'Illegitimität und voreheliche Sexualität auf dem Land: Unterfinning, 1671–1770', in R. van Dülmen (ed.), *Kultur der einfachen Leute: Bayerisches Volksleben vom 16. bis zum 19. Jahrhundert*, Munich 1983; Gitta Benker, 'Ehre und Schande: Voreheliche Sexualität auf dem Lande im ausgehenden

18. Jahrhundert', in Johanna Geyer-Kordesch and Annette Kuhn (eds), *Frauenkörper, Medizin, Sexualität: Auf dem Wege zu einer neuen Sexual-moral*, Düsseldorf 1986.

51 For records of such cases, see StadtAA, Scheltbücher, 1509–50, 5 vols. On English sexual slander, see Martin Ingram, *Church Courts, Sex and Marriage in England, 1570–1640*, Cambridge 1988, pp. 292–320.

52 Compare women's problematic relationship to anger: Davis, *Fiction in the Archives*, pp. 77–110.

53 StadtAA, Urg., 7 Sept. 1532, Matheis Dietl.

54 StadtAA, Urg., 14 Nov. 1528, 'denn sie ein Ander lieb gehabt vnd guet vertrawen zusamen gesuecht'.

55 Compare Ruth Harris on nineteenth-century Parisian murderess' use of vitriol and handguns: Ruth Harris, 'Crimes of Passion', *History Workshop Journal*, 25, 1988, pp. 31–63.

56 Here I have been influenced by the work of Elizabeth Gross. See, for example, 'Philosophy, Subjectivity and the Body: Kristeva and Irigaray', in Carole Pateman and Elizabeth Gross (eds), *Feminist Challenges: Social and political theory*, Sydney and London 1986; and Frigga Haug *et al.*, *Female Sexualization*, trans. Erica Carter, London 1987 (first published in German, 1983).

57 Valverde, *Sex, Power and Pleasure* p. 167.

58 StadtAA, Urg., 6 March 1534, Hans Mair.

59 StadtAA, Urg., 11 Oct. 1496, Hans Rotklinger.

60 StadtAA, Urg., 6 March 1534, Hans Mair; 7 Sept. 1532 Matheis Dietl.

61 See Barbara Duden, *Geschichte unter der Haut*, Stuttgart 1987, pp. 64–6, on the cultural specificity of nakedness. See the following expression in the criminal records: 'what did he want with her in her petticoat? she should undress.... Upon which Froschin undressed herself (naked); ('was er Jr Jm vnder rock wölle sie solle sich ab Ziehe ... Vff das die Froschin sich nackend ab Zogenn'), StadtAA, Urg., 3 March 1534, Lienhart Numenbeck; 'the sister saw Mair quite undressed in [his] front; likewise the girl also quite undressed' ('hab die schwester den Mair Vomen gar emplosst, dessgleichen des Medlin auch gar emplosst gesehenn'), Urg., 6 March 1534, Hans Mair; and see also the witness statement of the 'girl' in this case, 'unfastened himself and laid himself naked on her' ('sich Auf geöschtelt vnnd ploss auf sie gelegt'). In many of these cases, nakedness seems to mean not nudity but the undressing of certain parts of the body. But nudity was not unknown! See Natalie Zemon Davis, 'On the Lame', *American Historical Review*, 1988, p. 578. I am grateful to Barbara Duden for her help in exploring this.

62 See Patricia Simons, 'Women in Frames: The eye, the gaze, the profile in Renaissance portraiture', *History Workshop Journal*, 25, 1988, pp. 4–30; and on nakedness and concepts of the body, Barbara Duden, *Geschichte unter der Haut*.

63 StadtAA, Urg., 3 March 1534, Lienhart Numenbeck.

64 StadtAA, Urg., 6 March 1534, Waltpurg Frosch.

65 StadtAA, Urg., 12 Sept. 1533, Hans Hieber, 'Er krame keiner nichts sie verdiene Es dan vmb Jne.'

66 'Doch hab er Allweg die schoch zuuor abzogenn.'

67 'abe sie Jne nye kusst Wann er es Jr sagte so tho er Jr Onrecht'.

68 'Ein mal seie er vber sie komenn Vnnd mit Jr zu schaffen gehabt des sie geliten Also vermeint Er hab Jr die Junckfrauschaft genomen Wie wol er dan mocht sie nit gar gewynnen noch zu Jr ein komenn mogen.'

69 See my 'Going to Church and Street'.

70 'Er hieber liege Alls ein Bosswicht dan Er seie wol hundert mal bei Jr

gelegenn Daruff Er erZornet sie lieg Alß ein huor dan er hab sie zu einer huorenn gemacht.'

71 StadtAA, Urg., 28 Jan. 1544, Hans Dempff, Anna Has. The case began in the marriage court but was transferred to the council.

72 'Er hab ainmal der hesin die Ee Versprochen vnnd sie zu fall dardruch pracht.'

73 'hab die hesin thon wie ein tochter, die gern ein man hete gehapt, vnd die weil dempf ein feiner Junger gesel. so wol wirken kind, sey, hab er Jr besser dan er gezeug vnd ander gefallen'.

4 Sexual utopianism in the German Reformation

When the first clerical marriage took place in defiance of church law, the Reformation embarked on a course which involved far more than mere tinkering with the moral regulation of the priesthood. Clerical marriage necessitated a reconsideration of one of the oldest Christian conundrums, the relationship between the holy and the body. Now that a life of celibacy was no longer mandatory for the clergy, and sexual abstinence was no longer considered to be the estate most pleasing to God, reformers had to build a new accommodation between sexuality and the sacred.[1] Sexual renunciation and holiness, once indivisible, had been riven apart.

At a time when it is fast becoming an orthodoxy that the Reformation's legacy in the field of marriage and sexuality was the elevation of marriage and the imposition of discipline and moral order,[2] it is important to remind ourselves of the variety and profusion of views on marriage and sexuality which flourished well into the early years of the Reformation's institutionalization. In this chapter I want to explore not only some of the solutions to the problem of the relation between sexuality and holiness which were proposed by Protestant evangelicals, but also some of those propounded by radicals who were not part of established mainstream churches. Sexual utopianism and marital experiments were an accompaniment of much Anabaptist and radical idealism, and drew on a long tradition of free-thinking religious radicalism.[3] Nor were speculations about the nature of marriage, which – so reformers averred – was the cornerstone of social and political order, confined to Anabaptists and radicals. The homilies of mainstream reformers about marriage masked underlying uncertainty about what in fact counted as wedlock. The reworking by the reformers of their own monastic heritage of sexual renunciation into a Protestant familialism was a more troubled and incomplete process than is allowed by any triumphalist reading of the evangelical past, coloured by images of the Bible-reading seventeenth-century Protestant household.

Not all of this mainstream evangelical thought on marriage was new. As reformers turned to constructing a marital morality, they could draw on existing theologies of marriage and even take over much of the old marriage guidance literature intact.[4] In part, too, when they came to construct their own system of jurisdiction over marital matters to replace that of the Roman church, they could adopt and develop the rich tradition of secular law regulating behaviour. Much of this had been based on the distinction between the public sins, such as cohabitation, which publicly affronted the social institution of marriage and were punishable by secular authority, and private sins, such as discreet liaisons, which did not.

However, these continuities in literature and prescription cannot conceal the shift which had occurred. The place of marriage in the sixteenth-century evangelical cosmology had moved. For if correct marital behaviour was no longer the conduct enjoined on those lay people who had not opted for the holier estate, but was instead the estate expected of all but the rarest Christian, lay and clergy alike, then a new marital theology had to be developed. Paradoxically, though reformers no longer considered marriage to be a sacrament, they greatly magnified the moral burden this institution now had to bear. The marital relationship became the showcase of Christian living, open to general scrutiny, so that couples who 'lived like cat and dog' were guilty of moral, civic and religious inadequacy. The clergy were cast in the role of models of married life – much to the discomfort of clerics who found their marital quarrels the subject of parish gossip and church censure. This new place of marriage in turn involved not only orthodox Protestant reformers but also radicals of every stripe in an uneasy reconsideration of the relationships between sexuality and the natural, between lust and the social institution of marriage, between the Christian and society, and between spirit and body.

I shall chart some of the varieties of approach to marriage and morals in Protestantism by considering first a range of Anabaptists, spiritualists and sexual radicals and exploring the nature and limits of the marital experiments they devised. Second, I shall consider the reactions of mainstream reformers to these 'Anabaptists'[5] and suggest that despite the ferocity of their invective, reformers and Anabaptists confronted a common dilemma: the question of the relation between sexuality and holiness. Only when seen through the prism of the reformers' attacks on the Anabaptists, whom they viewed as disorderly, diabolical and undisciplined, can one understand the logic of Reformation morality which ultimately cast Anabaptists as the 'other'. It was, after all, in tandem with their attacks on Anabaptism that reformers began to develop that Reformation watchword, discipline. Third, I shall consider the affair of the bigamy of Philip of Hesse, the event which starkly revealed the extent of the commonalities between Philip's Lutheran and evangelical advisers and the Anabaptists whom they execrated.

I

The range of the critique of marriage as a social institution among Anabaptists emerges in a series of marital experiments within different sects, culminating most notoriously in the polygamy practised by the Anabaptists at Münster.[6] All aroused fierce discussion within the Anabaptist movements and were a propaganda gift to their opponents. For orthodox reformers, marital experimentation served as a dire warning of the ultimate outcome of such 'flesh-loving' sects. Even the bloody defeat of Anabaptists at Münster did not sound its death knell: Anabaptists were still to be found proposing group marriage or defending polygamy in the troubled years that followed.[7] The Hutterites' communitarian organization of marriage and sexual relations and that of some modern communities must also be understood as the inheritance of the possibilities opened up by the critique of marriage within early Anabaptism.[8]

The Anabaptist critique of marriage covered a broad spectrum. Though it is usually taken to spring from crude sensuality, it is better understood as deriving from a physical theology in which the body was saturated in moral and religious significance. A frequent theme of early Anabaptism was the need for the Christian disciple to undergo the experience of suffering to attain salvation. This emphasis on bodily experience made the question of sexual conduct within marriage a peculiarly difficult and urgent problem for Anabaptists. On the one hand, spiritualists and radicals, drawn to making a sharp distinction between spirit and body, could be attracted towards the idea of mortifying the flesh – an emphasis which could make it difficult to accommodate marriage in their practical theology at all. On the other, those who did not take the path of sexual renunciation tried instead to purify and spiritualize sexual expression, for in Anabaptist thought, the sensual could not be conceived as religiously indifferent.[9]

The radical apocalypticist Thomas Müntzer, who preached in the Peasants' War of 1524–5 and was executed for his part in the peasant cause, exemplifies the latent asceticism in the formative years of Anabaptist and radical thought which could lead both to the renunciation of sexuality and to its spiritualization. Though not an Anabaptist, he certainly influenced radicals and Anabaptists, and was held by Luther to be the father of the movement. Müntzer's abhorrence of 'the creaturely' as alien to the spirit of the godly in the dangerous last times suggests how thorny a matter it was to incorporate the realm of the senses into his theology.[10] His radical separation of flesh and spirit made it impossible for him to develop a theology of marriage. At the same time, however, hints within Müntzer's personal history and writings have led his biographer Walter Elliger to suggest that he may have been toying with the idea of spiritualizing the sexual within marriage. At about the time of his own marriage, Müntzer made the extraordinary claim that he had given up his manhood like Origen and killed the sexual in himself.[11] This tortuous relationship with sexuality is a recurrent feature of ecstatic, experiential sects which aim at Christian perfection: early Methodism was to share it two centuries later.[12] Luther, with his vigorously affirming, naturalistic attitude to the sexual functioning of the body, did not face a similar contradiction.

Later Anabaptists and radicals developed Müntzer's ambivalent asceticism. Their solutions could lead in several directions. For some, new forms of marriage led to a renewed patriarchalism, in which women remained closely subordinated to their husbands. For others, it led to a reformulation of the concept of marriage which could allow women considerable sexual initiative. For yet others, it could simply result in a firm adherence to the moral values of conventional society.[13] Common to most Anabaptists and radical sects, however, was their conviction of moral superiority over those of the 'world' from whom they had separated. They castigated orthodox Protestants and Catholics alike for their loose living and indiscipline, and claimed they were creating a morally pure, disciplined kingdom of the perfect.

In the years which followed, a series of sects were to pose the issues of sexual morality, asceticism and sexual utopianism very sharply. The unusual marital practices of one group of Anabaptists, the so-called Dreamers, came to the authorities' attention in 1531. A group of largely illiterate peasants from the region around Erlangen, they were rounded up and captured by the local authorities.[14] To the disbelieving ears of their interrogators they recounted their marital theology and responded in detail to questioning about their unorthodox sexual behaviour, describing how they had entered into 'new' marriages in obedience to the Spirit, some leaving spouses to whom they had long been married. Several ringleaders were eventually executed on grounds of belonging to a prohibited sect and for having entered into illicit divorces and remarriages.[15] Our evidence for their beliefs derives from their interrogations conducted at first without and then with the application of torture.

The Dreamers have often been presented as sexual libertines, unreflectingly overturning marriage as they surrendered to lust. However, their own statements of their belief suggest they tried not to reject marriage but to refashion it. Their advocacy of a new, spiritual marriage sprang rather from their attempt to apply the highest spiritual principles to the earthly institution of marriage. As Michael Maier put it, it was the disorder, unfaithfulness and quarrelling which they saw every day among married folk which led to their reforms.[16] This was a sentiment which would have been familiar to reformers and civic authorities alike, concerned as they were to regulate the evils which arose from disorderly marriages. City councils daily bewailed the violence and indiscipline of incorrigible married couples, and tried to 'speak them together again', in a kind of ceremonial renewal of the marriage.[17] In their attempts to purify marriage and make it a more morally perfect relationship, Anabaptists confronted the same dilemmas as the orthodox preachers, who were trying to create a marital theology for laity and clergy. Spiritual marriage, as the Dreamers explained it, usually entailed parting from the old spouse and beginning again, listening to the 'voice' (*stim*) of God which came from within the believer. To the Dreamers' detractors, the 'voice' they obeyed was to be identified as fleshly lust,[18] but for the members of the sect themselves, the voice called for a spiritualization and purification of lust. Far from following bodily desires (indeed, one poor Dreamer found his body incapable of doing the voice's bidding!),[19] the Dreamers held that one should listen to the 'voice', and only at His command should intercourse take place.[20]

This investment of the sexual act with spiritual significance served both to purify the body of lust and to sanctify the new monogamous matrimonial relations, conducted now according not to the flesh but to the spirit. Consequently, several Anabaptists were anxious to stress during their interrogations that they had first entered a period of sexual renunciation, giving up sexual relations with their spouses before embarking on the new marriage.[21] This, too, can be seen as a spiritualizing resolution of the moral burden which the companionate marriage bore in reformed practice as well as within Anabaptism.[22] For how could an estate which was so holy and pleasing to God, the cornerstone of the reformed order, no longer second to celibacy, be so full of meanness and so unworthy in daily practice?

For the Anabaptists' interlocutors, however, the Dreamers' self-presentation as sexual ascetics was a charade. Their confession that the 'voice' commanded intercourse two or three times in one night was, to the ears of the orthodox, merely proof that the 'voice' was a symptom of immodest lust where the appetites took over. When the Dreamers tried to demonstrate their distance from sensuality by pointing out that 'some nights' the 'voice' would not command union, they did their cause little good with their interrogators.

There were, however, points of contact between Dreamer belief and reformed practice. Shocking and unfamiliar though these marriages seemed to the authorities, the form of Dreamer marriage was actually uncomfortably close to orthodox marriage.[23] Indeed, if neither of a Dreamer couple had previously been married, secular authority had no grounds on which to prosecute, since the Dreamers could always argue (stretching the truth just a little) that they had indeed taken one another in marriage, but fully intended going to church to confirm the wedding.[24] After all, popular marriages were entirely valid according to the pre-Reformation practice if concluded in this fashion,[25] and reformed areas were not able to impose the church ceremony on all couples.

Anabaptists were no more refractory than ordinary peasants, faced with the attempts of secular authority to extend control over entry into marriage.[26] So far as externals were concerned, a 'spiritual' marriage could pass for a normal marriage. The Anabaptists' radical desacramentalization of religion was replaced with a hyper-spiritualization of all aspects of life which concerned internal matters. The elderly Dreamer couple who, unwilling to choose new spouses, 'remarried' each other in a kind of spiritual dedication ceremony, were not committing an offence.[27] Only when the marriage entailed adultery did Anabaptist practice clearly offend against secular norms.

And there were further similarities between Dreamer concerns and those of reformers. At the heart of the Dreamers' unease about marriage lay the question – as troubling to reformers as to radicals – of the place of sexuality, the realm of base bodily lusts, in God's scheme of holy matrimony. The solution posed by the Dreamers was to confer spiritual value on intercourse: marriages which were not of the spirit and sex which was not spiritual were not real unions at all, but worldly, false marriages. Reformers, however, were similarly convinced that the right ordering of sexual relations was fundamental to marriage; indeed, it was constitutive of marriage itself. They held that adultery sundered a marriage, enabling the innocent party to marry again. So integral to the marriage tie was fidelity that, as the reformer Johannes Bugenhagen spelt it out, if an adulterous spouse should be reconciled with his or her partner and taken back into the marriage bed, then 'it is once again a new marriage' and the innocent spouse could not sue for divorce.[28] The first marriage, dissolved by the adultery, was followed by a new marriage once sexual relations resumed. Even an orthodox Protestant theologian like Martin Bucer might later employ a similar moral emphasis on sexual expression in marriage to justify divorce in the case of adultery, advocating remarriage for innocent and guilty spouses alike.[29]

What did the new marriages of the Dreamers mean in practice? Most strikingly, the Dreamers' redrawing of marriage involved reciprocal spouse exchange among a small circle of believers, many of whom were related. Since marriage was fundamentally a social institution – an interpretation which the Dreamers did not question – the spiritual marriages entailed a series of changes to domestic arrangements in the small village homesteads where they lived. Many of the new marriages brought inversions of status. Hans Schmid married his maid while his old wife took Michael Maier in marriage; Jerg Kern, a manservant, married Baltasar Freund's wife. The overcoming of social difference was further strengthened by the web of kinship relations in which they were enmeshed – nearly all the group was related to the Maier and Kern families. (Here it is interesting to note that until they were interrogated under torture, most deliberately denied that the group had a leader, insisting that all were equal before God.) In this consolidation of kinship, familial bonds were intensified by the spiritual family created through the new marriages, so that, as one man put it, the two fathers held their children in common just as they held their goods in common.[30] Marital relations were here used to overlay kinship with a series of incestuous linkages, and sexual desire was pressed into the service of communitarian bonding. The resulting marriages made sexual relations intensely endogamous, so that their spiritualization involved a figurative relocation of the sexual into the family, re-enacting, perhaps, the primal sexual scenes of childhood. Infantile erotic interest, which in early development is first directed towards the child's parents, could thus remain forever locked within the family.

The Dreamers' new marriages did not, however, lead to the disintegration of the household or its internal order. Else Kern, the former maid, became mistress of Hans Schmid's house when she married him, even though his old wife still resided in the house.[31] In this sense the arrangements were patriarchal – the man's status determined that of his wife, not vice versa. Nevertheless, women were at pains to insist, against their own interest of self-preservation, that they themselves had suggested the union at the prompting of the 'voice' even if they also admitted that the man had first suggested the union following a dream.[32] And one woman clearly took the initiative. Travelling to Alt-Erlangen, she candidly informed Marx Maier that he was to be her spouse.[33] This was a direct inversion of expected feminine demeanour and involved a claim to a kind of sexual equality which cannot simply be dismissed as the mirage of male sexual fantasy. Open expression of female desire of this kind was sufficiently shocking to contemporaries for such a woman's reintegration into sixteenth-century society to require an acknowledgement of her shame and guilt.[34] Anabaptist marriage practices were therefore disconcerting evidence to their interrogators of the power of unfettered female desire, a power with which the authorities were only too well acquainted.

The Dreamers were struggling to create a new understanding of the relationship between the mind and the body. Whereas the world around them saw sexuality as the expression of the will, which could either curb or surrender to the anarchic, lustful flesh,[35] the Dreamers made the division between the flesh and the will even sharper. They rendered the sexual act good by alienating it from the human will altogether and making it an act of obedience to a divine, not a natural command.[36] Other Anabaptists, too, grappled with the question of the will, tending often to be drawn towards an insistence on the freedom of the will in contradiction of Lutheran theology.[37] This conception sprang from a deep-rooted Anabaptist straining after moral perfection. But it also led some Anabaptists and spiritualists to attempt a kind of asceticism of sensuality, where the sexual became sanctified by replacing human will with obedience to the divine. This transformation reached its apotheosis in the theology of the Thuringian bloodfriends, who held the sexual act to be the only sacrament.[38] For them, sexual union with the other members of the sect (the *cristirunge* as they called it) became the means of grace.[39] They resolved the opposition between the body and the holy by making the body itself the gateway for the divine.

II

The events in Franconia were soon followed by new kinds of marital experimentation elsewhere. In Strasbourg, the radical Claus Frey, who had been influenced by the Dreamers, arrived with the woman with whom he had entered a bigamous relationship, creating dissension among Anabaptists, radicals and other followers of Melchior Hoffman in the town.[40] Frey's theology of marriage is even more difficult to reconstruct than that of the Dreamers, since the full records of his interrogations at Strasbourg have not survived and our principal source is the hostile biographical pamphlet by the humanist reformer Wolfgang Capito.[41] Yet Frey, too, was no libertine. He insisted even until the moment of his death that his spiritual marriage to Elisabeth Pfersfelder, wife of the nobleman George Pfersfelder, was valid. He repudiated his first wife – who, in a piece of timely theatre, arrived at Strasbourg with their children in tow and presented herself as the faithful, obedient model of wifely deportment.[42] Such pathos and tragedy enacted before the riveted audience of Strasbourg preachers and councillors the dreadful and inhuman behaviour to which rejection of orthodoxy might lead. As the Strasbourg preacher Wolfgang Capito pondered, how was it possible for a man who had begotten eight children with his wife, the fecundity proof of the marriage's sexual health, suddenly to reject her?

Frey's spiritual marriage recalls those of the Dreamers. For him, however, it became not a prescription for spiritual renewal of marriage for all, but a symbolic enlargement of his own marital drama, transformed into a re-enactment of biblical chronology. His first wife, he claimed, represented the serpent of Genesis whose head must be trodden underfoot. His second wife, like Mary, brought the promise of salvation of all and was mother of all.[43] Frey's theology is a *bricolage* of various radical elements, many current in Strasbourg. After fighting with the Hoffman circle, he was eventually to be considered neither an Anabaptist nor a Lutheran, Zwinglian or papist.[44] But he was clearly formed by the intellectual world of radical theology. The serpent as symbol of evil was also a strong motif in the visual theology of the Strasbourg spiritualist and gardener Clemens Ziegler, whose simple diagrams show a kind of physiological location of the struggle between good and evil. The inner man, nestling like an organ in the body, fights the gut-like serpent.[45] Ziegler's dramatic representation of the spiritual battle between the old and new man was not so far removed from the moral theology of the

Strasbourg preachers. However, in Frey's hands, the transformation went further. The serpent has become both externalized as his old wife, and simultaneously located within his own extended 'marital flesh', so that only purification through separation from the old wife and entrance into the new spiritual marriage could bring salvation.

Frey's individualism also led him to a more limited reconceptualization of marriage. He called his wife his 'marital sister' (*eeswester*),[46] an expression not used by the Dreamers. As his sister, Pfersfelder was a fellow believer, unlike his old wife. The term can also be read as marking an insistence on equality in marriage, since it derives from the egalitarian, fraternal model of Anabaptist greeting. Certainly Elisabeth Pfersfelder, as the vehicle through whom all would attain salvation, occupied a powerful position within Frey's symbolic universe. But the model of brother–sister relations is perhaps better related to the rejection of matrimony as involving sexual relations of difference. As his 'marital sister' rather than his wife, Frey could retain his marriage partner endogamously within the family, as it were, so that bonds of kinship and similarity rather than difference could spiritualize the relationship. Indeed, this could even lead to the denial that their sexual relations resembled ordinary unions. Like the Virgin Mary, Pfersfelder remained 'a virgin before, during and after the birth'[47] – even though unlike Mary, Pfersfelder had not actually given birth.

However, this conception of marriage could also retain a grounding in the fundamental axioms of sixteenth-century patriarchy. The proof of his old wife's faithlessness was that she had not followed him to Nuremberg when he left Windsheim as an obedient wife should. By contrast, his spiritual wife was a paragon of obedience.[48] Even for Capito, the Strasbourg reformer who roundly condemned Frey's bigamy, this uncomfortable fact required some explaining. Concerned as he was to portray Frey's first wife as a devoted spouse and mother, he had at once to present her timely arrival at Strasbourg as proof of her eternal obedience while glossing over her earlier refusal to sell the house and follow her husband to Nuremberg.[49] Here, too, the Strasbourg preachers' insistence that long-term desertion was an offence against marriage serious enough to justify not only divorce but also remarriage had found its dreadful apotheosis in Frey. Her desertion – albeit for a shorter time than a Strasbourg court might have countenanced – was cause for divorce under Strasbourg legislation.[50]

III

All the reformers' predictions about the true nature of Anabaptism seemed to have been fulfilled when Anabaptists at Münster embraced polygamy. Here, it seemed, was ultimate proof that doctrinal deviance led to libertinism and indiscipline of every sort. Held up as a terrible warning, Anabaptist polygamy showed how far all Anabaptists had wandered beyond the pale of true belief and both natural and Christian behaviour. Yet, as we shall see, there was rather too much bluster in this polemic, for the advocacy of polygamy turned out not to be so utterly removed from mainstream Reformation thought. It must be seen as part of the general debate over marriage in which, despite the puffing of polemicists, principles were neither fixed nor unquestioned.

The Anabaptist experiment in polygamy has puzzled most modern historians, being seen as an inexplicable aberration or else passed over in silence. Yet for most inhabitants of Münster it must have been the most radical and most personally experienced transformation wrought by the new religion. It can be seen as the resolution of the personal problems of Jan of Leyden, who was already married to a daughter of the mayor Bernd Knipperdolling. When the movement's leader Jan Matthys had been killed, Jan of Leyden needed to retain the charisma of his powerful and beautiful widow by marrying her, but could not afford to alienate the powerful support of the Münster politicians by divorcing his wife. Such an explanation, however, cannot account for the adoption of polygamy by an entire city.[51]

Both Otthein Rammstedt and Ronnie Hsia have offered a suggestive explanation of its wider attraction.[52] In a city with a vast majority of single women and wives deserted by their husbands, it made sense to incorporate them within the institution which was the fundamental unit of the civic polity, the household. We might argue that polygamous marriage in Münster, taking its cue from the reformers' own insistence on the importance of female subordination within marriage, was grounded in the principles of the sixteenth-century household craft-workshop, where production and domestic unit were the same. Such an adaptation of the household workshop ideal was one to which a movement like Münsterite Anabaptism, recruiting widely from local craftsfolk and upper citizens, was naturally drawn.[53] As such, the Münster movement shares a similar impulse with the wave of moral reformism which can be seen in many cities throughout the 1530s and 1540s, where a Reformation movement, supported now by citizens and guildsfolk, attempted to create a disciplined city by applying the ethics of the household workshop to the whole town.[54] The Anabaptists of Münster, then, did not present so much an assault on marriage as a working out of the patriarchal potential within marriage to create an even more patriarchal institution. Having more than one spouse was an option for men only: women were not allowed to have more than one husband.

These, surely, were the key dynamics of polygamy – though it may be that the community of wives which the new households also created may have allowed female bonds to be strengthened beneath the patriarchal lines of obedience. Marriage and discipline were thus crucial issues for the self-definition of the city of the godly. Once again, what appears to be sexual libertinism was in fact rooted in an ascetic moral code, for in Münster adultery and even desire for another woman were punishable by death.[55] Polygamy proved to be compatible with a rigid sexual moralism. Nor did the Münsterites abolish marriage. Divorce was permissible, but this too arose from the need to order sexual relations so that all were contained within 'marriage' and marital behaviour – wifely obedience, cohabitation, marital faithfulness – might be upheld. We might say that polygamy in Münster was motivated less by the need to purify sexual relations and spiritualize marriage (as it was in the case of Frey or the Dreamers) than by the need to arrive at a model of social organization which would deal with the large numbers of unattached women. Fear of the anarchic power of female lust once it was released from the 'good training' which marriage provided meant that women had to be incorporated into households.[56] What Anabaptists shared with reformers was both the belief in the disorderly capacities of female lust and their diagnosis of the cure: marriage. The path taken by the Münsterites was to turn all women into wives, a solution that followed from the premises of evangelical theory.

Modern historians have attempted to rehabilitate Anabaptism by arguing that most Anabaptists were well-behaved moral individuals, and by distancing the movement from its radical, sexually unorthodox fringe. As James Stayer brilliantly argued for the Anabaptist doctrine of pacifism,[57] a 'recovery' of this kind risks distorting the plurality of Anabaptist theology and underestimates the activist, revolutionary wing within Anabaptist thought. Similar arguments must be made for the sexual libertinist groups within Anabaptism, so often consigned to the nether reaches of religious deviance and even characterized as insane.[58] Dismissal of such radicals invokes moralist arguments to obliterate these groups from the Anabaptist canon, and in so doing, makes unintelligible one of the major currents within Anabaptist and radical movements, namely the critique of marriage. Marriage radicals were trying to reformulate the place of the body and sexuality in relation to the holy, by purifying marriage of sin and creating a morally perfect relationship. Even historians who are aware of the diversity of Anabaptist thought on marriage tend to align marital experiment with the most negative attitudes to women, an equation which oversimplifies the range of views by implying that sexual freedom is inevitably associated with the exploitation of women. I now want to argue that Anabaptists and radicals were not alone in rethinking marriage. As their reactions to Anabaptists show, mainstream reformers were grappling with the same issues.

IV

When reformers came to devise their own moral standards, they turned to secular authorities to create Discipline Ordinances and Discipline Courts which would institutionalize the moral standards binding on all people, lay and clergy alike.[59] The preachers' call for discipline, however, was intimately bound up with the campaign against the greatest threat to their authority, Anabaptism. Anabaptism was the catalyst for the moral debate. For the preachers, it represented the manifest failure to create a united godly community. Anabaptist assault on the new clergy's authority meant that the issue of moral authority became inseparable from defeating the radicals. Thus at Strasbourg, the preachers constantly called for a new Discipline Ordinance and firmer discipline during the build-up to the great Synod of 1533, the event which was designed publicly to disprove the doctrines of the Anabaptists and restore a united faith to the religiously fractured citizenry. Demands for moral reform and doctrinal unity were constantly coupled in their submissions to the council.[60] In Constance, too, calls for a campaign against the Anabaptists and demands for more discipline went together.[61] Luther, whose genealogy of Anabaptism has so often been adopted by later historians, saw all Anabaptists as descended from Müntzer and Carlstadt. According to Lutheran propagandists, all religious radicals were united by their claim to an inner truth but were driven in reality by the Devil, and were liable to fall victim to the lusts of the flesh.[62] Thus sexual licence, the very complaint Anabaptists made against the soft-living church of the reformers, was used as a brush with which to tar the Anabaptists.

For Anabaptists, on the other hand, discipline was the issue which had led many of them to separate from the church in the first place.[63] Infant baptism, with its inclusive incorporation of saints and sinners, pure and impure, represented all that was ungodly in the church of the evangelicals. Only a believers' church, Anabaptists held, bound together by believers' baptism, could be a real community of saints. This was a position which could unite those Anabaptists who held that all believers, once saved, were incapable of sinning, with those who placed emphasis on the strict congregational discipline of the saints. Separation from the church and entry into the community of believers was the consequence of both views within Anabaptism. Baptism symbolized the radically different approaches of evangelicals and Anabaptists to discipline.

It was the Strasbourg preacher Martin Bucer, the theologian of discipline, who had the surest feel for the centrality of the issue for Anabaptists, and who, in one of the only such incidents in the Reformation, succeeded in winning back a group of Hessian Anabaptists to the Hessian territorial church by persuading them of the sincerity of his attempt to 'create godly discipline' in the territory.[64] Indeed, Bucer's theology, with its emphasis on the congregation's duty to undertake the disciplining of its own members and to punish offenders, was not always a comfortable partner for secular authority. Secular power naturally wished to retain the authority to punish all offences itself, and feared the new church might ultimately, like the old church, rival its own power. Bucer's plans for a congregationally-based programme of discipline were, in 1547 and 1548, to lead him on a collision course with the Strasbourg Council; and the Strasbourg design was defeated.[65] Discipline, as the authorities understood the term, was a vehicle for educating and training the totality of subjects, not an instrument for gathering a perfect community by winnowing out the sinners.

In Strasbourg itself, however, accommodation with the Anabaptists had proved impossible. This was partly because of the sheer variety of Anabaptists, spiritualists and radicals who made the city their home when they fled persecution elsewhere. It was also because the issue sharply exposed the disarray among the official Strasbourg preachers. The preacher and humanist Wolfgang Capito, for one, was sympathetic to spiritualist and Anabaptist doctrines, and even began to talk of the baptism of faith.[66] Other preachers also provided shelter to refugee radicals and lent an ear to unorthodox views. Increasingly, Bucer began to see the defeat of the Anabaptists as a prerequisite for restoring the unity and authority of the Strasbourg church. A breakthrough seemed to have been made when, in the Strasbourg pre-Synod of 1533, Bucer apparently re-established authority over the other preachers, but his hold on power was still so slender that there was at first no unanimity among the Strasbourg preachers on such basic tenets as compulsory baptism.[67] But the balance shifted decisively towards the established Strasbourg church when Wolfgang Capito finally broke with the Anabaptists.

Interestingly enough, it was the issue of sexual discipline which set the seal on Capito's public return to the orthodox camp. In 1534 he issued a pamphlet roundly condemning the doctrines of the spiritualist Claus Frey.[68] But, as the pamphlet makes plain, it was Claus Frey's bigamy which was for Capito the final proof that spiritualist doctrines were of the Devil, not of God.[69] 'By their fruits ye shall know them': if the fruits of spiritualist faith were sexual indiscipline, then the doctrine stood condemned.

Capito's pamphlet is illuminating because it exemplifies widespread views about the nature of Anabaptism and its connection with sexual experimentation. Capito, an unusually sympathetic orthodox observer, had a sharper eye than most for the nuances of spiritualist thought. An attractively mild and scholarly individual, a man after modern historians' tastes, he is in many ways an atypical sixteenth-century figure.[70] At the same time he was merely one of many, Anabaptists and orthodox, who were fascinated by the underlying question of the relation between the sexual and the holy. He fully shared his culture's puzzlement over the nature of woman and its concern to discipline female sexuality. In his conviction that discipline and the fight against Anabaptism were two sides of the same coin he was typical of the Strasbourg preachers. Like them, he recognized the challenge which Anabaptism posed to the nature of marriage. Capito's pamphlet is no blistering invective, though its condemnation of Frey is no less far-reaching for its (by sixteenth-century standards) mild tone. Melchior Hoffman replied to the pamphlet with a bloodthirsty pseudonymous pasquill written from his prison cell, in which he reckoned Capito among the 'bloodhounds' of the Strasbourgers. He recognized that Capito's final shot, the allegation that Hoffman's 144,000 elect would use the sword to usher in the Final Days, was a highly dangerous attack on the Melchiorite movement, the followers of Melchior Hoffman.[71]

Hoffman's venom was not misplaced. Even though Capito carefully distinguished between the maverick Frey and the other unorthodox, Frey's history was for him a morality play which proved the corrupting power of sexual obsession lying beneath the surface of all religious unorthodoxy. Capito's narrative portrays a tragedy of human lust. Sexual discipline was the issue which completed his parting of the ways with radical spiritualism, and marked his final return to the conservative evangelical moralism of his fellow-preachers at Strasbourg.

Yet despite its simple message, Capito's pamphlet is riven with contradiction as he tries to relate sexual to doctrinal unorthodoxy and to distinguish the different sexual natures of women and men. At one level the pamphlet is an indictment of the lustful Frey. But it is the career of Pfersfelder, Frey's second 'wife', which captures his attention. Capito wishes to present Pfersfelder as the reformed victim of lust, and she is therefore an Eve-figure. But drawing on this topos inevitably invokes the accompanying theme of female sexual guilt and responsibility. It was women's greater susceptibility to lust which led Pfersfelder to seduce Frey, according to Capito. And, in Capito's set-piece dialogue – redolent for his sixteenth-century readers with the imagery of immodest passion which might, in women's case, lead to subjection to the Devil himself – Pfersfelder describes how 'there came an urge in me . . . I should go and make myself subject to this man, with body, honour and good, that he should do with me as he wished'.[72] In similar vein, Capito implies her attractiveness was the temptation which led Frey astray, and supplies a dialogue in which she rues her relationship with Frey, telling how she had refused an offer of 200 gulden for her honour.[73] This innuendo both testifies to her attractions and, given the conventions of procuring, implies that she was not above flirtation. Female sexual agency thus accomplishes Frey's fall.

However, Capito also wants to present Pfersfelder as innocent victim of Frey's machinations, and Anabaptism, not sexual desire, as the ultimate cause of Frey's fall. Helpless victim of the lechery which Frey arouses in her, she is at the mercy of the forces within the cauldron of the female body. Indeed, the path to salvation which he proposes for her now that Frey has been executed is one of modesty, penitence and purification,[74] a course of treatment which, the reader feels, the good doctor Capito will superintend to assure full recovery. Like a penitent prostitute, Pfersfelder can be saved through renouncing her lust.

Capito's own biography is apposite here. He himself had contemplated marrying the Anabaptist 'queen' Sabina Bader, the widow of the executed Anabaptist 'king', Augustin Bader. Thanks to Bucer's machinations, however, he eventually took Wilbrandis Rosenblatt, the widow of the 'orthodox' reformer Oeclampadius, as his wife.[75] Marriage to a woman like Bader stood squarely in the medieval tradition of the virtuous deed of marrying a prostitute and ensuring her rescue. That he entertained the idea testifies both to Capito's fascination with Anabaptism and to his interest in redeeming 'fallen' women. Writing the pamphlet about Frey enabled Capito to restage the drama of female sexuality, allowing him to show that female desire can never be exorcised, because all women may fall prey to their own natures. Yet the very unruly sexual femininity which Capito found so compelling had to be suppressed and purified, disciplined in marriage. To these dilemmas, both doctrinal and sexual, the compelling simplicity of the moral condemnation of adultery provided the resolution: since adultery is wicked, it follows that whatever doctrines gave rise to it must be of the Devil.

The effects of the preachers' campaigns against Anabaptist 'indiscipline' were deeply ambivalent. Try as they might to present the Anabaptists as completely alien to the evangelical movement, the campaign exposed the contrary logic beneath. The susceptibility of even such a reformer as Capito, linked with the innermost circles of reform in Strasbourg, to spiritualist and Anabaptist doctrines, shows how close the seeming polar opposites of spiritualism and evangelicalism might draw. When Capito contemplated marrying Sabina Bader, he replayed within his own life – within his own marital 'flesh' – the drama of the expulsion and reintegration of the Anabaptist 'other'. Reformers, like Anabaptists and spiritualists, had to cut a marital ethic from the prickly cloth of a monastic heritage. Because they were only too aware of the competing forces of holiness and physicality they tried hard to desacralize the sexual act. They rendered it an 'indifferent thing' so far as holiness was concerned, denying that abstinence had any relation whatsoever to the divine and rejecting the age-old 'forbidden times'. Sexuality had instead to be disciplined and channelled into the social institution of marriage where it would no longer be a disruptive force but a pillar of social stability.

Anabaptists, who rejected the authority of the preachers and seceded from the universal church, were thus cast in the role of sexual deviants.

Their rejection of society meant that they were sure to be seen as creatures of indiscipline and lust, even regardless of their interest in marital experiment. The problem, however, was that sexual indiscipline could not be exorcized so easily. Earthly marriages stubbornly refused their appointed role as guarantors of social order and were occasions of quarrelling, disorder and enmity, while sexual sins continued to flourish outside the marital pale. Worse still, reformers were left with a view of the relations between spirit and nature which remained locked in dualism. The other side of Reformation morality was a sexual prurience convinced of the awesome power of female desire. Capito's ascription of Frey's fall to the agency of the beautiful Elisabeth Pfersfelder, or the invocation of the legendary beauty of Jan Matthy's widow as part of the explanation for Jan of Leyden's introduction of polygamy in Münster, testify to evangelical fear of the consequences of feminine sexual attraction.[76]

V

Indeed, despite the reformers' vigorous denunciation of the marital practices of the Anabaptists, an underlying instability can be discerned in the reformers' own doctrines of marriage. The most notorious case in point is the advice given by Luther and Melanchthon to Philip of Hesse to commit bigamy. This episode is often taken to be a freak incident, exemplifying Luther's naïveté in the political realm. But Luther was neither alone in his support of the bigamy, nor was his 'confessional advice' a departure from his theology of marriage. In this final section, I shall argue that Reformation theology, too, was open, in its early years, to uncertainty about the institution of marriage, and that it had not satisfactorily resolved the relation between the flesh and the will.

When the reformers argued that marriage should not be counted among the sacraments, they also undermined the principles of indissolubility. As a non-sacrament, moreover, marriage became the province of secular, not church, authorities who were now to deal with the myriad legal cases arising from disputed marriage promises, child support, desertion, adultery and other grounds for divorce. Reformed marriage doctrine thus engendered a host of problems. On the one hand, reformers lauded marriage and made it the cornerstone of evangelical morality. On the other, the preachers, having rejected the principle that marriage was a sacrament, allowed secular authorities far greater potential scope for invasion into the marital sphere. Even worse, their anti-sacramentalist view of marriage raised the hard question of what, if not the sacrament, is constitutive of marriage.

Luther's instinct when faced with moral conundrums was pastoral rather than legalist. His emphasis on sexual expression and childbearing as fundamental elements of marriage led him to propose that if a woman could not have children by an impotent husband she was then entitled to have intercourse secretly with a surrogate who could produce children and give her sexual satisfaction.[77] In this way, the public institution of matrimony would be upheld while the individual conscience found a remedy. It was thus in accord with Luther's established pastoral principles that he should have advised the Landgrave to enter into a second, secret marriage rather than endanger his conscience further by committing adultery and remaining unable to take communion. Precisely because marriage was such a serious relationship, it could not lightly be dissolved by divorce. Instead, when Philip's bigamy later became public knowledge, Luther somewhat unconvincingly condemned the Landgrave – not for having married bigamously, but for having publicly defended his act. In a sense, Luther's sharp distinction here between public and private harked back to the older notions. It rested on the distinction between 'public' adultery, which was a punishable offence, and 'private', which was a matter for confessional discipline alone. This was a distinction which some territorial Discipline Ordinances were to retain long after it had been jettisoned by many similar urban ordinances.[78]

Yet even moralists like Bucer for whom the public/private moral categories were untenable in the new, pure urban morality of the godly city, were to be found offering Philip support. Indeed, when the evangelical movement adopted the principle of biblicism as the sole judge of morals, they found that the Old Testament furnished several examples of unorthodox marital arrangements, and Zwinglian insistence on the primacy of scripture made such evidence hard to dismiss, predisposing them towards a possible accommodation with bigamy. Indeed, the concept of bigamy was itself fluid. Reformers seriously considered the question of whether remarriage for clergy ought to count as serial bigamy.[79] Bucer's attitude to the Hessian scandal was complex.[80] Much to his chagrin, he was widely suspected of having composed a notorious dialogue in defence of polygamy. Among the Strasbourg radicals the followers of the spiritualist Caspar Schwenckfeld seized on the charge with glee, because it nicely turned the tables on the Strasbourg moralists.[81] And not without reason, for Bucer's continuing support of Philip and his close involvement in discussions concerned with the affair[82] showed that evangelical morality and Münsterite polygamy might not be so far apart after all.

It is easy to charge Philip with cynical misuse of Reformation doctrine. When the reformers proved niggardly in their public support, the Reformation hero contemplated securing a papal dispensation for his bigamous marriage instead.[83] It was a tactical masterstroke to have manoeuvred Melanchthon, Eberhard von der Thann, the electoral Saxon representative, and Martin Bucer into acting as witnesses to the wedding.[84] But Philip's dilemma of conscience was a genuine one, and it fitted squarely into Reformation understandings of sin and the body. The Landgrave felt himself unable to take communion because he was an adulterer. Like the reformers, he regarded the sexual appetite as an integral part of human nature, something which could not be altered. He argued that he was so made that he could not remain faithful to one wife. Marriage, which reformers insisted was the remedy for sin, was therefore the solution: a second marriage would accommodate his sexual nature and render what were now sinful acts innocent. In an adroit application of the reformers' own arguments against clerical celibacy, he claimed that those who argued against bigamy were hostile to marriage itself, and hostile to women. They were like the priests who pretended to praise marriage while regarding women as the sink of iniquity and marriage as incompatible with religious office. It was precisely Philip's full-blooded support of marriage which led him to want more of it rather than less![85] In all this, the Landgrave sailed uncomfortably close to central contradictions within Reformation theology. If marriage was designed to be an outlet for human sexual nature, what happened if sexual ardour simply refused to be disciplined into marriage? If, as the reformers had argued, sex was not a matter of rational decision but of human nature, and if one could not choose to slough off nature and adopt the celibate life, what then was the relationship between the human will and the flesh? How then could Anabaptists be safely condemned as slaves to lust?

Philip's own preachers struggled to defend their ruler's bigamy, and a thoroughgoing public pamphlet war ensued, much to the embarrassment of Luther, Bucer and other reformers.[86] Their efforts show a willingness, albeit a tentative one, to rethink conventional assumptions about marriage. The anonymous author of the first of the Landgrave's pamphlet defences, the *Dialogus*,[87] argues at first the very limited case that every biblical reference purporting to condemn bigamy does not unequivocally do so. In the final passages of the pamphlet, however, the writer begins to engage imaginatively with the possibility of bigamy. He justifies it as a solution for a few individuals who are so fashioned by God that they cannot do otherwise, but warns all such to be careful not to mistake evil lusts for what is their God-given nature.[88] Trying to steal the discipline card, he argues that those who are opposed to bigamy are indifferent to far greater breaches of discipline.[89] Opposition to bigamy, so he claims, springs from an underlying low estimation of marriage: these people

> [hold] marriage and its service to be an impure and unholy thing, so that the best thing for mankind is never to enter the marital state, and the next best thing to enter it only once and stay there as briefly as possible.[90]

He even toys with the idea that bigamy may have the advantage of increasing marriage, helping 'all women, whom God has created for marriage, to enter matrimony'[91] and enabling Christian humanity to increase and multiply. These, of course, are arguments which are familiar to us from the theories of the Münster Anabaptists. They also justified bigamy on the grounds of the Old Testament dispensation and the injunction to increase and multiply.[92] The writer's unsatisfactory wrestling with the dilemma of sexual human nature and its relation to the will also recalls the struggles of other reformers with the same issues.

The arguments of the *Dialogus* were disowned by other evangelicals. Luther and Bucer rapidly distanced themselves from such speculation about marriage and bigamy. However, the fact that such debates were possible and that other reformers, too, might conceive of circumstances in which bigamy could be considered shows how far evangelical theology was from an unproblematic advocacy of marriage.[93] As late as 1689, it was possible to defend polygamy for princes.[94] Nor did evangelical censure force Philip to change course. He continued in his bigamous marriage until the death of his first wife in 1549. In Hesse, for the best part of a decade, the ruler's bigamy was not a matter for social obloquy. It was accepted fact.

The limited, but remarkable, temporary convergence between orthodox and radical views of marriage and sexuality was no mere quirk of fate. Evangelicals and radicals, after all, shared a common concern over the nature of marriage. Both were alarmed by the disorder and quarrelling within what ought to be the holy estate of matrimony. Both took sexual expression to be constitutive of marriage so that adultery sundered the bond. Both grappled with the question of the place of sex within marriage, and struggled to come to terms with a tradition of sexual renunciation which was as strong a part of the religious formation which most of the reformers underwent as it was of the medieval mysticism to which Anabaptists and spiritualists were the heirs. Evangelicals and radicals arrived at different solutions, but the issues they confronted were the same. Some Anabaptist solutions led to an intensified patriarchalism where men could rule over several wives but women could be punished for adultery. Other solutions issued in a kind of incestuous communalism, where female desires were as important as male.

For mainstream reformers, on the other hand, it was the adoption of the principles of evangelical morality and the universalization of household workshop values which both ensured the orthodox movement popular support and steered it away from its revolutionary potential.[95] The debate over marriage and discipline was central to the conservatization of the Reformation and its demonization of its opponents. Reformers advocated a sanctified patriarchalism, marked by the attempt to discipline human behaviour so that appropriate male and female behaviour would be clearly defined. But the victory of the conventional marital mode was not at first assured, even within mainstream Protestantism.

If one were to hazard an overview of the long-term course of these developments, it might run as follows. The repudiation by early evangelicals of the obligation of clerical celibacy opened up a new consideration of the relation between the holy and the body. The early years of the Reformation witnessed some sexual and marital experimentation, and mainstream reformers, appalled at the prospect of social anarchy and disorder, embraced a rigid morality and built their new church on the foundations of discipline. But in so doing they proved unable to resolve entirely the place of sexuality. Perhaps it was this spectre which was to return so powerfully in the guise of those sexually anarchic, malign female accomplices of the Devil, the witches.

NOTES

1 See, for the earlier period, Peter Brown, *The Body and Society: Men, women and sexual renunciation in Early Christianity,* New York 1988; and the interesting review article by John Bossy, 'Vile Bodies', *Past and Present,* 124, 1989, pp. 180–7.

2 Such a criticism could be made of my own work! See *The Holy Household. Women and morals in Reformation Augsburg,* Oxford 1989. See also Steven Ozment, *When Fathers Ruled: Family life in Reformation Europe,* Cambridge, Mass. 1983; on the English Reformation Patrick Collinson concludes 'It was here that the family as we know it experienced its birth': *The Birthpangs of Protestant England. Religion and cultural change in the sixteenth and seventeenth centuries,* London 1988, p. 93.

3 Claus Peter Clasen deals briefly with the issue in *Anabaptism: A social history 1525–1618: Switzerland, Austria, Moravia, South and Central Germany,* Ithaca, NY 1972, pp. 136–9, 200–7. Hans Peter Duerr, in *Der Mythos vom Zivilisationsprozess, I: Nacktheit und Scham,* Frankfurt am Main 1988, argues that there was a tradition of religious and sexual radicalism (pp. 308–23), but oversimplifies the varied and complex resolutions of the spirit/body dilemma which the sects reached.

4 Merry Wiesner, 'Women's Response to the Reformation', in R. Po-Chia Hsia (ed.), *The German People and the Reformation,* Ithaca, NY and London 1988, p. 151.

5 I shall be using the term 'Anabaptist' loosely in this chapter, rather as Luther might have used it to refer to non-mainstream Protestants, because my interest here is not in what defines and differentiates Anabaptist sects but in the spectrum of radical views.

6 Klaus Deppermann, *Melchior Hoffman: soziale Unruhen und apokalyptische Visionen im Zeitalter der Reformation,* Göttingen 1979, p. 293. This excellent biography places Hoffman within the wider Anabaptist tradition, giving a slightly different assessment of the role of sexual radicalism from the one I shall develop here.

7 James M. Stayer, 'Vielweiberei als "innerweltliche Askese": neue Eheauffassungen in der Reformationszeit', *Mennonitische Geschichtsblätter,* NF, 32, 1980, pp. 24–41. I am grateful to Professor Stayer for providing me with a copy of his article. Jan van Batenburg and his followers, and later those of Johan

Willems in the 1570s and 1580s, continued to practise polygamy: L.G. Jansma, 'Crime in the Netherlands in the Sixteenth Century: The Batenburg bands after 1540', *Mennonite Quarterly Review*, 42, 1988, pp. 221–35, at 223, 234. David Joris was defending the overcoming of sexual shame at Strasbourg in 1538: see Manfred Krebs, Hans Georg Rott *et al.* (eds), *Quellen zur Geschichte der Täufer*, Elsass, Gütersloh 1959 (hereafter cited as *QGT*, Elsass), vol. 15, Elsass iii, pp. 156–231 for debate between Joris and other Strasbourg Anabaptists; and Deppermann, *Melchior Hoffman*, pp. 313, 315–17. Joris's vision was of a sinless sexuality.

8 Clasen, *Anabaptism*, pp. 260–75 on the Hutterites.

9 On asceticism, not sexual promiscuity, as the impulse behind polygamy, see Stayer, 'Vielweiberei'.

10 See, for example, ' "Auslegung des Unterschieds Danielis", Alstedt 1524', in Günter Franz with Paul Kirn (eds), *Thomas Müntzer: Schriften und Briefe: Kritische Gesamtausgabe*, Gütersloh 1968, pp. 241–63, esp. 251–3. On the origins of Anabaptist views of marriage and on Müntzer, see Stayer, 'Vielweiberei'.

11 Walter Elliger, *Thomas Müntzer: Leben und Werk*, 2nd edn, Göttingen 1975, pp. 376–9; and see also Ulrich Bubenheimer, *Thomas Müntzer: Herkunft und Bildung* (Studies in Medieval and Reformation Thought 46), Leiden 1989, pp. 168–70.

12 Henry Abelove, 'The Sexual Politics of Early Wesleyan Methodism', in J. Obelkevich, L. Roper and R. Samuel (eds), *Disciplines of Faith: Studies in religion, politics and patriarchy*, London 1987.

13 Marion Kobelt-Groch, 'Why did Petronella Leave Her Husband? Reflections on marital avoidance amongst the Halberstadt Anabaptists', *Mennonite Quarterly Review*, 42, 1988, pp. 26–41; M. Lucille Marr, 'Anabaptist Women of the North: peers in the faith, subordinates in marriage', *Mennonite Quarterly Review*, 41, 1987, pp. 347–62. However, I am not convinced that advocacy of monogamy is linked with a more favourable position for women.

14 K. Schornbaum (ed.), *Quellen zur Geschichte der Wiedertäufer*, vol. 2, Bayern i, Markgraftum Brandenburg (hereafter cited as *QGT*, Brandenburg), Leipzig 1934, pp. 249ff.; Clasen, *Anabaptism*, pp. 131–6. Some of the Dreamers had fallen foul of the authorities before and had been imprisoned for Anabaptism.

15 *QGT*, 2, Brandenburg, pp. 327–9.

16

Dieweil gott die ehe gemacht und eingesetzt hab, dass beide zwo seel und ein leip sollen sein, und dieweil sie dan gesehen haben, dass in der ehe vil zank und unwillens gewest ist, auch eins von dem andern gelaufen und sunst ausgebulet haben, so haben sie vermeint, es sei kein rechte ee von gott.

(*QGT*, 2, Brandenburg, pp. 311–12)

17 Roper, *The Holy Household*, pp. 165–205.

18 Or, as others argued, it was the voice of the Devil: *QGT*, 2, Brandenburg, pp. 263–7, Gutachten der Nürnberger Theologen und Juristen über die Baiersdorfer Wiedertäufer, pp. 268–9, Ansbach Statthalter und Räte.

19 *QGT*, 2, Brandenburg, p. 316, Philipp Jacob.

20 *QGT*, 2, Brandenburg, pp. 287, 312, Michael Maier; p. 313, Hans Kern.

21 *QGT*, 2, Brandenburg, p. 272, Hans Schmid; p. 316, Philipp Jacob; p. 323, Else Kern.

22 Here one might compare the practice of 'marital avoidance': separation from the unbelieving spouse, which as Marion Kobelt-Groch has argued in 'Why did Petronella Leave Her Husband?' was a consequence of the spiritual burden which sexual intercourse bore in Anabaptism.

23 John Klassen has argued that ordinary Anabaptist marriages in fact

approximated to the old clandestine marriages: 'Women and the Family Among Dutch Anabaptist Martyrs', *Mennonite Quarterly Review*, 40, 1986, pp. 548–71, at 555.

24 *QGT*, 2, Brandenburg, p. 277, Appolonia Kern.
25 Roper, *The Holy Household*, p. 157; Michael Schröter, 'Wo zwei zusammen kommen in rechter Ehe . . .': *Sozio- und psycho-genetische Studien über Eheschliessungsvorgänge vom 12. bis 15. Jahrhundert*, Frankfurt am Main 1985, pp. 340–5.
26 Thomas Robisheaux, 'Peasants and Pastors: Rural youth control and the Reformation in Hohenlohe, 1540–1680', *Social History*, 6, 1981, pp. 281–300.
27 *QGT*, 2, Brandenburg, p. 321, Thomas Kern.
28 Johannes Bugenhagen, *Vom Ehebruch/ und Heimlichen weglauffen*, Wittenberg, Joseph Klug 1541 (1st edn 1539), fo. M iiiv: 'so ists auffs newe eine newe Ehe'.
29 Walter Köhler, *Zürcher Ehegericht und Genfer Konsistorium* (Quellen und Abhandlungen zur schweizerischen Reformationsgeschichte x), ii, Leipzig 1942, pp. 436–7. See Roper, *The Holy Household*, pp. 194–5, n. 54.
30 'und die kinder, so der Schmid zuvor mit benanter frauen gehabt, dieselben erhalten sie jezo in gemein mit einander, wie sie dann sunst andere guter auch in gemein haben': *QGT*, 2, Brandenburg, p. 287, Michael Maier.
31 *QGT*, 2, Brandenburg, p. 303.
32 *QGT*, 2, Brandenburg, p. 302.
33 *QGT*, 2, Brandenburg, p. 277, Katharina Kern.
34 Roper, *The Holy Household*, pp. 199–205.
35 See Chapter 3.
36 Justus Menius was shrewdly observant of the processes of displacement here: see his *Von den Blutfreunden aus der Widertauff*, Erfurt, Servasius Sthürmer 1551, fos D iv–D ii r.
37 Hans Jurgen Goertz, *Die Täufer: Geschichte und Deutung*, Munich 1980, pp. 67–76.
38 Paul Wappler, *Die Täuferbewegung in Thüringen von 1526–1584* (Beiträge zur neueren Geschichte Thüringens 2), Jena 1913, pp. 189ff., 481–94: according to Jorg Schuchart's interrogation, sexual intercourse by a 'pure' one could bring salvation to the partner, if she were of his faith and if she had intercourse willingly and believed (p. 481).
39 Unfortunately there is not space here to deal in detail with the Bloodfriends. But see Menius, *Von den Blutfreunden*; Clasen, *Anabaptism*, pp. 136–9; G. Franz, *Urkundliche Quellen zur hessischen Reformationsgeschichte 1525–1547* (Veröffentlichungen der historischen Kommission für Hessen und Waldeck 11/2), iv, Marburg 1954, pp. 324–7; Karl Wilhelm Hochhuth, 'Landgraf Philip und die Wiedertäufer', *Zeitschrift für die historische Theologie*, 29, 1859, pp. 182–96; Wappler, *Die Täuferbewegung*, pp. 189–206, 408–94.
40 It also occasioned a split between him and the Strasbourg followers of Melchior Hoffman and other Anabaptists. The Münsterite advocacy of polygamy in 1534 was apparently not accepted by Melchior Hoffman in Strasbourg, who was the Münster movement's supposed inspiration. The issue continued to split the Strasbourg and Münster Melchiorites.
41 Published in *QGT*, 8, Elsass, ii, pp. 321–42.
42 *QGT*, 8, Elsass, ii, shortly before 22 July 1533.
43 According to Capito's account, *QGT*, 8, Elsass, ii, p. 327.
44 *QGT*, 8, Elsass, ii, pp. 121–2, Hedio to Musculus, 23 July 1533.
45 Deppermann, *Melchior Hoffman*, Tafel 1–4, pp. 155–69.
46 *QGT*, 8, Elsass, ii, pp. 92–3, interrogation of Claus Frey.
47 *QGT*, 8, Elsass, ii, pp. 208–9: 'Sein Pfertzfelderin sey ein jungfrau vor der geburt, in der geburt und nach der geburt, dann sie hab sich jm vnterwürffig

gemacht', interrogation of Claus Frey. Frey seems to be claiming that her subordination to him confers the virginal status upon her.

48 *QGT*, 8, Elsass, ii, pp. 92–3, interrogation of Claus Frey: 'In summa: er will die Pfersfelderin haben vnd sein erste eefrau nit. Sagt, sie hab jne vff den fleischbanck wollen geben. . . . Aber nachdem die erst nit mit jme ziehen wollen, hab er alle macht gehabt, ein andere zu nemmen' (p. 93).

49 *QGT*, 8, Elsass, ii, Capito, p. 324 – he mentions the departure from Windsheim but not Frey's wife; he omits her refusal to sell the house (pp. 92–3) but describes her attendance at the pair's 'wedding' in Nuremberg (p. 326); her obedience and virtue are stressed (pp. 329–40).

50 Köhler, *Zürcher Ehegericht*, ii, p. 396: the stipulations of the ordinance of 1531 allowed for divorce after desertion, and the deserted party could bring the case for examination by the Marriage Court judges after a year.

51 R. Po-Chia Hsia, 'Münster and the Anabaptists', in *idem* (ed.), *The German People and the Reformation*, pp. 55–6.

52 Otthein Rammstedt, *Sekte und soziale Bewegung: soziologische Analyse der Täufer in Münster, 1534–5* (Dortmunder Schriften zur Sozialforschung 34) Cologne 1966, pp. 95–100; Po-Chia Hsia, 'Münster and the Anabaptists', pp. 55–6; 59; and see also Stayer, 'Vielweiberei'.

53 Rammstedt, *Sekte und soziale Bewegung*, pp. 104–14, 121–7, argues that Münster Anabaptism was not a movement of the poor but of the crafts and upper bourgeoisie. Karl Heinz Kirchhoff, in *Die Täufer in Münster, 1534–5: Untersuchungen zum Umfang und zur Sozialstruktur der Bewegung* (Geschichtliche Arbeiten zur westfälischen Landesforschung 12) Münster 1973, pp. 86–9, reaches a similar conclusion. Taira Kuratsuka has argued that the movement included lower strata cityfolk but was led by the middle class: 'Gesamtgilde und Täufer: der Radikalisierungsprozess in der Reformation Münsters: von der reformatorischen Bewegung zum Täuferreich 1534/5', *Archiv für Reformationsgeschichte*, 76, 1985, pp. 231–69.

54 Roper, *The Holy Household*, ch. 4.1.

55 Rammstedt, *Sekte und soziale Bewegung*, p. 99.

56 The preachers explicitly defended themselves against the credible charge that polygamy had been instituted because of 'der Viller Weiber Lust': Rammstedt, *Sekte und soziale Bewegung*, p. 98.

57 James Stayer, *Anabaptists and the Sword*, 1972, 2nd edn, Lawrence, Kan. 1976.

58 As Schornbaum, the compiler of the Bavarian documents on Anabaptism put it in the index for his second volume, the Anabaptists of Creglingen and Baiersdorf were

> not . . . Baptists, but mentally ill people who were confused by halluci-
> nations and in this condition deluded themselves that they were hearing
> the voice of God or of the Holy Spirit, who ordered them (amongst other
> things) to arbitrarily separate their marriages and live in adultery or
> bigamy.
>   (Karl Schornbaum (ed.), *QGT*, 5, Bayern, ii, Reichsstädte, Gütersloh 1951,
> p. 312, index)

59 Köhler, *Zürcher Ehegericht*, ii; and on discipline, see Paul Münch, *Zucht und Ordnung: Reformierte Kirchenverfassungen im 16. und 17. Jahrhundert (Nassau-Dillenburg, Kurpfalz, Hessen-Kassel)*, Stuttgart 1978, pp. 183–9; and William J. Wright, *Capitalism, the State, and the Lutheran Reformation: Sixteenth-century Hesse*, Athens, Ohio 1988, esp. pp. 161–86.

60 See, for example, *OGT*, 7, Elsass, i. pp. 233, 548–50; *OGT*, 8, Elsass, ii, pp. 263, 266, 357, 421, 473–4.

61 Jörg Vögeli, *Schriften zur Reformation in Konstanz, 1519–1538* (Schriften zur

Kirchen und Rechtsgeschichte 39, 40, 41), 2 vols, Tübingen 1972–3, i. pp. 441ff. The Discipline Ordinance, reproduced in full by Vögeli (pp. 442–64), forms a natural climax to his history of the introduction of the Reformation into Constance.

62 John S. Oyer, *Lutheran Reformers against Anabaptists: Luther, Melanchthon and Menius and the Anabaptists of Central Germany*, The Hague 1964, pp. 115–16; 132–9, 248–9.

63 On the theological underpinnings of discipline in Anabaptist thought, allied with Anabaptist critique of the clergy, see Goertz, *Die Täufer*, pp. 67–76.

64 Martin Bucer, *Deutsche Schriften*, ed. Robert Stupperich, Gütersloh 1960–, vol. 8, pp. 249–78; Münch, *Zucht und Ordnung*, pp. 110–16; Emil Sehling (ed.), *Die evangelischen Kirchenordnungen des xvi. Jahrhunderts*, Leipzig and Tübingen, 1902–77, 8/I, Hessen, Tübingen 1965, pp. 82–91; 101–12, 148–54, and introduction, pp. 10–23; *QGT*, 15, Elsass, iii, p. 293.

65 Werner Bellardi, *Die Geschichte der 'Christlichen Gemeinschaft' in Strassburg, 1546–1550*, (Quellen und Forschungen zur Reformationsgeschichte 18), Leipzig 1934; Jane Abray, *The People's Reformation: Magistrates, clergy and commons in Strasbourg 1500–1598*, Oxford 1985, pp. 197–8.

66 Deppermann, *Melchior Hoffman*, pp. 169–74; but for a different view see James Kittelson, *Wolfgang Capito: from humanist to reformer* (Studies in Medieval and Reformation Thought 17), Leiden 1975, pp. 183–6. He argues against seeing Capito as very deeply influenced by Anabaptism and spiritualism.

67 Deppermann, *Melchior Hoffman*, pp. 251–2.

68 Reprinted in *QGT*, 8, Elsass, ii, pp. 321–42.

69 Kittelson, *Wolfgang Capito*, pp. 186–206, argues that Capito returned to orthodoxy by 1531–2; but as late as November 1533 Bucer's correspondence rejoices in Capito's return to the faith: *QGT*, 8, Elsass, ii, pp. 207–8.; *Briefwechsel der Brüder Ambrosius und Thomas Blaurer 1509–1548*, ed. T. Schiess, Freiburg 1908–22, i, pp. 441, 453.

70 Kittelson, *Wolfgang Capito*. This excellent biography does not, however, deal in detail with Capito's troubled married life nor his attack on Frey.

71 Deppermann, *Melchior Hoffman*, pp. 306–7.

72 'Es kam ein sollicher trib in mich vnnd redet on vnderlass in mir, ich solte hingon vnd mich disem man underwürfflich machen, mit leib, eer vnd gut, das er mit mir machte wie er wolte'; *QGT*, 8, Elsass, ii, p. 324. Capito claims these were her written words.

73 *QGT*, 8, Elsass, ii, p. 325.

74 *QGT*, 8, Elsass, ii, pp. 337–9.

75 Deppermann, *Melchior Hoffman*, p. 247; Roland Bainton, *Women of the Reformation in Germany and Italy*, Minneapolis, Minn. 1971, p. 85.

76 See, for example, *Newe zeittung von den Widderteuffern zu Munster: auff die Newe zeittung von Munster D. Martini Luther Vorrhede . . .*, n.p. 1535, fo. A iv; and *Newe Zeytung/die Widerteuffer zu Münster belangende 1535*, n.p. 1535, fo. A iiv. Interestingly, in one of the few images we have of Divara, queen of Münster (a copy after Heinrich Aldegrever), the clothing Divara is wearing is the same as that used by Aldegrever to depict Potiphar's wife in a series about her temptation of Joseph: Hans Galen (ed.), *Die Wiedertäufer in Münster: Katalog*, Münster 1982, pp. 190–1. She, too, is a beautiful, lustful female.

77 Martin Luther, *De captivitate Babylonica ecclesiae praeludium*, 1520, in *D. Martin Luthers Werke: Kritische Gesamtausgabe. Werke*, 60 vols, Weimar 1883–1983, vol. 6, pp. 558–9.

78 See Köhler, *Zürcher Ehegericht*. Interestingly, the distinction was also retained among the imperial Police Ordinances. The Reichspolizeiordnung of 1530 contains a paragraph 'Von leichtfertiger Beywohnung' which condemns the

toleration of 'offentlich Ehebruch' (p. 257); and the editions of 1548 and 1577 extend this with a further paragraph on adultery: *Aller des heiligen römischen Reichs gehaltene Reichstage, Abschiede, etc (1356–1654)*, Mainz, Nicolas Heyll 1660, pp. 256, 468.

79 Bucer, *Deutsche Schriften* vol. 7, pp. 242–3: it was when Capito was about to marry the widow Wibrandis Rosenblatt that the question arose.

80 Hastings Eells, *The Attitude of Martin Bucer Toward the Bigamy of Philip of Hesse*, New Haven, Conn. 1924, pp. 58–131.

81 *QGT*, 15, Elsass, iii, pp. 511, 512, and see the satirical poem against Bucer and 'Schriftgelehrten' pp. 516–19.

82 He even advised Philip on writings connected with the affair: William Walker Rockwell, *Die Doppelehe des Landgrafen Philipp von Hessen*, Marburg 1904, pp. 226–8.

83 Ibid., pp. 25, 35ff.; and see Paul Mikat, *Die Polygamiefrage in der frühen Neuzeit* (Rheinische Westfälische Akademie der Wissenschaften Voträge G294), Opladen 1988.

84 Rockwell, *Die Doppelehe*, pp. 42–3.

85 Philip's attitude is generally characterized by this robust affirmation of marriage. See Gerhard Müller, 'Landgraf Philipp von Hessen und das Regensburger Buch', in Marijn de Kroon and Friedhelm Krüger (eds), *Bucer und seine Zeit* (Veröffentlichungen des Instituts für Europäische Geschichte Mainz 80), Wiesbaden 1976: his marginal annotations characteristically note 'Ist wieder got und paulum; teuffels lerre, die ehe zu verbiten; wellen weisser seyn dan got', p. 115. He was a firm advocate of clerical marriage.

86 Rockwell, *Die Doppelehe*, pp. 101–54.

87 *Dialogus/ das ist/ ein freundtlich Gesprech zweyer personen/Da von/Ob es Göttlichem/ Natürlichem/Keyserlichem/und Geystlichem Rechte gemesse oder entgegen sei/mehr dann eyn Eeweib zugleich zuhaben*, n.p., n.d. It is generally agreed to have been written by Johannes Lening, pastor of Melsungen in Hesse. By a nice irony of fate, it is catalogued in the Bodleian Library, Oxford, under Bucer.

88 'das sie sich selbst wol prüfen/vnd das recht vnderscheyden möge[n] was bei jnen böse fleyschliche lüst/vnd was bey jnen Gottes beruff vnd geschöpff sei': *Dialogus*, fo. Aa ii v.

89 *Dialogus*, fos AAr–AAv.

90 'die Ee vnnd jren dienst/für etwas vnreyn vnd vnheylig gehalten/darumb den menschenn das best sein solte/in die Ee nimmer kommen/das nechste nur eyn mal in die Ee kommen vnd kurtz in der bleiben': *Dialogus*, fo. Aa i v.

91 'so alle weibs bilder/so Gott zur Ee geschaffen zur Ehe kommen mochten': *Dialogus*, fo. Aa i v.

92 Rockwell argues, *Die Doppelehe*, pp. 14ff., that the Landgrave was not influenced by Münsterite arguments for polygamy, since the use of the biblical examples and the injunction to multiply are obviously going to be used by any defender of polygamy. But while Rockwell may be correct to maintain there was no formal influence, the arguments are clearly similar and derive from a shared milieu.

93 Philip's court preacher Melander was rumoured to have committed bigamy: Rockwell, *Die Doppelehe*, pp. 84–92.

94 A librarian by the name of Bögner argued for polygamy in 1698; a pastor supported Edward IV Ludwig of Württemberg's bigamous marriage to his mistress: Paula Sutter Fichtner, *Protestantism and Primogeniture in Early Modern Germany*, New Haven, Conn. and London 1989, p. 77.

95 See Roper, *The Holy Household*, ch. 1.

Part II

5 Blood and codpieces: masculinity in the early modern German town

> A male person must pay attention to many things when he goes amongst
> people. He must think of the many virtues that he must allow to appear
> in him. But a woman has no need of this. She has only one virtue to
> which she need attend, namely, to *Zucht* (modesty).[1]

In this passage from Johannes Jhan's School Ordinance, we seem to
possess a clear statement of how sixteenth-century people understood
the difference between men and women. Female virtue is understood in
bodily terms and it ultimately means chastity; male virtue, by contrast,
is plural and concerns a host of qualities which must be manifested in
public, 'when he goes amongst people'. Such contrasts seem to be the
very stuff of sixteenth-century wisdom about the sexes: male is opposed
to female, public to private, activity to passivity, and female honour, by
extension, is primarily a matter of chastity, male honour, of deeds. Here,
it seems, in the comfort of cliché, is the place to start an analysis of the
meaning of manhood. We might proceed to investigate masculinity as
a group system, structured around the axioms of honour and celebrated
in ritual. In such a project, gender history and a social history heavily
influenced by anthropology might, from their different directions, con-
verge. Such a study would analyse masculinity as a socially learnt
system of behaviour, paralleled by a sexually bifurcated system of meanings, which assured men dominance and upheld a male-dominated
social order. And it would satisfy a political imperative too, for if we
understood the nature of masculinity, we might have the key to unlock
the strongbox of patriarchy.

However, I want to suggest that such an approach is misconceived.
What first strikes the historian of the early modern town about masculinity is its sheer disruptiveness. Men posed a serious public order
problem, young bloods endangering the safety of the streets at night,
drunken husbands beating their wives to within an inch of their lives,
guilds fostering a male brotherhood which might even foment political
unrest. Masculinity and its routine expressions were a serious danger
to civic peace rather than a prop of patriarchy. Important as the worlds

of guild and public life were to masculinity, an investigation which confined itself to these phenomena would be misleading. The quotation I have just offered is an equally unreliable guide to sixteenth-century sexual identities, for masculinity, just as much as femininity, concerned the management of the body. In this chapter, I want first to sketch the public urban culture of masculinity, a culture which is increasingly familiar to us, and then go on to investigate the paradox of masculinity more closely by examining not the archetypal male virtues but those disruptive masculine sins, fighting and drinking. From there, I shall consider the understandings of the male body such writings elaborate, in order to take us closer to masculinity, seeing it not as a set of vices or virtues 'which a man must allow to appear in him', but as a psychic phenomenon which has a history none the less.[2]

MASCULINITY AND MALE HONOUR

There is certainly an important sense in which masculinity was a matter of adherence to a public code of manhood. The first thing we can establish about this public culture is that masculinity and male honour were primarily related to the group.[3] Collective events, like public dances, special dances performed by a craft, processions, ritual oath-swearings, military musters and official receptions for foreign guests were occasions which gave expression to the individual male citizen's sense of political belonging and his consciousness of being a man. The group to which a man belonged would be made very visible in ritual – sometimes all would wear clothing of the same colour, sometimes the men would march in a body, sometimes married and unmarried men might be assigned separate tables.[4]

For craftsmen, masculinity was certainly connected with achievement: the masterpiece, which was a requirement for entry into the guild, had to be completed and judged by his seniors. Only as a recognized master could he fully attain the status of *Hausvater*, politically adult and ruler over a little universe of wife, children, servants, journeymen and apprentices. 'Masculine duties' did not merely consist in 'leading the house and supplying it with all its needs', but included, in Wolfgang Perister's words, duties in the public realm, 'the public offices, town hall, church, school'.[5] Symbolically, masculinity was guaranteed when a man took up weapons and defended his city, so that the insult 'traitor', often used against men, was a devastating blow against a man's honour. (By contrast, the insult most frequently used against women, 'whore', impugned a woman's chastity, her bodily integrity and not her deeds.)[6]

Men had a whole chain of corporations to which they belonged and which publicly defended and validated the honour of the group: trade associations, journeymen's bands, military units, political corporations. Commissioned histories of guilds, like Clemens Jäger's history of the shoemakers' guild of Augsburg, provided potted biographies of the heroes of the guild's past and created a genealogy of brotherhood to rival the fashionable family chronicles of patricians. Women, by contrast, had no developed institutions which might celebrate their economic or religious role – they barely make an appearance, for example, in Jäger's chronicle. Instead, since their honour was primarily concerned with their sexual reputation, it had also to be individually defended. This is not to say it was a private matter, for a woman's dishonour could contaminate her menfolk, but female honour lacked the corporate dimension which male honour enjoyed.

Masculinity, however, was not a simple matter of public celebration and confirmation. For the very rituals which were meant to display masculinity were also the events which repeatedly led to disorder and destructive competition within the city. Guild honour could only be established in competition with other guilds, a competitive display in which the honour of other guilds was constantly put into question. Events in the festive calendar of guild life – its processions, dances and shooting matches – had periodically to be banned because they so often ended in fisticuffs. Even weddings, the occasions on which the honour of an entire guild was celebrated, ended all too frequently in blood and tears, as the dance floor might become the stage for an insult and its revenge. And, in order to preserve the honour of the guild, the leaders of trades and guilds regularly excluded those who were not honourable or who could not bring proof of legitimate birth, a complex and thorny procedure in which town councils rapidly became enmeshed as they were forced to adjudicate between guilds and those who wished to enter the guild. Because a guild could best ensure its honour by a policy of exclusivity, demonstratively rejecting illegitimate applicants and rigidly limiting the rights of, for example, widows to continue a workshop, it was in the guild's interest to adopt strict criteria for admission. But this inevitably placed it at odds with the council, whose chief duty was to maintain civic harmony among the citizens, and who owed fairness to all.

Even within the house itself, masculinity – supposedly the cornerstone of patriarchal order – was an ambivalent commodity. The house father, who was supposed to govern his wife, children and servants with wisdom and represent the benevolent paternal authority of the council within the confines of the workshop, was constantly suspected by the council of excessive drinking, violence and frittering away his goods. These were the archetypal male sins, condemned by church and council. The patriarchal order which sanctioned his right to beat an unruly wife and confirmed his control over a couple's material assets thus put the domestic patriarch in a position to imperil the household's economic existence if he so chose. At its most stark, the marital contract was a treaty between unequal partners. This was an apprehension hinted at

when, for instance, even marriage literature warned against the 'tyrannical' husband,[7] a word which captured the political dimension of such
abusive but, within certain ill-defined limits, licit behaviour.[8] There could
be an unpleasantly hard-headed realism about male domestic violence
in such jokes as that of the husband who, having hunted his wife out
of the house, says he's sure she will soon be back. Claus the Fool
remarks coolly that 'if she's pious, she will come back, but if she's
wicked, she'll be off to another'. The message is simple: a sound beating
sorts out women, for a good wife comes back no matter how hard she
is hit, but you're well rid of a whore.[9] Increasingly, urban councils
found themselves involved in such marital conflicts, intervening in the
household and imposing contracts on each side and dealing with complaints. Willy-nilly the council was forced into a continual engagement
with the darker side of patriarchal authority. Patriarchal authority was
not a seamless web.

DRINK

It was drinking that caused civic authorities the most severe problems.
This was a thorny issue, for social drinking was an important part of
male conviviality. Guild drinking rituals, for example, bound its members together. Drinking often took place in guild parlours, where pur-
chasing a round of drinks for all the guild brethren was an important
expression of comradeship. So closely was drinking bound up with
honour that to refuse a drink and the friendship that was proffered
with it was a serious insult. Though excessive drinking was castigated
in council prohibitions, and though tavern closing times were policed,
ritual drinking remained an important part of all guild assemblies –
indeed, even the city fathers themselves took care to provide a good
wine for the visit of dignitaries. As an expression of amity and exchange,
the drinking of wine had a legal import – it sealed a deed of sale and
might even confirm a contract of marriage. Indeed, the place sixteenth-
century tricksters often chose when they wanted to entangle a couple
in a promise of marriage was the inn – there was a ready audience for
the couple's exchange of vows, and a drink would seal the contract.[10]
In the guild world, eating and drinking with the guild members was
the occasion for work to be distributed, a journeyman to be found a
post. A round of drinks, sometimes at the collective expense of all the
guild members, would celebrate the purchase of guild property, or a
newcomer might be required to pay his dues by buying all the masters
a drink.[11] Special drinking vessels and plate which represented the
honour of the entire guild and depicted its noble origins, decorated
the walls and strengthened a consciousness of the guild's tradition – a
tradition which, however, was represented by male heads of household
alone.[12]

It was, however, precisely this male world which was repeatedly the locale for fights, insults, drunkenness and excessive behaviour. In the course of the sixteenth century, councils attempted to extend their control over such haunts of misrule. Their targets were inns, the rowdy culture of the streets at night and, to a lesser extent, the guilds themselves. Discipline Ordinances and church ordinances became ever more extensive, widening their moral concerns. The Discipline Ordinances were especially condemnatory of drunkenness, which they presented as the root cause of evils of every kind – a genealogy of vice which was also common to sermons. As the Augsburg Discipline Ordinance put it, in moralizing rhetoric which encapsulated the regular themes of moralist campaigns against excessive drink:

> Even if excessive wining and drunkenness had not been so greatly accursed in both divine and heathen writings, and everyone had not already been warned against it, daily experience of what misery and disorder, such as the transformation of noble reason into animal insensibility, destruction of soul, body and life, honour and good visibly follows from it, should justly teach us to utterly avoid it.[13]

At every turn, then, civic authorities found themselves confronted with the anarchic disruption caused by masculine culture – the feckless husband, the drunkard, the threatening collectivities of guild and gang. So far as its public manifestations were concerned, masculinity was far from functional for the patriarchal society of the sixteenth century.

THE BODY OF THE DRUNKARD

Is masculinity then exclusively group-related, a matter of deeds and comportment, as the quotation with which we began the chapter assumes? Masculinity certainly had a physical register and was accompanied by a specific understanding of the nature of the male body. To explore this further, we need to consider the masculine sins of drinking, gambling and fighting, about which an elaborate literature developed from the early tracts of humanists and moralists against such vices.

Certainly, it was not exclusively men who were guilty of drunkenness, gambling and fighting. But there was none the less a distinct sexual stereotyping which the moral literature elaborated. At times this is betrayed by accidental slips: the reader is warned that the consequences of vice are dangers for 'wife and child'. But the lusty drunkard is nearly always portrayed as a man. Polemicists knew how to go for the jugular: mock the imagined link between drinking and masculinity. As Matthäus Friderich complained in his *Sauffteufel*, 'every man wants to prove his manhood with drinking';[14] while Eberhard Weydensee resorted to heavy-handed irony against 'the strong heroes and beer-warriors, who

can prove their manhood with knightly deeds'.[15] Often, the drunkard is
a household head and husband. So, for instance, this portrait of the
husband you should pray God will *not* send you rolls up a host of male
miscreants into one stock character:

> a lazy sod and drip, a lay-about and lie-abed, who does nothing but
> eat and drink, . . . and gamble, who has learnt nothing and can do
> no work, but is a *schlueffel*, accustomed to a life of ease, and wants
> to nourish himself with lazy days, and lets his wife and children
> suffer dire need at home.[16]

Yet though this conception of male sins, shared by council, moral writers
and preachers – each, of course, inflecting their discussion differently –
seems to have focused on the disruptive deeds of the drunkard, it also
rested on a particular way of imagining the male body. Man is understood as a creature who is always breaking through the boundaries of
his own body, to the point that he threatens social order. He is a
volcano of drives and fluids which constantly threaten to erupt, spilling
outwards to dirty his environment through ejaculation, bloodshed, vomiting, defecation. Drinking, which, in the view of the preachers, released
all social inhibitions, gave free rein to lusts.

So, for instance, in the writings of moralists, the male body could be
described as a container into which alcohol was poured until it over-
flowed: 'For what are such people but true lye-sacks? They pour more
and more wine and beer in at the top, and when it is full, they let it
run out the bottom, yes, sometimes it climbs out the top.'[17] Excessive
eating and drinking led to an excess of semen, which had also then to
run off. Another of the 'impurities', a daughter of gluttony, was the
impure emission of fluid 'of the body which may occur waking or
asleep'.[18]

These bodily fluids were imagined as dirty and polluting. So Hans
Sachs, exploiting a cliché of much humanist writing, describes the return
of the drunkard, vomiting and dirtying his own bed.[19] A similar view of
the economy of bodily fluids and the danger of drink can be discerned
in the views of secular authorities. The Hessian Discipline Ordinance of
1543 speaks of 'the great indiscipline, which is committed when one so
shamefully vomits and consumes God's gifts in such an unclean fashion
and brings them up again'.[20]

This discourse circles around the correct use of food, bodily excess
and masculine dirt. Man, who is actually the most rational being, is
understood as a creature whose rational capacities can only master his
polluting body with the greatest of difficulty. He threatens to transform
himself into an irrational, pig-like creature at any moment. The most
natural man is the savage, who exploits, enjoys and pollutes his sur-
roundings without compunction. Even the normal patriarch, who after
all was constantly exposed to the temptations of conviviality and wine,

can barely maintain the discipline of his own body, let alone control his wife, children and servants. One might summarize the body-image of the sexes in the following fashion: while women had to fear the invasion of their bodies, and thus the dirtying and destruction of their honour, the polluting bodies of men threatened constantly to dirty themselves and others.

At the same time, the man's internal body could be imagined as a container of vice. Once the demon drink had entered the body, then a host of other devils would follow – the devil of lust, of envy, of swearing, so that all the body's functions, linguistic, sexual, active, would be perverted. Indeed, one dire fable recounted how a man, forced by the Devil to commit one sin alone of a trio of drunkenness, adultery and murder, chose drunkenness, only to end up committing both the other sins in his stupor.[21] The often shrill tones of preachers' sermons against drink reflect a certain desperation, for in attacking alcohol, preachers were attacking a cornerstone of male conviviality itself.[22]

FIGHTING

Fighting was another integral part of male culture, fisticuffs an attendant part of guild processions and dances. Violence took many forms. It could be honed into its own art form, formalized in a variety of sports, the most well known of which was the noisy magnificence of the noble tournament, with its clash of colour, weapons and horses at full tilt, and its own proud history – pamphlets reeled off the litany of the dates and number of all imperial tournaments since 935.[23] Wrestling, with its dance-like precision, elaborated the science of how to put maximum pressure on points of your opponent's body, and it too developed its own artistic genre of pictorial wrestling manuals; while fencing spawned its own arcane 'teach yourself' literature, whose function seems to have been less practical – the instructions, as Jan-Dirk Müller has shown, are often incomprehensible or plain nonsensical – than symbolic.[24] Imperial tournaments rested on the powerful mythology that only those not guilty of sins – no adulterer, moneylender, perjurer, rapist and so on – might participate, and neither might any man not of noble birth. Such a vision must have functioned as a kind of glamorous world of the imagination for citizens, who could not themselves joust, but in whose towns these contests were held. In these pamphlet celebrations, its social exclusivity was underlined. But its rules were also slightly transposed into the moralizing categories of urban communes, so that its heroes might seem men of civic as well as knightly virtue.

The raw energy of fighting, disciplined into art, was a pleasure for the senses: nightly urban street fights were far rougher affairs. However, they too had their rules. The nature of the insults which sparked a fight had to be noted, and sometimes verbal exchange was highly formalized, insult followed by counter-insult. It was important to note the words of insult, who struck the first blow, who first drew their weapon, and as soon as a drop of blood was shed, the fight was transformed into a breach of the peace. Bystanders could bid the peace, but if their peace-making was ignored, the fight became more serious because the common civic peace, proposed by a fellow citizen to whom the combatants were bound by the fellowship of the civic oath, had been spurned. The structure of brawling thus depended in part on civic rituals, a dependence which town councils sought to strengthen by requiring all those involved in a fight to report to the mayor, and binding the civic guards to seek out brawlers and force them into the night lock-up to sober up. A court was specially charged with the duty of fining offenders according to a fixed tariff. Councils thus strove to impose a discipline of sorts on brawling rather than to abolish it outright.[25]

Nor was the council the only authority to punish fighting. Guilds, too, had their own internal courts for dealing with disorder that occurred on guild premises. This was a privilege that they guarded jealously until, after mid-century, a series of towns developed Discipline Ordinances and courts to try moral offences, sometimes run by a coalition of clergy and councillors. These courts gradually sought to encroach on guild jurisdiction over their members' morals. The late fifteenth-century *mannzucht* of the Augsburg shoemakers shows what offences had originally come under their purview: calling someone a liar, cursing him, striking him on the mouth, drawing a knife and throwing a jug, drinking vessel or glass, or whatever else.[26] This lurid list of misdeeds, however, also testifies to the degree to which physical violence between members was the accepted concomitant of guild brotherhood. Guild fraternity, after all, rested on an uneasy balance between brotherly amity and fratricidal competition. There were the masters, who contended with each other for raw materials, markets and good journeymen, and there was the structural rivalry between masters and journeymen, which could sometimes break out into strikes and open warfare, threatening to split and destroy the craft organization altogether. Though guilds fostered an ethic of the group, of men bound to one another by a common history and a shared artisanal pride, and though they seemed an oasis of guild control outside the full control of the council, they were also islands of murderous dissension. Not surprisingly, this aggression was often turned outwards. Guild culture, with its ritualized drinking, could foment gang warfare. So in 1560, for instance, masons and weavers came to blows at the shooting grounds in the Rosenau at Augsburg, seriously wounding over eight people,[27] and bands of Freiburg journeymen caused havoc in the countryside for several years, retaliating against village youths who had offended them.[28]

Yet though violence threatened to undo the ties of brotherhood, it could also cement them further, because the 'licensed' fighting area of guild premises was also an effective container of conflict.[29] It shielded the culprits from council punishment, so that misdeeds were tried by one's peers. Fighting sanctioned the close physical contact between men and taught youths to know each other's bodies and assess their vulnerabilities. The brotherhood of bloodshed, linking youths in violence, was a resilient bond. For the individual man, fighting established his honour. It enabled a man to rehabilitate his reputation with physical force, placing his body as a pledge of manhood. Attacking an opponent also entailed recognizing him as an equal, and to vanquish him was an achievement. For the group, gang warfare was another, if unsanctioned, means of advancing the honour of the guild or journeyman band.

Indeed, fraternity was so compelling a value that it long remained a rival to the ambitions of civic governments, eager to extend their control over the citizenry. In 1587, two young civic guardsmen were tried for failing to report a fight at a weaver's wedding dance.[30] A dozen men, mainly weavers, had forcibly ejected a young student who wanted to join the dance, beating him up in the process. It was no accident that the incident took place at a wedding. The wedding dance, in which all honourable members of the guild might take part, was a powerful celebration of guild identity – the student who wormed his way in was an intruder. But the young guardsmen were also weavers, and one of them was leading the dance himself. The council naturally suspected that the guardsmen's loyalty to the craft had triumphed over civic duty – that they were shielding their fellow tradesmen. Indeed, the loyalty of guardsmen was an enduring problem, for they were not always willing to police the rough male culture to which, after all, they still owed allegiance, while the corporation of guardsmen itself was also riven with the kind of antagonisms which seem to have accompanied any sixteenth-century male grouping. Later that year, one of these same guardsmen was sacked for fighting with his fellow guards.[31]

Fighting, indeed, shows how inadequate a simple model of patriarchy is, for it was the rough culture of fighting men which the council was trying – and generally failing – to police. The council was in constant battle with the men whose interests it apparently represented and whose rough male culture threatened to undermine civic order. In consequence, civic fathers inclined to a dour view of the male culture which caused it such problems, inveighing against the youths who did nothing but drink, fight, whore and gamble. But much as the council sought to identify this culture with youth, experience did not confirm such a comforting view of masculine excess as no more than a passing adolescent phase. The men whom the council condemned for gambling and fighting were often patriarchs themselves, and even as prominent a member of town society as the venerable Gereon Sailer, doctor and humanist, could find himself caught up in a fight with the knight

Sebastian Schertlin – though he turned and ran, accusing Schertlin of not acting in a knightly way, his actions made sense only in terms of the culture of fighting to whose rules he also adhered. He was refusing to fight a nobleman who was his social superior, not his equal.[32]

Ultimately, despite its disruptive nature, it was upon the citizens' preparedness to physically fight to defend the city that civic society and the power of the council depended. Military musters were civic events, as much a male public self-display to their participants as a bureaucratic exercise – 'a pleasure to see and well rigged out in armour' as a Regensburg chronicler proudly described his local civic muster in 1543.[33] The political community was akin to the military community: the citizen was also the weaponed man; the woman, who did not bear arms, was also never fully a political subject. And despite its avowed intention to punish violent men, a council might find itself enmeshed in the culture of honour which supported physical violence. So the Augsburg Council, for one, granted exemption from punishment for the man who drew his weapon first should it transpire that 'someone had touched the other with such insulting words, injurious to honour, that the injured party was incited and caused to draw his weapon first in order to save his honour'[34] – a concession which, directly counter to the declared aim of the ordinance, fully recognized the legitimacy of defending male honour with the sword, the symbolic nexus on which the culture of fighting depended.

CAIN AND THE BODY OF THE KILLER

Violence remained a defining characteristic of the male. The first murderer, Cain, was often represented as a repulsive but recognizably masculine figure. In one dramatization of the Bible story by Hans Sachs, we encounter him hanging out with his mates, drawing his strength from their culture of fighting and drinking – in sharp contrast to his obedient brother Abel, well-schooled in creed and prayer, clean and upright.[35] In Sachs's drama, Abel is a mother's boy who complies with her command to wash in preparation for God's visit: Cain revels in the filth of the field, preferring the society of his mates (a convivial world which has many of the characteristics of the male drinking societies excoriated by sixteenth-century preachers) to the demands of his mother.[36] It is hard not to see a sense in which, much as the author strove to create in Abel a model of obedient manhood, measured and meek, the writing actually revels in Cain's technicolour masculinity. Cain provides some delightful comedy. When God asks to hear his catechism, Cain spouts forth a wonderfully blasphemous garbled version of the Creed[37] – a transgressive wish-fulfilment which every sixteenth-century child, forced to parrot the Lord's Prayer, Catechism and Creed, must have relished.[38]

The figure of Cain exemplifies a number of sixteenth-century imaginative obsessions. Cain is the savage man, untamed by religion or law. Yet in the Bible story, he is a crop-grower whose agricultural offering to God failed to compete with Abel's animal offering. And it is he, once punished, who produces offspring from whom the human race is descended – the prestigious urban craft of the smiths and metalworkers, for one, could claim him as an ancestor. Cain is portrayed by sixteenth-century poets and dramatists as a man who exults in violence to the point that he is 'running with blood'. In Sachs's version, he enjoys going about covered in blood, and refuses to be washed. Erasmus Alberus has Cain declaim: 'when I see blood, that is my lust', and 'if I would like to be scrubbed, then I run again amongst the boys on the street, then we shall scrub each other until the blood runs down our cheeks'.[39] Here, the medium of washing becomes blood itself, as Cain rejects any form of civilization. In a kind of mutual sado-masochistic orgy of violence, he takes on the characteristics of the man of excess, whom we have already encountered in the literature on drunkenness, bursting his bodily boundaries and vomiting and defecating with abandon. Cain, too, is firmly located in the world of male brotherhood. He is thus the archetypal excessive man, a creature of lust who breaks the fragile rules of civilization as happily as he ruptures his bodily boundaries, and who is ultimately a killer. Yet of course he is also a part of human history, and his eventual disciplined incorporation into society recognizes the necessity of his extravagant manhood.

TROUSERS AND CODPIECES

To this point, I have been arguing that a superficial analysis of male culture as a set of socially functional behaviour patterns fails to recognize the persistent trouble sixteenth-century masculine culture caused the authorities. To get at the elusive pulse of masculinity, I explored two masculine vices, drinking and fighting. On each occasion they led us back to the male body itself, conceived as a turbulent cauldron of lusts and energies. Now I want to speculate on sixteenth-century understandings of the male body a little further, by considering the sixteenth-century literature on male clothing.[40]

The issue which provoked most explicit discussion of the male body was the codpiece. Yet moralists like Musculus, author of the *Hosenteufel*, condemned the codpiece not because it paraded the phallus, but because it was a form of nudity. It displayed the penis to lascivious eyes which would only too easily be incited to lust. There is a strange unease in this kind of moralism, because it casts the male in the role of sexual quarry.[41] It is male flesh which titillates, and the author explicitly assumes that a woman may be allured.[42] At one level, this should come as no surprise in a society which held women to be the more lustful sex. But while women might happily be imagined as pleasure-seekers, it was quite another thing for them to take sexual command of a man, appraising his attractions. This discomfort is apparent in the writing, which presents the naked codpiece as shameful in part because it puts men in the female position – the target, perhaps, of the attentions of the paedophilic *Knabenschender*.

At another level, however, the youthful codpiece wearers are sexual cyphers. These flamboyant sexual primitives flaunt their attractions polymorphously, to both men and women. Their precocious virility was disturbing because it was an excess of masculinity so extreme as to escape sexual categories altogether. Thick and padded, assuming outlandish shapes and colours – one is described as boasting a trinity of flies – the codpiece was outrageous. Its hyperbolic exaggeration punctured phallic authority. Where decorum required the phallus to be decently hidden, the codpiece riotously displayed the penis as a massive joke.

Young men's clothes were compared to 'hellish flames', their ruffles and slashes evoking the fires of Hades licking about the body. The mercenary, a byword for luxurious expenditure on dress, epitomized this style and embodied its contradiction. Woodcuts depict him swaggering in ridiculously exaggerated ruffles and feathers, his attire a self-flattering advertisement of the agility and physical strength through which he earned his keep. There was more than a touch of the feminine in such narcissism, as the woodcuts slyly insinuated. Yet the mercenary was also the fierce fighter, coarse and cruel, whose reputation was so fearsome that even the Devil, in one comic poem of Hans Sachs, declined to allow such vicious monsters into his Hellish kingdom.[43]

The attack on young men's clothing took up all the themes of the old sumptuary legislation, in particular its concern that extravagant spending on clothes was wasteful consumption, a spending on self which would weaken and ultimately destroy the urban economy. But it had a particular animus in the case of young men's dress. This arose partly from the implied parallel with the ills of masturbation – seed, instead of being put to productive use, was being squandered in self-display – partly because it was also the vehicle for a general assault on young men's culture and partly because it raised the issue of sexual identity in such a disturbing fashion. Young men's clothes, with their bright, figure-hugging silhouettes, lending emphatic decoration to the muscular outline of legs, shoulders and arms, comprised a distinctive style which set them apart from their sombrely attired elders, clad in garments which did more to conceal than to enhance the body's outline. Dress was well suited to serve as the issue which represented the antagonism between a youth culture of pleasure, dancing and excess, and the measured comportment of older men. This conflict of styles, however, as I shall now go on to argue, was more apparent than real.

It is hard to know what to make of such ostentatious condemnation of young masculinity. A simple reading might view the matter as the struggle between the cultures of old and young men. But part of the pleasure of the text derives from its linguistic exhibitionism, exuberantly paralleling the clothing it purports to condemn – occasionally, to the point of titillation. So the prefatory poem to the *Hosenteufel* apostrophizes those who wear such fine codpieces that one would guess there was the sweetest honey inside![44] The apparent battle between youthful and elderly views of masculinity betrays not so much a cultural conflict as a shared vision. There is certainly an Oedipal strain in much of the uproarious culture of young men, exultantly parading their newly acquired potency. They are manifestly waging war against the patriarchs who must be toppled from their smug monopoly on political power, household authority and women. But this combative culture had also formed the patriarchs, and it was one to which they still owed allegiance.

Indeed, both competing cultures are perhaps better seen as in necessary coexistence in the same individual man, who could oscillate between the disciplined moderation required in the council chamber and the hedonistic abandon of the tavern at night. Different individuals might arrive at different resolutions along this spectrum. A man like the writer of the *Zimmersche Chronik*, a nobleman whose youthful companions included townsmen, could adopt a full-blooded endorsement of the world of excess (at least in his chronicle), poking fun at the failed knight who preferred sewing handkerchiefs to jousting, or the learned doctor who, not knowing how to conduct himself at a drinking bout, was absurdly ashamed when he lost bodily control and vomited.[45] Hans Sachs, the 'poet of morality' as Maria Müller has dubbed him, with his virtuous condemnation of the conduct he so aptly depicts, offers another solution.[46] In his case, the rigour of repression sits more or less easily alongside the exuberance of excess. Just as the culture of guildsmen and councillors, old and young, drew much of its strength from alcohol and the bonds forged by brotherly carousing, so both were implicated in the culture of violent exhibitionism, displaced with only partial completeness on to the culture of youth.

Finally, I want to pre-empt one possible line of criticism of what I have been saying and return to the problem we originally posed, the relationship of masculinity to power. It might be tempting to resurrect a normative masculinity for sixteenth-century society, and to argue that the meaning of masculinity is to be sought in the moral prescriptions of council, guild and preacher. The good man is he who keeps to the mean. His intake of alcohol is measured, his comportment dignified, his rule is not brute tyranny but a gentle yoke. However, such an anodyne conclusion would be a false resolution. Sixteenth-century masculinity drew its psychic strength not from the dignity of the mean but from the rumbustious energy which such discipline was supposedly designed to check. After all, the city ultimately required brute fighting men to keep order and defend the town. The man of excess, the figure who epitomized masculinity, was also a cultural creation. What seems at first to be uncivilized 'wildness' was in fact carefully structured by the rules of civic society. Discipline was not so much a matter of repression of the lusts as of their dramatization. The rowdy guild culture which caused council authority such irritation did serve, in the final analysis, to shore it up, but it did so in mortal combat, not by functional suitability.

NOTES

1
Ein Mansperson mus auff viel achtung geben/ wenn er vnter den leuthen ist/ Er mus auff mancherley tugend dencken/ dz er sie an jm erscheinen lasse/ Ein weib aber bedarff das gar nicht/ sie hat nicht mehr/ dann auff eine tugent achtung zu haben/ nemlich/ auf die Zucht.
(Johannes Jhan, *Jungfraw Schulordenung zu Torgau*, Leipzig, Jacobus Berwaldt, 1565, fo. q iv, v)

2 On recent literature on masculinity, see among others, Alan Bray, 'Homosexuality and the Signs of Male Friendship in Elizabethan England', *History Workshop Journal*, 29, 1990, pp. 1–19; Norbert Schindler, 'Nächtliche Ruhestörung. Zur Sozialgeschichte der Nacht in der frühen Neuzeit', in *idem, Widerspenstige Leute. Studien zur Volkskultur in der frühen Neuzeit*, Frankfurt am Main 1992; Stanley Chojnacki, 'Political Adulthood in Fifteenth-Century Venice', *American Historical Review*, 91, 1986, pp. 791–810; Alex Potts, 'Beautiful Bodies and Dying Heroes: Images of ideal manhood in the French Revolution', *History Workshop Journal*, 30, 1990, pp. 1–21; Maria E. Müller, 'Naturwesen Mann. Zur Dialektik von Herrschaft und Knechtschaft in Ehelehren der Frühen Neuzeit', in Heide Wunder and Christina Vanja (eds), *Wandel der Geschlechterbeziehungen zu Beginn der Neuzeit*, Frankfurt am Main 1991; Lynn Segal, *Slow Motion*, London 1990; Mike Roper and John Tosh (eds), *Manful Assertions*, London 1991; T. Carrigan, B. Connell and J. Lee, 'Towards a Sociology of Masculinity', in H. Brod (ed.), *The Making of Masculinities. The new men's studies*, London 1987.

3 On honour, see Martin Dinges, 'Die Ehre als Thema der Stadtgeschichte. Eine Semantik am Übergang vom Ancien Regime zur Moderne', *Zeitschrift für historische Forschung*, 16, 1989, pp. 409–40; Susanna Burghartz, 'Disziplinierung oder Konfliktregelung? Zur Funktion städtischer Gerichte im Spätmittelalter: Das Zürcher Ratsgericht', *Zeitschrift für historische Forschung*, 16, pp. 385–408; and Susanna Burghartz, 'Rechte Jungfrauen oder unverschämte Töchter? Zur weiblichen Ehre im 16. Jahrhundert', in Karin Hausen and Heide Wunder (eds), *Frauengeschichte – Geschlechtergeschichte*, Frankfurt am Main 1992; and see also Hermann Heidrich, 'Grenzübergänge. Das Haus und die Volkskultur in der frühen Neuzeit', in Richard van Dülmen (ed.), *Kultur der einfachen Leute. Bayerisches Volksleben vom 16. bis zum 19. Jahrhundert*, Munich 1983.

4 See Lyndal Roper, 'The Common Man, the Common Good, the Common Woman: Gender and meaning in the German Reformation commune', *Social History*, 12, 1987, pp. 1–22.

5 It included not only 'Haus wol furzustehen vnd dasselbige mit aller notturfft zuuersorgen', but also 'öffentliche Aemter, Rathause, Kirchen, Schule': Wolf-

gang Perister, *Lob vnd Trostschriefft/ Sambt notwendigem Bericht/ aus Gottes Wort. Vom heiligen Ehestande*, Berlin, Nickel Voltz 1582, fo. G i v.

6 See Merry Wiesner, 'Guilds, Male Bonding and Women's Work in Early Modern Germany', *Gender and History*, 1, 1989, pp. 125–37; Lyndal Roper, *The Holy Household. Women and morals in Reformation Augsburg*, Oxford 1989; and on the gendered nature of insults, see Laura Gowing, 'Gender and the Language of Insult in Early Modern London', *History Workshop Journal*, 35, 1993, pp. 1–21; and *idem*, 'Women, Sex and Honour: The London Church Courts, 1572–1640', Ph.D. diss., University of London 1993; David Sabean, *Property, Production and Family in Neckarhausen, 1700–1870*, Cambridge 1990, pp. 139–46, 334–9.

7 See Jhan, *Jungfraw Schulordenung*, fo. q iii v, who however cautions that women must endure a 'Tyrannisch' husband.

8 Rainer Beck, 'Frauen in Krise. Eheleben und Ehescheidung in der ländlichen Gesellschaft Bayerns während des Ancien Regime', in Richard van Dülmen (ed.), *Dynamik der Tradition*, Frankfurt am Main 1992; Roper, *The Holy Household*, pp. 165–205. On the way in which a tyrannical husband could expose the troubling lack of limitations on a patriarch's power, see Cynthia Herrup, 'The Trial of the Earl of Castlehaven for Rape and Sodomy', forthcoming.

9 Claus Narr [Wolfgang Büttner], *Sechs hundert sieben vnd zwantizig Historien von Claus Narren*, Eisleben, V. Gaubisch 1572, fo. L 4 v, no. 54.

10 I am grateful to Laura Gowing for pointing this out.

11 The drinking rituals of the shoemakers' guild of Augsburg are described in Clemens Jäger's chronicle of the guild, *Die Chroniken der deutschen Städte*, ed. Historische Kommission bei der Bayrischen Akademie der Wissenschaften, Leipzig, 1862–1931, vol. 34, Augsburg 9, pp. 316, 326. Some were abolished in the late fifteenth century, including one which involved every member drinking from a common cup when a new member came – this was abolished because of fear of syphilis.

12 See, in detail on the subject of the social meanings of drink and its control in the early modern city, Ann Tlusty, 'Das ehrbare Verbrechen. Die Kontrolle über das Trinken in Augsburg in der frühen Neuzeit', *Zeitschrift des historischen Vereins für Schwaben*, 85, 1992, pp. 133–55.

13
> Wann die vbrige Beweinung vnd Trunckenhait gleich nit so hoch in Götlicher vnd haidnischer Schrifft verflucht/ vnd menigklich daruor verwarnet were/ Sollte vnns doch die täglich erfarenhait/ was jamers vnd vnrats/ als verstellung der Edlen Vernunfft/ in vihische vnsinnigkait/ verderbung der Selen/ leibs/ lebens/ Eren vnd Guts/ augenscheinlich daruss eruolgt/ billich daruon gantz vnd gar abhalten
>
> (*Ains Erbern Rats/ der Stat Augspurg/ Zucht vnd Pollicey Ordnung*, Augsburg 1537, fo. a iiii r)

14 'ein jeglicher seine Mannheit mit Sauffen beweisen . . . wil', Matthäus Friderich, *Sauffteufel*, 1557, in Ria Stambaugh (ed.), *Teufelbücher in Auswahl*, 5 vols, Berlin and New York, 1970–80, vol. 5, p. 12.

15 'Das seind dann die starcken Helden vnd Bierkrieger/ die Künden also jre mannhait mit Ritterlicher that beweisen', Eberhard Weydensee, *Ain schöne ermanung an alle Christen/ das sy sich des grausamen vnd vnmenschlichen Lasters/ des vbertrinckens enthaltend*, c. 1540.

16
> einen faulen schlingen vnd tropffen/ einen müssiggenger vnd langschleffer/ der allein frisset vnd seuffet/ toppelt vnd spielet/ nichts gelernet hat/ vnd keine arbeit thun kan/ sondern ist ein schlüffel/ vnd des müssig-

ganges gewonet/ vnd wil sich mit faulen tagen neeren/ vnd lest daheim
sein Weib vnd Kinder not leiden

(Heinrich Salmuth, *Hochzeit Predigten*, Leipzig 1580, fo. K iii v)

Paulus Rebhun describes the evil husband in the following terms: 'Die spieler
aber/ vnnd lose volsauffer/ die da mutwillig das jre verzeren/ vnnd die
Weyber lassen not leiden/ die sindt nicht ehren werd/ sollen auch (wens
recht zugieng) von der Oberkeyt hart gestraffet/ vnd zur arbeyt getrieben
werden' (Paulus Rebhun, *Hauszfried. Was für vrsachen den Christlichen Eheleu-
ten zubedencken/ den lieben Haussfriede in der Ehe zu erhalten*, Nuremberg,
Johann Berg vnd Vlrich Newber 1555, fo. f); while Georg Reuter describes
how the Devil destroys a couple's love: 'wann der Teuffel thut erwecken/
Jns Mannes Hertz/ welches ist ein schrecken/ Lust zu spielen/ fressen vnd
sauffen/ Thut andern Weibern auch nachlauffen', *Ehrenkrånzlein Ehristlicher
Eheleute*, Breslaw, Georg Bawman 1607, fo. B 3 r.

17 'Dan- was seind solche lůte/ dan- recht Laugenseck? Giessen jmer mer Wein
vnd Bier oben ein/ vnd wenns zu lange worden ist/ lassen sy es vnden
wider auss lauffen/ ja es steigt zu zeiten wol oben wider auss.' Weydensee,
Ain Schône ermanung, fo. C i v.

18 'wan einer ein vnreinen flůß hat des leibs das dan mag geschehen wachen/
oder in dem schlaf', Johannes Altenstaig, *Von der Füllerey ein müter aller vbel
vnd laster/ vnd was schaden vnd vnfal da von entston Auch arzeneien darwider*,
Strasbourg, Johannes Grienynger 1525, fo. L; and compare:

Dann dises laster ist nimmbert allein/ dann die trunckenheit machet offt
das der Mensch sündiget wider seinen willen/ wann er vom wein ange-
zůndet würt. Dann auß der trunckenheit volgen schantliche vnd ergerliche
wort/ vnzüchtige geberden/ die zur vnreinigkeyt reitzen/ es volget
darauß Gotteslesterung/ fluchen vnnd [B v v] schwőren/ sie gibt vrsach
zur vnzucht/ Ehebruch vnnd anderer bůberey.

(Jsaac Kessler, *Dialogvs/ Oder gespråch zwischen einem Geystlichen Lehrer/
vnnd Kind/vom Neüen Jar . . .*, Strasbourg, Samuel Emmel 1568, fo. B v r–v)

19

Dann stinckt er wie ein widhopff-nest
Bringt sie in inn das peth zu-lest
Und deckt ihn zu wol und genaw,
So gröltzt vnd fartzt er wie ein saw.
Vil-leicht pruntzt er auch inn das pett.
Ein saw wol bey im narung het.

(Hans Sachs, 'Die vier wunderberlichen Eygenschafft vnd würckung des
Weins', in Adalbert von Keller and Edmund Goethe (eds), *Hans Sachs*, 26
vols, Tübingen 1870–1908, vol. 4, p. 241 (Flegmaticus))

20 'der grossen vnzucht, so begangen wirdet, indem dass man sich so schend-
lich bricht und die gottsgab so unsauber verschwindet und durchbringt',
Kirchenzuchtordnung 1543, in Emil Sehling *et al.* (eds), *Die evangelischen
Kirchenordnungen des 16. Jahrhunderts*, Leipzig 1902–11, Tübingen 1963–,
Hessen I, p. 149.

21 Matthäus Friderich, *Widder den Sauffteufel*, 1557, in Stambaugh (ed.), *Teufelbücher*, vol. 5, pp. 22–3.

22 So Melchior Ambach, in his introduction to *Von Zusauffen vnd Trunckenhait/
sampt jren schônen früchten*, Frankfurt am Main, Herman Gülferich 1544,
complains that those who want to be the world's friend must not attack 'this
pig-like vice' of drunkenness, fo. A ii r. Friderich, in his *Sauffteufel*, makes
the typical complaint that those who preach against drink are mocked:

Das sie aber so offte darwider predigen/ geschicht auch billich/ denn es ist ein solch laster/ das man jetzund vor kein laster und Sůnde/ sondern vor eitel Recht und tugent helt/ wie man siehet/ das die gelobet und gerômet werden/ die nuhr wol sauffen kônnen/ Dagegen die verachtet und verspottet werden/ die es nicht thun kônnen oder wôllen.
(Friderich, *Sauffteufel*, in Stambaugh (ed.), *Teufelbücher*, vol. 5, p. 35)

and the same author suggests that one should refuse a drink offered by a social superior, because one ought to obey God more than man (ibid., p. 41).

23 See, for example, Bartholomaeus Clamorinus, *Thurnierbůchlein. (Kurtz vorzei-chnuβ vom Alter, Ankunfft vnd Thaten der Freyherren auff Tautenberg)*. Dresden, G. Bergen 1591, see fo. CCii r ff., FF i ff. Clamorinus was a preacher. Hans Sachs's *Der Thurnier spruch. Alle Thurnier/ wo/ wie vnd wenn sie inn Teutschlandt gehalten sind worden*, Nuremberg, Hans Guldenmundt 1541 offers a similar enumeration and a list of those excluded: fo. A iii r–v.

24 See, for example, *Hye in disem büchlin kindt man die recht kunst und art des Ringens... lernen*, [Strasbourg, M. Hüpüpff 1510?], and perhaps the most famous example, Fabian von Auerswald's *Die Ringer-kunst*, Wittenberg 1539, reprinted with commentary Leipzig 1987; and on *Fechtbücher*, Jan-Dirk Müller, 'Zwischen mündlicher Anweisung und schriftlicher Sicherung von Tradition. Zur Kommunikationsstruktur spätmittelalterlicher Fechtbücher', in H. Kühnel (ed.), *Kommunikation und Alltag in Spätmittelalter und früher Neuzeit*, Vienna 1992 (Veröffentlichungen des Instituts für Realienkunde des Mittelalters und der frühen Neuzeit 15).

25 On violence and male night culture see Schindler, 'Nächtliche Ruhestörung'.

26 Die Schusterchronik von Clemens Jäger, *Chroniken der deutschen Städte*, vol. 34, Augsburg 9, p. 313 and n. 1.

27 *Die Chroniken der deutschen Städte vom 14. bis ins 16. Jahrhundert*, vol. 33. Paul Hector Mair, Augsburg 8, pp. 54–5.

28 Tom Scott, *Freiburg and the Breisgau. Town–country relations in the age of Reformation and Peasants' War*, Oxford 1986, pp. 110–13; Thomas Robisheaux, *Rural Society and the Search for Order in Early Modern Germany*, Cambridge 1989, esp. pp. 118ff.

29 Similarly, as Norbert Schindler has shown, the calendar could act as a kind of container for violent, disruptive behaviour: behaviour of a far more physically violent, disruptive kind was expected at carnival, constituting part of its fun. Norbert Schindler, 'Karneval, Kirche und verkehrte Welt. Zur Funktion der Lachkultur im 16. Jahrhundert', in *idem*, *Widerspenstige Leute*, pp. 163ff.

30 Stadtarchiv Augsburg (hereafter cited as StadtAA), Urgichtensammlung (hereafter cited as Urg.), 26 Feb. – 5 March 1587, Thomas Mair and Adam Schneeweiss. The dance also occurred on carnival Monday.

31 StadtAA, Urg., 10 Oct. 1587, Thomas Mair, with Urgicht of March.

32 For Paul Hector Mair's description of this fight, see *Chroniken der deutschen Städte*, vol. 33, Augsburg 8, pp. 65–6.

33 'lustig zu sehen und warlich wol angethan mit harnasch', *Die Chroniken der deutschen Städte vom 14. bis ins 16. Jahrhundert*, vol. 15, p. 214.

34 'Doch/ ob yemandt den anndern dermass/ mit Schmåhlichen/ errletzlichen wortten/ beleget vnd antastet/ Das der Verletzt/ zu rettung seiner Eren/ am Ersten/ zum Wôrzucken geraitzt vnd verursacht wurd', Augsburg/ Zucht vnd Pollicey Ordnung, 1537.

35 Hans Sachs, 'Comedia. Die ungleichen kinder Eve, wie sie Gott, der herr, anredt', in von Keller and Goethe (eds), *Hans Sachs*, vol. 1, pp. 53–87.

36 *Hans Sachs*, vol. 1, pp. 62–4.

37 Sachs, 'Comedia'; and see also *Von Eua der ersten Mutter/ vnd Abel/ Seth/ vnd Cain. . . . Aus einer des Herrn Philippi Melanthonis Epistel/ gezogen vnd verdeutscht*, 1544, fo. B ii v, and Erasmus Alberus, *Ein Gesprech/ von der verfurung der Schlangen vnd der Gnade Christi vnsers Heilandts/ zwischen Gott/ Adam/ Eua/ Abel vnd Cain*, Nuremberg, Friedrich Gutknecht n.d., fos c iv v–C v r.

38 See Gerald Strauss, *Luther's House of Learning: Indoctrination of the young in the German Reformation*, Baltimore, MD and London 1978 on sixteenth-century methods of catechism teaching.

39 Erasmus Alberus, fos b v v–b vi r. Cain says: 'wenn ich Blut sehe/ das ist mein lust'; 'Wenn ich gern gezwagen were/ so wolt ich wider vnder die Knaben auff die Gassen lauffen/ da wolten wir vns einander zwagen/ das vns das Blut die Backen herab kendeln sol.' Sachs has a similar passage.

40 See, for excellent illustrative material, Gundula Wolter, *Die Verpackung des männlichen Geschlechts. Eine illustrierte Kulturgeschichte der Hose*, Marburg 1988.

41 On the problems of representing the male nude, see Potts, 'Beautiful Bodies and Dying Heroes'.

42 A similar anxiety about the way men's extravagant dress style may make them feminine is to be found in Joachim Westphal's *Hoffartsteufel*, Stambaugh (ed.), *Teufelbücher*, vol. 3, p. 185: 'wenn sich die Man und junge gesellen so zart und Weibisch überkleiden und auff den kauff polliren'.

43 Hans Sachs, *Der Teuffel lest Keyn Lantzknecht mehr in die Helle faren*. Nuremberg, G. Merckel 1558.

44
    Der latz muß auch so geputzt sein/
    Als wer süsse honig sehm drein.
          (Andreas Musculus, *Vom Hosen Teuffel. Anno M.D.LV.*, prefatory poem by
                Gregorius Wagner, in Stambaugh (ed.), *Teufelbücher*, vol. 4, p. 5)

45 *Die Chronik der Grafen von Zimmern*, ed. Hans Martin Decker-Hauff, 3 vols, Stuttgart 1967, vol. 3, pp. 42, 59.

46 Maria E. Müller, *Der Poet der Moralität. Untersuchungen zu Hans Sachs*, Europäische Hochschulschriften Reihe 1, no. 800, Berne, Frankfurt am Main and New York 1985.

6 Stealing manhood: capitalism and magic in early modern Germany

How might we begin to explore the meanings of masculinity in the past? One starting-point must be the workings of business and the getting of money, the exercise central to many men's sense of manhood and identity.[1] In the early modern town, maleness and business went together: the masculine sex was held to be the more rational, and the merchant exemplified reasoned decision-making. Later writers, too, were apt to see in him the man of calculation, shrewd, forward-looking and modern. Feminist historians' interest in economic history has tended, by contrast, to concentrate on women's work experience and the sexual division of labour, or on the few examples of successful merchant women, leaving the mysteries of business theory, banking and exchange rates for men to master. However, what we know about women's participation in the economy tells us about only some of the links between economic structure and gender.

Here I shall explore issues which mainstream economic history, still largely uninterested in questions of gender, has left untouched, by considering not the construction of maleness but its loss. What might men in the early modern period have meant when they complained – as they regularly did – that their manhood had been stolen, bewitched away from them by sorceresses making secret ligatures in string? To untie this knot of meaning, I shall examine one criminal tale about a merchant whose life and business were coming to an end. He lived in a time when capitalist venture trading, still in its infancy, was entering a period of uncertainty. I shall bring three unlikely themes to bear on the story: early modern capitalism, the meaning of masculinity and love magic.

In 1564, the healer Anna Megerler came before the Augsburg town council's judges accused of using maleficent magic against a young boy who had just died of a *verseerung*, a consuming wound inflicted by sorcery. This was a banal tale of healing gone wrong, in which the suspicions of the the boy's parents had turned instead to the failed healer: she had been imprudent enough to suggest that their son's illness was a botched spell intended for the mother, not the son.

But in the course of her interrogation, Megerler came up with a truly sensational story. She claimed that the greatest merchant capitalist of the day, Anton Fugger, had not only had her taught crystal-ball gazing, but had employed her to give him occult knowledge which he used in his business. The man who had been the emperor's banker, who unashamedly used his financial muscle to become a powerful player on the stage of international politics, who had a network of business interests spanning Hungary, Austria, England and the New World, who was a local land magnate and member of the imperial nobility had, according to Megerler, been consulting a village crystal ball-gazer, and a woman at that, to run his massive trading empire.[2] Like Nancy Reagan's Ronald, leader of the western world yet reliant on the astrologer's say-so, Fugger (on Megerler's account) had in the last years of his life been hopelessly ensnared in the nets of a common quack healer, low-level magic-maker and ex-priest's whore.

Megerler claimed Fugger had assured her his name would protect her. And so indeed it proved. Invoking his name when the questioning became sticky, Megerler's story wrought consternation among the council. After four sessions of intensive questioning on her links with the Fuggers they decided against torture, since in this case such searching interrogation had, as they put it, every sign of leading to 'complications'.[3] This decision undoubtedly saved her skin. Insisting upon her innocence, she was released on oath to forswear crystal ball-gazing for ever more, and expelled.[4] She lost her livelihood, but kept her life.

How is the historian to make use of such an archival fragment? Are we dealing here with evidence about the meaning of manhood – indeed, can we term this 'evidence' at all? It is not possible now to determine whether Megerler's tale was true or false. Fugger himself was safely dead when she told her story, and the council failed to produce witnesses who could shed further light on matters. I have found no material which would corroborate or disprove her account – but then Megerler's story concerns transactions which, by their very nature, are unlikely to have left historical trace. The search for verification of our source rapidly runs up against the wall of what we cannot know about the past.

But the historian's obsession with establishing the facts – a concern which is always keener when the 'facts' seem tainted with the poisonous breath of the irrational – would here deflect us from the more interesting issues. For whether or not the facts were as Megerler said, the story was credible in the context of that culture. Its credibility, not its accuracy, is important to the historian interested in the connections of cultural meaning – here, between capitalism, manhood and magic. These links were not unique to this case. The late sixteenth-century fascination, especially among merchants, with the promise of alchemy, and the interest in divination and crystal-gazing were part of this cultural milieu.

Certainly, the contemporary town council which dealt with the case did not dismiss it as incredible. Instead, it tried to catch Megerler out on details of fact, convicting her of misremembering whether Fugger's room was wallpapered or upholstered, or of mistaking the route she had taken to Fugger's friend's chamber. Its interrogators failed, without torture, to shake her story. Its uncharacteristic reluctance to further rake over the coals, and its anxiety about the 'complications' that might ensue were the case developed, indicate that it did not consider the combination of sorcery and capitalism to be implausible. And with reason. We know from later evidence that the Fuggers were to become embroiled with magic practitioners of various kinds: with alchemical experimenters,[5] with blackmailing tricksters threatening them with witchcraft.[6]

We know too that the council would have been aware of the problems Fugger's business was facing: the rapid period of expansion under Jacob Fugger and his nephew Anton had been followed by a period of economic uncertainty and lowered confidence. We may speculate that the Fugger family's central role in the reintroduction of a reformed Catholicism into a largely Protestant Augsburg, their passionate support of the Jesuits and their interest in exorcisms may have predisposed them towards a more receptive attitude towards connections between the material and the spiritual world – we know that some members of the family seriously entertained belief in the transmigration of souls.[7] And we know that magic and early science were often closely connected, and that both found interested audiences among the educated urban merchant élites.

Here, of course, we have entered the quagmire of the probable and the plausible – unfriendly territory, the reader might object, for the historian. But such an objection seeks to restrict the historical imagination to the narrowly factual at the expense of meaning, and if we are investigating manhood, the object of our quest is as much mental and psychological as it is physical. This is not to say that historical meanings can be deduced without evidence – far from it. They must always painstakingly be located in a historical context, pieced together from as much evidence as possible. But evidence may be both more and less than fact. In what follows I want to examine not whether what Megerler said was 'true', but rather to explore how it could be that the mental universes of early capitalism (which we assume to be rational) and sorcery (which we now identify with the irrational) might coincide.

I am suggesting that this distinction between the rational and the irrational is not useful for comprehending early modern culture. And, taking business practice as my example, I want to argue that the meaning of manhood itself, that sex which contemporaries identified as the more rational, was enacted in both unconscious and conscious ways which defy any equation of rationality with the market. To understand

Plate 6.1 Sixteenth-century portrait of *Anton Fugger* by Hans Maler

Source: By kind permission of the Kunsthalle, Karlsruhe.

how this might be, I shall examine crystal-gazing to show how the logics of sorcery and early capitalism were interwoven. From there, I shall return to the meaning of manhood.

There were good reasons why an early modern merchant might find crystal ball-gazing attractive. Merchants like Anton Fugger faced particular difficulties for which such magical techniques offered solution. Head of an international concern with agents and factors scattered from Tyrol to the Indies, Anton Fugger, like any merchant, had above all to rely upon the work of men he could not see. In this his trade set him apart from most other early modern workers. Craftsmen worked in a household workshop where they could supervise their workmen constantly, their employees living (in theory) above the shop; the peasant could survey his labourers. But the early modern capitalist faced different problems. Work was carried out by individuals posted to particular regions, with power to act in the firm's name, to receive and to lend money. The extent of independence they might attain, far from home and from the boss, was considerable; yet the merchant was entirely reliant on their good faith for his firm's prosperity.

Communications were a major problem of early modern business. It is no accident that it was early capitalists who devised the first news networks, or that a postal system should have developed in tandem with business.[8] But letters, however frequent, were at best an uncertain method of controlling one's subordinates, as Anton Fugger had himself painfully discovered in the late 1550s. Despite repeated admonition to his factor, Michael Ortel, in Antwerp to avoid giving too much credit to the Netherlands court, Ortel had continued to lend, and no amount of furious letter-writing on Anton's part seemed able to stop him.

Anton then sent a man instead of a paper. He dispatched his trusted servant, Michel Mair, with elaborate instructions to get full accounts from Ortel and stop the loans. But once in the Netherlands, Mair proved equally recalcitrant and, worse, took Ortel's part, arguing for the continuation of the loans. Faced with this double insubordination by those bound to him by contract, Fugger turned to kin: he sent his son Hans to try to sort out the mess.[9] Fugger's disquiet was well founded, for the Spanish crown defaulted on the Netherlands and Spanish loans in 1557, leaving Fugger to write off a total of almost 5 million florins in exchange for bonds of little worth.[10] As bankruptcy loomed, the message seemed clear that one could not trust factors, men whom one could not see, and whose interests were not those of the family.

In the crystal ball, Anton Fugger could behold his subordinates. He could see, Megerler testified, what they wore, 'how they housed'. With this wonderful piece of early modern satellite spy-equipment, Fugger could see without being seen[11] – a powerful fantasy of perfect visual mastery over a group of factors upon whose loyalty and devotion he was in real life utterly dependent. To his dismay, he noticed in the crystal ball that 'my servants are better dressed than I!' – tangible proof, in an age where the splendour of one's clothing was an exact social indicator – that his factors were overtaking him.[12] (Indeed, one of Fugger's oldest servants, his bookkeeper Mathäus Schwarz, even commissioned a 'costume autobiography' – a wonderfully narcissistic monument of 137 portraits of himself by Augsburg artists in various outfits.)[13]

How to bind one's subordinates to oneself remained a nagging problem of early capitalism, one which early merchant adventurers sought to circumvent by basing their ventures firmly in family capital, so that, clan-like, the members would obey the head. The Fugger firm – strictly a one-family enterprise into which, unlike other firms, non-relatives and even relatives by marriage were not admitted[14] – was a firmly patriarchal structure headed by a single individual, Anton Fugger.[15] And it was precisely in the late 1550s that this structure began to creak. Other relatives began to strike out on their own (some even employing the hated Ortel) and unruly factors began to make money on their own account, developments which, Fugger believed, were responsible for the firm's slide into bankruptcy. The ageing Fugger responded by taking the reins of control into his own hands once more, restricting the powers of the factors and concentrating power at the centre.[16] Such an individualized mode of control, with a magus at the centre of a web of information relying on awesome power, shares the same structure as the fantasy of the crystal ball.

And it may be that there was a further connection between Fugger's concerns and those of the crystal-gazer, though my speculation here is tentative. Megerler explained that her crystals contained two banned spirits who carried out the tasks she commanded. A powerful sorceress had banned the spirits into the crystals with which Fugger had supplied her. The ball's inhabitants were the lost souls of those who had been executed, and whose sins excluded them from Paradise, condemning them to wander through the air. One of these spirits, she reported, was named Jonas Olsesser.[17]

I do not think this was a coincidence. Jonas Olsesser was almost certainly Joachim Elsässer, a notorious criminal who died a gruesome death and was a likely lost soul: in 1559, he was executed at Augsburg for poisoning his wife. But he was also rumoured to have been involved with Georg Frölich in a scandalous plot to murder the Prince Bishop of Würzburg, a conspiracy in which Silvester Raid was suspected of participating. Raid was a former factor and confidante of the Fuggers who had turned against them, joining with Fugger's rivals after his dismissal and ultimately turning to robbery.[18] To have the infamous Elsässer's wandering soul forced to work for Fugger in the crystal was thus a fine form of punishment for a criminal Fugger had good reason to dislike. And perhaps it represented the ultimate revenge: in the crystal ball, Fugger's opponents were not only brought finally under his control and rendered harmless, but their evil creative powers were set to work for Fugger's own gain, in a kind of cannibalistic ingestion of the enemy's potency. There is certainly a recognizable logic of fantasy here. By exercising the ultimate control – imprisonment in crystal – over a criminal who could stand for all Fugger's rivals and insubordinate factors, Fugger could finally overcome the antagonisms and enmities unavoidably generated by business. We cannot now discover from Fugger whether this was why these particular crystals were chosen, even if he could have articulated such a connection. But perhaps we may see here a further element of magical thought, an unconscious congruence between the crystals and the wishes of an early modern merchant man like Fugger.

Megerler, employed like any other professional on an *ad hoc* basis, gave Fugger occult knowledge. By looking into the crystal balls provided by Anton himself, she could inform him of what was happening in each part of his trading empire and – a time-honoured application of crystal ball magic – tell him where treasure was to be found. When she saw a mountain with silver in the crystal, Anton determined to acquire it. The silver mountain was a visionary solution of his bankruptcy fears – money in tangible, shining form instead of the worthless assurances the Spanish crown was offering against his claims.[19] And it was a merchant fantasy with a shared life: in the mid-1560s, the Haug–Langnauer–Linck firm of Augsburg, which had English mining interests, attempted to use alchemy to convert quicksilver to silver to boost its flagging income.[20] George Fugger, Anton's nephew, had a strong interest in alchemy, even installing his own experimental workshop and alchemical kitchen at Trent. He shared this preoccupation with his brother Ulrich, who was rumoured to possess the 'stone of wisdom' which would turn all to gold. And in 1570, Anton's own son, Marcus Fugger, was reputed to have entered into a contract with an alchemist in the hope of increasing his mining profits.[21]

Using crystal balls to find treasure – the hope of a tangible wealth – was a powerful mid-sixteenth-century longing which every class of people might share, all the more seductive in a world of nightmare bad copper coinage and uncertain paper bonds. Crystal ball-gazers were called upon to divine the whereabouts of treasure, organizing neighbours and friends to dig at midnight, like one Nuremberg cunning woman caught in Augsburg in 1544 with crystals, incense, Bible and bells, mining for untold wealth in the backyard of a suburban house.[22]

Finding treasure was an integrative social fantasy which resolved an underlying early modern ambivalence about wealth. For sixteenth-century people, wealth was a malignant force. People got rich only by making others poorer. Only by finding treasure – whether the treasure of the Indies or the silver deposits of the Tyrol or New World – could one become harmlessly rich. Within the city, wealth was inherently limited, goods were finite and the crucial economic issue was perceived as being the *division* of resources, not the creation of wealth. When Augsburg craftsmen of the 1560s diagnosed the city's economic ills they laid the blame at the door of the newcomers, people who clogged up the crafts, creating too much competition and taking away work, putting pressure on the housing stock and burdening the poor relief system. Immigration control was the craftsmen's nostrum for the city's economic plight.[23]

But popular opinion might also, in the 'murmurings' feared by councils throughout the century, identify the wealthy capitalists as the source of the problem, because they had cornered supplies and taken an unfair share of the wealth. This kind of murmuring against 'the big jacks' was a lingering source of social instability, a threat serious enough for the big merchants to be careful to provide free bread in times of famine and leave rich legacies to the poor and needy. In the weaving industry, the town's foremost employment, council and craftspeople responded to economic crisis by attempting to share out the misery. Limits were imposed on the numbers of looms each master might work and the putting out system was suppressed.[24] Instead of restructuring to allow the big merchants their head, guild protectionism won the day in a triumph of the belief that wealth was finite and that the common good ought to take precedence over individual gain.

Capitalists too, however, could share this conception of wealth as limited and believe their own enterprises to be of doubtful morality. The view of wealth as finite inclined them to pursue monopolies – to gain complete control over a limited raw material, a practice which was widely viewed as both unfair and immoral though it was central to early modern business strategy.[25] Economic theology had, furthermore, only recently – and controversially – resolved the problem of usury.[26] Since money was not a 'good', how could one charge for its use? – a position which Luther, among others, continued to hold.[27] Thus it could be believed that those who lent money were practising a form of economic activity which was morally questionable. Indeed, just over ten years later, the Fuggers were to find themselves under attack from their erstwhile allies, the Jesuits, who wanted to restrict interest-taking and threatened to refuse absolution to those who continued such usurious practices.[28]

Augsburg's own civic secretary, Conrad Peutinger, had stoutly defended the rights of merchants to make money, exercise monopolies and lend money at the Imperial Diet of 1530.[29] But although Peutinger had a conception of the economy as a whole, even his defence of early modern capitalism remained ultimately locked in the paradigms of individual action.[30]

To account for economic outcomes, Peutinger turned to the notion of fortune. Fortune could explain how an individual became rich or how others faced bankruptcy, and it was their willingness to gamble with fortune that justified the profits businessmen made in long-distance trade.[31] Such a theory of Madame Fortune as the engine of economic success was of course not very far from the presumptions of crystal ball-gazing, where the 'lucky ones', 'Sunday's children',[32] are able to look into the crystal balls and see past, future and present.

The individualism of economic theory further contributed to the merchant's anxiety, and accorded with magical beliefs. In the centuries before the development of *limited liability* for companies, merchants faced individual responsibility should their firm experience bankruptcy.[33] The unfortunate merchant who reneged on his debts could wind up in prison – as indeed a succession of once-proud Augsburgers did in the 1550s, 1560s and 1570s.[34] By failing to honour his contract with an individual and repay debt, the merchant had committed an offence and a sin which he had individually to expiate.[35] Consequently, in legal terms, business failure was attributable to personal fault rather than market conditions; and yet businessmen moved in a world of uncertainty, unfairness and unpredictability, of debt repudiation and ships lost at sea.[36]

Magic, with its prospect of unrivalled information – through crystal balls one could see exactly what was happening in all parts of the business empire – and its promise of individual, personal control of all one's subordinates, could thus offer immense attractions to the merchant facing disgrace. It held out the hope of enhanced personal performance for the individual upon whom, so the merchant believed, all depended. Consequently it is not surprising that many of the local élite as well as ordinary townsfolk dabbled in crystal ball-gazing – the Count of Ottingen, another member of the Fugger family, even the ex-mayor Leonhard Christof Rehlinger were all named as clients by another crystal ball-gazer some years later.[37] The balls themselves, precious stones, were far beyond the pocket of most Augsburgers, and it was usually the patrons who provided the balls for the seers.

Crystal-gazers frequently maintained they merely used balls which had already been *zugericht*, that is, the spirits of dead souls which floated about in the air and which accomplished the magic had already been banned into the balls. Consequently, the seer had only to manipulate the machinery, and could disclaim direct dealings with the spirits themselves.[38] In part this was a defence tactic, for to admit to conjuring spirits was to court condemnation by the council – which did not always distinguish between spirits and devils – for truck with the diabolic. Increasingly, under the influence of Reformation thinkers, crystal-gazing was thought to involve the Devil.[39] But even the most circumspect seer might occasionally fall prey to the temptation to frighten the neighbours by claiming commerce with spirits. We have noted Anna Megerler's claim that the spirits of two executed criminals inhabited her balls. Teased beyond endurance by the drunken father of the child she was healing, she could not forbear to threaten him with banning into her crystal balls. Though he had scoffed at Megerler's crystals, his own residue of belief in her powers was sufficient to provoke him to a violent rage.

But if it sometimes suited seers to leave their powers ominously vague, what consistently emerges is a kind of tactical suspension of belief on the part of both seer and client. So Regina Koch claimed 'she had no belief in such nonsense' when she was first approached by the treasure-seeker who wished to dig up her garden.[40] Professing disbelief while permitting the magic to proceed allowed them to present themselves later to the council as innocent. And it also enabled them to limit their dealings with the occult, acting as pure instrumentalists, not magicians. Tactical suspension of belief could thus work to restrict the invasion of external forces – whether spiritual or demonic – into the individual. By limiting one's understanding of the supernatural world and refusing to participate in it – while yet making use of its energies – sacred power could be appropriated.

This manipulation corresponds to the relation between layperson and the sacred power wielded by the priest and husbanded by the church: the layperson, who could not perform the miracle of transforming the bread into the body of Christ, could none the less make use of the consecrated Host.[41] Laypeople, too, might nurture a healthy scepticism about the efficacy of particular saints' cults, reviling them for bad performance, propitiating them in the hope of good.[42] In a similar fashion, the early capitalist manipulated the economic levers of exchange rates and monopolies, while disclaiming knowledge of the underlying economic forces, the province of Dame Fortune.

If the individual alone were liable for personal economic failure, then he needed to use the best forces he could muster and play his cards close to his chest. Keep your plans dark and do not let others know what you intend – such exhortations were typical of Fugger's interactions with his factors; and indeed his motto was 'silence is golden'.[43] And this is precisely his strategy as represented in Megerler's account. Like a good capitalist, he took care early on to gain a monopoly on her services, binding her to come only to him. They met secretly, she travelling to the Fugger's patronage church of St Moritz's where he would give her an agreed sign if he wished her to gaze for him. No one was to see her comings and goings, food and drink was brought to them by a servant who simply handed it to Fugger and departed, and the room in which they met was a business room in the heart of the Fugger palace. As such, the knowledge Megerler offered was occult, special and private.

The pair's meetings thus had all the hallmarks of an illicit sexual relationship – secretiveness, a man and woman alone, church trysts. Yet the council never questioned Megerler on any sexual misdealing. Whether because the protagonists' age or physical attractions made this unlikely, the council treated what would normally have been considered 'suspicious indications' of an adulterous liaison as behaviour appropriate to occult knowledge of this kind.[44] The intimacy of the occult, the creation of a private space and the assumption that Megerler possessed something which only a woman could give, paralleled sexual friendship:

the relationship between client and seer was a kind of inverted, non-sexual liaison where the woman's capacity was purchased by the man.

Early modern business practice relied heavily upon names. The name, against which the recipient of letters of credit would pay an agreed amount of money, represented one's creditworthiness and honour. Refusal by one's peers to honour one's name and pay out on a bill secured on it was the ultimate proof that bankruptcy loomed and one's business standing was lost. So in the last years of his life, we know that Anton Fugger fretted that his name might no longer be honoured. Peppered through his correspondence are references to how this or that transaction will affect his honour.[45] The name could thus be used as a powerful sign. It was a means of making deals happen when the name's owner was miles away. In this way, the virile *name* about which Fugger worried so much functioned like a magical token.

Names in magical and religious thinking have a similarly active power. The name of Jesus features, for instance, as a key part of the meditations of mystics, with its own especial power akin to that of any other bodily part – heart, feet, wounds – by which devotion might be inspired.[46] If the name of Jesus, and, likewise, of demons, could also be put to use in incantation and conjuring,[47] names had great potency in more mundane magic. One could command an individual by possessing parts of his or her body, and, similarly, one could gain power over someone by means of their name. So one woman told of a magical remedy to discover whether one's husband were alive or dead: the name of both husband and wife had to be written on an egg with a string passed through it, and the egg put in a fire.[48] The 'naming' of the two spirits who were locked in the crystal ball was the means of dominating and ruling them. Naming was a means of controlling the world, both mundane and spiritual. To Adam, the first man, God had given the power of naming the orders of the world.

For the early modern capitalist, the name was a potent and powerful means of doing business. Its health embodied the enterprise's prosperity: when one's name could no longer accomplish anything, one's business credibility was gone. Fugger's name, representing the family of which he was the proud head, was redolent with his honour. Anxiety about his name and its potency, and fear lest it become a thing of no value, were thus a very powerful way of imagining the loss of manhood. In the last year of his life, the year in which Megerler claimed to have been advising him, Fugger, weakened with illness and racked by the breakup of his family, sought to hold the business together by ceaseless business activity. Trying to disengage from the disastrous financing of royal houses, he hung on to the old Silesian mining interests although they no longer made him a profit, and moved further into land investment around Augsburg. He even seems to have toyed with the notion of staging a comeback in the old Hungarian mining interests in the very last year of his life, and to have considered unlikely new projects in an attempt to preserve his name and honour in a final burst of creative energy.[49]

What I have been moving towards here is a tentative explanation for the plausibility of Fugger's consulting a woman. On the face of it, a woman was a strange choice for Fugger to make. Crystal ball-gazing could be practised by men as well as women, and it was also employed in high intellectual magic.[50] Fugger could certainly have afforded the services of a male élite intellectual magician. But, as her interrogation makes plain, it was precisely Megerler's local fame as a village healer, as a woman with access to supernatural kinds of knowledge and as an expert in emotions and love magic, which drew Fugger to her.

Why might this be? Women's magic was of a different order. Though their genitals were not as magical as men's were,[51] they were also less prone to suffer maleficent harm. Their interior bodies, however, housed mysteries. As the ones who bore children, nursed the sick and cared for the dying, they had access to mysterious bodily products such as cauls, dead infants, milk and blood; but often they needed substances from others to work their magic. They collected herbs which could transform both taste and bodily states, they were mistresses of the chemistry of cooking and, having captured men's seeds in their wombs, they carried out the alchemy of turning food into nourishment for the foetus and blood into milk for the newborn child.[52] Women were mistresses of transformational science.

But all these were also the ambivalent processes which easily went wrong. As Heide Wunder has pointed out, the causal chains of women's work often went awry: cream curdled, the cheese spoiled, butter failed to churn, the fever did not settle and the patient died.[53] In all such cases, female sorcery was feared. Women controlled the resources of body magic, and since their bodies lacked the magical phallus, they knew in compensation how to manipulate and control men's organs, making men fall in love with them, and robbing them of manhood.[54]

For the merchant world, manhood and virility were presumed to reside in the control of things, and in the honour and power of one's name. Women, by contrast, were widely held to be the manipulators of emotion, inspiring love and hatred and using strange arts to divine, foretell and control. Perhaps one might suggest that Anton Fugger, in the twilight of his life, experiencing bodily weakness and decay and with the power of his own name in question, also feared his manhood might be stolen once and for all – a predicament for which the acknowledged effective cure was to turn to a cunning woman, a specialist in love magic.

There are further connections between love-magic and capitalism. The magical sight of his subordinates, which the council seems to have thought it not inconceivable for Fugger to have used crystal balls to achieve, was designed to give Fugger visual mastery over his factors. But crystals were also commonly used to view a lover, and discover whether or not he or she were faithful. Love for another involves trusting them when they are invisible. This was especially true in the early modern period when men often travelled long distances in search of work, and trust might be sorely tried if, for example, a marriage promise had not been made binding, or if the man went off to war.[55] Like the capitalist, the lover – frequently a woman – wanted to know what the beloved was doing, 'with whom they housed', and so they frequently turned to the crystal ball-seer to give them visual mastery over the beloved.

What did manhood mean for merchants? Early capitalists were nourished in a civic, guild-dominated culture, built on the bedrock of male honour. Honourable brotherhood bound the masters of a guild together,[56] and the defence of 'men's honour' (*Manseer*) could prove a potent rallying cry for the journeymen and apprentices who hoped to graduate some day into the masters' world.[57] Guild insignia, silver plate and coats of arms of all the brothers studded the walls of the guild rooms where men drank together. Guild processions, dances and church ales bristled with phallic symbols such as grotesque noses, codpieces and poles.[58] Yet this extravagant profusion of phallic imagery testified to the fragility of maleness. Male honour had perpetually to be re-established through competition – guilds rivalled each other in processional display, young bloods fought at dances and a guild's reputation could best be secured by impugning the respectability of its competitors.

For the merchants, increasingly a class set apart from guildsfolk as the century wore on, masculinity bore a related but different significance. Less surely anchored in a collective sense of honour than were guildsmen, early capitalists' claim to honour was linked with individual struggle and success. Reputation was conferred partly on the family, in a kind of insecure approximation to the blood nobility of the patricians who dominated the towns and outlying countryside, and with whom they intermarried;[59] but its link with individual success could endure even after the uneasy transition from merchant to aristocrat. The honour of the merchant thus ultimately depended on his own success – the family name, even such an illustrious name as that of Fugger, with its accolade of imperial nobility and urban patrician status, was never quite beyond attack.

Sixteenth-century culture can clearly be described as a phallic culture, though we are still far from knowing what that term might mean. This was a culture where, after all, the symbol of the central Christian mystery of the Incarnation was the Infant Jesus's naked penis.[60] It was a culture whose carnival world was peopled with walking penises, and phalluses on sticks. In some images of the witches' night ride, the witch was depicted astride the penis, a woman 'on top' wildly riding to the witches' sabbath.[61] It was also a culture still obsessed with the myth of Jewish ritual murder,[62] the belief that Jews sought to steal Christian children and drain their blood to use in religious rites.[63] As the myth developed, the sacrifice increasingly required a male Christian child for its efficacy.[64] In a woodcut of the popular Simon of Trent case, eager rabbis crowd around in anticipation of the Christian blood, their knives pointed perilously at the infant's penis.[65] Though not always expressed as fear of castration, the fear of the theft of manhood, whether through loss of honour and credit or through love sorcery, was a common cultural theme.

Beneath the phallic confidence of sixteenth-century German culture was a distinct awareness of the fragility of male potency and an anxiety about female power, a sexual dynamic which may have more than a little connection with the themes of the witch fantasies. In order to explore the extent of this cultural perception, however, and define its location, we need to understand what men feared when they worried about the theft of manhood. Masculinity, I have been arguing, for the archetypal virile entrepreneur of the early modern period, was intrinsically bound up with honour, the name, access to treasure and the control of other people. In the sexual economy of early modern magic, men might more often control objects: women, the emotions, the body and the penis. Crystal ball-gazing, a technique which is not exclusively attached to either sex, can show how this sexual division of powers operated and reveal how such pervasive magical assumptions affected quite other spheres of life. Put another way, what I have been trying to suggest is that the roots of witchcraft accusations, sexual antagonism and commerce in the emotions lie not in some underworld of sixteenth-century German culture, the province of marginals and outcasts, but at its very heart. We shall not understand either capitalism or masculinity unless we can place them within the magical culture in which they grew.

NOTES

1 See Leonore Davidoff and Catherine Hall, *Family Fortunes: Men and women of the English middle class*, London 1987, which brilliantly explores these connections in the eighteenth- and nineteenth-century English context. I have also been greatly influenced by the work of Michael Roper on business and masculinity. See his 'Masculinity and the Evolution of Management Cultures in British Industry 1945–85', Ph.D. diss., University of Essex 1989; and *idem*, 'Recent Books on Masculinity', *History Workshop Journal*, 29, 1990, pp. 184–6. For other ways of analysing masculinity in early modern Europe, see Alan

Bray's path-breaking, 'Homosexuality and the Signs of Male Friendship in Elizabethan England', *History Workshop Journal*, 29, 1990, pp. 1–19.

2 Stadtarchiv Augsburg, Urgichtensammlung, 28 Feb. 1564, Anna Megerler (hereafter cited as StadtAA, Urg.)

3 Extract from council minutes, 'allerley weyterung', 13 March 1564, in StadtAA, Urg. 28 Feb. 1564, Anna Megerler.

4 StadtAA, Strafbücher des Rats, 1563–71, fo. 24 v, 14 March 1564. Where maleficent magic could not be proven, crystal-gazers tended to be punished with exile and confiscation of the crystals: Strafbücher des Rats, 1563–71, fo. 27 v, 30 May 1564, Walburga Mair; Strafbücher des Rats, 1588–96, fo. 32 v, 18 Feb. 1589, Hans Wanner; fo. 33 r, 23 Feb. 1589, Maria Marquart; fo. 75 r, 24 July 1590, Anna Widenmann. The Imperial Law Code (Carolina, 1532) specified the death penalty for maleficent sorcery, but left punishment flexible for non-maleficent sorcery: A. Kaufmann (ed.), *Die Peinliche Gerichtsordnung Kaiser Karls V von 1532 (Carolina)*, Stuttgart 1975, art. 109.

5 [Achilles, P. Gasser], in M. Welser, (ed.), *Chronica der Weitberuempten Keyserlichen Freyen dess H. Reichss Statt Augspurg . . .* , trans. E. Werlich, Frankfurt am Main, Christoph Egen[olffs] Erben 1595, pp. 128–9.

6 StadtAA, Urg., 11 Feb. 1591, Paulus Mairat. Mairat attempted to gain money from Jacob Fugger by giving him a letter which purported to detail the plots of witches against him.

7 Martha Schad, *Die Frauen des Hauses Fugger von der Lilie (15.–17. Jahrhundert). Augsburg–Ortenburg–Trient* (Studien zur Fuggergeschichte 31), Tübingen 1989, pp. 25–41, 49–70, 53.

8 Augsburg and the Fuggers were prominent in these developments: Hermann Kellenbenz, 'Wirtschaftsleben der Blütezeit', in G. Gottlieb *et al.* (eds), *Geschichte der Stadt Augsburg*, Stuttgart 1985, pp. 267–8; Beatrix Bastl, *Das Tagebuch des Philipp Eduard Fugger* (Studien zur Fuggergeschichte 30), Tübingen 1987, pp. 254–60; Hermann Kellenbenz (ed.), *Europäische Wirtschafts- und Sozialgeschichte vom ausgehenden Mittelalter bis zur Mitte des 17. Jahrhunderts* (Handbuch der europäischen Wirtschafts- und Sozialgeschichte 3), Stuttgart 1986, pp. 881–2.

9 Götz Freiherr von Pölnitz, *Anton Fugger*, 3 vols, Tübingen 1958–86, second part of vol. 3 co-authored with Hermann Kellenbenz, *Anton Fugger 1555–1560*, (Studien zur Fuggergeschichte 29), Tübingen 1986, pp. 124–34.

10 Richard Ehrenberg, *Das Zeitalter der Fugger. Geldkapital und Creditverkehr im 16. Jahrhundert*, 2 vols, Jena 1896, vol. 1, pp. 163–5; Pölnitz and Kellenbenz, *Anton Fugger*, vol. 3, ii, pp. 119–28, 342.

11 On the gaze and the understanding of its power in Renaissance Europe, see Patricia Simons, 'Women in Frames: The eye, the gaze, the profile in Renaissance portraiture', *History Workshop Journal*, 25, 1988, pp. 4–30.

12 Clothing ordinances were becoming much more precise in this period. See, for example, StadtAA, *Eines Ersamen Rahts der Statt Augspurg der Gezierd vnd Kleydungen halben auffgerichte Policey ordnung*, Augsburg, Valentin Schöningk 1582; and the wedding ordinance of 1575, *Ains Ersamen Raths. der Statt Augspurg/ Hochzeit Ordnung*, Augsburg, Valentin Schöningk 1575 which made clear distinctions in permitted clothes and gifts according to social rank; and H. Lenk, *Augsburger Bürgertum in Späthumanismus und Frühbarock 1580–1700* (Abhandlungen zur Geschichte der Stadt Augsburg 17), Augsburg 1968, pp. 30–3; and on sumptuary law, Diane Owen Hughes, 'Sumptuary Law and Social Relations in Renaissance Italy', in J. Bossy (ed.), *Disputes and Settlements: Law and human relations in the west*, Cambridge, 1983.

13 Pölnitz and Kellenbenz, *Anton Fugger*, vol. 3, ii, pp. 188, 361: Kellenbenz acidly refers to Schwarz's *Kleidernarretei*, p. 188.

14 Ehrenberg, *Das Zeitalter der Fugger*, vol. 1, pp. 88, 139, 196.

15 Pölnitz and Kellenbenz, *Anton Fugger*, vol. 3, ii, pp. 357–9: Pölnitz cites Schiele's judgement that Fugger's power was like that of an 'absolute monarchy'.

16 For Pölnitz's view, see Götz Freiherr von Pölnitz, *Die Fugger*, 2nd edn, Frankfurt am Main 1960, pp. 256–70. Fugger seems to have been interested in dealings with Russia: Pölnitz and Kellenbenz, *Anton Fugger*, vol. 3, ii, pp. 116–8, and see 131–4.

17 The other spirit was named Jacob Seibold. I have not as yet been able to trace him.

18 On Elsässer's fate, Gasser, *Chronica*, p. 98; StadtAA, Strafbuch des Rats, fo. 105 v, 16 March 1559, (where he is named Elsesser). On Elsässer, Raid and Frölich: Pölnitz, *Anton Fugger*, vol. 3, i, pp. 255, 257, 312, 316, 363–4, 380, 385–6, 415, 469, 495–7, 499, 513. Pölnitz and Kellenbenz, *Anton Fugger*, vol. 3, ii, pp. 171, 188.

19 Spanish silver intended to meet the claims of the Fuggers had been impounded in 1557, Ehrenberg, *Das Zeitalter der Fugger*, vol. 1, p. 163; Pölnitz and Kellenbenz, *Anton Fugger*, vol. 3, ii, p. 124.

20 Wolfgang Zorn, *Augsburg. Geschichte einer deutschen Stadt*, Augsburg 1972, pp. 200–2.

21 Pölnitz and Kellenbenz, *Anton Fugger*, vol. 3, ii, p. 238; Paul von Stetten, *Geschichte der Heiligen Römischen Reichs Freyen Stadt Augsburg . . .* , 2 vols, Frankfurt am Main and Leipzig 1743–58, vol. 1, p. 592.

22 StadtAA, Urg., 27 May 1544, Regina Koch, 31 May 1544, Hans Meichssner, Jorg Nestle, Clain Jorg Hess, Clas Schmid, Hensle son of Regina Koch; Reformationsakten, Schwenckfeldiana, 29 May 1544, draft copy of letter to Nuremberg Council from Augsburg concerning the case.

23 Lyndal Roper, *The Holy Household. Women and morals in Reformation Augsburg*, Oxford 1989, pp. 27–40.

24 ibid., p. 30; Claus Peter Clasen, *Die Augsburger Weber. Leistungen und Krisen des Textilgewerbes um 1600* (Abhandlungen zur Geschichte der Stadt Augsburg 27), Augsburg 1981, esp. pp. 237–60, 330–2.

25 Ehrenberg, *Das Zeitalter der Fugger*, vol. 1, p. 117; Reinhardt Hildebrandt, 'Augsburger und Nürnberger Kupferhandel 1500–1619. Produktion, Marktanteile und Finanzierung im Vergleich zweier Städte und ihrer wirtschaftlichen Führungsschicht', in H. Kellenbenz (ed.), *Schwerpunkte der Kupferproduktion und des Kupferhandels im Europa 1500–1650* (Kölner Kolloquien zur internationalen Sozial- und Wirtschaftsgeschichte 3), Vienna 1977, pp. 196–8; and Ekkehard Westerman, 'Tendencies in the European Copper Market in the 15th and 16th Centuries', in H. Kellenbenz (ed.), *Precious Metals in the Age of Expansion* (Beiträge zur Wirtschaftsgeschichte 2), Stuttgart 1981, on the oligopolistic structure of the copper supply; Joseph Höffner, *Wirtschaftsethik und Monopole im 15. und 16. Jahrhundert*, Jena, 1941, pp. 36–49.

26 For an excellent analysis of the debates around 1514–15 in which the Fuggers were centrally involved over the legitimacy of collecting interest in capital investments, see Heiko Oberman, *Masters of the Reformation: The emergence of a new intellectual climate in Europe*, trans. Dennis Martin, Cambridge 1981, pp. 130–51; and for Peutinger's contribution, Heinrich Lutz, *Conrad Peutinger. Beiträge zu einer politischen Biographie* (Abhandlungen zur Geschichte der Stadt Augsburg 9), Augsburg 1958, pp. 106–9.

27 Martin Luther, 'Von Kaufshandlung und Wucher, 1524', in *D. Martin Luthers Werke: Kritische Gesamtausgabe*, 60 vols, Weimar 1883–1983, vol. 15, pp. 279–322; Luther, 'An die Pfarrherrn, wider den Wucher zu predigen, Vermahnung 1540)', *Luthers Werke, WA*, 51, pp. 325–424; and see Jakob

Strauss, 'Dass Wucher zu nehmen und zu geben unserem christlichen Glauben entgegen ist', in A. Laube and H. Seiffert (eds), *Flugschriften der Bauernkriegszeit*, Cologne and Vienna 1978, pp. 178–89; Höffner, *Wirtschaftsethik*, pp. 147–51 on the attitudes of Luther and Zwingli.

28 In 1576 the Jesuits, particularly Peter Canisius, began to preach against it and refuse absolution to those who refused to desist from making money out of interest charges. Once again, the Fuggers, strongly associated with Canisius and the Jesuits, were particularly sensitive on the issue. Schad, *Die Frauen des Hauses Fugger von der Lilie*, pp. 35ff.

29 Lutz, *Conrad Peutinger*, pp. 300–7; Clemens Bauer, 'Konrad Peutingers Gutachten zur Monopolfrage. Eine Untersuchung zur Wandlung der Wirtschaftsanschauung im Zeitalter der Reformation', *Archiv für Reformationsgeschichte*, 45, 1954, pp. 1–43, 145–96.

30 Clemens Bauer, 'Conrad Peutinger und der Durchbruch des neuen ökonomischen Denkens in der Wende zur Neuzeit', in Hermann Rinn (ed.), *Augusta 955–1955 Forschungen und Studien zur Kultur und Wirtschaftsgeschichte Augsburgs*, Munich 1955, pp. 222–6. Bauer interestingly shows how important the irrational was in Peutinger's account of economics.

31 Bauer, 'Conrad Peutinger', p. 225; Bauer, 'Konrad Peutingers Gutachten', pp. 193–4, and p. 41 for Peutinger's use of *fortuna*.

32 StadtAA, Urg., 2 July 1590, Anna Stauder.

33 So, for example, the Polizeiordnung of 1553 for Augsburg continued to stipulate that debtors should be confined until their debt was paid. *Die Chroniken der deutschen Städte vom 14. bis ins 16. Jahrhundert*, 36 vols, Leipzig 1862–1931, vol. 33, Augsburg 8, pp. 36–7, n. 2. In 1560 Hans and Marquart Rosenberger met this fate, as had the Höchstetter before them (*Chroniken*, vol. 3, p. 36). Sometimes the marriage portion of the debtor's wife was exempt from seizure for debt, sometimes not: Elmar Lutz, *Die Rechtliche Struktur süddeutscher Handelsgesellschaften in der Zeit der Fugger*, 2 vols, Tübingen 1976, vol. 1, pp. 466–8.

34 Lutz, *Die rechtliche Struktur*, vol. 1, pp. 465–7; Jakob Strieder, *Das reiche Augsburg*, ed. H. Deininger, Munich 1938, p. 46: there were seventy bankruptcies in Augsburg between 1564 and 1584. Augsburg experienced an unusually large number of bankruptcies partly as a result of the earlier defaults of the Spanish and French crowns.

35 In 1574, in the wake of numerous bankruptcies, the Augsburg Council formulated a distinction between simple bankruptcy and bankruptcy caused by fraud; but in 1580, it decreed that 'all' debtors were to be imprisoned and considered dishonourable. Reinhard Hildebrandt, 'Zum Verhältnis von Wirtschaftsrecht und Wirtschaftspraxis im 16. Jahrhundert. Die Fallitenordnungen des Augsburger Rates 1564–1580', in Anita Mächler *et al.* (eds), *Historische Studien zu Politik, Verfassung und Geschichte*, Bern and Munich 1976, pp. 158, 152–61. See also J. Hellmann, *Das Konkursrecht der Reichsstadt Augsburg*, Breslau 1905.

36 Insurance was in its infancy: Kellenbenz, *Europäische*, pp. 885–6.

37 StadtAA, Urg., 2 July 1590, Anna Stauder. Gasser describes another case of a woman who claimed to be from the von Wolffstein family and dabbled in crystal-gazing, making great profits from interested Augsburgers and people from the surrounding area until she was unmasked as a fraud: Gasser, *Chronica*, p. 120.

38 Some astrologers and magicians had to make use of 'seers', often 'innocent' people such as virgins or children, to gaze (scry). John Dee, the seventeenth-century English astrologer, needed a medium to see: Nicholas H. Clulee, *John Dee's Natural Philosophy. Between science and religion*, London 1988,

pp. 141–2; and William Lilly also used a woman to see: *Mr William Lilly's History of His Life and Times, from the Year 1602 to 1681*, London 1715, pp. 101–2. According to Megerler's testimony, Fugger could scry, but had harmed his sight doing so and thus needed her help. Even so, he still engaged another woman to teach her.

39 H. Bächtold-Stäubli, *Handwörterbuch des deutschen Aberglaubens*, 10 vols, Berlin and Leipzig 1927–42, vol. 5, pp. 583–7: Luther and Hans Sachs believed this. See also *Luthers Werke, WA*, Tischreden 4. nr 3618A, 3618A, 3618B, pp. 159–60, where the notion of a diabolic pact concluded in exchange for the crystal is evident; and for story of crystal destroyed by the Lutheran layman, Lazarus Spengler, F. Nork (F. Korn), *Die Sitten und Gebräuche der Deutschen*, Stuttgart 1849, pp. 647–8; and tale of crystal associated with monk, Heinrich Pröhle, *Deutsche Sagen*, Berlin 1863, pp. 232–3, nr 173.

40 Koch gave the following account of her conversation with the treasure-seeker: 'Sie hab Jrs abgeschlagen vnnd gesagt, wass sie mit dem Narren weiss vmb gee, Sie weiss von khain Schatz, hab auch khain glauben an solhe ding'. StadtAA, Urg., 27 May 1544, Regina Koch.

41 On the materialist conception of the workings of the sacred, see Bob Scribner, 'Cosmic Order and Daily Life: Sacred and secular in pre-industrial German society', in *idem, Popular Culture and Popular Movements in Reformation Germany*, London 1987. On clerical control of the sacrament, see Charles Zika, 'Hosts, Processions and Pilgrimages: Controlling the sacred in fifteenth-century Germany', *Past and Present*, 118, 1988, pp. 25–64.

42 Scribner, 'Cosmic Order', p. 13.

43 'Stillschweigen stehet wohl an', Ehrenberg, *Das Zeitalter der Fugger*, vol. 1, p. 167; Pölnitz and Kellenbenz, *Anton Fugger*, vol. 3, ii, p. 358: 'sondern solches alles in guter Stille und geheim bei uns und unter uns'.

44 Indeed, in 1558 the council had even decreed that anyone found in a suspicious place or with suspicious people should be admonished, and, if there were sufficient indices of suspicion, punished corporally. StadtAA, Ratsbuch 30/II, fos 80 r–v, 29 Oct. 1558, and transcribed as an addition in Zucht and Executionsordnung 1553, Schätze ad 36/5, fo. 37 v.

45 Thus in 1554, Anton Fugger, short of cash, demanded that Ortel send him money at any price, for his credit relied upon it ('denn mir steht darauf mein Credito') and went on to add that he was more concerned about the mockery of people than the business itself ('Mir ist schier so viel am Spott der Leute gelegen, als an der Sache selbst'): Ehrenberg, *Das Zeitalter der Fugger*, vol. 1, p. 157. In 1557, after the crash, he decreed that Ortel should raise no money in Anton Fugger's name ('dass er auf meinen Anthoni Fuggers Namen nichts mehr soll aufbringen'): Pölnitz and Kellenbenz, *Anton Fugger*, vol. 3, ii, p. 129. In 1558, he expressed concern about the firm's alleged involvement in the illegal silver export business of Urban Mair because it touches honour, and no honourable man would want to be involved with such a one: Pölnitz and Kellenbenz, ibid., 'Denn es trifft die Ehre an, würde kein ehrlicher Mann mit einem solchem zu tun wollen haben', p. 196.

46 Ulinka Rublack, 'A Late Medieval German Nun and Her Infant Jesus Doll', unpublished paper, Institute of Historical Research, London June 1989.

47 See Charles Zika, 'Reuchlin's *De Verbo Mirifico* and the Magic Debate of the Late Fifteenth Century', *Journal of the Warburg and Courtauld Institutes*, 34, 1976, pp. 104–38.

48 StadtAA, Urg., 2 July 1590, Anna Stauder.

49 Pölnitz and Kellenbenz, *Anton Fugger*, vol. 3, ii, pp. 259ff; Pölnitz, *Die Fugger*, pp. 256–70.

50 See note 38 above.
51 There does not seem to be a German equivalent for the powerful magical use of the vagina in crop fertility magic: see Luisa Accati, 'The Larceny of Desire: The Madonna in seventeenth-century Catholic Europe', in Jim Obelkevich, Lyndal Roper and Raphael Samuel (eds), *Disciplines of Faith. Studies in religion, politics and patriarchy*, London 1987, esp. pp. 78–9.
52 Thomas Laqueur, 'Orgasm, Generation, and the Politics of Reproductive Biology', in Catherine Gallagher and Thomas Laqueur (eds), *The Making of the Modern Body. Sexuality and society in the nineteenth century*, Berkeley and Los Angeles, Calif. 1987, esp. pp. 8–9; and see Ian Maclean, *The Renaissance Notion of Woman. A study in the fortunes of scholasticism and medical science in European intellectual life*, Cambridge 1980, pp. 28–46.
53 Heide Wunder, 'Frauen in der Gesellschaft Mitteleuropas im späten Mittelalter und in der Frühen Neuzeit (15. bis 18. Jahrhundert)', in H. Valentinisch, (ed.), *Hexen und Zauberer*, Vienna 1987, pp. 123–54.
54 For similar domination of body magic and love-sorcery by women, see Ruth Martin, *Witchcraft and the Inquisition in Venice 1550–1650*, Oxford 1989; and on witches causing impotence, see Emmanuel Le Roy Ladurie, *Jasmin's Witch. An investigation into witchcraft and magic in south-west France during the seventeenth century*, trans. Brian Pearce, London 1987.
55 One famous example is explored by Natalie Davis in *The Return of Martin Guerre*, Cambridge, Mass. 1983. The autobiography of the eighteenth-century Parisian journeyman glazier, Jacques Ménétra, describes the hero's various escapes from the rich widows to whom he nearly promised marriage: Jacques-Louis Ménétra, *Journal of My Life*, trans. Arthur Goldhammer, New York 1986, pp. 46–8, 68, 72, 79. He is able to continue on his journeys: the widows have to wait for tokens from him.
56 On male honour and its relationship to work identity, see Merry Wiesner, 'Guilds, Male Bonding and Women's Work in Early Modern Germany', *Gender and History*, 1, no. 2, 1989, pp. 125–37.
57 Lyndal Roper, *The Holy Household*, pp. 31–40.
58 I have explored this theme in more detail in Chapter 3.
59 On the importance of marriage in creating networks between patricians and merchants in Augsburg, see Katarina Sieh-Burens, *Oligarchie, Konfession und Politik im 16. Jahrhundert. Zur sozialen Verflechtung der Augsburger Bürgermeister und Stadtpfleger 1518–1618* (Schriften der philosophischen Fakultäten der Universität Augsburg 29), Munich 1986; and on the position of the Fuggers, members of the imperial nobility but of the urban patriciate from only 1538 on: Olaf Mörke, 'Die Fugger im 16. Jahrhundert. Städtische Elite oder Sonderstruktur?', *Archiv für Reformationsgeschichte*, 74, 1983, pp. 141–62; and Olaf Mörke and Katarina Sieh, 'Gesellschaftliche Führungsgruppen', in Gottlieb *et al.* (eds), *Geschichte der Stadt Augsburg*.
60 Leo Steinberg, *The Sexuality of Christ in Renaissance Art and in Modern Oblivion*, London 1984.
61 This theme is developed in Charles Zika, 'Fears of Flying: Representations of witchcraft and sexuality in sixteenth century Germany', *Australian Journal of Art*, 8, 1989–90, pp. 19–48.
62 Even as late as 1560, a servant woman was banished from Augsburg for having attempted to sell a little boy to the Jews at Oberhausen. *Chroniken der deutschen Städte*, vol. 33, Augsburg 8, pp. 48, 50; StadtAA, Urg., 19 (July 1560), Anna Paur.
63 See R. Po-Chia Hsia, *The Myth of Ritual Murder. Jews and magic in Reformation Germany*, New Haven, Conn. 1988.
64 ibid., p. 52.

65 This image was compellingly depicted in Hartmann Schedel's *Nuremberg Chronicle*, 1493, which was rapidly pirated and widely diffused. There were also popular broadsheets commemorating the case: Hsia, *Myth of Ritual Murder*, pp. 46–50, 49 for image.

7 Drinking, whoring and gorging: brutish indiscipline and the formation of Protestant identity

I

Around the time of the Renaissance and Reformation, European people altered in some fundamental way, or so most historians seem to agree. Whether for better or for worse depends on your point of view. To those who regard the regulation of the free, instinctual life of medieval man as a tragic fall, the birth of the modern era saw the repression of a vigorous populist culture; to those who seek to trace the increasing civilization of European culture, it betokened the beginnings of the well-ordered state and its subject, the domesticated, responsible citizen. Historians who study popular culture posit the growth of a great divide between the culture of the little people and the culture of élites, or investigate the imposition of the culture of the urban bureaucrat on the peasant. Historians who study religious change document a growing sense of confessional identity – that is, the formation of a sense of denomination – in the years following the turbulence of the religious reformations of the early sixteenth century. For those whose theme is the development of the self the story begins around the sixteenth century; others who study poor relief notice an attempt to inculcate the work ethic. In all these narratives, the sixteenth century occupies a pivotal position. It marks the beginning of a transformation of the religious, political and psychological identity of the European person.

The unwritten assumptions and influences on this kind of work are drawn from many sources, not always explicit. Important among them is the concept, first developed by Norbert Elias, of social disciplining.[1] Elias's work is a powerful tool of synthesis which offers the prospect of integrating psychoanalysis with a historically informed sociology. With its help, historians can transform the quaint detail of the history of cleanliness, or the intimate details of sexual practice in the past into the building blocks of a strong narrative of social and cultural change. Such seeming trivia are indices of the process of social disciplining, a transformation by which the developing state of the early modern period gradually managed to inculcate order in its citizens. This process was not merely accomplished at the level of the state alone: in the sixteenth and seventeenth centuries, people underwent psychological change of the kind necessary to submit themselves to the authority of a civilized society. The attractions of such a theory to modern historians are immense.

In this chapter, I want to question the assumptions on which such views rest. I shall explore their use in one corner of the debate, that which concerns religious change in sixteenth-century Germany. A key term here is confessionalization, which has been defined as 'the formation of religious ideologies and institutions in Lutheranism, Calvinism and Catholicism'.[2] This, too, can be seen as part of the process of social disciplining. Taking its cue from Elias's studies of the development of absolutism in France, in which the development of the early modern absolutist state is seen as part of the 'civilizing process', this literature views the growth of religious identities in the sixteenth and seventeenth centuries in Germany as part of a parallel process of civilization. Confessionalization is a wide-ranging term which breaks the confines of narrowly religious history to include moral behaviour, cultural forms and the increasing power of the religiously zealous state within its scope. It applies not just to particular confessions but stresses the similarity of developments in states of differing religious character. It typifies Counter-Reformation Bavaria as well as Calvinist Geneva. So far as its social aspects are concerned, confessionalization has generally been seen as an aspect of the 'social discipline' which the development of the state required. When people became truly Calvinist, so the argument would seem to run, they gave up drinking, whoring and gambling and whole communities began to live godly lives – ironically, an idealizing application of social history worthy of the most zealous nineteenth-century Protestant historian.

Late sixteenth-century Protestantism seems to fit perfectly the model of the birth of the controlled, disciplined modern subjectivity. But here I shall argue that it bursts the bounds of the paradigm altogether. I shall do so by exploring three major problems which bedevil the confessionalization debate as they apply to Protestantism: there are similarities but also important differences in the case of Catholicism. They relate to the use which has been made of Elias's work. The first is the too easy fit assumed between political transformation and behavioural regulation. The second concerns the failure to distinguish how 'discipline' and state formation affected different groups in different ways. And the third is the way 'regulation' is itself understood, and the model of the human instincts which underpins this concept. The word 'regulation' implies the simple imposition of controlling measures on human behaviour: I want to suggest that we may need another vocabulary altogether if we are adequately to imagine the contradictory effects on human beings of disciplinary legislation.

II

But first, we need to consider the phenomenon of discipline and how it may be related to religious and political change. As religious historians began to seek an understanding of how the state acquired legitimacy, it was perhaps natural that discipline should have been a key focus of their interest, for the concept is at once religious and secular.[3] Recent work such as that of Heinz Schilling, Thomas Robisheaux and William Wright on the Reformation and discipline has enormously extended our understanding.[4] These historians are suggesting that the roots of the early modern state can be seen in the increased kinds of powers early modern authorities – civic ones at first – took over their subjects as they assumed powers and functions which had formerly belonged to the church. They assumed the duty of patrolling the moral lives of their citizens, supplementing the moral suasion of the confessional with new morals courts and punishment of those who gave in to the temptations of the flesh. They entered into the regulation of marriage, Protestant areas setting up marriage courts with secular representation to determine which were valid marriages and who might be awarded a divorce. And in many towns and territories, they embarked on a programme of poor relief, taking responsibility for the systematic care of the indigent instead of permitting the fate of the poor to depend upon the strength of charity among their fellow Christians.

Discipline, however, was not an early modern invention. The origins of Discipline Ordinances lay in the late medieval period, when authorities, working with concepts of 'public' and 'private' sins, issued mandates against such public sins as cohabitation with prostitutes or drunkenness. Public sins could be punished by secular authorities; private ones, which did not cause offence to one's neighbours, were a matter for the church's confessional. The Reformation's achievement was to link the concept of discipline with evangelical fervour, creating a far more compelling and integrated vision of a disciplined society.[5] So, for example, Jörg Vögeli, city clerk of Constance, concluded his epic narrative of the Reformation in his home town with the introduction of its Discipline Ordinance. This set the seal on the Reformation. Now the godly city was to be created, and the discipline of its people would set the city apart from the godless outside. Discipline was essential to his sense of being neither Anabaptist nor papist but an evangelical, a citizen of a purified city of God.[6]

Throughout German towns and territories, Discipline Ordinances were drafted and published during the 1530s, 1540s and well into the second half of the century. Imperial Discipline Ordinances were published in 1530, 1548 and 1577.[7] Although in German discussions, confessionalization has primarily been treated as a phenomenon of the late sixteenth century and contrasted with the religious flux of the early part of the period, the supposedly disciplined society of the post-1550 years cannot be understood in isolation from its origins earlier in the century: rather, the period needs to be seen as a whole. Nor was discipline a mere matter of words. A series of new disciplinary bodies were set up with powers to punish.[8] The institutionalization of discipline was an important element of the Reformation's establishment. As Vögeli was well aware, the signs of a reformed city were the abolition of the mass, evangelical preaching and discipline. Perhaps the Common Man knew the Reformation had arrived not when he received the sacrament in two kinds, but when he found himself hauled up before the Discipline Lords for swinish drunkenness.

The morals campaign was fired by evangelical hope. It proposed a world where each individual had duties according to his or her place; the master, mistress, children and servants each having a particular set of moral obligations. It powerfully invoked the certainties of the household workshop where everyone knew their place, their work and their social duties, and it was an immensely attractive creed. Order and right living were its watchwords. It called for punishment of the sins of drunkenness, evil living and godlessness, and it exhorted secular authority to act to bring the godly society into being.

III

What is the link between religiously influenced movements of moral regulation and political change? The first problem with the model proposed by the theory of social disciplining is that it assumes a natural homology between political structure and social behaviour. It takes for granted that the development of the state will be matched by changes in the way people behave. In the religious version of this story, Protestantism generates disciplined behaviour and the state builds its edifice on the foundations of a disciplined group of subjects. In the hands of Norbert Elias and those who have been influenced by him, the story becomes a narrative of progress and civilization, even when it is conceded to move in fits and starts rather than ineluctably upwards. Gradually behaviour becomes more disciplined and the boundaries of shame move ever inwards. The bodily functions become hidden as the social control necessary for political authority is created. Street-fighting gives way to the use of courts, people begin to use handkerchiefs to blow their noses and table manners become more complex in polite society.

In variants of the Elias interpretation such as that developed by the authoritative French *History of Private Life: Passions of the Renaissance* (Elias is explicitly invoked in Roger Chartier's introduction to the volume),[9] the Elias schema bestows a causal primacy on the political.[10] This is curious, for it can result in social history which leaves the grand narratives of the rise of the state unchallenged: politics, it transpires, is the Final Instance. But it is a strange kind of politics, for the abstract Rise of the State is notoriously difficult to pin down. Meanwhile, political revisionist historians are busily questioning the existence of such wholesale transitions, or even advocating the relinquishing of such terms as 'absolutism' altogether.

Discipline, I would argue, was not the natural outcome of the progressively expanding state. It was a moral theology which appealed to particular groups of people, and its acceptance had to be fought for through politics. The adoption of new Discipline Ordinances was frequently the result of intense struggles within towns and territories. The most immediate political conflict it caused was, first of all, with the new church. If secular authority was to administer moral discipline, it was clearly invading the area which had chiefly been the preserve of the church, where the clergy had employed control of morals through the confessional, backed up with the ultimate sanction of excommunication. In this struggle between church and secular authority the outcome varied. Some ordinances allowed a considerable degree of latitude to the church in administering congregational 'warnings' and even exclusion from communion (though often the local town council or secular authority's approval for excommunication was required); others excluded the church from the processes of discipline altogether.[11]

The second authority with a claim to discipline was the guild system. Guilds had previously exercised moral supervision over their own members, fining those who were rowdy or were excessively drunk on guild premises. In some areas this transition did not lead to open conflict. In the city of Augsburg, prominent guildsmen already occupied key positions on the town council. These men happily swapped the backroom parlours of guild affairs for the wider stage of urban politics.[12] In the town of Lindau, however, the same development issued in a different arrangement. There, guild opposition apparently led the council to vest control of discipline in the guild's hands, relinquishing its own claims. This solution was not a stable one and in 1554 the council resumed control over morals. But it was not an easy victory, as its own prescription betrays: when the council redrew the ordinance, it decreed that any who mocked the ordinance should be accounted 'those who hold authority in contempt' (*Verächter der Obrigkeit*).[13] In Nuremberg where guild influence was minimal and the patrician controlled council had already secured tight ascendancy over its citizens, moral control does not appear to have featured strongly in evangelical rhetoric. The brothel even remained open throughout the Reformation, a situation unthinkable in Augsburg, Constance or Ulm.[14]

'Discipline' is not a natural accompaniment of the rise of centralized authority, but a concept around which rival political claims could be staked out. Its appeal was neither natural nor inevitable, but varied. The concept of discipline owed much to the guild and civic ordinances of the fourteenth and fifteenth centuries. And sometimes it might be the bastions of resistance to the modernizing institutions of the state who fought hardest for discipline: in Augsburg it was guildsmen who called for moral reform, in Lindau the guilds attempted to keep control of discipline themselves. As Thomas Robisheaux has persuasively argued for Hohenlohe, in rural areas it might be village elders who saw the discipline campaign as furthering their interests, and who embraced Lutheranism most fervently.[15] Nor was the appeal of discipline confined to the evangelically orthodox. In Hesse, too, as the example of the Anabaptists who charged the Hessian church with laxness suggests, discipline could alike be longed for by evangelicals and anarchistic sectaries hostile to any manifestations of the modern state.[16]

But is discipline a zero sum game in which, regardless of the aims of the players, the state can only win? I don't think so. Though reformed moralism remained a powerful political force, its enforcement was episodic rather than consistent, despite the plethora of discipline courts. A redraft of the Discipline Ordinance, usually carried out every twenty years or so, was the occasion for renewed moral vigour; and visitations were the immediate spur to a moral spring clean. In Constance, the ordinance Vögeli had greeted as the dawn of a new evangelical age was not being observed, and only a decade later, Ambrosius Blarer, its author, was fighting a losing battle against godless political opponents in the council to secure a 'new Reformation'.[17] Prosecution patterns in Augsburg bear this out – there tends to be a regular trickle of cases accompanied by the occasional mass panic. The hold of the ideology of discipline on actual behaviour was always fragile. The rise of 'discipline' did not secure a disciplined, modern subjectivity.

Movements of moral reform need to be understood in more complex ways. They move by fits and starts rather than ineluctable progression. And after all, as the example of many a tele-evangelist reminds us, the priests of moral perfection are not always its paragons. Gereon Sailer, prominent Augsburg Zwinglian, doctor and humanist, quietly kept a mistress on the side; the evangelical former prior of the Augsburg Carmelites consorted with a prostitute.[18] Discipline is not guaranteed by ordinances, nor does punishment suffice to root out the sins of the flesh. This does not show that evangelical moralism was mere cant. As I shall argue below, it suggests, rather, that the relation between the high-water mark of moralist doctrines and actual behaviour is not straightforward. The abolition of the civic brothel, the campaign against prostitution and the growing Protestant execration of the prostitute as Whore of Babylon may have made the prostitute a far more sexually compelling inhabitant of the ex-prior's or Sailer's imaginative worlds than she would otherwise have been.

IV

How are we then to understand the impact of these Discipline Ordinances? Historians writing on the imposition of 'discipline' later on in the century tend to assume that discipline and moral reform operated in a uniform fashion on an undistinguished body of subjects. Taking its cue from the older discussion of absolutism, much of this work assumes that the state succeeded in creating a unified body of subjects, and addressed them as such. As Gerhard Oestreich, one of the most important exponents of the idea of social discipline, put it, the process of 'social disciplining' encompassed almost all areas of life, and practically all 'estates, groups and professional strata'.[19] It was a process of a 'spiritual–moral and psychological structural transformation of the political, military and economic human being' through which individuals came to discipline themselves in accordance with the demands of society. We might notice in passing that this is a series of categories which excludes women.

Discipline Ordinances, however, do not bear out the idea that discipline was a uniform, universal process. They suggest, rather, that the impulse of the ordinances was often to make distinctions between the ruled – the mechanism which some recent historians of absolutism are arguing was also crucial to the development of the early modern state.[20] It is not just that discipline affected different groups at different times – the cities first, the freer life of the court perhaps somewhat later – but that the process of ordinance-making itself, so far from creating the uniform subject, advanced social distinction. The ordinances identify and thus define vagabonds and outsiders as particular categories of person.

Commonly, the ordinances distinguish between members of the polity, subjects, and those outside it. So, for instance, non-citizens guilty of adultery were to be banished from the body politic while their citizen peers were given prison sentences and eventually reintegrated. Similarly, because much of the rowdy behaviour which the ordinances aimed to punish occurred either outside in the streets or in guild rooms, patrician youths, with their exclusive patrician dance parlours, were not as subject to the regulations as were their non-aristocratic brethren. Status differences were made explicit, interestingly enough, in one ordinance, by erecting sexual taboos. Triple penalties attached to adulterous liaisons between master and maid, or mistress and manservant.[21]

But the distinction I particularly want to consider here is that between men and women. In Oestreich's discussion of the process of social disciplining, sexual difference, central though the regulation of sexual behaviour is to any argument about morals, is generally not discussed. Instead we learn how 'man' became more subject to control by the state, or we read of how the bureaucrat, soldier or courtier became created.

These examples are universals, ideal types like the concept of social disciplining itself, but the use of the abstract universal here is symptomatic. It leaves us without an account of the disciplining process of women. Elias does make some remarks about women when he deals with sexual relations, describing their increasing modesty as analogous to men's disciplining. Where gender difference does enter his argument more directly, women tend to be treated as a natural resource whose exploitation by men is gradually reined in by the process of civilization: after the middle ages, women become less subject to rape by men acting on their powerful sexual drives. The court society demands much more restraint from men and consideration for women, allowing them a 'first wave of emancipation'. In consequence, women come to be the exception to the general psychological theory the example is used to document. Medieval men were the owners of strong sexual drives, while women apparently did not suffer so much from the attacks of such instincts (a conception which would have surprised their medieval and male contemporaries, who believed women's lusts to be greater than their own). As a result, women lack the historical interiority accorded their menfolk. Perhaps they have already developed the internal superego which enables them to be the quiescent objects of male domination; perhaps, weaker psychologically, they are but a paler reflection of general transitions.[22]

However, I think any account of the effect of moral movements must accord gender difference a central place. Gender difference is not a matter of deviation from the male norm. Projects of disciplining are centrally concerned with what it ought to mean to be a man or a woman, and with setting out appropriate behaviour for the sexes. Throughout the Discipline Ordinances we have been considering, male and female behaviour is understood in different ways, and the ordinances in fact deal with it under different headings. Men and women were problematic in different ways to early modern governments. Men were seen as in thrall to the twin dangers of alcohol and gambling – the two devils as they were sometimes imagined. Men's addictions led to violence, creating a serious public order problem for the early modern state. Again, we see the insidious effect of universalist language which is actually about men. Though in principle the sections of Discipline Ordinances which dealt with drinking and gaming were usually not gender specific, the intention clearly was. *Zutrinken*, or competitive drinking, where if your drinking companion cannot equal your toast he insults you, was a particular target of censure. A male custom, it was the cornerstone of artisan brotherhood.[23] Gaming, too, was primarily a male pursuit: many ordinances inveighed against the harm it caused 'to wife and child'. And though women, too, could be violent and engage in punch-ups at market or on the street, it was male violence which was perceived as the real problem. Stabbings and woundings in a society where most men carried a dagger or sword were routine. If the state wished to monopolize the means of force, it had to attempt some kind of control of men.[24]

Women, by contrast, are chiefly included in the sections concerned with sexual misbehaviour: adultery, fornication and procuring, although men also faced punishment for such sins. These sections often included a paean of praise to marriage, elaborating the roles thought proper to man and wife. They thus gave voice to a powerful set of notions about appropriate female behaviour as chaste, modest and silent.

It is evident that the ordinances propose different understandings of male and female behaviour, and of the sexed body. Men's bodies were viewed as potentially anarchic and undisciplined. Here, we might notice the fascination of several ordinances with vomiting, which they describe in some detail.[25] Gorging themselves and vomiting in an animal manner, men could not be controlled – they broke all the boundaries of civilized life. When drunk, men became violent and their aggression spilled out into the street. In particular, the ordinances castigated male drunkenness because it led men to lose control over bodily functions, and this represented their relinquishing of reason. It was men's greater capacity for thought which raised them above womankind and which distinguished them from animals. Men's drunkenness therefore offered the imaginative possibility of the loss of male superiority. Men's grip on bodily boundaries – their inherent cleanliness – was imagined to be tenuous in the extreme!

Women's bodies, by contrast, were thought to have weak boundaries in a sexual sense. Sexually permeable, their wombs were constantly alive, and open to male invasion. The Lindau city fathers found it hard to believe in female innocence at all, setting very low compensation fees for loss of virginity and denying seduced women all compensation, even for childbed expenses, if 'she ran after him more than he her'.[26] We might say that male bodies were imagined as constantly breaking their boundaries, polluting the world around them with violence and vomit. Female bodies, by contrast, could bring pollution on society through their sexual openness.

As a result, these ordinances positioned men and women in different ways, and this meant that the experience of discipline for men and women was very different. While women were primarily prosecuted for their sexual misconduct and evil tongues, men were disciplined for rowdy behaviour, drunkenness, gambling and blasphemy. The project of discipline affected men and women differently, and it contributed greatly to the elaboration of the distinct natures men and women were presumed to have. Indeed, this sexual dynamic of the ordinances was one of their most important impulses, as their composers sought to pin down and define what behaviour was appropriate to the two sexes God had created.

The ordinances also set out the ideal of the *Hausvater*, that icon of Protestant manhood, who was to rule his servants and journeymen, cautioning them for blasphemy or evil words and superintending their moral behaviour. But as the ordinances had implicitly conceded, the Protestant patriarch proved remarkably reluctant to assume his moral mantle, frequently living it up in taverns and gambling his earnings away. In consequence, the authorities straddled an uneasy divide between wanting to invade the household and police the male miscreant, and treating him as a respected ally whose household authority would buttress their own. The household, the institution which composed society and which was the essential backdrop for any discussion of ideal masculinity and femininity – as if, like a child's drawing, you could not have mummy and daddy without the house – thus occupied an ambivalent position. On the one hand, the craft household was the school of godly life, the mirror of order and the microcosm of the state. On the other, it was the scene of violent marital fights, and its artisan ruler was likely as not a gambling drunkard. This led to an ambiguity in policing tactics. While sixteenth-century authorities lauded the household and gave it a role in policing morals, they also greatly increased the scope for official intervention into the domestic, allowing officials to search the house for illegal drinking, and permitting wives to cite their husbands for unfair beating.[27]

In this way, what had once been the impermeable skin of the household became ruptured. Whereas crossing the threshold and entering the territory of the house was, in the medieval period, an act which violated the honour of the household,[28] now the interior world of the household was to be open to scrutiny, should the council wish to make use of its powers. The household, the container of the two sexes, was thus no longer a sealed body. Therefore, at one level the ordinances can be understood as trying to contain bodies and isolate the individual subject. But the project of making the individual rather than the guild or house the unit of subjection also undermined the intactness of the household. If Protestantism aimed to make the household holy, it did not revere its own creation. We might say that what began as a project of consecrating the household order led to increased intervention and supervision of its little realm by the authorities of church and state, in the name of patriarchal virtues. Who would not want a perfect family, a cradle of ordered calm in a rough street world, with a benign patriarch ruling a happy commonweal? Such a vision only made the actual tyranny of drunken, brutish, debauched masters the more unbearable, encouraging wives and servants to cite such men before the authorities. The Reformation's idealization of the household consequently fostered its actual instability, as real households failed to live up to the ideal and authorities felt compelled to offer discipline from without as a remedy, however ineffective, for its ills.

V

The third and major problem which I wish to consider here is that such analyses of confessionalization and discipline are premised on an unsatisfactory account of sexuality. They rest on a notion of social control which views sexuality as a matter of simple physical drives and regulation as restraint of these drives. These assumptions derive from the adoption of the key concepts of Norbert Elias. So far it is striking that in Germany, at least, it has been the instinctualist account of sexuality to be found in Elias's work rather than the discourse approach of Michel Foucault which has dominated work on the subject.[29] Even in France, Elias and not Foucault is invoked as the inspiration of the magisterial *Passions of the Renaissance*, the Annales school's account of the relationship between discipline and absolutism. In part, this has to do with historical territorialism: Elias, working within a Weberian historical frame which accords primacy to the growth of the bureaucratic state, sees the key developments as occurring in the early modern period; Foucault, however, whose project was a pessimistic re-evaluation of the rationalist legacy of the Enlightenment, locates the major historical transitions in the eighteenth century.[30] But although early modernists may be drawn to Elias's privileging of their own period of study, the ambivalent effects of sexual regulation about which Foucault wrote so incisively can be dated to well before the eighteenth century. Whatever the problems of the Foucauldian approach, it has at least the merit of a more sophisticated understanding of the body and sexuality, one that enables the historian to explore the construction of sexual desire through language, broadly interpreted. This is the method that I shall first adopt here, because I think it takes us further in conceptualizing the contradictory effects of legislation on human beings; although, as I shall later argue, it does not take us far enough.

Dancing, that obsession of Protestant divines, urban oligarchs and beleaguered rural officials, is a particular case in point. When the authorities fulminated against the sexual gyrations, the embracings, the leapings and the unseemly way women's skirts flew up during dances, they were not merely imposing a stricter policing of the body or suppressing popular culture. Their diatribes also served to endow these dance styles with an enhanced sexual significance. As the preacher Melchior Ambach put it:

> To the music of sweet strings and unchaste songs people practise easygoing, whorish gestures, touch married women and virgins with unchaste hands, kiss one another with whorish embraces; and the bodily parts, which nature has hidden and covered in shame, are uncovered by lechery; and under the cloak of diversion and entertainment, shame and vice are covered.[31]

When parishioners heard from his pulpit not to dance lasciviously they also learnt how. To see these ordinances as resulting in the purification and desexualization of dance would be to share the naïve optimism of sixteenth-century Calvinists. And one would miss the distinctly sexual tone of the Calvinists' own fascination with the way the body moved in dancing, with the 'unchaste gestures, words and work' which constitute 'venereal dancing'.[32]

Nor is Ambach's erotically-charged tone an unfortunate lapse. The literature of moral reform is mesmerized by the ills it purports to exorcize, and one could draw examples to illustrate this point from countless works. Indeed, moralism spawned its own genre of highly successful Devil Books, reaching its apogee around the middle of the century, each devoted to such heroes as the Trousers Devil, the Marriage Devil, the Whoring Devil or the Drunken Devil.[33] The dissection of sin became an art of entertaining, the diabolic characters not so much fearsome denizens of Hell as domestic figures of fun, and the books themselves, endlessly reprinted, were often bound together to make impressively thick compendia, tricked out in leather and gold. Or one might think of the female allegories of the seven deadly sins which a sculptor like Peter Dell modelled for his sophisticated patrons. The slatternly drunkard who depicts greed is magnificently gross; her sister Lust bares her leg, daring the owner to touch its sensual wooden surface – the statuettes, vice you can stroke, are just small enough to hold in the hand. The art of moralism was animated by an eroticism of bodily excess, encompassing the sensuality of all bodily orifices, oral, genital and anal.

VI

Similarly, instead of viewing the Rabelaisian literature of Fischart, Scheidt and Dedekind as the last fling of a medieval bodily freedom, we might see it as inherently connected with the rise of sexual moralism.[34] In part this literature has its roots in the old vision of Schlaraffenland, the land of Cockaigne, of gorging, plenty and excess, which was a familar theme for the visual arts as well.[35] But temporally its elaboration is linked with the rise of moralism. Moralist genres and the literature of excess exploit similar literary techniques, and these similarities extend to the morals ordinances themselves. Sometimes drafted by clergy, the morals ordinances from the 1530s onwards were couched in a histrionic rhetoric, denouncing the 'shameful sin and great vice of drunkenness', the animal habit of excessive eating, 'useless and undisciplined dancing' and other forms of 'brutish indiscipline'. They were made to be read aloud, but they employ a highly literary style. They heap up adjectives and strive for emotive effect, adopting techniques which owe much to both moralist preaching and to earlier humanist and medical writings against sin.[36] Soon they became too long for oral delivery.

Their rhetoric of moral outrage rapidly found imitators. The morals campaign was accompanied by a flurry of evangelical writings on the evils of gaming, drunkenness, dancing and whoring, which threatened to become an entire sub-genre in itself. Borrowing their language from the morals ordinances, writers like Cyriakus Spangenberg, Melchior Ambach or Matthäus Friderich wrote fulsomely on discipline and on the duty to punish sinners, legitimating as they did so the secular authorities who were hallowed by their moral task. The vast treatises which writers like these produced (many purported to be sermons, but no congregation would have lasted the distance) developed a momentum of their own.

In the mid-sixteenth century, this kind of writing reached its full flowering in wonderful comic creations. With writers like Johann Fischart, these finally crossed the boundary from the originally oral techniques of the Discipline Ordinances to a literate culture in love with the possibilities of language itself. Now the moralist stratagems of repetition, piling up of adjectives and employing animal comparisons were employed to devastating effect. Johann Fischart's famous litany of drunkards, the eighth chapter of the *Geschichtklitterung*, his massively extended reworking of Rabelais's original, is a celebration of drunkenness which draws from the moral literature against drinking, finally breaking down into exuberant linguistic incoherence as the alcohol works its miracle.[37] In 1572, Fischart had written his own rhyming version of *Till Eulenspiegel* which transforms the figure of Till from the cunning, calculating peasant into a grotesquely gargantuan figure; the anonymous *Lalebuch* features a similar hero whose location is the world of the town, not the country.[38] Now, the creature of excess could be one's neighbour, oneself. Dedekind's uproarious development of the figure of Grobian is a fantasy of bodily anarchy which similarly derives its imaginative pull from the condemnation of bodily excess: this is what makes it transgressive.[39] It is, moreover, an intellectual's pleasure. Larded with learned references, the first edition appeared in Latin and was subsequently translated into German by Caspar Scheidt.[40]

The repressive literature and the literature of excess are two sides of the same coin, for the negative and positive attitudes towards bodily function are held simultaneously. They are a single, related process, and not the operation of a repression on prior, natural drives. The condemnation of violent, rowdy behaviour, and the fulminations against vomiting as the paradigmatic anarchic loss of control in the male body were thus integrally connected with the fascination with bodily excess, the body where the 'drives' were given free rein.

Hans Sachs offers an interesting example of a midpoint between the literature of moral censure and the celebration of excess. In his poem

'The Four Miraculous Properties and Effects of Wine', a doctor describes the four types of humour and how they are affected differently by wine.[41] The lucky Sanguinius is sociable, peaceful and forgiving when in his cups, and sleeps the sleep of the just, but the irascible Colericus is to be found cursing, swearing and terrifying the poor servants when he drinks too much. The last type, Melancolius, becomes entertaining and ape-like, chattering and laughing and up to all sorts of japes when drunk.

But it is the third character, Flegmaticus, who particularly interests me here. Flegmaticus embodies excess. When drunk, he discards all the bodily containments of civilized man – he defecates and vomits with enthusiasm. The poetry is not moralistic – the reader is meant to laugh and even enter into the infantile dream of transgression, the loss of control of social and bodily boundaries as we read how he no longer knows which house is his own and tries to enter others. But the loss of the house, of outer social identity, is just a metaphor for his loss of bodily control, which, however, is envisaged with gusto rather than horror. He 'dirties himself in manure like a pig/ and lies a while in a dung heap'.[42] When he at last reaches home, his poor wife must undress him even though he stinks, and when she has at last managed to tuck him up well in bed, he belches and farts like a sow. But the best is yet to come. Even in bed, this filthy creature cannot be contained by the orderly sheets: he suffers an attack from 'the cellar department' which produces 'a big heap of lumps', and he urinates in the bed so that 'a sow could even get a meal off him'.[43] Comical scenes ensue next morning when Flegmaticus awakens to his hangover.

In his conclusion to the poem, Sachs, distancing himself from the medical role, resumes his own narrative persona and offers a general statement about the dangers of alcohol excess for everyone. But this moralistic postscript does not remove the poem's ambivalence. Indeed, his earlier use of the theory of the humours serves to entrench the idea that intolerance to wine is a matter of physical constitution rather than of moral failing. Sachs, the poet of morality,[44] explicitly commends modest drinking in his final authorial coda, and then goes on to suggest that alcoholic excess can reveal psychological truth. Like the removal of clothing, drinking uncovers a man's 'true character' – in his cups, one sees whether a man is 'feminine and timid' (*weybish vnd klainmütig*) or 'unruly, wild and fierce' (*rumorisch toll vnd wütig*). Ironically, the disorderly, wild character, who poses such a problem for order-loving governments, is at least a real man. It is interesting that Sachs's phrase at this point is 'opens his secrets' (*öffnet seine heimligkeyt*), an expression which could be understood sexually.

In the age of 'social discipline', the supposed era of the growth of table manners and the period which we are asked to believe saw the development of social hygiene, filthiness exercised a powerful grip on the imagination. Take, for instance, Till Eulenspiegel's often repeated advice on how to get the lion's share of food at table: you place one finger over one nostril, blow two or three times, roll the snot into a ball and smear it over the food. Even the author of *Grobianus* found this a bit much: he recounts the tale but goes on to suggest doing the same thing with 'pepper or sour milk'.[45] His squeamishness points to the substance this desecration of manners is really about: excrement.

Indeed, the equation of vomit, excrement and food is a constant theme of the literature of excess. Often, it is connected with the animal world and with the dirtiest of animals, the pig. In the woodcuts which illustrate several of the pamphlets against drunkenness, pigs lick up the vomit which floods from the drunkards' open mouths, or nose eagerly around the stream of excrement. In the world of the release of bodily inhibition, dirt becomes clean and nourishing. The body's products – snot and faeces – are powerful dirt which enable the individual to extend his ego, claiming possession of food. Grobian often extols the power of breaking wind. Like incense, his farts can perfume the whole house, they are so noisy they sound like trumpets, they climb up into the air and, like an *alter ego*, wander about on their own like an untamed ruffian.[46]

The pleasures of this kind of writing, however, are not just the result of playful Bakhtinian reversals, transforming dirt into its opposite, cleanliness,[47] but have to do with the way such texts mobilize the forgotten physical pleasures of defecation. It is as if the laughter excited in the reader reproduces the release of control experienced in defecation. Here, the language of moralism, so far from imposing repression, enables the reader to gain access to an eroticism of anal sensation, and this is what makes the extended, absurd joke enjoyable. I do not think that we can gauge the pleasure of this writing without some use of psychoanalytic ideas,[48] but they may be employed, however, not to delineate a social psychology, as Elias might have done, but to explore the psychic pleasures which particular kinds of writing may incite.[49]

The two literatures of Grobian and of moralism were thus closely related. After all, Grobian claims to be an inversion with a didactic point: in Scheidt's German preface, the author states that since people always do the reverse of what they are warned to do, he will teach the reader how to be the complete oaf. This ironic inversion of moralism betrays the symbiotic relationship of the two genres. Hans Sachs's moral condemnation of drinking similarly owes its verve to its borrowings from the literature of drunken excess. In a man like Johann Fischart, Calvinist moralist and high priest of excess were rolled into one. The writer of the *Geschichtklitterung*, who reworks his Rabelaisian source to extend the scenes of excessive eating,[50] who scatters baroquely excessive streams of verbs in repeated fits of linguistic pyrotechnics, and who greatly develops the scatological elements in Rabelais's original, was also responsible for hymns of truly nauseating sentimentality.[51] Though Fischart sprinkled liberal doses of moral commentary over his reworking of Rabelais's *Gargantua*, the effect of the cocktail is to explode its own pomposity – it is as if the po-faced moralist cannot contain a belly laugh, and neither can his readers.[52]

VII

Both the prohibitions – what historians, misleadingly as I hope I have persuaded you, have named 'social discipline' – and the breaking of these taboos have to be understood together. The ordinances are not a simple literature of repression. Rather, they are one half of a cultural process which consisted of both the luxuriation in imagined bodily excess and its condemnation. Ordinances, moral literature and the literature of excess played with language in similar ways. Social discipline thus 'is' a matter of drinking, gorging and whoring, and it is an obsession rather than a mere repression. It was the prism through which sixteenth-century people thought about the boundaries of the body. They imagined control both in bodily and political terms: it was no accident that moralist movements should have been a key discourse for creating political legitimacy.

I think there are two methodological issues of more general interest which might arise from what I have been saying. The first concerns how we understand human psychology. Here I have been arguing against the still widespread view that the history of sexuality is the story of the imposition of regulations and repressions. This leaves us with the inadequate account of human psychology as a matter of containment of instincts. We have to pay attention to the extent to which many of these 'drives' are developmental, cultural creations, and we need to see 'repression' as part of a double process which also creates, rather than represses, its opposite. However, although I have argued here against Norbert Elias's model of social transformation in Europe, Elias formulated important questions. He was right to make us think about the relation between society and psyche. In this chapter I have sometimes drawn on Michel Foucault's work to criticize Elias, but I have resisted the temptation to view the process of discipline as the mere creation of discourse. The anatomizing of discourses, it seems to me, will not of itself supply us with an adequate psychology, nor explain the appeal and transformation of discourses. Though it will continue to be through language that we find out about people in the past, a history of sexuality which confines itself to linguistic taxonomy will be a poor thing.

The second concerns how we understand the contrast between prescription and practice. This contrast has been the bread and butter of social historians, who have claimed a privileged access to 'how it really was in practice despite the letter of the law'. I have argued elsewhere against seeing historical documents, themselves complex cultural products, as simple reflections of 'reality'. Here I would like to suggest that we might do better to understand the ordinances, too, not as the straightforward opposite of 'real daily life' but rather as pieces of writing which can equally benefit from literary techniques of analysis if we are to mine their psychological significance. This project requires us to replace them within the wider cultural context from which they came. Excess must be restored to the literature of discipline.

NOTES

1 Norbert Elias, *The Civilizing Process. Sociogenetic and Psychogenetic Investigations*, trans. Edmund Jephcott, 2 vols, Oxford 1978, 1982 (first published Basel 1939): vol. 1, *The History of Manners*; vol. 2, *State Formation and Civilization*; idem, *The Court Society*, trans. Edmund Jephcott, Oxford 1983 (first published Darmstadt and Neuwied 1969). For a critique of Norbert Elias, see Hans Peter Duerr, *Der Mythos vom Zivilisationsprozess*, vol. 1, *Nacktheit und Scham*, Frankfurt am Main 1988; vol. 2, *Intimität*, Frankfurt am Main 1989: vol. 3, *Obszönität und Gewalt*, Frankfurt am Main 1992; and reply by Michael Schröter, 'Scham im Zivilisationsprozess. Zur Diskussion mit Hans Peter Duerr', in Hermann Korte (ed.), *Gesellschaftliche Prozesse und individuelle Praxis. Bochumer Vorlesungen zu Norbert Elias' Zivilisationstheorie*, Frankfurt am Main 1990.

2 R. Po-Chia Hsia, *Social Discipline in the Reformation: Central Europe 1550–1750*, London and New York 1989, pp. 4–5.

3 Gerhard Oestreich, following in Elias's footsteps, raised these questions in relation to absolutism, and his work has been very influential among Reformation historians. But for him, 'social disciplining' was a secular, not a religious phenomenon whose success depended on the decline of religious feeling in the era following the wars of religion. Gerhard Oestreich, 'Strukturprobleme des europäischen Absolutismus', in his *Geist und Gestalt des frühmodernen Staates*, Berlin 1969; idem, *Neostoicism and the Early Modern State*, trans. David McLintock and eds B. Oestreich and H. Koenigsberger, Cambridge 1982. Oestreich's ideas have been interestingly developed by, among others, Robert Jütte in 'Poor Relief and Social Discipline in Sixteenth-Century Europe', *European Studies Review*, 11, 1981, pp. 25–52. Winifried Schulze, in a nuanced development of Oestreich's views, has pointed out that authorities during the Reformation were engaged in the same process, but he too argues that their religious concerns were incidental to the process of social disciplining, which sprang from needs which were fundamentally secular (Schulze, 'Gerhard Oestreichs Begriff "Sozialdisziplinierung in der frühen Neuzeit"', *Zeitschrift für historische Forschung*, 14, 1987, pp. 265–302). Elias also does not consider religious change to be of prime importance to the growth of manners and civilization. See J. Goudsblom, 'Responses to Norbert Elias's Work in England, Germany, the Netherlands, and France', in P. Gleichmann, J. Goudsblom and H. Korte (eds), *Human Figurations. Essays for Norbert Elias*, Amsterdam 1977, pp. 75–6.

4 Heinz Schilling, 'Die Konfessionalisierung im Reich. Religiöser und gesellschaftlicher Wandel in Deutschland zwischen 1555 und 1620', *Historische Zeitschrift*, 246, 1988, pp. 1–45; idem, 'Die "Zweite Reformation" als Kategorie der Geschichtswissenschaft', in H. Schilling (ed.), *Die reformiertie Konfessionali-*

sierung in Deutschland Das Problem der "Zweiten Reformation", Gütersloh 1986, pp. 387–438; Thomas Robisheaux, *Rural Society and the Search for Order in Early Modern Germany*, Cambridge 1989; William J. Wright, *Capitalism, the State, and the Lutheran Reformation: Sixteenth-century Hesse*, Athens, Ohio 1988; Georg Schmidt, 'Die "Zweite Reformation" im Gebiet des Wetterauer Grafen-vereins. Die Einführung des reformierten Bekenntnisses im Spiegel der Modernisierung gräflicher Herrschaften', in Schilling (ed.), *Reformierte Konfessionalisierung*; Paul Münch, *Zucht und Ordnung. Reformierte Kirchenver-fassungen im 16. und 17. Jahrhundert (Nassau-Dillenburg, Kurpfalz, Hessen-Kassel)*, Stuttgart 1978; Thomas Winckelbauer, 'Sozialdisziplinierung und Konfessionalisierung durch Grundherrschaft in den Österreichischen und böhmischen Ländern im 16. und 17. Jahrhundert', *Zeitschrift für historische Forschung*, 19, 1992, pp. 317–40. For confessionalization in Catholic areas see Wolfgang Reinhard, 'Gegenreformation als Modernisierung? Prolegomena zu einer Theorie des Konfessionellen Zeitalters', *Archiv für Reformationsgeschichte*, 68, 1977, pp. 226–52; for the argument that disciplining was well underway in towns before the Reformation, Werner Buchholz, 'Anfänge der Sozialdiszi-plinierung im Mittelalter. Die Reichsstadt Nürnberg als Beispiel', *Zeitschrift für historische Forschung*, 18, 1991, pp. 129–48. The material on confessionaliz-ation has been well summarized and developed in Hsia, *Social Discipline in the Reformation*. For an interesting application of similar ideas to a later period, see Marc Raeff, *The Well-Ordered Police State: Social and institutional change through law in the Germanies and Russia, 1600–1800*, New Haven, Conn. and London 1983.

5 Walter Köhler first alerted historians to the centrality of discipline in the early appeal of evangelicalism in south German areas. He located it in early evangelicalism, as an integral part of the appeal of the early Zurich Refor-mation of the 1520s. But whereas Köhler saw the phenomenon as a con-fessional and geographical one – part of what distinguished urban Zwinglians, who cared desperately about discipline, from Lutherans, who did not – we now need to understand 'discipline' more broadly: Walter Köhler, *Zürcher Ehegericht und Genfer Konsistorium*, 2 vols (Quellen und Abhandlungen zur schweizerischen Reformationsgeschichte 7, 10), Leipzig 1932, 1942.

6 Jörg Vögeli, *Schriften zur Reformation in Konstanz, 1519–1538*, 2 vols (Schriften zur Kirchen- und Rechtsgeschichte 39, 40, 41), Tübingen 1972–3, vol. 1, pp. 441ff. The Discipline Ordinance is reproduced in full by Vögeli and forms the natural climax to his narrative. See, on the Constance ordinance, Fritz Hauss, 'Blarers Zuchtordnungen', in Bernd Moeller (ed.), *Der Konstanzer Reformator Ambrosius Blarer 1492–1564. Gedenkschrift zu seinem 400. Todestag*, Constance and Stuttgart 1964; and Hans–Christoph Rublack, *Die Einführung der Reformation in Konstanz von den Anfängen bis zum Abschluss 1531* (Quellen und Forschungen zur Reformationsgeschichte 40), Gütersloh 1971, pp. 87–93.

7 *Aller des heiligen römischen Reichs gehaltene Reichstage, Abschiede etc. 1356–1654*, Mainz 1660, pp. 246–59, 455–73, 847–68; and see Josef Segall, *Geschichte und Strafrecht der Reichspolizeiordnungen von 1530, 1548 und 1577* (Strafrechtliche Abhandlungen 15), Breslau 1914.

8 Köhler, *Zürcher Ehegericht*; and Lyndal Roper, *The Holy Household. Women and morals in Reformation Augsburg*, Oxford 1989.

9 Roger Chartier (ed.), *A History of Private Life*, vol. 3, *Passions of the Renaissance*, trans. Arthur Goldhammer, Cambridge, Mass. 1989, pp. 15–17; and see also the introduction to the whole volume by Philippe Ariès, ibid., 'Introduction', pp. 4, 9.

10 Interestingly, Elias's own work need not be read in this way, since he also

accords an important role to the increasing subdivision of labour in leading to 'civilization'.

11 As is well known, even in Calvin's Geneva, the consistory had to struggle against secular authority and did not have clear power to excommunicate individuals until 1555. The range of solutions devised in southern German and Swiss cities are discussed in Köhler, *Zürcher Ehegericht*.

12 See Roper, *The Holy Household*, pp. 74–82.

13 Emil Sehling (ed.), *Die evangelischen Kirchenordnungen des xvi Jahrhunderts*, Leipzig and Tübingen 1902–77, vol. 12, Bayern II, Lindau Zuchtordnung 1533, pp. 186–97, and note p. 197, n. v from 1554 redaction of the ordinance, section headed 'Dass niemand wider die zuchtordnung reden soll'; Bekanntmachung zur Einschärfung der Zuchtordnung 1539, pp. 198–9; and introduction pp. 181ff. On the Reformation in Lindau, see Johannes Wolfart, 'Political Culture and Religion in Lindau, 1520–1628', Ph.D. diss., University of Cambridge, 1993.

14 Merry E. Wiesner, 'Paternalism in Practice: The control of servants and prostitutes in early modern German cities', in Phillip N. Bebb and Sherrin Marshall (eds), *The Process of Change in Early Modern Europe. Essays in honor of Miriam Usher Chrisman*, Athens, Ohio 1988, pp. 193–5: the brothel was finally closed in 1562, but even then the council doubted whether its decision had been prudent.

15 Thomas Robisheaux, 'Peasants and Pastors: Rural youth control and the Reformation in Hohenlohe, 1540–1680', *Social History*, 6, 1981, pp. 281–300.

16 Martin Bucer, *Deutsche Schriften*, ed. Robert Stupperich, Gütersloh 1960–, vol. 8, pp. 249–78; Sehling, *Die evangelischen Kirchenordnungen*, vol. 8/I, Hessen, pp. 82–91, 101–12, 148–54 and 'Introduction', pp. 10–23.

17 The timely arrival of the plague helped him to gain the councillors' attention, but the new Reformation was never realized and Blarer's dream of creating a pious people was not fulfilled. Hauss, 'Blarers Zuchtordnungen', pp. 120–1.

18 Roper, *The Holy Household*, pp. 86–7, 20.

19 Gerhard Oestreich, 'Policey und Prudentia civilis in der barocken Gesellschaft von Stadt und Staat', in Brigitta Oestreich (ed.), *Strukturprobleme der frühen Neuzeit. Ausgewählte Aufsätze*, Berlin 1980, p. 371.

20 See, for example, William Beik's brilliant *Absolutism and Society in Seventeenth-Century France. State power and provincial aristocracy in Languedoc*, Cambridge 1985, esp. pp. 336ff.

21 Sehling, *Die evangelischen Kirchenordnungen*, vol. 12, Bayern II, Lindau 1533, p. 194.

22 Elias, *The Civilizing Process*, vol. 1, pp. 169–91, much of which concerns Erasmus's attitudes to women; vol. 2, pp. 77–82, 90: here, where Elias makes interesting observations about women and Minnesang, and the different position of women in a male-dominated society, it is largely male attitudes to women and the role of women in the male warrior psyche which he is describing. Women do not feature in the following section in vol. 1 'On Changes in Aggressiveness' (pp. 191–205). For a development of some of the possibilities within the Elias framework, see Schröter, 'Scham im Zivilisation-sprozess', esp. pp. 76, 82–5.

23 See the forthcoming doctoral dissertation of B. Ann Tlusty on drink in the early modern town, 'The Devil's Altar: Drinking and society in early modern Augsburg', Ph.D. diss., University of Maryland 1994.

24 For an excellent recreation of the social history of night life and the ambivalences of policing tactics see Norbert Schindler, 'Nächtliche Ruhestörung. Zur Sozialgeschichte der Nacht in der frühen Neuzeit', in *idem, Widerspenstige Leute. Studien zur Volkskultur in der frühen Neuzeit*, Frankfurt am Main 1992.

25 Sehling, *Die evangelischen Kirchenordnungen*, vol. 12, Bayern II, Lindau 1533, p. 190; vol. 8, Hesse I, 1543, p. 149, mentions 'the great indiscipline which is committed when one vomits so shamefully and consumes and then brings up the gifts of God so filthily'.

26 ibid., vol. 12, Bayern II, Lindau 1533, p. 196; and in Basel, the youth had to pay only 5 shillings compensation if the woman took the sexual initiative: Susanna Burghartz, 'Jungfräulichkeit oder Reinheit? Zur Änderung von Argumentationsmustern vor dem Basler Ehegericht im 16. und 17. Jahrhundert', in Richard van Dülmen (ed.), *Dynamik der Tradition*, Frankfurt am Main 1992, p. 15.

27 On marital violence and women's use of the courts, see Rainer Beck, 'Frauen in Krise. Eheleben und Ehescheidung in der ländlichen Gesellschaft Bayerns während des Ancien Regime', and Rebekka Habermas, 'Frauen und Männer im Kampf um Leib, Ökonomie und Recht. Zur Beziehung der Geschlechter im Frankfurt der Frühen Neuzeit,' in van Dülmen (ed.), *Dynamik der Tradition*.

28 Hermann Heidrich, 'Grenzübergänge. Das Haus und die Volkskultur in der frühen Neuzeit', in Richard van Dülmen (ed.), *Kultur der einfachen Leute. Bayerisches Volksleben vom 16. bis zum 19. Jahrhundert*, Munich 1983.

29 See, for example, Günther Pallaver, *Die Verdrängung der Sexualität in der frühen Neuzeit am Beispiel Tirols*, Vienna 1987, which regards the Catholic church as having been instrumental in the process of 'disciplining' through its use of the confessional in the period after the Reformation and explicitly draws on Elias; Heinrich Richard Schmidt, 'Die Christianisierung des Sozialverhaltens als permanente Reformation. Aus der Praxis reformierter Sittengerichte in der Schweiz während der frühen Neuzeit', *Zeitschrift für historische Forschung*, Beiheft 9, 1989, pp. 113–63; Thomas Kleinspehn, *Der flüchtige Blick. Sehen und Identität in der Kultur der Neuzeit*, Reinbek bei Hamburg 1989; on disciplining the clergy, Bruce Gordon, *Clerical Discipline and the Rural Reformation. The synod in Zürich, 1532–1580*, Berne and Frankfurt am Main 1992; and see Michael Schröter's work, including *"Wo zwei zusammenkommen in rechter Ehe". Sozio- und psychogenetische Studien über die Eheschliessungsvorgänge vom 12. bis 15. Jahrhundert*, Frankfurt am Main 1985; and 'Zur Intimisierung der Hochzeitsnacht im 16. Jahrhundert', in Hans-Jürgen Bachorski (ed.), *Lust und Ordnung. Bilder von Liebe und Ehe im 16. Jahrhundert*, Konstanz 1991.

30 Michel Foucault, *The History of Sexuality*, vol. 1, *An Introduction*, London 1979.

31
>   Leichtfertige/ hürische geberden übet man nach süssem seytenspil/ vnnd vnkeuschen liedern: da begreifft man frawen vnd junckfrawen mit vnkeuschen henden: man küst einander mit hürischem vmbfahen: vnd die glider/ welche die natur verborgen vnnd scham bedeckt hat/ enntblöst offtmals geylheyt vnd vnder dem manttele einer kurzweil vnnd spiles/ wirdt schand vnnd laster bedeckt....

>   (Melchior Ambach, *Von Tantzen/ Vrtheil/ Auss heiliger Schrifft/ vnd den alten Christlichen Lerern gestelt*, Frankfurt am Main 1564, fo. B iv v)

32 See Ambach's rhetorical climax, 'Was ist aber tanzen anders/ dann vnkeusch geberde/ wort vnnd werck?', Ambach, *Von Tantzen*, fo. C ii v, 'venerisch Tanzen', fo. C iii r.

33 Ria Stambaugh (ed.), *Teufelbücher im Auswahl*, 5 vols, Berlin 1970–80.

34 This was a point which Marx made in his 1847 attack on Karl Heinzen. Ostensibly condemning the petty-bourgeois nature of this kind of writing, he speaks of the 'aesthetic revulsion' it arouses, but follows this with a wonderfully Grobianesque sentence which zestfully borrows the punning, excessive style it purports to revile:

Flat, bombastic, bragging thrasonical, putting on a great show of rude vigour in attack, yet hysterically sensitive to the same quality in others; brandishing the sword with enormous waste of energy, lifting it high in the air only to let it fall down flat; constantly preaching morality and constantly offending against it; sentiment and turpitude most absurdly conjoined; concerned only with the point at issue, yet always missing the point; using with equal arrogance petty-bourgeois scholarly semi-erudition against popular wisdom, and so-called "sound common sense" against science; discharging itself in ungovernable breadth with a certain complacent levity; clothing a philistine message in a plebeian form; wrestling with the literary language to give it, so to speak, a purely corporeal character, willingly pointing at the writer's body in the background, which is itching in every fibre to give a few exhibitions of its strength, to display its broad shoulders and publicly to stretch its limbs; proclaiming a healthy mind in a healthy body; unconsciously infected by the sixteenth century's most abstruse controversies and by its fever of the body; in thrall to dogmatic, narrow thinking and at the same time appealing to petty practice in the face of all real thought; raging against reaction, reacting against progress, incapable of making the opponent seem ridiculous, but ridiculously abusing him through the whole gamut of tones; Solomon and Marcolph, Don Quixote and Sancho Panza, a visionary and a philistine in one person; a loutish form of indignation, a form of indignant loutishness; and suspended like an enveloping cloud over it all, the self-satisfied philistine's consciousness *of his own virtue* – such was the *grobian literature* of the sixteenth century.

(Karl Marx and Friedrich Engels, *Collected Works*, vol. 6, London 1976, pp. 312–13)

35 For a superb discussion of carnival and the culture of laughter see Norbert Schindler, 'Karneval, Kirche und verkehrte Welt. Zur Funktion der Lachkultur im 16. Jahrhundert', in *idem, Widerspenstige Leute*.

36 One famous predecessor was Johann von Schwarzenberg's *Der Zudrincker vnd Prasser Gesatze, Ordnung vnd Instruction*, Oppenheim 1512–13, who was later a supporter of the Reformation. His pamphlet was reissued and incorporated into Matthäus Friderich's Devil Book against drinking in 1557. See also Heinrich Stromer von Auerbach, *Eine getrewe, vleissige vnd ehrliche Verwarnung Widder das hesliche laster der Trunkenheit*, translated into German and published by the Lutheran Georg Spalatin at Wittenberg 1531. Sebastian Franck wrote *Von dem grewlichen Laster der Trunkenheit*, Nuremberg 1531; Leonhard Schertlin, *Dialogus von Künstlichem vnd höflichem, Auch vihischem vnd vnzüchtigem Trinken*, Strasbourg 1538; Jörg Wickram, *Dialog von dem mächtigen Hauptlaster der Trunckenheit*, Strasbourg 1551. Important work on this literature and its relation to the actual social customs of drinking is being done by Ann Tlusty at Augsburg: Tlusty, 'The Devil's Altar'.

37 For a different assessment of Fischart, see Mikhail Bakhtin, *Rabelais and His World*, trans. Hélène Iswolsky 1968, Bloomington, Ind. 1984, pp. 62–3: Bakhtin sees Fischart as a moralist in whose pages the original, primitive folk culture of the Rabelaisian original still survives despite the German moralist tendency to define the material as indecent. I think Bakhtin does not fully recognize the pleasurable nature of the 'disgust' the German moralists tried to incite in their readers.

38 *Eulenspiegel Reimensweiss*, Frankfurt am Main 1572; *Das Lalebuch*, 1597, reprinted Stuttgart 1970; see Peter Honegger, *Die Schiltburgerchronik und ihr Verfasser Johann Fischart*, Hamburg 1982, pp. 118–21.

39 See Peter Stallybrass and Allan White's stimulating *Politics and Poetics of*

Transgression, London 1986. They contrast the 'grotesque' with the 'classical' body, which they term 'bourgeois', although 'bourgeois' moralism creates both; but this formulation also carries with it the idea of an Elias-influenced model of historical transformation: ibid., pp. 22, 31, 89–90, 188, 197.

40　Friedrich Dedekind, *Grobianus. De morum simplicitate*, Frankfurt am Main 1549; *idem, Grobianus. Von groben sitten*, trans. C. Scheidt, Worms 1551. The original was extended and even developed to include a female Grobian: *idem, Grobianus und Grobiana*, trans. C. Scheidt, Frankfurt am Main 1567. For a modern edition of the 1551 version, *Neudrucke deutscher Literaturwerke des XVI und XVII Jahrhunderts*, nos 34, 35, reprinted Halle 1966.

41　Hans Sachs, *Die vier wunderberlichen Eygenschafft vnd würckung des Weins*, Nuremberg, G. Merckel 1553.

42

    Vnd bsult sich im kot wie ein schwein.

    Leyt etwan ein weyl inn eim mist.

(fo. A iiii v)

43

    Vil-leicht pruntzt er auch inn das pett.

    Ein saw wol bey jm narung hett

(ibid.)

44　Maria E. Müller's apposite phrase. See her *Der Poet der Moralität. Untersuchungen zu Hans Sachs* (Europäische Hochschulschriften series 1, Deutsche Sprache und Literatur, vol. 800), Berne 1985; and for her different interpretation of similar material, see pp. 213–42. On the technique of negative didacticism, see her 'Der andere Faust. Melancholie und Individualität in der Historia von D. Johann Fausten', *Deutsche Vierteljahrsschrift für Literaturwissenschaft und Geistesgeschichte*, 60, 1986, pp. 572–608.

45　Dedekind, *Grobianus*, modern reprint *Neudrucke*, p. 35.

46　ibid., pp. 36, 43, 55–6.

47　This is the approach taken by Bakhtin in *Rabelais and His World*.

48　See Sigmund Freud, *Der Witz und seine Beziehung zum Unbewussten*, in Alexander Mitscherlich *et al.* (eds), *Freud: Studienausgabe*, 10 vols, rev. edn, Frankfurt am Main 1989, vol. 4, pp. 13–219, which, however, deploys a mechanistic, economically influenced model of psychic expenditure and repression that I found less helpful in interpreting this humour.

49　We might note that the inverse of this set of excremental themes is of course that racist stereotype beloved of sixteenth- and seventeenth-century polemicists, the Jewish sow. Here the Jew is depicted as nourished by the sow, who is the creature of dirt. The Jew is therefore a shit-eater, one who is totally unclean and subject to others. If the Christian man is imagined as being omnipotent, through the phallic magic of his excrement, the Jew, nourished on the excrement of others, lacks a phallus – something which may help to explain why the myth that circumcised Jews were in league to capture and kill Christian boys was so powerful among Christians. Jews were believed to use Christian blood in rituals. Woodcut images of such scenes often show the rabbi's knife pointing at the boy's penis. On this myth in Germany see R. Po-Chia Hsia, *The Myth of Ritual Murder. Jews and magic in Reformation Germany*, New Haven, Conn. and London 1988.

50　Florence M. Weinberg, *Gargantua in a Convex Mirror. Fischart's view of Rabelais*, New York 1986; and on Fischart, popular culture and language, Pia Holenstein, *Der Ehediskurs der Renaissance in Fischarts Geschichtklitterung. Kritische Lektüre des fünften Kapitels*, Berne and Frankfurt am Main 1991.

51 See G. Below and J. Zacher (eds), *Johann Fischarts geistliche Lieder, christliche Kinderzucht und Lob der Lauten*, Berlin 1849, for example, pp. 90ff.

52 See also Anna Leblans, 'Grimmelshausen and the Carnivalesque: The polarization of courtly and popular carnival in *Deer abenteuerliche Simplicissimus*', *Modern Language Notes*, 105, no. 3, 1990, pp. 494–511.

Part III

8 Exorcism and the theology of the body

How a culture imagines the body is one of its most fundamental and revealing elements; and how individuals imagine their own bodies relates to their identity at the most profound level.[1] Theories of the body, whether explicit or implicit, may assume a sharp division between the body and the mind, or they may articulate a profound interconnection between what is mental, physical and spiritual. Among the issues which cluster around concepts of the body are questions of individuation, how we define the boundaries of a person and his or her bonds with other people, living or dead; the causal links between illness or other kinds of physical harm and psychic, emotional or spiritual powers; and the nature of what we might call a 'person' and his or her relation with the divine.

Some of the distance between our world and that of early modern Europe can be measured in the foreignness – and familiarity – of its concepts of the body. Souls could be thought to exist without bodies, the body could be the battleground of demons, and other people's malevolent sorcery could cause illness. Times of social and cultural upheaval are likely to bring with them changes in the way the body is understood. Because such concepts are so primary, any disturbance in them is likely to create a ripple of troubling changes which cannot be contained in a closed philosophical or theological context. Sixteenth-century Germany, I shall argue, was a society in which shifts of these kinds were taking place, as people fought over the relations between God and mankind, flesh and spirit, body and soul, sorcery and the demonic. To chart these shifts properly we need to explore not only the terrain familiar to the historian of concepts, the theological debates between Catholics and Protestants, but also what seems at first to be the marginal realm of sixteenth-century culture, the province of sorcerers, practitioners of magic and their clients.

Sixteenth-century Augsburg, a large and powerful imperial city, furnishes an interesting case study of these transitions. Augsburg in the later sixteenth century was a ferment of different religious attitudes. Majority Protestant, it was none the less ruled by a system of religious balance imposed by the Catholic Emperor Charles V following the city's defeat in the Schmalkaldic War.[2] Power was shared between Catholics and Protestants and concentrated in the hands of merchants and patricians, so that Catholics enjoyed far greater political influence than they had numbers. Guilds, which the emperor viewed as the seed-beds of Protestantism and of insurrection, were abolished and the influence of guildsfolk curtailed. The 1560s and 1570s, however, saw the emergence of a revitalized Catholicism. Under the influence of the Jesuit Peter Canisius, Catholicism began to win new and powerful converts. Chief among the newly militant Catholics were the Fuggers, Augsburg's internationally famous banking family.[3] By the 1570s Augsburg had become a theatre for the debates between Counter-Reformation Catholics and Protestants in southern Germany, and by 1579, with the founding of the Jesuit College, the institutions of the Counter-Reformation had an assured position in the town.[4]

These same years also saw a growth in criminal cases connected with magic, so that by the end of the century, sorcery had become part of the staple fare of criminal justice. Why should the issue of sorcery have suddenly become something with which routine criminal justice began increasingly to concern itself? Part of the explanation, I want to suggest, must be sought in the volatile religious debates of the later sixteenth century.

CATHOLIC AND PROTESTANT THEOLOGIES OF THE BODY

Underlying the battle of theologies between Protestants and Catholics in late sixteenth-century Augsburg were arguments about the nature of the relationship between human beings and supernatural powers. So fundamental were these disputes that, rather than finding their expression in intellectual debate alone, they were in large part internalized to the point where religious conflict became dramatized in the body itself. For Catholics, false religion was expressed physically: the body, in revolt against heresy, could sicken. Its healing required the restoration of true belief or even the expulsion of demons. Conversion to Catholicism was experienced above all through a long and dramatic process of struggle. This might be intellectual struggle, or it might involve physical struggle with demons who could hurl the sufferer on the ground, subjecting the body to violent contortions and pain. Counter-Reformation priests sought to demonstrate the truth of their doctrine by performing exorcisms which graphically illustrated their authority. In a series of dramatic cases from 1563 onwards, these priests carried out first private and then public exorcisms, accomplishing by their means remarkable and shocking conversions of élite Protestants, particularly women, to Catholicism. The powerful Fugger family played a key role in these events, and servants from the family's houses supplied most of the subjects for the exorcisms.[5] Indeed, so important were these events to Jesuit success in the city that one might argue that the Counter-Reformation in Augsburg progressed by means of exorcisms. Crowds thronged to witness them, and numerous reconversions resulted. Protestants were compelled to discuss the issue. The passionate religiosity of the Fugger households, nurseries of the renascent Catholicism, was fuelled by the emotional turmoil of exorcism and reconversion – sometimes, indeed, to the alarm even of Jesuits like Peter Canisius.[6]

The resonances of these lurid episodes in sixteenth-century society derived from a fundamental theological shift brought about by the Reformation in the understanding of the relationship between flesh and spirit. Though it has received less attention from Reformation historians than other doctrinal changes, its significance was deep and its implications long-lasting. Protestants greatly weakened the link between the physical and the divine. As they did so, they forced a reassessment of the theological understanding of the body. This can be seen most clearly in four key changes which the Reformation accomplished.

First, Protestants permitted clerical marriage, thereby denying that clergy had to be celibate, and separating virginity from holiness. What we might term the Protestant domestication of sexuality rested partly on the Protestant belief in human nature: all humans, a few special individuals aside, were sexual in nature, and their sexuality was a matter of human constitution, not something which an individual could renounce by means of vows. Associated with this was a second major shift, the conviction of man's fundamental sinfulness and an emphasis on the distance between the human and the divine. This issue became focused on the question of the nature of Mary, as Protestants sought to relegate her to the status of a purely human model for the believer. Her human nature, mired in sin, could never be united with the divine, they argued, for only Christ, the son of God, could participate in God's glory. This position rested on a sharp demarcation of the godly and human natures, a separation of categories so fundamental to Protestant thinking that some theologically unorthodox thinkers like Caspar Schwenckfeld, grappling with the problem of how the divine could be manifest in human form, even went so far as to claim that Christ himself must have had two separate natures, a human and a divine.[7] Third, Protestants denied that divine forces could be captured in the physical, whether representations of saints or saints' relics, or even, as the radical Zwinglian position had it, in the host itself. The holy could not therefore be manifest in parts of the human body, a theological position which widened the gulf between things of the divine world and matters of the flesh. And fourth, the more Protestants stressed the difference between the profane and the religious, marking the boundaries between the two worlds more sharply in ritual and abolishing those popular customs which threatened to elide the two, the more they were drawn to making a sharper distinction between the divine and the body. The world of carnival and of carnality could have no place in the church's sacred territory.[8]

Catholicism of the Counter-Reformation responded to the challenge Protestants posed to the relation between body and spirit by reiterating and even strengthening the connection between the two. Catholic writers like Peter Canisius, the Jesuit active in Augsburg, re-emphasized the cults of saints and wrote forthrightly in favour of relics and of blessings. They advocated pilgrimages, the regimen of fasting and feasting, they emphasized the cult of the Virgin, forming new sodalities in her honour, and they commended images.[9] Sacred power could indeed be inherent in material things, and the holy could be manifest in the body of a saint. Virginity, they insisted, was an estate especially pleasing to God, and they exalted the special role of the priest who was a custodian of divine things. The priest had also to be chaste. Not only, unlike his Protestant compeers, must he be an unmarried man, but as performer of the divine miracle in which the Host becomes flesh, he must now be seen to be celibate, removed from the entanglements of earthly flesh.

These contrasts, however, should not be overdrawn. Protestants, like Catholics, could believe in demons and think God and the Devil were active in the natural world, though their resolution of the relation between the spiritual and natural worlds was often uncomfortable.[10] And the relation between body and soul sometimes confused even the Catholic faithful as well. Much to Canisius's dismay, Ursula Fugger and Johannes Fugger seriously entertained belief in a kind of transmigration of souls, holding that the souls of the dead could migrate into the bodies of living people.[11] Heretical views of this kind were a product of theological instability. For Catholics as for Protestants, the precise relationship between bodies, spirits and demons proved hard to define.

EXORCISM

It was exorcism which provided the issue that inflamed the battle between the confessions in the decades of the 1560s and 1570s, and dramatized the questions of the relationship between body and soul. In 1564, circumstances impelled Canisius to deviate from his planned text and to preach a sermon on possession.[12] He was responding to a series of cases of exorcism, carried out by priests at Augsburg. The temperature of debate rose, and in 1568 the council stepped in, banning public exorcisms and, in an even-handed manner, also banning the Protestants from preaching too vigorously against the Catholics.[13] Polemicists in and beyond the city began to debate the status of exorcism, and in 1571 a veritable pamphlet war was joined as Matheus Eisengrein publicly defended Canisius's miraculous exorcism of the seventh Devil from a maid from Augsburg in Our Lady's Chapel at Altötting. None the less, the issue was never an easy one for Catholics, since it exposed their own unresolved theology of body, soul and demons. The leaders of the Jesuit order were reserved on the question of exorcism. Loyola never participated in one and Laynez was mistrustful of them.[14] Indeed, Canisius met with criticism within his own order for his exorcisms, and seems to have found what rapidly became the Fugger women's mania for exorcism difficult to moderate. Writing to his superiors he expressed reservations about the journey to Rome of his star convert, Ursula Fugger, who was hoping to secure successful exorcisms for another two of her servants there.[15] Both Canisius's precise attitude to exorcism, and his theory of demonic possession, are difficult to reconstruct.[16]

Exorcism posed the question of the nature of the relation between body and spirit in peculiarly stark form because it represented religious truth in a way that depended on physical sensation. What particularly struck contemporaries about possession, even Protestants like the chronicler Paul Hector Mair, was its intensely physical character: it was the wide open mouth, the distension of the tongue, and the hands outstretched to Heaven which captured Mair's imagination when he recounted the curious case of a possessed woman who had jumped out of the window of her house.[17] It was as if the body had itself become a kind of blank sheet, with horror written clearly upon it, transparent evidence of the Devil's presence.

Accounts of exorcism by Catholic propagandists also stressed the writhing, pain and agony of the subject. The famous exorcism of the seventh Devil from Anna Bernhauser at Altötting took three days. This, too, was an exorcism in which the Fuggers played lead roles. In his description of the woman's torments, Matheus Eisengrein drew attention to the twenty-four tortures she was to undergo – five of which, according to the demon, were on account of the Fuggers![18] The successful exorcism required her master Marx Fugger to hold her in his lap while others present – his wife Sibilla, Canisius and another priest – strove to support her as the Devil threw her about.[19] In this kind of physical witnessing of religious struggle all those who surrounded the possessed individual had an active part to play, supporting the sufferer with their hands, and becoming aware of the awesome strength of demons through touch and motion as they battled to hold the sufferer still. Intense religious experience could thus be expressed in the physical language of holding and comforting. Physical contact could even be permitted to override class boundaries without arousing the taint of suspicion of sexual impropriety. For the active onlookers, the possessed person's suffering offered a kind of struggle by proxy, indeed, sometimes literally so. Thus the Fugger wives, Catholic converts who had undergone the agony of conversion to the faith,[20] did not themselves experience exorcism – instead it was their serving women who provided the subjects for the exorcisms. There was deep psychological truth in Eisengrein's claim that five of the 'torments' had been for the Fuggers: just as the Catholic could accumulate works on another soul's account, so Anna Bernhauser's body suffered pains on their behalf.

But it was above all on the body of the possessed individual that the drama of exorcism focused. The signs of spiritual disruption could be smelt, seen, heard and felt in his or her body. A loathsome stench was emitted as demons left the body, and its limbs were endowed with unnatural strength – even five people could not hold Anna Bernhauser still.[21] As the individual writhed in torments of agony, normal social comportment and bodily discipline were forgotten. So also, Susanna, the daughter of Michael Roschman, suffered from frenzies in which she would attack strangers, or fall senseless on the floor, sweat profusely, scream and ask for knives.[22] When she was given holy water, she began to let out piteous piercing cries, and doubled herself up so that her head almost touched her feet – and when Dr Scheibenhart attempted to exorcize her, she pulled up her bound feet to her head so that 'she uncovered her own nakedness most wretchedly'.[23] Veronica Stainer, another possessed woman whose story was told by Sebastian Khueller, sought to leap out of the window;[24] Anna Bernhauser was thrown about so harshly that the onlookers thought she would be dashed in a thousand pieces.[25] The physical dislocation and disorganization of the individual were expressed in the loss of ordered functioning of the limbs. The body might even change shape, swelling grotesquely as Khueller described Veronica Stainer, until head, neck and breast became deformed.[26] As the individual's bodily silhouette became warped and distended, so, too, his or her outer social identity was sloughed off. The body became the glass within which its demonic inhabitants cavorted.

These inversions extended even to the point of reversing gender. Instead of using Anna Bernhauser's female voice and comportment, the Devil spoke through her 'with a coarse and almost masculine voice'.[27] Witnesses heard the Devil raging in Michael Roschman's daughter, speaking in a 'quite coarse man's voice', saying 'Ho, ho, ho, priest, I'm not leaving the house.'[28] Veronica Stainer had two voices, one her normal voice, 'natural, small, feminine and virginal', the other 'strange, coarse, unnatural, heavy, masculine snuffling and rasping'. With the latter, she cursed God and sang ribald drinking songs, spewing forth a torrent of insults.[29]

The disturbance in the religious realm – time and again Catholic pamphlets blamed the Lutherans for the disorder – was thus expressed somatically. This marked a change from the form which religious upheaval had taken earlier in the century. Early evangelicalism was not marked by somatic outpourings. Protestants exhorted individuals to live chaste disciplined lives, to shun excess and seek their own salvation. At the same time, while evangelicals sharpened the distinction between

things of the spirit and things of the world, their arguments tended to
sever the chains of causation between the divine and the mundane. In
early mainstream evangelicalism, extreme bodily states were not taken
to mark out an individual as possessed of especial spiritual gifts. Protestantism in its early years brought not so much a secularization of the
world as a desomatization of the spiritual. This is not to say that
evangelicals had no concept of the physical manifestation of spiritual
states: the individual's journey of salvation was often imagined as leading through the stages of despair in which the individual might groan
aloud over his or her own sin. But the physical expression was not in
itself required, nor did it demand the witnessing of others. Indeed, so
little were individuals held to be capable of being temporarily absent
from their own body that even drunkenness was considered not to
absolve them from full moral responsibility for their actions. Instead, as
an additional sin, it provided grounds for increased punishment.

Exorcism directly addressed Protestant theology of the body and its
belief in the distance between the human and the divine. Here one
crucial issue was the status of Mary. For Protestants, she was to be
regarded as the human mother of Jesus, not the divine Queen of Heaven.
Protestants had no female figure who might represent the divine. But
Counter-Reformation Catholics advocated Mary's veneration, and she
played an active role in exorcisms. The liturgy of exorcism often made
use of repeated Hail Marys, vindicating the efficacy of prayer to the
Virgin, and exorcists taught the prayer to Protestant victims of possession as a sure remedy against the Devil's power. Their Protestant
opponents smelt a rat whenever the prayer was used – to them it was
a sure sign that the Devil, not God, was at work. One Protestant minister
noted approvingly that a poor young sick woman whom the Jesuits
were tormenting with attempted exorcisms steadfastly refused to pray
to Mary, holding by her evangelical faith.[30] Canisius invoked Mary's aid
as he began the exorcism at Altötting, and Mary appeared to Anna
Bernhauser accompanied by two angels while Anna recovered from the
demon's assaults.[31] Catherine Gutleb, another member of the Fugger
household, went into trances and beheld the Virgin in her heavenly
blue cloak.[32] Demons were particularly noted for their irreverence to
Mary.[33] Just as Catholic militants sought to make Protestants confess the
power of the Virgin, so the blaspheming demon at Altötting was finally
forced to bow to Mary, kissing the earth seven times and begging her
forgiveness. These events were described at length by Matheus
Eisengrein in a tract depicting the miracles which the Virgin had performed at Altötting and advertising the virtues of Marian pilgrimages
to the site.[34] Taken up by Albert V of Bavaria, the shrine, which had
sunk into obscurity, became an important pilgrimage place once more.[35]
Canisius himself, in a stupendous work containing 4,000 biblical refer-

ences and 10,000 from patristic and scholastic authors, was later to create a monument of scholarship endorsing her cult.[36]

Theologically, the Protestant changes in attitudes towards images, clerical celibacy and relics discussed above contributed to an attenuation of the links between the physical and the spiritual. In their battles with the Catholics, Protestants could sometimes seem to represent a religion utterly divorced from the bodily. So Johann Marbach concluded his lengthy attempted refutation of the miracle at Altötting with a list of Protestant 'miracles' to counter those of the Papists.[37] The six miracles of Lutheranism he enumerated – the demolition of the papacy and the uncovering of Antichrist, the useless resistance of the Pope, the endurance of Lutheran teaching, the hindering of the Devil's work, the power of the sacrament and, finally, the German Bible – were, however, forbiddingly abstract. As wonders of doctrine, they were hardly likely to out-miracle the Jesuits. They involved no intervention of the divine in the bodies of human individuals. Protestant miracles of this sort are characterized by a kind of somatic evacuation of the divine.

For the Lutheran Marbach, one of the signs that Canisius's exorcisms were in reality 'collusions' with the Devil was the fact that the exorcisms lasted so long and involved physical struggle. True exorcisms, he maintained, were effected instantaneously and without pain.[38] This claim amounted to a rejection of the concept, so central to Catholic narratives, of religious conversion as a physical struggle which needed to be waged over time. Marbach, and others like him, repudiated the spectacle of pain which testified to the physical struggle with demons. Religious truths, so far as Marbach was concerned, were not mapped out in the body of the believer as a sign for pious onlookers to interpret, nor could the body, through agony, 'speak' divine things.

Interestingly, too, one of Marbach's chief targets – indeed, one of his proofs that the alleged miracles were diabolic collusions – was Mariolatry.[39] Condemning what he saw as wrong-headed worship of a human being, Marbach was concerned to insist upon the distinctness of the natures of God and man, and to elaborate the doctrine of original sin:

> the son of God did not take on the Virgin Mary and unite his godly nature personally, but from her flesh and blood alone he took on true human nature, and therefore she could not then have been absorbed into the Holy Trinity, since her flesh and blood had been taken on by the son of God. She is and remains outside the Holy Trinity, a pure human being, with and amongst other creatures.[40]

He condemned the exorcism because it had employed the godless Hail Mary. Mariolatry, a litmus test of Protestant separation of the divine and the human, was at stake in exorcism. For Protestants, its involvement was yet further evidence of wrong belief; for Catholics, Mary ought to be invoked in exorcism and the help she gave vindicated her veneration.

There was more than one stand, however, which Protestants might take on the question of exorcism. Indeed, the issue exposed the range of Protestant views surrounding the basic theology of the body. Some, like Marbach, argued that the whole Altötting affair was a trick of the Devil, and insisted that no exorcism had taken place. Marbach did admit, however, that genuine exorcisms were possible. At least one Protestant pastor attempted to beat the Jesuits at their own game at Augsburg and undertake exorcisms – without success. Others, like the doctor and humanist chronicler Achilles Pirminius Gasser who reported this case with some amusement,[41] remained determinedly contemptuous of such priestcraft, preferring a natural, physiological explanation for illness and deriding what they held to be superstition. Gasser poked fun at the credulous crowds who flocked to the village of Mühlhausen in 1564, prominent citizens among them, because they believed a rumour that all the devils and witches for miles around were to meet there for a sabbath.[42] He ridiculed the possessed women's attempts at Greek and Hebrew – as garbled as that of their priestly teachers, he noted – and he laughed at the comically homespun names of their demons, 'Doghead', 'Ravenfoot', 'Horsedirt' and so on.[43]

Scepticism of a more measured kind was the mode of attack adopted by Christoph Jacobellus, a Lutheran preacher, in an account (which probably circulated privately) designed to rebut the allegations that he had turned Catholic when confronted with a successful Jesuit exorcism.[44] The subject was a woman in the city hospital and the event had been staged under the aegis of Jörg Fugger's wife in the Fugger palace. For Jacobellus too, however, it was bodily comportment which offered the decisive proof as to whether demonic possession was involved. When the Jesuits tried to stage a public exorcism, he avers, the woman's comportment was modest and chaste, evincing no signs of demonic perturbation – clear proof that her ailment was of natural not demonic origin. Her sighs and groanings were to be diagnosed, he claimed, not as the outpourings of a body in the grip of satanic power, but as the toiling of the soul weeping over its own sins, a familiar stage along the path of the individual towards salvation through faith alone.[45] However, even his meticulous account had to concede that Dr Wendel had successfully exorcized another woman of the Fugger household earlier on.[46] Moreover, the framework of his analysis, and the importance he attached to bodily comportment, served to underpin rather than undermine the belief that bodies could indeed house demons.

Other Protestants even tried to press the diabolic into the service of propagandist comedy. One Protestant mock poem celebrated the case of a Jesuit who supposedly disguised himself as a Devil and hid in the bedroom of a maid who worked for the Fuggers.[47] This missionary desperado hoped to shock the young Protestant serving woman into renouncing her belief. He met a sticky end, stabbed to death by a fearless Protestant, who was surprised when the Devil did not dematerialize at the first blow. A wonderful inversion of the domestic conversions in the Fugger household, the incident offered rich comic pickings – sexual innuendo, and diabolic sleight of hand – which by implication suggested that trickery, if not sexual impropriety, was to be suspected whenever the Fuggers and their ilk claimed to command the Devil.

But even when Protestants adopted an attitude of forthright scepticism, they were not excused from putting their sceptical beliefs to the test. Those who derided diabolic diagnoses had to demonstrate to the public the efficacy of the naturalistic cures they advocated.[48] Nature, however, did not always oblige. In the case of one of the possessed maids, Gasser diagnosed womb trouble, but he and other doctors failed to heal the patient. Unfortunately for them, she was later successfully exorcized.[49] In this atmosphere of heightened religious controversy, matters of belief had to be decided in the bodies of those who suffered.

Although it was primarily in the religious realm that the relation between the body and supernatural forces was debated, the argument was never the province of theologians alone. Chief among the other areas in which these issues were worked out was sorcery. Sorcery, like Catholicism and Protestantism, had no unitary attitude either to the body or to the nature of the powers of which sorcerers made use. This was especially true in the 1580s and 1590s, before diabolism had begun to be imported as an all-purpose explanation of the nature of magic.

MAGIC AND THE BODY

Before 1560, trials for magic and sorcery in Augsburg were exceedingly rare – the council dealt with only four such cases between 1500 and 1560. But in the two decades between 1560 and 1580, the years of the exorcism mania in the city, eleven individuals were tried for such crimes, and between 1580 and 1600, when the Counter-Reformation was becoming firmly established, at least thirty-six people were interrogated about offences relating to magic.[50] The motley collection of sorcerers, crystal-ball-gazers, treasure-seekers and healers rounded up between 1530 and 1600 occasionally included individuals suspected of witchcraft but none was sentenced to death for such a crime until 1625. Over the whole course of the seventeenth century, only seventeen individuals met with the fate of execution – an eighteenth died in prison. Though Augsburg avoided the large-scale witch panics of some of its neighbours, it had a steady trickle of witchcraft and sorcery cases none the less.

Many of these sorcerers and healers were semi-competent fraudsters rather than wizards, and the council sometimes showed a lack of zeal in pursuing them. Georg Schot, for instance, though repeatedly named as ringleader in a case of treasure-seeking in 1578, was not himself brought before the judges until the following year, and then on a different charge.[51] Like his two companions, he escaped with a warning.[52] Maria Marquart, repeatedly mentioned as a healer using spells throughout the 1570s and 1580s, was not subjected to criminal interrogation until 1589 – when, however, she was exiled for life.[53] Maria Dorner came before the council in 1579 and again in 1591 when she, too, was banished for life. Her banishment was confirmed in 1594 and 1611, but this did not stop her from seeing clients from Augsburg – she was mentioned in a case in 1599, still plying her trade from nearby Kriegshaber.[54]

Once discovered, the fates of the sorcerers were various. Some were tortured and subjected to banishment, others escaped with a mere caution; but in the sixteenth century, none was executed or convicted of truck with the Devil.[55] The council's attitude towards sorcery in this period was complex. At times it seemed to be almost agnostic about sorcery, pursuing cases spasmodically in response to complaints. But over the years it increasingly concerned itself with magic and the power of the Devil so that, by the end of the century, judicial authorities were conversant with sorcery and had a developed sense of which were the most serious cases and which involved mere deception.

As it was practised in late sixteenth-century Augsburg, magic made much use of the body in several different ways. Detached pieces of bodies, living or dead – nails, hair, cauls and the like – could be used as magical objects to protect from harm, or to cause it, to bring luck or cause transformations of various kinds. In a related use, discarded or stolen pieces of a person's body (or clothes which were invested with their owner's personality) might be used to exercise control over that individual. Pain might be invoked as an intensifier of a spell. Magical spells could bring about harm to an individual's body. All of these usages rested on the belief in the profound interconnectedness of supernatural forces and the body. In this way, they shared the world-view of pre-Reformation and Counter-Reformation Catholicism. Magic of this sort was thus practically impossible to combine with a radical disjuncture between flesh and spirit.

In several aspects, the so-called 'white magic' of the late sixteenth century in Augsburg echoed the themes of its Counter-Reformation context. These features of magic were age-old, but their iteration in a changed religious context gave them new meaning. As we have seen, Catholicism of the second half of the sixteenth century insisted on the connectedness of the spiritual and bodily worlds. Exorcism vindicated the efficacy of holy water, showed that fasting worked, and demonstrated that relics, blessings and making the sign of the cross were effective against the Devil.[56] Relics played a prominent role in the exorcism of Veronica Stainer – when Philip de Taxis hung a fragment of the cross around her neck, she resisted wildly and then fell unconscious. Susanna Roschman's sceptical Protestant parents were forced to concede the efficacy of Catholic sacramentals when their possessed daughter had a fit after being given holy water to drink.[57] Magic could be viewed as an applied version of cognate beliefs, showing that supernatural forces could be located in bodies and objects. As the Counter-Reformation reaffirmed the power of relics, so believers in magic transformed pieces of the body into magical tokens: one woman gave a man a caul to use to bring him luck;[58] two men carried bits of a condemned criminal's finger.[59]

Magic was often frankly parasitic on Catholic belief. Frequently, magical spells relied upon iterations of prayers and of the Creed, and especially of Hail Marys, devotional practices which had been bitter targets of Protestant polemicists. In the second half of the sixteenth century, however, numerical repetitions of prayer-formulae of this kind were increasingly being advocated by a more confident Catholicism. The exorcism of Anna Bernhauser proceeded with the recitation of particular numbers of Our Fathers and Hail Marys;[60] and the reaffirmation of the efficacy of the Rosary and of the Hail Mary was a strong theme of Eisengrein's Catholic defence of Altötting.[61] Just as Canisius argued for the usefulness of charitable donations for the donor's soul, so also several sorceresses ordered specific numbers of alms to be given as part of a process of removing a spell or bringing about the return of lost objects.[62]

Even the structures of magical formulae could be lifted from Catholic liturgy. Indeed, much of the 'white magic' uncovered by the council was precisely for this reason difficult to fault. Its use was more often a kind of unauthorized appropriation of the rites and power of orthodox Catholicism, like the penumbra of sacramentals, or the superstitious use of sacred power to protect. Elisabeth Rormoser would kneel on a grave, and command Christian souls to plague a thief until he returned that which was stolen. In a prosaic application of the power of the Passion, she prayed 'Jesus was lost, Jesus was found again, that my things be found again, so help me God and his holy five wounds', following this up with three Our Fathers, three Creeds and three Hail Marys. Maria Marquart described a spell-lifting cycle which was largely a kind of imitation para-liturgy of the Passion. Apart from the simple introductory spell, the ingredients came from the church. The cycle began on a Thursday, with an invocation of Jesus's suffering on the Mount of Olives, and lasted until Saturday. It involved increased repetition of orthodox prayers: the Our Father and Hail Mary were to be repeated three, five and seven times respectively, followed by the Creed.[63] The technique seems to have involved a magical strengthening of the power of the blessing by a sort of imaginative exercise of invocation of the Passion, as if the bodily suffering of Christ could be manipulated by the user of the spell. In a case such as this, a devotional exercise of the kind being advocated in Counter-Reformation Augsburg, based on imaginative identification with bodily suffering, was being turned to magical use.[64]

Exorcisms, with their dramatic proof of the priest's power, greatly enhanced priestly authority. They showed the priest to be a figure who, with divine assistance, could exercise control over non-earthly forces. More than a mere 'servant of the Word' and representative member of his congregation, as Protestants might have described their ministers, the Catholic priest of the Counter-Reformation enjoyed a special relation with the divine.[65] But, in the unsettled world of the early Counter-Reformation, the possibility that a priest could mediate in this highly dramatic way between the bodily and spiritual world could serve to strengthen the belief that other individuals, too, might exercise similar control over the supernatural. Just as the drama of the exorcism required a priest for its efficacy, and testified to his authority, spells confirmed the power of the magician and worked to strengthen faith in individual magical performers.

Perhaps most striking of the commonalities with Counter-Reformation religiosity is the hypostasization of pain. This rested on a conception of the body which Counter-Reformation Catholicism revived. Physical sensation, in this way of imagining the body, could be represented as divorced from the body which experienced it. So, for example, Anna Stauder appealed to the pain which Mary experienced as she gave birth as part of a spell;[66] and Maria Marquart, in the cycle we have just described, explicitly invoked first the bloody sweat of Christ at Gethsemane, then the honour of the holy sufferings of Christ and finally the seven sufferings of God and the heart's pain which his mother endured. This kind of imaginative abstraction of bodily sensation was also characteristic of Counter-Reformation religiosity. Intense physical sensation could be the vehicle for expressing religious experience: one might think of the orgasmic reception of the spirit which Bernini's sculpture of S. Theresa depicts. A stronger insistence on the need for the believer to feel – to imitate in one's soul, for example, the sufferings of Mary – was combined with the belief that these were salvific, so that sensational identification by the believer with a saint's suffering was itself a way of experiencing the divine. By 1605 in Augsburg, Good Friday processions to mark the Stations of the Cross, a ritual which depended on the individual imaginatively experiencing the Passion for him- or herself, had taken on definitive form.[67] While an emphasis on sentiment in religion was not in itself new, what we are seeing here is the reaffirmation and intensification of belief in the active power of bodily sensations such as pain, as Catholicism reaffirmed the inter-relation of body and soul.

I have been arguing that sorcery, like exorcism, raised the question of the relationship between body and spirit in a parallel and highly troubling manner. Perhaps it is not insignificant that there were connections between the milieu of the exorcisms, dominated by the Fugger households, and that of the sorcerers. So Maria Marquart claimed that the stone she used as a crystal ball had been given to her on a rosary by the late Georg Fugger.[68] This was almost certainly the husband of Ursula Fugger-Lichtenstein, the ex-Protestant who featured so prominently in exorcisms.[69] There were further connections: Marquart's assistant boy crystal-gazer was employed carrying wood 'into the master Fuggers' houses'.[70] Hans Fugger had accompanied Ursula Fugger on her pilgrimage to Rome, where two other Fugger servants had been exorcized, and his wife Elisabeth, like Ursula, was another convert from Protestantism.[71] Anna Stauder claimed to have done crystal ball-gazing for 'Herrn Hans Fugger', while in 1579, Maria Dorner claimed that the sorcery she was thwarting was directed against Hans Fugger's gardener. She described the container of hair and bones which she had detected in her crystal ball and discovered under the lintel of the stable and shed, and she told how she and her companion had informed Hans Fugger's wife about the pot.[72] Dorner even tried indirectly to present the sorcery as aimed at the Fuggers themselves, accusing the woman she suspected of casting the spell of having maligned Hans Fugger. Countering sorcery was thus connected with combating threats against the Fuggers. Once again, the drama of sorcery and disenchantment was being enacted by the Fugger servants. The world of the sorcerers was loosely connected with the world of the Fuggers, the Catholic converts, and of exorcism. For Catholic converts, leaving Protestantism entailed abandoning its asceticism of the flesh, and confessing the somatic power of both benign and malign forces. Perhaps this is why exorcism, sorcery and conversion could share some associations.

THE LOGIC OF SORCERY

As we have seen, Catholics and Protestants in the late sixteenth century were proposing radically different theologies of the body. At this point we need to investigate more closely the understanding sorcerers themselves presented of the body and of their magical techniques, in order to see in what sense the body was possessed of magical powers, and how it might be a target of sorcery.

The most striking feature of sorcery is the way it functioned by employing a concatenation of magical forces. Pieces of the body would seldom be used alone, but in conjunction with spells and prayers. Magical effects could be obtained by piling up magical forces and incantations in a fundamentally syncretistic fashion. Thus spells regularly concluded with religious references, or might include prayers. They demonstrated a willingness to employ whatever might work, whether church-sanctioned power or other force, as a kind of magical potpourri.[73]

Of those interrogated on suspicion of sorcery, Maria Marquart was one of the most confident and articulate. No stranger to council interference, she had previously been ordered to desist from healing. And she was almost certainly identical with the Maria Marquart who fought an attempt by the barber-surgeons' trade to ban her from healing nearly two decades before, proudly describing how she had helped many with medicine and with 'the gifts and arts granted her by God'.[74] She insisted she healed out of 'Christian sympathy and mercy', not for money, and presented her healing squarely in the tradition of Christian charity. Marquart was married to a watchmaker, a highly prestigious trade, and she was a citizen of Augsburg. Old and ill when she was arrested in 1589,[75] she none the less gave a coherent and lengthy account of her techniques, and never sought to deny her powers. Central to her self-presentation was the concept of 'natural arts' (*natürliche künsten*): these, she claimed, were all she used. The spells she recounted to the council interrogators made much use of devotional techniques and prayers. She also employed needles and threads used in sewing corpses into shrouds as a kind of strengthening of spells, and used herbs and crystal balls. She was careful to deny any invocation of spirits. Instead, her spells reiterated parts of the body in a kind of protective litany, imitated and invoked Jesus's sufferings or relied on sympathetic magic.[76]

Maria Marquart was one of only a few individuals interrogated before 1600 who candidly professed white witchcraft. She was one of only two sorcerers who coherently argued they had used 'natural arts' – an admission which did little to help her cause. Despite her high social status, her age and infirmities, she was banished from the city for life.[77] What made the distinction between black and white magic so unstable was that nearly all other sorcerers persistently relied on ambiguity about the source of magical power. Their strategies of self-defence before the council were usually to insist upon their own ignorance about magical processes, or even to demonstrate their incompetence. All those accused of crystal ball-gazing, for example, protested that they had not prepared (*zugericht*) the crystal balls they had used. Instead, they used ones which had been made ready for use as magical objects by unnamed others. Presenting themselves as mere operators of technology, they never sought to deny the general understanding of how crystal balls worked, the belief that spirits, possibly evil spirits, inhabited the balls and were responsible for bringing about the magical powers of vision the balls afforded.[78]

This meant that the crystals, in which past, present and future could be seen, could be presented as part of 'natural magic' only in so far as their owners took pains not to enquire further into the nature of the power by which they worked. Instead, strategic, vague threats might be used. Thus, one woman was reported to have threatened to 'ban' a man into her balls, locking him in like the spirits. She was reported to have boasted of her control over the spirits, and to have commanded them by name.[79] Under interrogation, however, she firmly denied such powers and insisted that she had acquired the balls already in working order.[80] Similarly, the capacity to 'see' in the crystal balls, a talent which not everyone possessed, was presented as a matter of luck, not skill. 'Sunday's children', the 'lucky ones', had the ability – an ability represented as a natural capacity, not something acquired through magical technique.[81] Many of those who owned such balls stressed the non-occult way by which they had come across them: one said she had been given the crystals by Anton Fugger, another received them on a rosary given to her by Georg Fugger.[82] Maria Dorner claimed to have chanced upon her set of balls at a second-hand market in a job lot of household goods, their prosaic origin mirroring her unwillingness to ascribe any special art or talent to gazing. Anyone with the 'gift' might practise it, she averred.[83]

As far as possible, crystal ball-gazers sought to distance themselves from the powerful, hypothetical sorcerers who had set up the balls; but their reluctance to claim the power to conjure and their refusal to speculate on their mechanisms ultimately served to strengthen the belief that crystal magic did, in the last analysis, rest on the conjuration of very powerful spirits, by very powerful sorcerers. Indeed, the force of Maria Dorner's arguments, the only crystal ball-gazer to deny outright that the balls had to be *zugericht* if they were to work, was dented somewhat by her equally strenuous denials that she had employed any magic at all. Her victim, a love-sick young man, was all too visibly stricken with the malady after she provided the herbs which his would-be paramour placed under his straw mattress.[84]

There were, however, also cases which seemed to involve a more powerful kind of body magic. Those who cut bits off the bodies of condemned criminals were evidently dabbling in magic which could not be equated with a straightforward use of natural body magic. Yet despite the grisly trinkets they employed, these sorcerers were less disturbing, because the talismans either did not work or did not seem to involve supernatural power. Under interrogation, Leonhard Nadler presented himself as a magical innocent. He said he had heard that bones from a dead criminal could make you lucky at shooting and gambling – an extremely mundane application of sorcery. Indeed, Nadler recalled, it had not even worked – when he rushed off to try his success with his wonderful keepsake, he was soundly beaten at cards. Disgusted, he threw the bones back where he had taken them from.[85] Thomas Trummer, found with a chest full of objects for use in sorcery, strove to explain its contents: the hair and navel cords belonged to his wife, and one lot of hair to his dead mother; his wife could give account of these, he explained. He admitted owning a knuckle and cord from a dead criminal, also in the hope of luck at shooting and gambling.

An amateur, his passion was collecting. He 'had just enjoyed writing down and reading [the spells]'[86] – a hobby he had indulged to his wife's alarm. She had thrown his books on the fire!

The notion of the gentleman collector of curiosities was one which could easily be assimilated by an Augsburg councillor. The second half of the sixteenth century was the heyday of famed Augsburg humanist collectors of coins, antiquities, local historical objects and books. History itself, for the Augsburg antiquarians, was a matter of curiosities, of objects to be acquired with stories attached, and the historian might suspend judgement as to whether the tales were true or false.[87] Trummer succeeded not just in convincing the council that he was someone who had never practised harmful magic, but in persuading them that he was a collector only, an individual who had 'not used' his treasures.[88] All those who owned such talismans refused to speculate on the nature of the magic they employed.

As the century wore on it was difficult to argue for the natural arts a woman like Marquart claimed to practise, or to claim that the body itself could be a magical instrument. Instead, 'help of the Evil Enemy' must be suspected. Under the pressure of interrogation, sorcerers had already begun to vacate the argument that magic could be explained in non-demonic terms, by refusing to speculate on the nature of the magic they successfully practised, and by increasing their own power by leaving it tactically vague whether the source of their magic was benign or malign. The syncretistic nature of magical practice, together with the sorcerers' own self-aggrandizing attempts to hint at greater, possibly diabolic, powers which they might possess, helped to strengthen the view that the connection between body and spirit on which sorcery depended was ultimately diabolic, not 'natural'. In consequence, the theory of diabolism, with its elaborate explanation of the mechanisms of enchantment, began to displace alternative accounts of the nature of sorcery.

Support for a demonological explanation of all sorcery came both from the sorcerers themselves and from the lessons of the exorcisms of the 1560s, 1570s and 1580s. So, for instance, the owners of the mutilated parts of criminal bodies might claim ignorance, but it was hard not to believe that their real power came from the Devil, who took the souls of the damned. And in 1599, Maria Dorner, who had tried to present herself to the council as a practitioner of white, natural magic, who had been banished from Augsburg and was now safely ensconced in Kriegshaber, was to be found advising an Augsburg client to burn brandy in the name of the Devil if he wished to win back stolen goods.[89] On the other hand, Veronica Stainer, the possessed maid from Starnberg, was observed to know miraculously all sorts of private details about her visitors. This knowledge, which made her seem rather like a sooth-sayer or crystal-gazer, was merely further proof to Sebastian Khueller that the Devil was involved.[90] The sorceress herself, despite her protestations, might even bring diabolic possession about. In the infamous Vienna case of a young girl exorcized of 12,652 demons, it transpired that the girl's grandmother, a sorceress, had actually caused the infestation. She had sought to marry her granddaughter to the Devil, and had tricked her into eating a piece of apple which contained the demon.[91] Here, love magic led directly to the Devil itself. Thus from both directions, the distinction between natural magic and diabolism became harder to maintain, as an exorcism case like this one implicated sorcerers, and sorcery implicated the Devil.

THE SEXED BODY

To this point we have been describing the relation between the body and the non-material world. However, the body was always imagined as a sexed body. Men's and women's bodies had distinct magical capacities, and their use of magic was different. Because of the importance of concepts of the body in sorcery, magic, sexuality and sexual identity were linked. The ills for which magic was held to be an appropriate remedy often concerned sexuality, and love relations were an area in which magical intervention might often be sought – or suspected. Sexual capacity, even the essence of one's sexed body, could be threatened by the sorcerer. This is most clearly evident in the complaint frequently mentioned in connection with sorcery, impotence.

Impotence was the bodily ill for which men most often appear to have sought magical assistance, and which they feared women had brought about. Unlike womanhood, manhood was experienced as a fragile achievement, and masculine superiority was perceived as constantly subject to threat. Women who threatened 'that he should neither go up nor down with any love'[92] were fearsome creatures. In the phrase which was often used to describe this ability, 'stealing manhood', the interconnections between biological and cultural manhood found vivid expression. In this sense women were imagined to have the power of castration – and the power to restore potency.[93]

There was also a gendered specialization in the practice of sorcery itself. In part, this derived from the different patterns of men's and women's work. It emerges most vividly in the different ways male and female sorcerers made use of parts of the body in sorcery. Women made use of the corporal resources – fingernails, hair, cauls – and of objects associated with the body. As the ones who gave birth, women had access to a treasure trove of potentially magical bodily substances: cauls, dead infants, navel-cords, afterbirth. The division of labour in sixteenth-century Germany assigned the most intimate work of care for the body to women. They were closely associated with mourning and care for the bodies of the dead, an important source of magical objects.[94]

Maria Marquart employed thirteen nails from a bier which had been sent to her by another sorceress in a spell. She used needle and thread with which a dead body had been sewn into its shroud as a kind of magical strengthening in another spell.[95] Bath maids did the work of scratching, delousing and manicuring and they therefore had access to the waste products of the body through which magic might be exercised, to control the affections, desires and health. So Catherine Tenn feared lest the woman who pared her infant's nails at the civic bath should use them to cause her child harm.[96] The council eventually determined that Tenn was mentally disturbed,[97] but her unbalanced fear of the bath-keeper merely exaggerated a general social fact: nearly everyone was dependent upon the physical care of women, a dependence which could be turned to harm.

Men, however, tended to use parts of the body in more extreme fashion. Several are described as having negotiated with the executioner to get bits of the body of condemned criminals. Georg Schot asked the hangman of Schongau for a piece of the colon of a man who had recently committed suicide (and who was therefore accounted 'dishonourable' and buried by the executioner). Leonhard Nadler had taken 'a little piece' of the big toe of a corpse hanging on the gallows at Augsburg, and a fragment of the man's shirt.[98] According to the council at Regensburg, Thomas Trummer had virtually ransacked the corpse of a man who had been broken on the wheel. The entire body had been plundered for magical segments: the man's penis, all his fingernails, toenails, spokes of the wheel on which his body had been broken – all had been removed, the council wrote.[99] Just as the bodies of dead saints often had to be protected against relic-hunters, so here the exhibited corpse had become a collection of magical talismans, the pieces invested with supernatural power akin to the healing potential which relics contained.

Partly, this difference can be explained by the fact that most men had to obtain bodily parts through intermediaries because they did not ordinarily perform the work of bodily care. One sorcerer claimed to have got materials from his brother-in-law, a doctor.[100] His sorcerer's chest consisted mainly of non-bodily products, 'blessings, spells, herbs, roots, ointments, and hair'. Only under torture was he prevailed upon to admit that this hair was pubic hair he had taken from the 'secret parts' of a girl in Switzerland. How he had obtained it and what he intended to do with it remains unclear. Few apparently negotiated with women to obtain bodily products. This meant that their magical use of bodily relics was overlain by the magic deriving from dishonour. Criminal relics partook of the power of the juridical process and they were steeped in the dishonour which attached to those who came into contact with the executioner.[101] Indeed, one such enthusiast and his more reluctant companion had been banished from their trade association on account of the dishonour they incurred through coming into physical contact with the execution.[102] Male sorcerers tended more often to employ magic connected with written spells, books, herbs and what we might describe as more exotic bodily relics derived from criminals; women tended to apply magic by using spoken spells and the natural magical properties of the body.[103]

Exorcisms, too, had a sexual logic. As far as we know, in late sixteenth-century Augsburg they were exclusively carried out on women; and the famous cases at Starnberg and Vienna in Austria also involved young women.[104] All the women who figured in the Augsburg exorcisms were referred to as 'maids' or 'virgins'. Described as 'servants', even when they were of noble family, the women exemplified particularly well the subordinated aspect of female nature. Women were believed to be closer to the Devil, and they were therefore more subject to temptation and more enslaved to their physical natures than men were. In consequence, their bodies were more naturally suited to house devils.

In this way the drama of exorcism, accomplished by a male priest with Mary's assistance, was also a sexual script.[105] As unmarried women, the possessed maids were poised on the verge of sexual existence, a state held to be especially alluring. The accounts of the exorcisms did not shrink from supplying the occasionally titillating detail. The author of the account of Susanna Roschman's exorcism described how Susanna had said the Devil had visited her at night in her chamber, asking her to yield to him. Nor did the writer omit to mention how, under the sway of the Devil, writhing and twisting, the girl had exhibited her genitals.[106] In the case of another woman exorcized by Dr Wendel before 200 onlookers, there was the added spice that she had borne and murdered an illegitimate child, the product of an affair with a married man.[107] Exorcisms were often carried out on beds, where the possessed woman, rolling about and dress askew, sunk in the toils of complete bodily submission to the male Devil, recalled only too vividly the woman lost to the body and to lust.[108]

Indeed, the sexual logic of exorcism was central to its meaning. It was primarily the disruptions of normal womanly behaviour which testified to the Devil's presence, a conviction which could be as powerfully held by Lutherans as by Catholics. So for Christoph Jacobellus, the woman's chaste and appropriately obedient feminine deportment clinched the argument that her malady was not diabolic in origin but natural. She showed herself:

> disciplined and patient, and behaved in such a manner that not a single sign of a possessed person could be perceived in her. She only cried, and looked longingly at the [Protestant] preacher, and let out many a deep sigh. Otherwise she spoke not a word during the whole process . . . and once she spoke to the Jesuit in great humility.[109]

By contrast, the Devil spoke through Anna Bernhauser's body in a male voice, spitting at them all, and screaming 'Let me go, you whore' at the image of Mary in the church. Tossed about by the 'tyrannical mischief' of the Devil, she sinks into unconsciousness as he leaves off plaguing her; and when she comes to, she speaks 'voluntarily and in stillness', describing a beatific vision of Mary she has experienced.[110] Sebastian Khueller's narrative of Veronica Stainer's possession has the individual alternating between the two genders in accordance with the degree of diabolic disruption. Possession becomes a kind of hypermasculine caricature, as she displays all the emblems of the classic male vices – drinking, hunting, swearing and whoring. In her demonic personality, she sings the drinking song 'Dumle dich guts weinle, weinle dumle dich' ('Stagger about, my good little wine; my little wine, stagger about'), insults the company, overturns social boundaries by addressing her lord by the informal 'thou', sings scurrilous ditties and cavorts about like a frenzied hunter.[111] The success of the exorcism was proven when the woman resumed her feminine persona, purged of these masculine excrescences. The successfully 'liberated' maid was once again chaste, her bodily boundaries were no longer distorted and exceeded, and she spoke modestly. As Khueller described it, exorcism necessitated the expulsion of the masculine and the resumption of an unfragmented conventional sexual identity.[112]

But the sexual logic of exorcism was not exclusive to Catholic militants. Scathingly sceptical Protestants like Gasser adopted their own sexual logic, ascribing the exorcisms to an essentially female credulity and attachment to superstition. Whenever women were ill, Gasser argued, they wished to believe in charms, miracles and the like and they turned to the priests – not to his colleagues, the doctors. This was why they proved easy prey for the Jesuits. Gasser's own medical explanation of the illnesses of the maids, however, came straight from female biology and its susceptibility to female emotionality. He ascribed the women's illness to disorders of the womb and even to 'insane love'.[113] Sexualizing the nature of their disorder, he located it in the uterus, and in women's consequently sex-driven natures. So far from their bodies being the theatre of spiritual battles, Gasser saw women as inextricably caught in the snares of their own biology, enslaved to a sexuality which destroyed their reason and unbalanced their health. Deriding Mariolatry as superstition, Protestants like Gasser denied that the female body could ever represent the divine. Thus, in this case, a Protestant dualism about the body and spiritual forces served to underwrite women's consignment to the realm of the fleshly. Men, or at least right-thinking Protestant men, belonged to the realm of human reason.

Protestantism, with its potential for a radical dualism of flesh and spirit, had disturbed the relation thought to hold between the bodily and the divine, and had thrown the issue of the theology of the body into sharp relief. Magic's pragmatic use of whatever higher powers seemed to work, be they benign or malign, had relied on a world-view which saw the spiritual and the somatic as essentially interconnected. Late sixteenth-century fascination with sorcery must be sought partly in the ferment of ideas which challenged the Protestant understanding of body and spirit, and made the Devil seem to be active in real, not metaphorical bodies. Faced with the riveting evidence of diabolic power, Protestants wavered. Some claimed to have surer recipes for dealing with demons, others turned the fire of ridicule on the Catholics – not always, however, with convincing results. Few Protestants were willing to reject all allegations of magic, and not every case of sorcery could be unmasked as fraud. Here I have explored the Protestant sceptical reaction. There is another story, which cannot be told here, of how Protestants came to develop their own accounts of possession, and of the Devil's activity in the world.[114] In the end, sorcerers proved equally unable to elaborate a non-demonic account of the relation between body and spirit. Their understanding of the 'natural arts' and the natural magic of the body could not prevail against the logic of demonology.

Both sorcery and exorcism elaborated a vision of the body which contained a terrifying sexual logic. The exorcist might seem to expel the crude, masculine persona who blasphemed, growled and insulted the bystanders. He appeared to leave behind a purified, chaste maid, who spoke with a mild voice and venerated the Virgin. But not all exorcisms worked.[115] And who knew whether the woman would remain the exemplar of modest, subservient womanhood? Or who could tell in whose body the Devil might next alight? Though the devils were driven out, exorcisms strengthened the view that demons might make human bodies their home, and that female bodies were particularly vulnerable to the invasion. Even the most sceptical Protestants could agree with the Catholics that women were more vulnerable to the snares of the Devil – they differed merely in ascribing female susceptibility to superstition and biology. These were lessons which outlived the exorcism craze of the 1560s.

Sorcery, too, taught that women were fearful creatures. When women grew older, when their powerful sexual desires raged even though they could no longer bear children, when maturity gave them a measure of wisdom and authority, their femininity could no longer be so readily tamed and chastened. As the sex whose bodies housed mystery, and who possessed the monopoly of physical care, women could also turn that power against those who were dependent upon them. Increasingly in the years after 1560, older women began to be seen by Protestants and Catholics alike as the most likely source of physical injury, the ones who could take away love and consume limbs. As demonology triumphed, it began to hammer out the links between the sexual category of the possessed individual, a young, sexually prescient woman, and that of the most fearsome sorcerer, now understood as a mature woman, a witch who had the power to castrate.

NOTES

1 See Joyce McDougall, *Theatres of the Body: A psychoanalytic approach to psychosomatic illness*, London 1989; *idem*, *Theatres of the Mind: Illusion and truth on the psychoanalytic stage*, New York 1985.

2 See on Augsburg in this period, Paul Warmbrunn, *Zwei Konfessionen in einer Stadt: Das Zusammenleben von Katholiken und Protestanten in den paritätischen Reichsstädten Augsburg, Biberach, Ravensburg und Dinkelsbühl*, Wiesbaden 1983; and Bernd Roeck, *Eine Stadt in Krieg und Frieden: Studien zur Geschichte der Reichsstadt Augsburg zwischen Kalenderstreit und Parität*, 2 vols, Göttingen 1989. On the city's earlier religious history, see Friedrich Roth, *Augsburgs Reformationsgeschichte*, 4 vols, vol. 1, 2nd edn, Munich 1901; vols 2–4, Munich 1904–11; Philip Broadhead, 'Internal Politics and Civic Society in Augsburg During the Era of the Early Reformation 1518–1537', Ph.D. thesis, Kent 1981; Lyndal Roper, *The Holy Household. Women and morals in Reformation Augsburg*, Oxford 1989, pp. 7–27.

3 See Martha Schad, *Die Frauen des Hauses Fugger von der Lilie (15–17 Jahrhundert) Augsburg–Ortenburg–Trient*, Tübingen 1989.

4 Herbert Immenkötter, 'Kirche zwischen Reformation und Parität', in Gunther Gottlieb *et al.* (eds), *Geschichte der Stadt Augsburg*, 2nd edn, Stuttgart 1985, p. 405.

5 See Schad, *Die Frauen*, pp. 29–39, 51–9.

6 Schad, ibid., contains excellent material on this.

7 Robert Emmet McLaughlin, *Caspar Schwenckfeld: Reluctant radical*, New Haven, Conn. and London 1986.

8 See Peter Stallybrass and Allon White, *The Politics and Poetics of Transgression*, London 1986, for a different and stimulating interpretation of the relation between Protestantism and body symbolism.

9 John P. Donnelly, 'Peter Canisius', in Jill Raitt (ed.), *Shapers of Religious Traditions in Germany, Switzerland, and Poland, 1560–1600*, New Haven, Conn. and London 1981, p. 150.

10 See Stuart Clark, 'Protestant Demonology: Sin, superstition, and society (*c.* 1520–*c.* 1630)', in Bengt Ankarloo and Gustav Henningsen (eds), *Early Modern European Witchcraft: Centres and peripheries*, Oxford 1990.

11 Bernhard Duhr, *Geschichte der Jesuiten in den Ländern deutscher Zunge (im. XVI Jahrhundert)*, 4 vols, Freiburg 1907–13, Munich 1921–8, vol. 1, pp. 732–3; Schad, *Die Frauen*, p. 53. See also, on the phenomenon of exorcism, H.C. Erik Midelfort, 'The Devil and the German People: Reflections on the popularity of demon possession in sixteenth-century Germany', in Steven Ozment (ed.), *Religion and Culture in the Renaissance and Reformation*, Kirksville, Mo. 1989.

12 Duhr, *Geschichte der Jesuiten* vol. 1, p. 740.

13 Paul von Stetten d. Ä, *Geschichte der Heiligen Römischen Reichs Freyen Stadt Augsburg*, 2 vols, Frankfurt am Main and Leipzig 1743–58, vol. 1, p. 582.

14 Duhr, *Geschichte der Jesuiten*, vol. 1, p. 731.

15 ibid., p. 733.

16 See O. Braunsberger, *Beati Petri Canisii, Societatis Iesu, Epistulae et Acta*, 8 vols, Freiburg 1901, vol. 4, pp. 876–8, 883.

17 *Die Chroniken der deutschen Städte vom 14. bis ins 16. Jahrhundert*, 36 vols, Leipzig 1862–1931, vol. 33, Augsburg 8, pp. 208–9.

18 Matheus Eisengrein, *Vnser liebe Fraw zu Alten Oetting. Das ist. Von der Vralten H. Capellen vnser Lieben Frawen . . .* , Ingolstadt 1571, fo. 128.

19 Eisengrein, *Vnser liebe Fraw*, fos 128, 130.

20 See Schad, *Die Frauen*, pp. 25–39, 51–70.

21 Eisengrein, *Vnser liebe Fraw*, fo. 128.

22 *Eigentliche vnnd warhafftige verzeichnuss/ was sich auff// den 19 Iunii des drey vnd sechtzigisten jars zu Augspurg/ mit eines armen Burgers Tochter daselbst zugetragen/ welche vom bösen Geist angefochten vnnd besessen/ doch aber durch Gottes genadt vnd krafft von herren// Simon Scheibenhart/ der heiligen schrifft Doctorn// vnd Pfarherrn zu sanct Mauritzen/ in Augspurg/ aussgetriben/ vnd also die Besessen entbunden worden ist*, n.p., n.d.

23 'sich selbs ellendigklich emplösset', *Eigentliche vnnd warhafftige verzeichnuss*, fos A iv v; A iv r.

24 Sebastian Khueller, *Kurtze/ Warhafftige/ vnd summarischer weiss beschribne Historia/ von einer Junckfrawen/ wölche mit dreissig vnnd etlichen bösen Geistern/ leibhafftig besessen . . .* [Munich, Adam Berg 1574?], fo. A iii r. This exorcism took place in the castle chapel at Starnberg in Austria. I am including it here because the castle was that of the brothers Ferdinand, Philip and Joseph de Taxis, members of the Prague–Vienna line of the postmaster family which also had strong links with Augsburg (Wolfgang Behringer, *Thurn und Taxis: Die Geschichte ihrer Post und ihrer Unternehmen*, Munich and Zurich 1990, p. 197). Since the pamphlet was published in more than one edition in Munich, it is very likely that it circulated in Augsburg. Copies of distinct editions are to be found in the Deutsche Bibliothek, Berlin, and the Bayerische Staatsbibliothek, Munich, and I cite from the latter.

25 Eisengrein, *Vnser liebe Fraw*, fo. 130r.

26 *Kurtze Warhafftige . . . Historia*, fo. A ii v.

27 Eisengrein, *Vnser liebe Fraw*, fos 128 r–v.

28 *Eigentliche vnnd warhafftige verzeichnuss*, fo. B i r: 'gar groben mans stim', 'ho ho ho Pfaff/ auss dem Hauss kum ich nit'.

29 Khueller, *Kurtze Warhafftige . . . Historia*, fos A ii r–A iv r.

30 *Actus/ Der Ganzen verlauffenen/ handlung zwischen dem predigcanten Jm. Spital/ zu Augspurg/ Frawen Jörg Fuggerin, vnd den Jesuitern/ daselbst sich zugetragen*, Stadts– und Staatsbibliothek Augsburg, 4 Cod Aug. 146, fo. 51 v. There is also a copy in the Stadtarchiv Augsburg (hereafter StadtAA), Evangelisches Wesensarchiv, Akt 632.

31 Eisengrein, *Vnser liebe Fraw*, fo. 130 v.

32 Marcus Velserus, *Chronica der Weitberuempten Keyserlichen Freyen vnd dess H. Reichs Statt Augspurg . . .* , Frankfurt am Main 1595 (translation of Marx Welser's *Rerum Augustanarum Vindelicarum libri octo*, followed by Gasser's *Annals*), p. 125. Latin version of Gasser: Achilles Pirminius Gassarus, *Annales de vetustate originis, amoenitate situs, splendore aedificiorum, ac rebus gestis civium reipublicaeque Augsburgensis*, in J.B. Menckenii, *Scriptores rerum Germanicarum*, vol. 1, Leipzig 1728, no. xvii.

33 Eisengrein, *Vnser leibe Fraw*, fos 128 v, 131 v–132 r; Georg Scherer, *Christliche Erinnerung/ Bey der Historien von jüngst beschehener Erledigung einer Junckfrawen/ die mit zwölfftausent/ sechs hundert/ zwey vnd fünfftzig Teufel besessen gewesen*, Ingolstadt, David Sartorius 1584, p. 28. This sermon was dedicated to Philipp Eduard Fugger, son of Ursula Fugger: Schad, *Die Frauen*, p. 51.

34 Eisengrein, *Vnser liebe Fraw*, chs 14, 15 and throughout.

35 Schad, *Die Frauen*, p. 69.
36 *De Maria Virgine Incomparabili*: Donnelly, 'Peter Canisius', p. 150.
37 Johann Marbach, *Von Mirakeln vnd Wunderzeichen. Wie man sie ausz vnnd nach Gottes Wort/ flueur waar oder falsch erkennen soll*, n.p. 1571, fo. L [2] ii r.
38 ibid., fo. X iv v.
39 ibid., fos M ii v, N i r, U iv r.
40 ibid., fo. N i r:

> der Sohne Gottes nicht die Jungfrawen Mariam angenommen/ vnd seiner Göttlichen Natur personlich vereiniget hat/ sonder allein auss irem fleisch vnd blut die wahre menschliche Natur/ derwegen sie dann auch nicht in die H. Dreyfalitkeit ein gangen/ wie ihr fleisch vnd blut von Sohn Gottes angenommen/sonder ist vnd bleibt einweg wie die anderen ausserthalb der H. Dreyfaltigkeit/neben vnnd bey anderen Creaturen ein pur lauterer mensch.

41 Velserus, *Chronica*, p. 114.
42 ibid., p. 111.
43 ibid., pp. 122–3.
44 *Actus*, throughout. See also Warmbrunn, *Zwei Konfessionen*. pp. 244–5; Schad, *Die Frauen*, pp. 52–3.
45 *Actus*, fos 15 r–16 v.
46 ibid., fos 1 r–3 v.
47 *Warhaffter Bericht, wie ein Jeusuiter in teüffels gestalt: in wellichem er ein Euangelisch Mensch, vonn Jrem Glauben abzuschröckhen vermaint erstochen worden* (Stadt- und Staatsbibliothek Augsburg, 4 Cod Aug. 147). The incident supposedly occurred in 1569. A shorter printed version circulated with a woodcut, tantalizingly revealing the maid's naked breasts as she lies in bed, her hands raised above her head in fear: W. Strauss, *The German Single-Leaf Woodcut 1550–1600*, 3 vols, New York 1975, vol. 3, p. 1335, and reproduced in Schad, *Die Frauen*, following p. 24. See also Warmbrunn, *Zwei Konfessionen*, p. 244.
48 Because of the religious and sceptical conflicts in Augsburg, medicine functioned rather differently from what Giovanni Levi describes for seventeenth-century Italy. There, the scope of medicine's success was defined by the supernatural. Giovanni Levi, *Inheriting Power: The story of an exorcist*, trans. Lydia Cochrane, Chicago, Ill. and London 1988, pp. 24–8.
49 Velserus, *Chronica*, pp. 122–3: the events took place in 1568.
50 Figures are drawn from Wolfgang Behringer, *Hexenverfolgung in Bayern: Volksmagie, Glaubenseifer und Staatsräson in der frühen Neuzeit*, Munich 1987, pp. 431–69. One woman, a self-confessed witch, died under arrest in 1591, ibid., p. 157. See also Roeck, *Eine Stadt in Krieg und Frieden*, vol. 1, pp. 93–117, 445–55; vol. 2, pp. 539–53.
51 Wilhelm Koboltz and Niclaus Brestle named him: Stadt AA, Urgichtensammlung (hereafter Urg.), 10, 17 Oct. 1578, Wilhelm Koboltz; 17 Oct. 1578, Niclaus Brestle. He was interrogated on 9 and 11 Feb. 1579 about his spells and collection of magical goods.
52 StadtAA, Strafbuch des Rats, fo. 42 v, 23 Oct. 1578, Wilhelm Koboltz; fo. 43 r, 23 Oct. 1578, Niclaus Brestle; fo. 53 r, 12 Feb. 1579, Georg Schot.
53 StadtAA, Urg., 15, 20 Feb. 1589, Maria Marquart; Strafbuch des Rats, fo. 33 r, 23 Feb. 1589. She had been named by Wilhelm Koboltz: Urg., 10 Oct. 1578, Wilhelm Koboltz. The boy who did crystal-gazing for her was banished in 1589: Strafbuch des Rats, fo. 32 v, 18 Feb. 1589, Hans Wanner. On Marquart and sorcery, see Wolfgang Behringer, *Mit dem Feuer vom Leben zum Tod. Hexengesetzgebung in Bayern*, Munich 1988, pp. 205 ff.

54 StadtAA, Urg., 31 March 1579, Maria Dorner/Baur/Obermair; Strafbuch des Rats, fo. 58 r, 2 April 1579; fo. 109 v, 2 May 1591: she returned on 22 Nov. 1594 and was banished again, and re-exiled in 1611. Georg Strele named her in his testimony of 5 March 1599: Urg., 5 March 1599, Georg Strele.

55 There is one unclear case in 1563: Behringer, *Hexenverfolgung*, p. 434.

56 Scherer, *Christliche Erinnerung*, pp. 33, 34–5, 36–7. On the use of prayers and religious objects in late medieval sorcery, see Richard Kieckhefer, *Magic in the Middle Ages*, Cambridge 1990, pp. 65–85.

57 Khueller, *Kurtze Warhafftige . . . Historia*, fo. A ii v, *Eigentliche vnd warhafftige verzeichnuss*, fo. A iv r.

58 StadtAA, Urg., 21 Aug. 1560, Elisabeth Werlin.

59 StadtAA, Urg., 8, 11 Feb. 1577, Thomas Trummer.

60 Eisengrein, *Vnser liebe Fraw*, fos 127 r, 129 v, 131 v–132 r.

61 ibid., fos 136 v ff.; and note, for instance, ch. 15 of this encyclopaedic book on the wonders performed at Altötting, among which this exorcism has a prominent place.

62 StadtAA, Urg., 15, 20 Feb. 1589, Maria Marquart; 25 March–27 April 1591, Maria Dorner/Obermair.

63 StadtAA, Urg., 15, 20 Feb. 1589, Maria Marquart.

64 See also StadtAA, Urg., 9, 11 Feb. 1579, Georg Schot, for blessings invoking St John's mother, the Holy Trinity and Jesus. Anna Stauder appended five Our Fathers, five Hail Marys and five Creeds to a spell: StadtAA, Urg., 2–23 July 1590, Anna Stauder, and see Behringer, *Mit dem Feuer*, pp. 208ff. For a slightly different interpretation of this evidence see Roeck, *Eine Stadt in Krieg und Frieden*, vol. 1, pp. 103ff. Ruth Martin has found similar appropriation of religious objects and rituals in sorcery in Venice: Ruth Martin, *Witchcraft and the Inquisition in Venice, 1550–1650*, Oxford 1989.

65 Scherer concludes his pamphlet, *Christliche Erinnerung*, with a refutation of supposed Protestant exorcism, including scurrilous stories about exorcisms which Luther was supposed to have attempted.

66 StadtAA, Urg., 2–23 July 1590, Anna Stauder.

67 Louis Châtellier, *The Europe of the Devout: The Catholic Reformation and the formation of a new society*, trans. Jean Birrell, Cambridge 1989, p. 150.

68 StadtAA, Urg., 15, 20 Feb. 1589, Maria Marquart.

69 Schad, *Die Frauen*, pp. 30–41.

70 StadtAA, Urg., 15, 20 Feb. 1589, Maria Marquart.

71 Schad, *Die Frauen*, pp. 55–9.

72 Behringer, *Mit dem Feuer*, p. 210, StadtAA, Urg., 31 March 1579 and witness accounts 27 Feb. 1579, Maria Dorner/Baur/Obermair.

73 The same pattern emerges for Venice. See Martin, *Witchcraft*.

74 StadtAA, Handwerkerakten, Bader und Barbierer 1535–80, 20 Oct. 1571, Maria Marquart.

75 StadtAA, Strafbuch des Rats, fo. 33 r, 23 Feb. 1589.

76 StadtAA, Urg., 15, 20 Feb. 1589, Maria Marquart.

77 StadtAA, Strafbuch des Rats, fo. 33 r, 23 Feb. 1589. The other was Maria Dorner/Baur/Obermair, who in 1591 stoutly defended crystal-gazing as a 'free art', practised by princes and great lords: Urg., 25 March–27 April 1591, Maria Dorner/Baur/Obermair. She, too, was exiled for life: Strafbuch des Rats, fo. 109 v, 2 May 1591.

78 Anna Rasp addressed the balls when she or others wished to view, invoking the angels of the planets; Anna Megeler's spirits, however, had names and were the spirits of condemned criminals. StadtAA, Urg., 20 Aug. 1592, Anna Rasp; 28 Feb.–3 March 1564, Anna Megeler.

79 StadtAA, Urg., 28 Feb.–3 March 1564, Anna Megeler.
80 So, too, did Anna Rasp and Anna Beiss: StadtAA, Urg., 20 Aug. 1592 and 21 Aug. 1592, respectively.
81 StadtAA, Urg., 25 March–27 April 1591, Maria Dorner/Baur/Obermair; 20 Aug. 1592, Anna Rasp; 15, 20 Feb. 1589, Maria Marquart.
82 StadtAA, Urg., 28 Feb.–3 March 1564, Anna Megeler; 15, 20 Feb. 1589, Maria Marquart.
83 StadtAA, Urg., 31 March 1579, Maria Dorner/Baur/Obermair.
84 StadtAA, Strafbuch des Rats, fo. 80 r, 30 Aug. 1590, Anna Rheim/Mozart (the victim); fo. 109 v, 2 May 1591, Maria Dorner/Baur/Obermair; Urg., 25 March–27 April 1591, Maria Dorner/Baur/Obermair.
85 StadtAA, Urg., 20, 21 Jan. 1587, Leonhard Nadler.
86 'Allain sein lust damit gehabt dieselben abzuschreiben vnd zulesen', StadtAA, Urg., 8, 11 Feb. 1577, Thomas Trummer.
87 On humanists and history, see Stephanie Jed, paper given at 'History, Anthropology and the Renaissance Text' conference, London, 7 July 1990; and her 'The Scene of Tyranny: Violence and the Humanistic tradition', in Nancy Armstrong and Leonard Tennenhouse (eds), *The Violence of Represen-tation: Literature and the history of violence*, London and New York 1989.
88 StadtAA, Strafbuch des Rats, fo. 2 r, 14 Feb. 1577: 'Dieweil er solche [= zauberische sachen vnd kunsten] nit gebraucht.' He was let off, his beloved collection was burnt, and he was threatened with corporal punishment should he be found guilty again.
89 StadtAA, Urg., 5 March 1599, Georg Strele.
90 Khueller, *Kurtze Warhafftige … Historia*, fo. A iii r.
91 Scherer, *Christliche Erinnerung*, pp. 15–17.
92 StadtAA, Urg., 21 Aug. 1561, Elisabeth Werlin: 'dz Hans mit kaim Lieb solt vff vnd abghien'.
93 See Chapter 6; see also Martin, *Witchcraft*, throughout and p. 226 on women's domination of love magic.
94 See, for example, StadtAA, Urg., 3 April 1591, Magdalena Hofherr.
95 StadtAA, Urg., 15, 20 Feb. 1589, Maria Marquart.
96 StadtAA, Urg., 11 Oct. 1589, Catherine Tenn.
97 StadtAA, Strafbuch des Rats, fo. 49 v, 14 Oct. 1589.
98 StadtAA, Urg., 9, 11 Feb. 1579, Georg Schot; 20, 21 Jan. 1587, Leonhard Nadler.
99 StadtAA, Urg., 8, 11 Feb. 1577, Thomas Trummer, letter from Regensburg enclosed.
100 StadtAA, Urg., 10, 17 Oct. 1578, Wilhelm Koboltz.
101 See Ch. Hinckeldy (ed.), *Strafjustiz in alter Zeit*, Rothenburg 1980; Werner Danckert, *Unehrliche Berufe: Die verfemten Leute*, Munich 1963; Helmut Schuhmann, *Der Scharfrichter*, Kempten 1964; Franz Irsigler and Arnold Lassotta, *Bettler und Gaukler, Dirnen und Henker: Aussenseiter in einer mittelal-terlichen Stadt*, Cologne 1984, pp. 228–82. Kathy Stuart, 'The Boundaries of Honor. "Dishonorable people" in Augsburg 1500–1800', Ph.D. diss., Yale University 1993.
102 StadtAA, Urg., 20, 21 Jan. 1587, Leonhard Nadler; note of 20 July 1586 attached concerning Leonhard Nadler and Paul Mair.
103 Many of Koboltz's spells were written: StadtAA, Urg., 10, 17 Oct. 1578, Wilhelm Koboltz. He got Niclaus Brestle to write some 'blessings' down for him: 17 Oct. 1578, Niclaus Brestle. Georg Schot collected written spells: 9 and 11 Feb. 1579, Georg Schot.
104 Scherer, *Christliche Erinnerung*; Khueller, *Kurtze Warhafftige … Historia*.
105 The sexual logic of nineteenth-century spiritualism offers an interesting

parallel. See Alex Owen, *The Darkened Room: Women, power and spiritualism in late Victorian England*, London 1989.

106 *Eigentliche vnnd warhafftige verzeichnuss*, fos A ii r, A iv v.
107 *Actus*, fos 1 r–3 v.
108 *Eigentliche vnnd warhafftige verzeichnuss*, fos A iv r–v, B i v–B ii r: Susanna Roschman exhibited behaviour of a sexual kind, and was bound on a bed where the exorcism took place; *Actus*, fo. 13 r: the possessed woman was placed on a bed in a large room.
109 ibid., fo. 15 r:

> zichtig vnd gedultig erzaigt, vnnd sich so verhalten, das nicht ain ainiges zaichen, aines besössnen, an Jm hette vermörckt werden konnen, Allain hatt sy gewaint, den Predigcanten Sehnlich angesechen, vnd Manchen tieffen Seüffzen gelassen, Sonnst hat sy, weil dise ganze Action gewert, kain wort gerödt.... Da sy dann auch ain mal zum Jesuiter ganz diemmüetig gesprochen.

110 Eisengrein, *Vnser liebe Fraw*, fo. 130 v.
111 *Kurtze Warhafftige ... Historia*, fos A ii r–A iv v.
112 The flat description by Christoph Jacobellus of Dr Wendel's purportedly successful exorcism of Georg Fugger's servant has the demon speaking with 'grausamen bellen'. When it departs from the maid, it leaves her weak and quiet, confessing sadly to her sin which had caused the possession: *Actus*, fos 1 rff.
113 Velserus, *Chronica*, pp. 122–3, 125.
114 See Clark, 'Protestant Demonology'.
115 So, for instance, the woman successfully exorcized by Dr Wendel in 1568 had been exorcized by Dr Simon Scheibenhart before, only to have one stubborn demon named 'Hellhound' return: *Actus*, fo. 1 r.

9 Witchcraft and fantasy in early modern Germany

In January 1669, Anna Ebeler found herself accused of murdering the woman for whom she had worked as a lying-in-maid. The means were a bowl of soup. Instead of restoring the young mother's strength, the soup, made of malmsey and brandy in place of Rhine wine, had increased her fever. The mother became delirious but, as the watchers at her deathbed claimed, she was of sound mind when she blamed the lying-in-maid for her death. As word spread, other women came forward stating that Ebeler had poisoned their young children too. The child of one had lost its baby flesh and its whole little body had become pitifully thin and dried out. Another's child had been unable to suckle from its mother, even though it was greedy for milk and able to suck vigorously from other women: shortly after, it died in agony. In a third house, an infant had died after its body had suddenly become covered in hot, poisonous pustules and blisters which broke open. The baby's 7-year-old brother suffered from aches and pains caused by sorcery and saw strange visions, his mother suffered from headaches and the whole household started to notice strange growths on their bodies. And a fourth woman found her infant covered with red splotches and blisters, her baby's skin drying out until it could be peeled off like a shirt. The child died most piteously, and its mother's menstruation ceased. All had employed Ebeler as their lying-in-maid. Anna Ebeler was interrogated six times and confessed at the end of the second interrogation, when torture was threatened. She was executed and her body burnt on 23 March 1669 – a 'merciful' punishment practised in place of burning in the humane city of Augsburg. She was aged 67. Just two months had elapsed since she was first accused.[1]

Anna Ebeler was one of eighteen witches executed in Augsburg. As many more were interrogated by the authorities but cleared of witchcraft; others faced religious courts and yet further cases never reached the courts. Augsburg saw no witch-craze. Unlike its south German neighbours, it executed no witch before 1625 and its cases tended to

Plate 9.1 The case of Anna Ebeler, 1669, *Relation Oder Beschreibung so Anno 1669 . . . von einer Weibs/Person . . .*, Augsburg 1669

Note: These images might be used and reused for different cases. Thus, some of the same scenes are to be found in *Warhaffte Historische Abbild: und kurtze Beschreibung, was sich unlangst in (. . .) Augspurg (. . .) zugetragen (. . .)*, Augsburg 1654; and *Warhaffte Beschreibung des Urthels (. . .)*, Augsburg 1666.

come singly, one or two every few years after 1650.[2] Witchcraft of an everyday, unremarkable kind, the themes of the cases can tell us a great deal about early modern psyches. For Ebeler's crimes were not unusual. It was typical, too, that of her accusers all except one should have been

Plate 9.2 A: Anna Ebeler is abducted from a dance by the Devil and led to her house

women, and that her victims were young infants aged up to about six weeks and women who had just given birth.

One dominant theme in witch-trials in Augsburg is motherhood. Relations between mothers, those occupying maternal roles and children, formed the stuff of most, though not all, witchcraft accusations in the town.[3] To this extent, early feminist works which focused on birth and midwives in their explanations of witchcraft were making an important observation.[4] But though the trials were concerned with the question of motherhood they were not, it seems to me, male attempts to destroy a female science of birth nor were they concerned with wresting control of reproduction from women. What is striking is that they were typically accusations brought by mothers, soon after giving birth, against women intimately concerned with the care of the child, most often the lying-in-maid and not the midwife.

Many investigations of witchcraft proceed by trying to explain why women should be scapegoated as witches or what other conflicts may have been at the root of the case – conflicts involving issues with which we are more comfortable, such as struggles over charity, property or political power. However, I want to argue that the cases need to be understood in their own terms by means of the themes they develop. As historians, I think we may best interpret them as psychic documents which recount particular predicaments. Witchcraft cases seem to epitomize the bizarre and irrational, exemplifying the distance that separates us from the past. What interests me, however, is the extent to which early modern subjectivities are different or similar to ours. I shall argue that unless we attend to the imaginative themes of the interrogations themselves, we shall not understand witchcraft. This project has to investigate two sides of the story, the fears of those who accused, and the self-understanding of people who in the end, as I shall argue, came to see themselves as witches.

Our perplexity in dealing with witchcraft confessions derives in part from their epistemological status. In a profession used to assessing documents for their reliability, it is hard to know how to interpret documents which we do not believe to be factual. But witchcraft confessions and accusations are not products of realism, and they cannot be analysed with the methods of historical realism. This is not to say that they are meaningless: on the contrary, they are vivid, organized products of the mind. Our problem is not that early modern people had a different ontology to our own, believing in a world populated by ghosts who walked at night, devils who might appear in the form of young journeymen, severed arms carrying needles or wandering souls inhabiting household dust. Rather, all phenomena in the early modern world, natural and fantastic, had a kind of hyper-reality which resided in their significance. Circumstantial details were ransacked for their meaning for the individual, and for what they might reveal about causation and destiny. Causation, which could involve divine or diabolic intervention in human affairs, was understood in terms both moral and religious. Consequently, we need to understand confessions and accusations as mental productions with an organization that is in itself significant. This means analysing the themes of witchcraft not to tell us about the genealogy of magical beliefs – the approach taken by Carlo Ginzburg in his recent book[5] – but to tell us about the conflicts of the actors.

In the cases I have explored, witchcraft accusations centrally involved deep antagonisms between women, enmities so intense that neighbours could testify against a woman they had known for years in full knowledge that they were sending her 'to a blood bath' as one accused woman cried to her neighbours as they left the house for the chancellery.[6] Their main motifs concern suckling, giving birth, food and feeding; the capacities of parturient women's bodies and the vulnerability of infants. This was surprising, at least to me: I had expected to find in witchcraft a culmination of the sexual antagonism which I have discerned in sixteenth- and seventeenth-century German culture. The idea of flight astride a broom or pitchfork, the notions of a pact with the Devil sealed by intercourse, the sexual abandonment of the dance at the witches' sabbath, all seemed to suggest that witchcraft had to do with sexual guilt and attraction between men and women, and that its explanation might lie in the moralism of the Reformation and Counter-Reformation years, when Catholics and Protestants sought to root out prostitution and adultery, shame women who became pregnant before marriage and impose a rigorous sexual code which cast the women as Eve, the temptress who was to blame for mankind's fall.[7]

Some of the cases I found certainly dealt with these themes, but the primary issue in what we might term a stereotypical case of witchcraft was maternity. The conflicts were not concerned with the social construction of gender but were related much more closely to the physical changes a woman's body undergoes when she bears children.[8] While these clearly have a social meaning and thus a history, the issues were so closely tied to the physical reality of the female sex and to sexual identity at the deepest level that they seemed to elude off-the-peg explanations in terms of female roles and gender conflict. The stuff of much of the accusations made by the mothers was not femininity or genital sexuality, but was pre-Oedipal in content, turning on the relationship to the breast and to the mother in the period before the infant has a sense of sexual identity.[9] The primary emotion of the witchcraft cases, envy, also originates in this early period of life.[10] Witchcraft accusations followed a pattern with a psychic logic: the accusations were made by women who experienced childbirth and their most common type of target was a post-menopausal, infertile woman who was caring for the infant. Often, as in the case we have just explored, she was the lying-in-maid.

Here it might be objected that witchcraft interrogations and confessions cannot be used to give us insight into early modern psychic life in this way. They are stereotyped products, it might be argued, not of those interrogated but of the minds of the interrogators. These men wanted to know about witches' sabbaths, sex with the Devil and cannibalism and they forced this information out of the women using leading questions and even outright promptings, resorting to torture to gain the confession they needed to convict the woman. However, such an objection does not recognize the cultural attitude to pain nor its place in the dynamic of interrogation in early modern society. Witches were women who could not feel pain as normal women could. They were unable to weep and they did not sense the witch-pricker's needle.[11] A measure of physical pain, so the interrogators believed, was a process of the body which enabled the witch to free herself from the Devil's clutches, weakening her defences against the admission of guilt. The amount of pain had to be finely judged by the executioner, a scientist of the body. Using his knowledge of the victim's frailty, and in consultation with the council, he calculated the precise grades required at each stage of the process (from exhibition of the equipment, stretching on the rack without attaching weights, through to attaching weights of increasing size) so that the witch's integral, diabolic personality might be stripped away by the application of pain to uncover the truth.[12] Like a kind of medicine of salvation, it assisted her travail to return to the Christian community in contrition so that she might die in a state of grace. Torture was part of an understanding, shared by the witch and her persecutors, of the interrelation of body and soul: the skin of the outer person had to be flayed away to arrive at psychological truth. Those who did not crack under torture were set free despite the seriousness of the accusations against them, because they were said to have proven their innocence: they lacked a diabolic interiority of this kind.

Pain had a religious significance too. By experiencing the pain of flagellation, or participating in the procession of the Twelve Stations of the Cross, a ritual which reached its final form in the Counter-Reformation in Augsburg,[13] one could come closer to Christ by physical imitation of His sufferings. Maternity involved pain. Mary herself had borne Jesus in suffering, and the seven swords of grief piercing the suffering Madonna were a powerful Baroque image. Luisa Accati has written of the importance of the Madonna in agony to Baroque understandings of both Marian piety and motherhood.[14] Soothsayers told of spells in which they appealed to 'the suffering of Mary as she lay on her martyr-bed of straw'.[15] The witch, the woman whose capacity to feel pain was impaired, was thus an unmaternal woman, alienated from the realm of pain so manifestly experienced by the new mothers who accused her of sorcery. Devoid of maternal affection, the witch was incapable of feeling pity for her victims.

Moreover, the system of confession also rested on a measure of collusion between witch and questioner. The witch had to freely affirm her confession after it had been given, in the absence of torture. This was a requirement of the Imperial Law Code of Charles V of 1532, and it was certainly not honoured all over the empire.[16] But in a place like Augsburg which did not experience mass witch-hunts, the credibility of the phenomenon of witchcraft rested on the ultimate truth-telling of the witch. Witches could and did modify their confession: so, for instance, Anna Ebeler, who had confessed to having sex with the Devil a countless number of times, insisted at the last that she had only rarely had diabolic intercourse, a disclaimer incorporated in her final public condemnation. Witches were commonly supposed to have renounced God, Jesus, Mary and the saints, but Ebeler was able to maintain that she had never forsworn the Virgin, who had comforted her during diabolic assaults, and that she had never desecrated the Host as she had earlier confessed she had.[17] Another who firmly denied that she was a witch was not described as such in her denunciation, even though she was executed for having used witchcraft.[18]

This freedom was in some sense apparent rather than real: witches who confessed and then revoked their confession embarked on a long and hideous game of cat and mouse with their interrogators, as they were reinterrogated and tortured until their narrative was consistent. But interrogators knew when a confession was simply a result of torture or its fear, and they noted this. Crucial to their own understanding of their task was the belief that, by repetition and forcing the culprit to describe and redescribe the minutiae of the crime, checking with witnesses, the truth would eventually be uncovered. That truth took on a kind of talismanic quality, as the witch was forced to tell and retell it in up to ten sessions of questioning, making it consistent. Her statements were then read out in full to the assembled council before condemnation could be agreed; a summary of her crimes was recorded in the Council's Punishment Book and read out before her execution; and this material formed the basis for the broadsheets and pamphlets that were written about the case.[19] The reiteration fixed the details until there could be no doubt about the narrative. It was a truth which the witch herself freely acknowledged and for which she alone had provided the material. For despite the power of the stereotypes in the witch's confession, these do not explain the particular inflections individual witches gave to them, as they described how they went to a sabbath that was held just by the gallows outside Augsburg, or how the Devil appeared to them in a long black coat, dressed for all the world like a merchant.[20]

There is a further collusive dynamic at work in interrogation, that between witch and torturer. Torture was carried out by the town hangman, who would eventually be responsible for the convicted witch's execution. Justice in the early modern period was not impersonal: the act of execution involved two individuals who, by the time of execution, were well acquainted with each other. Particularly in witch-trials, torture and the long period of time it took for a conviction to be secured gave the executioner a unique knowledge of an individual's capacity to withstand pain, and of their physiological and spiritual reactions to touch. In a society where nakedness was rare, he knew her body better than anyone else. He washed and shaved the witch, searching all the surfaces of her body for the tell-tale diabolic marks – sometimes hidden 'in her shame', her genitals. He bound up her wounds after the torture. On the other hand, he was a dishonourable member of society, excluded from civic intercourse and forced to intermarry among his own kind. His touch might pollute; yet his craft involved him in physically investigating the witch, a woman who if innocent was forbidden him. He advised on the mode of execution, assessing how much pain the witch might stand, a function he could potentially exploit to show mercy or practise cruelty.[21] In consequence, a bond of intense personal dependence on the part of the witch on her persecutor might be established. Euphrosina Endriss was greatly agitated when a visiting executioner from nearby Memmingen inspected her. She pleaded that 'this man should not execute her, she would rather that Hartman should execute her, for she knew him already'.[22]

Once the torturer's application of pain had brought the witch to confess, she knew she faced execution, and she knew her executioner. In the procedure of interrogation itself, carried out in the presence of council interrogators, scribes and executioner, there is an unmistakable sado-masochistic logic, as the witch, in response to pain, might reveal details of her crimes only to deny them subsequently; or as she proffered scattered scraps of information about diabolic sex only then to tantalize her questioners with contradiction or silence. In this sadistic game of showing and concealing, the witch forced her persecutors to apply and reapply pain, prising her body apart to find her secret. Once it was found, she might herself identify with the aggressor: so, at the conclusion of her final confession as a witch, when it was plain she faced death, Anna Ebeler fell at her persecutors' feet in tears, asking for a merciful execution. 'She begged my lords for forgiveness for what she had done wrong. She thanked them for granting her such a good imprisonment and treatment.'[23] Masochism, however, has its twin in sadism. Even in death, the resolution of the game, the witch herself was believed able to retaliate against her tormentor. One hangman found his hands suddenly crippled after he executed two witches in 1685, and his colleague had to execute the third. Just before Barbara Fischer was executed, so one chronicler noted, a powerful rainstorm struck as if everything must drown: this witch, the writer observed, had shown no signs of contrition.[24] At every stage, the trial progressed through a combustion of sadism, retaliation and masochism, in which each actor might in fantasy veer from persecutor to victim to tormentor.

How can the historian make use of material generated in such circumstances? In spite of the geographical specificity and precision of detail we noted earlier in the confession material, witchcraft confessions certainly do possess a stereotypical aspect. There are elements, like the diabolic pact, the sabbath, the powder the Devil gave them to do harm, which appear in most confessions. But the basic psychic images of any society are usually the stuff of cliché. It is their commonness which makes these images seem banal, yet enables them to give form to inchoate, shared terrors and common predicaments. It is undoubtedly true that the pressures of interrogation and pain caused accused witches to shape their accounts of their own emotions and present a narrative of their psychic worlds in a particular way – the language of witchcraft forced them to present the Devil as their seducer and the ultimate cause of their fall. But narratives in which people try to make sense of their psychic conflicts usually involve borrowing from a language which is not at first the individual's own. We might say that coming to understand oneself can involve learning to recognize one's feelings in the terms of a theory, psychoanalytic or diabolic, which one might not originally have applied to oneself, and it can also entail a kind of violence.

What was the substance of the witches' crime? The grief and terror of the witnesses concentrated on the bodies of those who were the victims of witchcraft. Their bodies bore the signs of their martyrdom. As one mother put it, her dead child was covered in sores so that he looked like a devotional image of a martyr.[25] Strange signs were seen: nipples appeared all over the body of one infant, erupting into pussy sores. The legs of another were misshapen and bent.[26] Repeatedly, witnesses stress the physical character of the victim's agony, incomprehensible suffering which cannot be alleviated by the onlookers or by the mother, and which excite hatred, revenge and guilt feelings in part because of the sufferer's innocence. In emotionally-laden language, the witnesses describe the 'piteous' way a child died, and their own failure to get the child to thrive. It is in this collective world of gossip and advice that the rumours of witchcraft first began, in the grief and guilt of the mother at the loss of the tiny baby, and as the women around them sought to identify the cause of this inexplicable, unbearable suffering. Such gossip could be deadly. It was her employer's tongue, her 'wicked gob' as Barbara Fischer put it, using the term applied to animals' mouths, which caused one lying-in-maid to retaliate against her maligner by poisoning her.[27]

The themes of the injury are not only pitiful but frightening. These terrors circle around nourishment and oral satisfaction, evoking power-ful pre-Oedipal feelings. The breast, milk and nourishment were its key images. The food the witch gave the mother was sprinkled with white or black diabolic powders or the soups she was fed were poisonous, and these of course influenced the milk the infant received in a very immediate way. Attacks on the mother's food were thus attacks on her infant as well. When the witch killed, she often used poison, perverting the female capacity to nourish and heal. So one grandmother was inter-rogated three times and tortured because her young grandson suspected witchcraft when he felt queasy after drinking an aniseed water tonic she had given him.[28] The witch could be a kind of evil mother who harmed instead of nourishing her charge. The flow of nourishment could be dis-rupted so that the child dried out and died. In one case, the witch was accused of literally reversing the flow of the maternal fluids, herself sucking the infant dry and feeding on it. Its mother described how

> its little breasts had been sucked out so that milk had been pressed out from the child's little teats contrary to nature, . . . and from this time on the child had lost weight so that it looked as if hardly a pound of flesh remained on it.[29]

Another baby was found to be covered with a myriad of tiny teats as if it had become a mere drinking vessel for the thirsty witch; yet another baby's teats produced 'a little drop of white watery liquid'.[30] The signs that sorcery was afoot were clearly written on the infant's body. Its skin dried out for lack of fluid, or else erupted in sores as if evil fluids within its body were forcing their way out. Its entire little body might become 'red and blue, all mixed up, and rigid and hard, like a plank of wood'.[31] The infant might be unable to drink from its own mother, yet when given to another woman, be 'so hearty in sucking that it made her weep'.[32] (These themes could also emerge in cases which did not

Plate 9.3 B: Ebeler's night ride with the evil one; C: Ebeler at the witches'
dance; D: The witches' assembly and the diabolic feast

correspond to the classic accusation against a maid: so Regina Schiller
denied that she had had sex with the Devil. He had tried to seduce her
but instead 'had come to her breasts, and had tried to give her a little
powder so that she could harm people, especially children'.[33] Here, too,
a woman was thinking of herself as a witch who was the possessor
of a poisonous breast, harming children, again working the images of
pre-Oedipal nourishing rather than exploring fantasies of sex with the
Devil.) In all these cases, the infant's feeding had been disrupted so that
no satisfactory nourishing could take place and the relation between
mother and child was destroyed. Feeding had been reversed and the
infant's young rosy flesh was wasting away while the old witch thrived.

These beliefs rested on a whole economy of bodily fluids. A post-
menopausal woman, the old witch was in a sense a dry woman who,
instead of feeding others well, diverted nourishment to her own selfish
ends. Older widows were believed to have the power to ruin young
men sexually, and youths were warned against marrying such women
because they were sexually ravenous, and would suck out their seed,
weakening them with their insatiable hunger for seminal fluid and
contaminating them with their own impurities.[34] The old witch's fluids
did not flow outwards. Often her magic was directed against fertility,
making women barren.[35] As was well known, witches could not weep,
and old widows could neither menstruate nor suckle children. Instead,
so the science of demonology explained, she was nourishing the Devil.
The warts for which the executioner searched her naked body were the
diabolic teats on which the Devil sucked. Witches were also believed to
communicate without confessing, and to secrete the Host in their
mouths, taking it home to trample upon and dishonour. In doing so they
were not only misusing holy food but maltreating a child, the infant Jesus
whose saving death provided the Bread of salvation, squashing him

and making him suffer pain. This motif is clearly taken from the older myth of Jewish ritual murder, the belief that Jews were stealing the Host and torturing it to make it bleed, and that they stole Christian children so that they could use their blood in secret rituals.[36] Yet even this hoary fantasy was incorporated into the fabric of daily life: Anna Schwayhofer confessed to this crime in the apocalyptic year 1666, and described how, housewife to the fingertips, she had afterwards swept the crumbs of the desecrated Host off the floor of her lodgings with a broom.[37]

Witches were women who did not feed others except to harm them. Failed exchanges of food typified a witch's interactions with her neighbours. So one woman, suspected of being a witch, offered two sisters who lived in her house a dish of Bavarian carrots. Yet this was a two-edged peace offering. The woman insisted the sisters eat the food, and sat with them until it was all consumed. One of the two was pregnant, and the dish made her ill.[38] The witch said the food would strengthen the child within her, yet this wish for the child's health actually meant its opposite. Like the fairies of fairytale who are not invited to the baptism, the old woman's evil 'wishes' for the infant's future blighted its life. And this could happen in a trice, even without the witch's intention: Maria Gogel explained how 'if a person ate plain milk, peas, meat or cheese, and chanced upon a child and merely said "Oh, what a beautiful child" immediately it is bewitched'.[39]

Witches' other means of harming was by 'trucken', pressing down on the infant or its mother. The verb may also refer to the effort of pushing down in labour. In witchcraft it is used in at least three different contexts: to describe the way the Devil forces one woman to do evil, the smothering of an infant, and a mysterious kind of oppression felt by the woman who has just given birth. Georg Schmetzer's wife complained of feeling that something was coming to her at night, lying on her and pressing her so that she suffered from pain down one side. She suspected the lying-in-maid of coming to her bed in the evening and lying on top of her – a fear strengthened by the maid's unorthodox suggested remedy for her backache that she should undress and lie on top of her in a kind of all over massage.[40] Anna Maria Cramer believed a witch was coming to her at night and lying on her, pressing down on her pregnant body.[41] Another woman heard a mysterious voice crying 'druckdich Madelin, druckdich' (be pressed down, Maggie, be pressed down) and she felt something trying to bite her neck. Her lying-in-maid Euphrosina Endriss was finally brought to confess that she had 'pressed' the baby she carried about with her, squashing its skull so that it died.[42] The themes here do not appear to be directly sexual. Rather, what is described is a kind of heavy, deadly embrace, again typified by an ambiguous mixture of love and hatred which might kill the infant with a kind of excess of maternality. The mother's feelings have more to do with extreme depression, immobility and passivity. In all these cases, the mother

Plate 9.4 E: Ebeler's interrogation and confession of witchcraft; F: Ebeler
perverts two innocent children, a boy and a girl

seems to suffer from a kind of lassitude, unable to move or act to protect herself and her child beyond screaming for help – she cannot fight back, and the oppressive sensation of smothering symbolizes her inaction and the diffuse nature of the threat to herself and her child, causing harm not from within her own body but in a kind of anonymous pressure from without. As with the disturbances of nourishment, the violence is indirect, its source unclear and retaliation impossible.

Why should it have been motherhood which engendered these murderous antagonisms between women? Mothers in the early modern period spent the first few weeks of their child's life 'lying in', recuperating from the birth. These six or so weeks were set apart from normal life as the woman retreated into the lying-in-room, resting in the bed from which the husband would be banished. There she was the centre of the house, and there, lying in bed, she would entertain her female friends who had supported her during the birth, holding a women-only birth party with wine and delicacies to celebrate her delivery. If she could afford it, she would employ a lying-in-maid, whose job it was to care for both mother and child. During this period when her life was predominantly lived in the world of women, she could not leave the house and some believed her to be under the power of the Devil.[43] Evil influences might make their presence felt; ghosts might appear. At the end of this time she would go to church for the ceremony of purification or churching, which marked her return to marital cohabitation and public life, and the lying-in-maid would be dismissed. Today the attendant psychic conflicts of this period of the mother's life might be described as relating to the loss of the pregnant state and the ending of the unity of mother and child. Together with the incessant demands on time and energy that the new infant makes, these might be related to maternal depression and to a mixture of feelings towards the infant which may extend to anger, envy or even to wishing harm to the child.

What seems to emerge from these cases, however, is a different set of historically formed psychic mechanisms for dealing with this predicament. The time of separation of mother and child was clearly marked in ritual terms.[44] The mother's re-entry into society as a single being, uncontaminated by what can – if she bears a male child – seem to be the bisexuality of pregnancy, was celebrated in churching, a ritual which remained an important ceremony despite the Reformation's attempt to curtail it. These few weeks were also full of danger for mother and child. According to English figures, a woman had a 6 to 7 per cent chance of dying in childbed, and while this figure may seem low, it was an ever-present terror, doubtless added to by the stories passed around by her women visitors.[45] In the first few weeks of life the child was at its most delicate, as feeding had to be established, either with the mother, a wet-nurse or else by hand. Interestingly, it was during this period or else immediately after the lying-in-maid's departure that the child began to ail. But instead of seeking the source of her ills in post-natal depression, within herself, as we would, the mother's anxieties about the child's fate and her own ability to nourish it were directed outwards, so that harm to either mother or baby was believed to have been caused by another. Here we might make use of what Melanie Klein says about splitting, which allows intolerable feelings of hostility and malice to be projected on to another, so that the mother recognizes only benevolence in herself, projecting the evil feelings about herself on to the 'other' mother.[46] The lying-in-maid was thus destined for the role of the evil mother, because she could be seen to use her feminine power to give oral gratification to do the reverse – to suck the infant dry, poison the mother and her milk and, in the most extreme form of witch fantasies, to kill, dismember and eat the child at the witches' sabbath. At a time when the new mother's experience of giving birth and caring for an infant might raise memories of her own infancy, recalling the terrifying dependence on the maternal figure for whom she may have experienced unadmitted, intolerable feelings of hatred as well as love, there was another person playing the maternal role to hand. We might say that during the new mother's period of feeling complete inertia, 'pressed down upon', she finally gained the strength to retaliate, resolving her state by accusing the witch of harming her child. In this sense, so far from being a simple expression of misogyny, early modern society can be said to have taken the fears of the mother seriously, supporting her search for the culprit instead of describing her as suffering from post-natal depression or attributing a kind of madness to her – women today may attempt to use the defence of post-partum psychosis to argue that they were not legally responsible for crimes committed during the first few weeks after giving birth.

The lying-in-maid was almost over-determined as the culprit, should witchcraft be suspected. Old, no longer capable of bearing a child herself and widowed, she was a woman who housed alone and was a transitory member of the households of others. No longer at the heart of a bustling household of her own, she was a hired member of the family for whom she worked, privy to the most intimate physical secrets of the bodies of those she tended. An interloper, she was never accorded a real place of her own – one even had to share a cramped bed with a servant which was so narrow that she fell out of it in the night.[47] The lying-in-maid undermined the settled hierarchies of the household at a time when the new baby's arrival overturned the workshop's rhythm. For the six to eight weeks after the mother had given birth, she alone carried out the duties of a mother, dandling, washing and swaddling the baby, and caring for its mother, giving her nourishing soups. Just as she had no place in the house she might call her own, so also her work life left her humiliatingly dependent on others: on the midwife, who trained her, recommended her and from whom she might hear of her next job; on her employer, the mother, who might choose not to re-employ her and who could blacken or enhance her reputation by gossiping with other mothers about her. She lacked the midwife's qualifications and official status as an employee of the council, nor did she have the luxury of the midwife's official retainer to tide her over slack periods. Often, it was her very insecurity which was turned against her. One woman who went down on her knees to plead with her accusers only made them the more convinced that something was amiss; frightened people were likely to be caught in the Devil's snares.[48]

But she was also invested with awesome power. She had her particular recipes for strengthening soups, she had her methods for bringing up young infants, she 'alone cared for the child, and it was in no one's hand but hers' as one lying-in-maid accused of witchcraft put it.[49] She was strong at a time when the new mother was ill and weakened, and she was fulfilling her tasks. The new mother, sleeping alone in the marital bed, was not 'mistress of the household' in sexual terms: old, infertile and unhusbanded as the lying-in-maid was, she represented a double threat to the mother, standing both for the mother's own future and sometimes representing a sexual threat as well. If the husband were 'up to no good', the lying-in-maid, who in many cases had borne illegitimate children, might be suspected.[50]

The lying-in-maid dealt with the waste products of the body, she had access to the afterbirth and to cauls and she had the care of the infant's body.[51] One lying-in-maid was accused of purloining the afterbirth, burning it at night under her bed in a bid to harm mother and child, and it was only with great difficulty that she managed to persuade the judges that she had merely been attempting to clean a pewter bowl.[52] Another was foolish enough to accuse the midwife of hiding a baby's caul. Taking the 'little net' to the child's father in the hope of gaining a handsome tip for her trouble, she not only antagonized the midwife but led people to suspect that she had her own nefarious purposes for the caul.[53] Through the waste products of the body, things invested with their owner's power – hair, nails, afterbirth – the sorcerer could control the individual to whom they had belonged. These substances could be used to direct the emotions, causing the bewitched person to fall in love, and they could be used to harm. In this cosmology, emotions were highly sensitive to manipulation of the body. Emotions, like physical pains, could be the result of external events and could readily be ascribed to other people, their source sought outside rather than in the self.

As any mother knew, to antagonize a lying-in-maid was to court disaster. 'I gave her good words until she left the house', so one young mother said.[54] Many of the witnesses mention the time when the lying-in-maid was 'out of the house', a phrase which captures the element of menace the maid was thought to represent. Only then might an accusation be safely made, because then the maid could not revenge herself by bewitching the child. (One seer refused to help an ailing child until the maid had gone: then she succeeded in restoring its rosy flesh, but it began to waste away again when the maid returned shortly after to collect money she was owed.)[55] So fraught was the moment of the maid's departure that her formal relinquishing of responsibility could also become a test of whether the child had thrived. One woman repeated the ambiguous rhyme she had spoken on parting from the child:

My dear little treasure, now you are well recovered
Look master and mistress
Now I depart from the child
Whatever may happen to him now
I will not be held to blame[56]

Such a jingle, with its careful divestment of responsibility, has a menacing tone. It is a double-edged wish. An attempt to free the speaker of blame, it carries the implied threat that something *will* happen to the infant, and it prophylactically points the finger at someone else, by implication the mother, who now assumes the maternal role alone. Indeed, harm often came to the child after the lying-in-maid had departed. 'It was the first night . . . that the lying-in-maid was out of the house', one mother remembered, that strange things began to happen; it was just after the maid had left, another mother noted, when her child had suddenly sickened.[57] Something of the uncertain nature of the relationship between mother and lying-in-maid is caught in the way one maid kept referring to the presents she had received, listing them and naming their giver, in a fruitless attempt to determine the relationship as one of goodwill – yet even the mothers she thought had valued her care were now willing to testify against her conduct.[58] Her behaviour was always indeterminate, its meaning open to a subsequent hostile reinterpretation.

Above all, it was the lying-in-maid's maternal role which placed her in the role of suspect. Sometimes this might lead to straightforward conflicts over upbringing – Euphrosina Endriss was blamed for molly-coddling a child, giving it too many warm cushions.[59] Midwives and mothers suspected maids of bathing the child in water that was too hot, or of swaddling its limbs too tightly so that it might become deformed.[60] Injuries inflicted in the first few weeks of the infant's life might not manifest themselves for years: the failure of one child to speak, harm to one girl's reproductive organs, were all blamed on the lying-in-maid.[61] 'Why must it always be the lying-in-maid who is to blame?' asked one accused woman.[62] A woman who could not be trusted, a woman unable to bear children herself, she was tailor-made for the role of the ultimate evil mother. The very intensity of the bonds between her and the child, as the person who enjoyed a primary attachment to the baby in its first weeks of life, were also the reason to suspect her. As with all witchcraft, it was the powerful ambivalence of feeling which nourished witchery: witchcraft was to be feared not from those indifferent to you, but from those whose relationship was close and whose intimate knowledge of your secrets could be turned to harm. Consequently, every good wish a suspected woman might make for the health and well-being of an infant was charged with its opposite. So one young mother feared the frequent visits the lying-in-maid made to her infant's cradle, standing over it. She later discovered a knife underneath its crib.[63]

And the lying-in-maid had a motive: envy. Envy was the motor of witchcraft as seventeenth-century people understood it. One of the seven deadly sins, it was a feeling which could have material force. It is also an emotion which, according to Melanie Klein, first develops in the early months of an infant's life and is deeply connected to feelings of love and hate. Envy involves wishing harm towards an object. In the logic of sorcery, where emotions might be externalized on to things outside the person and where feelings had active force, the emotion itself was the wellspring of injury. Circumstances conspired to make the lying-in-maid appear a likely sufferer from envy and hatred. As seventeenth-century people saw it, she was poor and single; her employer had a workshop and was comfortably off. Infertile herself, she tended a mother who was surrounded by the love, attention and presents of other women, and who had a baby. By contrast her own children had been conceived illegitimately or had died in infancy. So Barbara Fischer had been raped by her stepfather twenty years before she found herself accused of witchcraft. The child of their relationship had died just a few days after birth. At the time, she had begged the council to let her marry, blaming her stepfather's refusal to let her wed for her own fall into sin with him. But the council had punished her by confining her inside the house for her shame, and, two decades later, she explained her fall into witchcraft as the consequence of not being

Plate 9.5 G: Ebeler is led to execution and branded with burning tongs

allowed to marry and become a mother.[64] Interestingly, her diabolic lover appeared to her in the form of a journeyman dyer, the trade her stepfather had followed. Admission of the envy she felt for the mother she tended was, in her case as in many others, the first step in her interrogation towards a full confession.[65] The witch, too, fully believed that to feel envy for a woman was to wish to harm her, and in this emotional world, where things were invested with meaning, emotions could also act directly. Anna Schwayhofer explained she had summoned the Devil when, conscious of her own sins, she despaired of God's mercy: she had taken communion without confession, and she felt 'great envy, resentment and enmity to various persons'.[66]

To this point I have been exploring the psychic world of those who made the accusation, arguing that it is best understood as invoking deep emotions from the early period of the mother's own infant life. She and those around her are able to crystallize her own ambivalence towards her infant by projecting intolerable feelings on to the lying-in-maid. I am not arguing that this always happened: in the vast majority of cases, the childbed was concluded happily and the maid was dismissed with mutual goodwill. But I am claiming that the social organization of mothering practices allowed this to happen, so that a certain kind of psychic dramatic script was available should things go wrong.

But the witch herself had an understanding of her own behaviour. Its main element concerned her own admission of envy. This was the breaking point which then catapulted her into a range of other confessions about the Devil. These form a distinct layer of testimony, elicited under torture and often given with a considerable degree of reluctance. In other contexts, however, where children were not the target of malice, the Devil could be a dominant theme: so the young Regina Schiller baffled authorities all over southern Germany for over a decade with her bizarre physical contortions and extravagant confessions, telling the authorities about her lurid pacts with the Devil and showing the written contract for so many years and so many days, the number indicated with little strokes of blood because she could not count so far.[67]

By contrast, the witches whose fates we have considered here were chary of admitting even to flying or attending the witches' sabbath, and when they did so they presented themselves as outsiders, women who hung at the edges of the wild assemblies, without finding friends among the fellow witches. One witch recalled that the others came from elsewhere, they wore masks and spoke with accents she could not understand, and they were well dressed, not of her class. She did not dance, and at the feast, few people sat at her table.[68] This was certainly a means of cutting down their involvement and guilt and yet the strong sense of being outsiders which their words convey suggests that the fantasies mirrored their current experience of isolation, socially marginal and shorn of friends who might succour them. Their relations with the Devil were distant and unsatisfactory. Even when conviction was a certainty, these accused witches still tried to minimize the extent of their sexual involvement with the Devil, Dorothea Braun insisting at the last that, contrary to her earlier confessions, she had never had sex with the Devil and had always resisted him; Anna Ebeler saying that she had told the Devil she was too old for such things; Anna Schwayhofer firmly denying that intercourse had ever taken place.[69] Indeed, Braun presents the Devil as a kind of peremptory employer, a master whose whims she was condemned never to satisfy. She was too slow learning the craft, she explained, and so the Devil beat her.[70] Their accounts usually give only the merest description of the Devil – he came as a journeyman, or dressed in black, he was a disembodied arm – and they try to argue that their bodies remained intact. Diabolic invasion presents a taboo from which they wanted to shield themselves. But genital sexuality is seldom their own explanation of what they do, even though the sexual narrative would excuse their deed with the culpability of Eve. Instead, dirt and degradation feature. This is most evident in the names of their diabolic lovers, which had names such as Hendirt, Gooseshit and the like, names which combine animality with excrement.[71] Common to almost all is the acknowledgement of the feeling of hatred and the sense of being deserted by God, exiled from the community of fellow Christians. Yet their deeds are projected on to the Devil: he whispers what they should do, he gives them the powder, he forces them to harm the children. In this way their hostile emotions (apart from the first feelings of hatred) could be projected on to the Devil and dissociated from themselves, in a kind of splitting characteristic of witchcraft at every level.

But if I am right that witchcraft could involve conflicts between women that have to be understood in psychic terms, we still need to explain why such conflicts were open to expression through witchcraft at a particular historical moment. After all, even in the town we have been considering here, there were witchcraft cases which followed this pattern or drew on these motifs for only a little over a century, and they were concentrated in the years from 1650 to 1700. After 1700, we can notice a dramatic inversion of the pattern. Now, children rather than their mothers became the objects of suspicion. Between 1724 and 1730, thirty-one child witches were locked up,[72] while after the death of one suspected witch in custody in 1699, no older women were condemned.[73] This reversal suggests to me that the dynamics of much witch hunting have to be sought in the relationship between mother and child which, after a certain point, switched to the child rather than its mother. I suspect that witch-hunting in the seventeenth century must in part be related to the idealization of motherhood in Baroque society. This is not simply a matter of misogyny: after all, it was because the state took the fears and accusations of suffering mothers seriously that cases could be prosecuted. Germany in the later seventeenth century was a society recovering from the ravages of the Thirty Years' War. In Augsburg, the population had halved: small wonder that people feared attacks on fertility.[74] Here the widow played a double role. On the one hand, attacks on old, post-menopausal women are a staple of misogynist tract from the late sixteenth century onwards. But on the other, the widow, I have been suggesting, was merely the mother's mirror image, a woman who could be the repository of all the fears about evil mothers. Maternal hostility and fears about evil mothers could not easily be expressed directly in a society where Mary was revered by both Catholics and Protestants, and where the image of the suffering Madonna was ubiquitous. Hence, too, the tendency in folktale to populate a story with evil stepmothers who alone can represent the bad mother, keeping pure the image of the good, dead mother.[75] Here it is no coincidence that this period also saw a dramatic increase in executions of the ultimate evil mother, the woman who commits infanticide: such women had to be executed. This rise occurred from the early seventeenth century onwards, even though the Imperial Law Code of 1532 had paved the way for such executions three generations before. Together with witchcraft, this accounted for the vast bulk of women executed in Augsburg in the seventeenth century.[76] The themes of much witchcraft, I would argue, are to be found not in a simple sexual antagonism between men and women, but in deeply conflicted feelings about motherhood. At this level, we can talk about misogyny: one trouble with modern psychoanalysis, I think, as with seventeenth-century witchcraft, is that in the end, a mother, or a figure in a maternal position, is made responsible for our psychic ills.

What I have been trying to do here is to explore the themes of early modern witchcraft not so much in order to explain that phenomenon, but in order to see, in the one area where we do have detailed documentation, whether early modern subjectivities were radically different from

Plate 9.6 H: Ebeler is executed and her body burnt to ashes

our own. That is, I have been asking whether and how there is a history of mind and emotion. It might be objected that I have used psychoanalytic categories in order to explore past mental phenomena, and to that extent, my argument is circular, but I think this conceptual difficulty is inherent in the productive use of ideas. One current problem is whether a body of theoretical work like psychoanalysis, designed in a particular historical period, can possibly do justice to the mental lives of people in quite a different time. It is certainly true that psychoanalytic theory can be used to reduce all symbolic worlds to the same meaning, so that everything speaks of phallologocentrism, or betrays the Oedipal complex. I do not think testimony should be read reductively in this way. In the material I was reading, basic psychic conflicts which did not accord with what I expected to find were emerging from witness statements. It seems to me that there are some primary areas of attachment and conflict – between those in maternal positions and children – which are pretty fundamental to human existence, but the form those conflicts may take and the attitude societies adopt to them may change.[77] This, it seems to me, is the territory of the historian. If historians declare the effects of primary emotions of this kind to be unknowable, they will be condemning us to use of a 'common-sense' model of psychological explanation which makes no sense at all because it leaves out of account the extent to which irrational, deep and unconscious feeling can determine human action – and it is hard to see how any history of witchcraft or even of religion can be satisfactory without exploring this dimension.

NOTES

1 Stadtarchiv Augsburg (hereafter cited as StadtAA), Urgichtensammlung (hereafter cited as Urg.), 28 Jan. 1669, Anna Ebeler.
2 StadtAA, Stafbücher des Rats, 1563–1703. For the indispensable, path-

breaking study of witchcraft in Bavaria, see Wolfgang Behringer, *Hexenverfolgung in Bayern. Volksmagie, Glaubenseifer und Staatsräson in der Frühen Neuzeit*, Munich 1987, pp. 431–69: there is one unclear case from 1563; one woman died under arrest in 1591 (p. 157), and another in 1699 (Strafbuch des Rats, 1654–99, 24 Sept. 1699, Elisabeth Memminger). See also Bernd Roeck, *Eine Stadt in Krieg und Frieden. Studien zur Geschichte der Reichsstadt Augsburg zwischen Kalenderstreit und Parität* (Schriftenreihe der Historischen Kommission bei der Bayerischen Akademie der Wissenschaften 37), Göttingen 1989, esp. vol. 1, pp. 113–16, 445–54; and vol. 2, pp. 539–52 on the witch-trial of 1625; and on the cases of 1654, see Wolfgang Wüst, 'Inquisitionsprozess und Hexenverfolgung im Hochstift Augsburg im 17. und 18. Jahrhundert', *Zeitschrift für Bayerische Landesgeschichte*, 50, 1987, pp. 109–26. On witch-hunting in the region as a whole, H.C. Erik Midelfort, *Witch Hunting in Southwestern Germany 1562–1684. The social and intellectual foundations*, Stanford, Calif. 1972.

3 Three of those executed were lying-in-maids, and a fourth was a failed midwife. Four of those heavily suspected were lying-in-maids and most were expelled from the town on other pretexts. Other cases were closely related. One executed witch killed her own child, another committed incest with her own son who later died, while a third had worked as a child-minder. In seven further cases, themes were borrowed from the same paradigm: the executed witches had harmed children for whom they were in some sense responsible.

4 Barbara Ehrenreich and Deirdre English, *Witches, Midwives and Nurses. A history of women healers*, New York and London 1973. See also, for a survey of feminist views of witchcraft, Dagmar Unverhau, 'Frauenbewegung und historische Hexenverfolgung', in Andreas Blauert (ed.), *Ketzer, Zauberer, Hexen. Die Anfänge der europäischen Hexenverfolgungen*, Frankfurt am Main 1990. Recently it has been argued that witchcraft accusations were an attempt to destroy a female science of birth control: Gunnar Heinsohn and Otto Steiger, *Die Vernichtung der weisen Frauen. Beiträge zur Theorie und Geschichte von Bevölkerung und Kindheit* (Part A, Hexenverfolgung, Kinderwelten, Menschenproducktion, Bevölkerungswissenschaft), Herbstein 1985. However, the cases the authors cite are actually about hostility to children, not about birth control: see, for example, pp. 149–56. For a critique of the Heinsohn-Steiger thesis, see Robert Jütte, 'Die Persistenz des Verhütungswissens in der Volkskultur. Sozial- und medizinhistorische Anmerkungen zur These von der 'Vernichtung der weisen Frauen', *Medizinhistorisches Journal*, 24, 1989, pp. 214–31. David Harley has argued that there is little evidence for the importance of midwives among those executed in England: 'Historians as Demonologists: the myth of the midwife-witch', *Social History of Medicine*, 3, no. 1, 1990, pp. 1–26; and for a similar argument, Peter Kriedte, 'Die Hexen und ihre Ankläger. Zu den lokalen Voraussetzungen der Hexenverfolgungen in der frühen Neuzeit – Ein Forschungsbericht', *Zeitschrift für historische Forschung*, 14, 1987, pp. 47–71, 60. While it may be true that the absolute figure of midwives accused or executed was small, they are none the less a recognizable occupational group in the German evidence where only a few other work patterns may be discerned. Their significance might be better related to the involvement of mothers, lying-in-maids and others connected with the care of mothers and infants.

5 Carlo Ginzburg, *Ecstasies. Deciphering the witches' sabbath*, trans. Gregory Roberts, London 1990 (first published in Italian 1989): interestingly, one of the effects of Ginzburg's brilliant analysis is that women's predominance as victims in the witch-hunt tends to slip from the explanation.

6 StadtAA, Urg., 15 July 1650, Ursula Neher, testimony Sabina Stoltz, 29 July 1650. Anna Ebeler screamed that her persecutors were sending her 'to the butcher's slab', 'to the raven stone': StadtAA, Urg., 28 Jan. 1669, Anna Ebeler, testimony of Catharina Mörz, and Anna Ebeler, 24 Jan. 1669.

7 See, on the sexual themes of images of witchcraft, Charles Zika, 'Fears of Flying: Representations of witchcraft and sexuality in early sixteenth-century Germany, *Australian Journal of Art*, 8, 1989–90, pp. 19–48; and on the themes of witch fantasy and their historical elaboration, Richard van Dülmen, 'Imaginationen des Teuflischen. Nächtliche Zusammenkünfte, Hexentänze, Teufelssabbate', and Eva Labouvie, 'Hexenspuk und Hexenabwehr. Volksmagie und volkstümlicher Hexenglaube', both in Richard van Dülmen (ed.), *Hexenwelten. Magie und Imagination vom 16.–20. Jahrhundert*, Frankfurt am Main 1987; Robert Rowland, ' "Fantasticall and Devilishe Persons": European witch-beliefs in comparative perspective', in Bengt Ankarloo and Gustav Henningsen (eds), *Early Modern European Witchcraft: Centres and peripheries*, Oxford 1990. On the project of sexual regulation in sixteenth-century Germany, Lyndal Roper, *The Holy Household. Women and morals in Reformation Augsburg*, Oxford 1989; and R. Po-Chia Hsia, *Social Discipline in the Reformation, Central Europe 1550–1750*, London 1989, pp. 122–73.

8 See Estela V. Welldon, *Mother, Madonna, Whore. The idealization and denigration of motherhood*, London 1988, for an illuminating attempt to deal with the issues of female psychosexual identity.

9 John Demos has also noticed the importance of pre-Oedipal themes in Salem witchcraft: *Entertaining Satan. Witchcraft and the culture of early New England*, Oxford 1982, esp. pp. 116ff, 179ff.

10 Melanie Klein, 'Envy and Gratitude' (1957), in *idem, Envy and Gratitude and Other Works 1946–1963*, London 1975.

11 See, for example, StadtAA, Urg., 20 Dec. 1685, Euphrosina Endriss, 6 March 1686, final observation that Endriss had often looked as though she were going to cry but not a single tear escaped from her; Urg., 28 Jan. 1669, Anna Ebeler: at the interrogation of 11 March 1669, Ebeler noted that the Devil had not allowed her to cry properly, but, as the scribe noted, she then began to cry heartily and to pray the Lord's Prayer, the Ave Maria, and deliver a 'beautiful' extempore confession. Urg., 11 Feb. 1666, Anna Schwayhofer, 15 March 1666, interrogators noted that she apparently felt no pain from the thumbscrews, a fact which the executioner explained by saying this was a mild form of torture. The executioner pricked a suspicious looking mark on Anna Elisabeth Christeiner but it disappeared, strong proof, he thought, of the Devil's work: Urg., April 1701, fourth interrogation, 3 Aug. 1701.

12 See Edward Peters, *Torture*, Oxford 1985; on the executioner, often a key figure in the generation of a witch-hunt, Helmut Schuhmann, *Der Scharfrichter, Seine Gestalt – Seine Funktion* (Allgäuer Heimatbücher 67), Kempten 1964; Ch. Hinckeldy, *Strafjustiz in alter Zeit*, Rothenburg 1980; Werner Danckert, *Unehrliche Berufe. Die verfemten Leute*, Munich 1963; Franz Irsigler and Arnold Lassotta, *Bettler und Gaukler, Dirnen und Henker, Aussenseiter in einer mittelalterlichen Stadt*, Cologne 1984, pp. 228–82. The duration of torture might also be measured by the time it took to say particular prayers, a technique which tacitly invoked divine assistance against diabolic power: see, for example StadtAA, Urg., 30 June 1650, Barbar Fischer, for the use of the Miserere and Lord's Prayer. In some Bavarian trials, torture becomes part of an almost physical struggle against the Devil's power: see Michael Kunze, *Highroad to the Stake*, trans. William E. Yuill, Chicago, Ill. and London 1987; and Wolfgang Behringer 'Hexenverfolgung als Machtspiel', R. Po-Chia Hsia and B. Scribner (eds), *History and Anthropology in Early Modern Europe. Papers from the Wolfen-*

habüttel conference 1991, forthcoming. Kathy Stuart has researched the role of executioners and dishonourable people in Augsburg in the early modern period, and she has a great deal to say about the executioner as an expert on the body and its capacity to withstand pain, knowledge which also made his skills as a healer greatly valued: Kathy Stuart, 'The Boundaries of Honor. "Dishonorable people" in Augsburg 1500–1800', Ph.D. diss., Yale University 1993.

13 Louis Châtellier, *The Europe of the Devout. The Catholic Reformation and the formation of a new society*, Cambridge 1990, p. 150.

14 Luisa Accati, 'The Larceny of Desire: The Madonna in seventeenth-century Catholic Europe', in Jim Obelkevich, Lyndal Roper and Raphael Samuel (eds), *Disciplines of Faith. Studies in religion, politics and patriarchy*, London 1987.

15 StadtAA, Urg., 2 July 1590, Anna Stauder. I have developed the theme of parallels between spells and Counter-Reformation religiosity in 'Magic and the Theology of the Body: Exorcism in sixteenth century Augsburg', in Charles Zika (ed.), *No Other Gods Except Me: Orthodoxy and religious practice in Europe 1200–1700*, Melbourne 1991.

16 *Die peinliche Gerichtsordnung Kaiser Karls V. von 1532*, 4th edn, ed. A. Kaufmann, Munich 1975, arts no. 48–58, pp. 50–6.

17 StadtAA, Urg., 28 Jan. 1669, Anna Ebeler, interrogations 28 Jan. to 23 March 1669; Verruf, 32 March 1669; and Strafbuch Des Rats, 23 March 1669, pp. 312–14.

18 She also denied intercourse with the Devil. StadtAA, Urg., 20 Dec. 1685, Euphrosina Endriss, 4 March 1686, and condemnation, 16 March 1686; Strafbuch des Rats, 1654–99, pp. 557–8.

19 The procedure is described in Staatsbibliothek München, Handschriftenabteilung, Cgm 2026, fos 1 v–5 r. For pamphlets describing the cases, see, for example, *Warhaffter Sumarisch: aussführlicher Bericht vnd Erzehlung. Was die in des Heyligen Röm. ReichsStatt Augspurg etlich Wochen lang in verhafft gelegne zwo Hexen/benandtlich Barbara Frölin von Rieden/vnnd Anna Schäflerin von Etringen . . .*, Augsburg 1654; *Relation Oder Beschreibung so Anno 1669 . . . von einer Weibs-Person . . .*, Augsburg 1669.

20 StadtAA, Urg., 28 Jan. 1669, Anna Ebeler, interrogation 6 March 1669; Strafbuch des Rats, 1654–99, 7 Feb. 1673, Regina Schiller, pp. 390ff.

21 In 1587 the 'evil custom' of allowing the hangman to carry out torture unsupervised had to be explicitly abolished in Augsburg: Behringer, *Hexenverfolgung in Bayern*, p. 158.

22 StadtAA, Urg., 20 Dec. 1685, Euphrosina Endriss, report of Hans Adam Hartman, 5 Feb. 1686: Hans Adam Hartman, executioner of Donauwörth, was the son of the Augsburg executioner Mattheus Hartman who had been crippled in both hands (see below).

23 'bitt in fine nochmalen fuessfellig vnd mit Weinen vmb Ein gnedig urthel, vnd Meine herrn vmb verzeihung, wass sie vnrechts gethan. bedankt sich auch dass man ihr so ein gute gefangnuss vnd tractament zukommen lassen', StadtAA, Urg., 28 Jan. 1669, Anna Ebeler, testimony of 21 March 1669. Anna Schwayhofer also concluded her final testimony by saying this was the confession by which she wanted to live and die, 'confessing also, that she was a heavy, yes, the greatest sinner, and therefore she would gladly die, only begging hereby for a merciful judgement': Urg., 11 Feb. 1666, Anna Schwayhofer, interrogation 31 March 1666. On sadism and masochism see Joyce McDougall, *Plea for a Measure of Abnormality*, London 1990 (1st edn, French 1978); Sigmund Freud, 'Three Essays on the Theory of Sexuality', in *On Sexuality* (Pelican Freud Library 7), trans. James Strachey, ed. Angela

Richards, London 1977; *idem.*, 'The Economic Problem of Masochism (1924)', in *On Metapsychology* (Penguin Freud Library 11), trans. James Strachey, ed. Angela Richards, London 1984.

24 Staatsbibliothek München, Handschriftenabteilung, Cgm 2026, fols 64 v–65 r, 61 r.

25 StadtAA, Urg., 11 Feb. 1666, Anna Schwayhofer, testimony of Margaretha Höcht, 19 Feb. 1666.

26 StadtAA, Urg., 15 July 1650, Ursula Neher, testimony of Susanna Custodis, 11 July 1650.

27 'nur vmb Jhres bösen Maules Willen', StadtAA, Urg., 14 June 1650, Barbara Fischer.

28 StadtAA, Urg., 13 May 1654, Anna Zoller.

29 StadtAA, Urg., 15 July 1650, Ursula Neher, testimony of Sabina Stoltz, 11 July 1650. See also Urg., 25 Jan. 1695, Barbara Melder, testimony of Judith Wolf, 23 Feb. 1695 who saw Melder, the suspected witch, suck her baby's breast.

30 StadtAA, Urg., 15 July 1650, Ursula Neher, testimony of Anna Erhardt, 29 July 1650: at the time, she interpreted this naturalistically and only considered sorcery when Stoltz and Vetter accused Neher.

31 'am ganzen leiblen ganz roht vnd blaw durcheinander, auch ganz stärr vnd hart, wie ein holz', StadtAA, Urg., 11 Feb. 1666, Anna Schwayhofer, testimony of Hans Adam Sperl, 19 Feb. 1666.

32 'da habe das kind so herzhafft angefallen vnd von Ihr getrunken dass sie Köfppin sich geJammert vnd dorüber Weinen müssen', StadtAA, Urg., 28 Jan. 1669, Anna Ebeler, testimony of Anna Maria Kopf, 13 Feb. 1669.

33 'Er ihr zu den Prüssten khomben, vnd ein pulverlin geben wollen, damit den Leüthen, vnd sonderlich Khinder zuschaden', StadtAA, Strafbuch des Rats, 1654–99, 7 Feb. 1673, p. 390, Regina Schiller.

34 See Fredericus Petrus Gayer, *Viereckichtes Eheschätzlein. Da ist: Die vier Gradus der Eheleute*, Erfurt, Johann Beck 1602, esp. fos C iii r ff. on widows' lust, D vii v ff. and E ii v where the writer warns that young men who marry old widows are likely to pine and die in their youth before their elderly wives do, because these old widows have concentrated impurities in them (presumably owing to the cessation of menstruation) and even have impure, poisonous breath.

35 See, for example, Emmanuel Le Roy Ladurie, *Jasmin's Witch. An investigation into witchcraft and magic in south-west France during the seventeenth century*, trans. Brian Pearce, London 1987, pp. 25, 43, 59–60: in rural communities in particular, the hostility to fecundity also involves destruction of the earth's fertility.

36 See R. Po-Chia Hsia, *The Myth of Ritual Murder. Jews and magic in Reformation Germany*, New Haven, Conn. and London 1988.

37 StadtAA, Urg., 11 Feb. 1666, Anna Schwayhofer, interrogation 19 March 1666.

38 StadtAA, Urg., 11 Feb. 1666, Anna Schwayhofer, testimony of Anna Corona Cramer, 19 Feb. 1666; 25 Feb. 1666, Anna Maria Cramer; testimony Anna Maria Cramer and Anna Corona Cramer, 13 March 1666; and interrogations.

39 StadtAA, Urg., 15 July 1650, Ursula Neher, testimony of Maria Gogel, 29 July 1650.

40 StadtAA, Urg., 20 Dec. 1685, Euphrosina Endriss, testimony of Georg Schmetzer, 24 Dec. 1685.

41 StadtAA, Urg., 11 Feb. 1666, Anna Schwayhofer, testimony of Anna Corona Cramer, 19 Feb. 1666; 25 Feb. 1666, Anna Maria Cramer; testimony Anna Maria Cramer and Anna Corona Cramer, 13 March 1666.

42 StadtAA, Urg., 20 Dec. 1685, Euphrosina Endriss, testimony of Magdelena Hornung, 24 Dec. 1685.

43 On churching, see Susan C. Karant-Nunn, 'A Women's Rite: Churching and the Lutheran Reformation', Hsia and Scribner (eds), *History and Anthropology*, forthcoming. See also, for example, *Andreas Osiander d. A. Gesamtausgabe*, eds Gerhard Müller and Gottfried Seebass, Gütersloh 1975–, vol. 5, Brandenburg–Nuremberg church ordinance 1533, p. 128: women who have just borne children should be instructed by the pastor and preacher that they are not under the power of the Devil, as had previously been believed: 'das sie nicht in gewalt des teuffels sein, wie mans bisshere nicht on sundern nachteyl der gewissen darfür gehalten und groeblich daran geyrret hat'.

44 For an excellent account of these rituals in England, see Adrian Wilson, 'The Ceremony of Childbirth and its Interpretation', in Valeries Fildes (ed.), *Women as Mothers in Pre-Industrial England*, London and New York 1990.

45 Patricia Crawford, 'The Construction and Experience of Maternity in Seventeenth-Century England', in Fildes (ed.), *Women as Mothers*.

46 See, for example, Melanie Klein, 'Envy and Gratitude' (1957), 'Some Theoretical Conclusions Regarding the Emotional Life of the Infant' (1952), 'On Identification' (1955), in *idem, Envy and Gratitude and Other Works*.

47 StadtAA, Urg., 28 Jan. 1669, Anna Ebeler, testimony of Anna Maria Schmuckher, 1 Feb. 1669.

48 StadtAA, Urg., 28 Jan. 1669, Anna Ebeler, testimony of Benedict Widenmann, 24 Jan. 1669.

49 StadtAA, Urg., 20 Dec. 1685, Euphrosina Endriss, pre-trial testimony of Endriss, 4 Dec. 1685.

50 For example, Ursula Neher, StadtAA, Urg., 15 July 1650; Barbara Fischer, Strafbuch des Rats, 1615–32, p. 397, 13 May 1623; tried as a witch in 1650.

51 On the different ways men and women used sorcery and bodily products, see Ruth Martin, *Witchcraft and the Inquisition in Venice, 1550–1650*, Oxford 1989; Ingrid Ahrendt-Schulte, 'Schadenzauber und Konflikte. Sozialgeschichte von Frauen im Spiegel der Hexenprozesse des 16. Jahrhunderts in der Grafschaft Lippe', in Heide Wunder and Christina Vanja (eds), *Wandel der Geschlechterbeziehungen zu Beginn der Neuzeit*, Frankfurt am Main 1991; Roper, 'Magic and the Theology of the Body'.

52 StadtAA, Urg., 15 July 1650, Ursula Neher, and testimony Hans and Jacobina Vetter, 11 July 1650.

53 StadtAA, Urg., 28 Jan. 1669, Anna Ebeler.

54 'immerdar guete worth gegeben, biss Sie aus dem haus kommen', StadtAA, Urg., 29 Jan. 1669, Anna Ebeler, testimony of Eleonora Schmidt, 1 Feb. 1669.

55 StadtAA, Urg., 15 July 1650, Ursula Neher, testimony of Sabina Stoltz, 29 July 1650.

56 StadtAA, Urg., 20 Dec. 1685, Euphrosina Endriss, qu. 47, and testimony of Georg Schmetzer, 4 Dec. 1685: 'mein Schäzle du bist wohl auf, sehet Herr und Frau, iezo gehe ich Von dem Kind, es geschehe ihm was da wolle, so will ich entschuldiget sein'. The next day, the child began to sicken.

57 StadtAA, Urg., 28 Jan. 1669, Anna Ebeler, testimony of Juditha Schorr, 13 Feb. 1669; Euphrosina Hayd, 1 Feb. 1669.

58 StadtAA, Urg., 29 Jan. 1669, Anna Ebeler, and interrogation, 19 Feb. 1669.

59 StadtAA, Urg., 20 Dec. 1685, Euphrosina Endriss, qu. 50.

60 StadtAA, Urg., 15 July 1650, Ursula Neher, testimony of Jacobina Vetter, 29 July 1650; testimony of Susanna Custodis, 11 July 1650.

61 StadtAA, Urg., 15 July 1650, Ursula Neher; testimony of Adam Schuster, 11 July 1650; testimony of Anna Erhardt, 29 July 1650.

62 'was die kellerin vmb solche sachen red vnd antwort geben', StadtAA, Urg., 28 Jan. 1669, Anna Ebeler, interrogation, 19 Feb. 1669, qu. 49.

63 StadtAA, Urg., 11 Feb. 1666, Anna Schwayhofer, testimony of Euphrosina Sperl, 19 Feb. 1666: the knife was her husband's but it had been moved.

64 StadtAA, Strafbuch des Rats, 1615–23, 13 May 1623, p. 397; and notes of 19 Oct. 1624, 30 Aug. 1625, 22 Nov. 1625, 29 Jan. 1626; Urg., 10 May 1623, Barbara Fischer; Strafbuch des Rats, 1633–53, 23 July 1650, fo. 337 r–v; Urg., 14 June 1650, Barbara Fischer.

65 StadtAA, Urg., 14 June 1650, Barbara Fischer, see interrogation of 20 June 1650.

66 'gegen vnderschidlichen Personen grossen Neid, grollen vnd feindtschafft getragen', StadtAA, Urg., 11 Feb. 1666, Anna Schwayhofer, interrogation, 31 March 1666; and see also Urg., 28 Jan. 1669, Anna Ebeler, throughout. On enmity and exclusion from community, see David W. Sabean, *Power in the Blood*, Cambridge 1984, pp. 31–60; for a strict Lutheran interpretation of confession and enmity, *Andreas Osiander d. A Gesamtausgabe*, vol. 7, p. 663, Kirchenordnung Pfalz-Neuburg 1543, no absolution to be granted if someone still bears enmity. On the role of envy and hatred in the bringing of witchcraft accusations see Heide Wunder, 'Hexenprozesse im Herzogtum Preussen während des 16. Jahrhunderts', in Christian Degn, Hartmut Lehman and Dagmar Unverhau (eds), *Hexenprozesse. Deutsche und skandinavische Beiträge* (Studien zur Volkskunde und Kulturgeschichte Schleswig-Holsteins 12), Neumünster 1983, esp. pp. 188–9; Robin Briggs, *Communities of Belief. Cultural and social tensions in early modern France*, Oxford 1989, pp. 7–65, 83–105.

67 Staats- und Stadtbibliothek Augsburg, 2o Cod Aug. 288, Schilleriana; Strafbuch des Rats, 1654–99, 7 Feb. 1673, Regina Schiller, pp. 390ff.

68 StadtAA, Urg., June 1625, Dorothea Braun, interrogation, 22 Aug. 1625.

69 StadtAA, Urg., June 1625, Dorothea Braun, statement, 18 Sept. 1625; Urg., 28 Jan. 1669, Anna Ebeler, interrogation, 23 Feb. 1669. Urg., 11 Feb. 1666, Anna Schwayhofer, interrogation, 26 March 1666; and Strafbuch des Rats, 1654–99, 15 April 1666, pp. 235–6.

70 StadtAA, Urg., June 1625, Dorothea Braun, interrogation, 22 Aug. 1625. An older witch also tried to teach her to fly on a cat, but the cat refused to carry her!

71 'Hennendreckele': StadtAA, Strafbuch des Rats, 1633–53, 23 July 1650, Barbara Fischer, fo. 337 r–v; 'Gänsdreckh', Strafbuch des Rats, 1654–99, 18 April 1654, Anna Schäffler, pp. 4–7.

72 Behringer, *Hexenverfolgung in Bayern*, p. 466; Stadt- und Staatsbibliothek Augsburg, 2o Cod Aug. 289, Acta puncto maleficii et tentationis diabolicae.

73 Wolfgang Behringer has noted a general rise in cases of child witches from the last quarter of the seventeenth century onwards. See his 'Kinderhexenprozesse. Zur Rolle von Kindern in der Geschichte der Hexenverfolgungen', *Zeitschrift für historische Forschung*, 16, 1989, pp. 31–47. StadtAA, Strafbuch des Rats, 1654–99, p. 722, Elisabeth Memminger: since she was considered to have been a witch, her corpse was publicly carted out and buried under the gallows. There were two further similar cases: Christina Haber, a lying-in-maid, was interrogated and tortured, 12 Dec. 1699, but eventually let out on recall: Strafbuch des Rats, 1654–99, p. 725. Anna Maria Christeiner and her daughter were accused of abducting and harming children, Verbrecherbuch, 1700–1806, p. 31, 20 Aug. 1701; Urg., 3 Aug. 1701. They were severely tortured but eventually freed on recall. By contrast, a case of 1700 to 1703 concerns the plight of the daughter of Hans Georg Groninger, a suspected girl witch aged 14 in 1702, who ate lice and her own excrement: Stadt-

und Staatsbibliothek Augsburg, 2o Cod Aug. 289, Acta puncto maleficii et tentationis diabolicae; StadtAA, Urg., 17 May 1702, Regina Groninger.

74 Barbara Rajkay, 'Die Bevölkerungsentwicklung von 1500 bis 1648', in Gunther Gottlieb *et al.* (eds), *Geschichte der Stadt Augsburg*, Stuttgart 1985; Roeck, *Eine Stadt in Krieg und Frieden*, vol. 2, pp. 775–85, 880–9.

75 Bernd Roeck argues that Marian devotion was a line of division between the two confessions, but his evidence from baptismal registers also shows that while Catholics favoured the name 'Maria' for girls, the most popular name choice among Protestants was 'Annamaria'. This name choice combined the names of both the mother of Jesus and her mother, suggesting the centrality of Marian ideals and motherhood to Protestant understandings of womanhood. Protestants also strongly favoured the names 'Maria' and 'Regina' (associated with the Queen of Heaven): Roeck, ibid., vol. 2, pp. 847, 862–5. See the rich paper of Marina Warner, 'The Absent Mother, or Women Against Women in the Old Wives' Tale', inaugural lecture, Tinbergen Professor, Erasmus University, Rotterdam 1991.

76 StadtAA, Strafbücher des Rats. Between 1633 and 1699 nine women were punished for this offence, six of whom were executed while a further six women and two men were suspected of the crime.

77 For a different, path-breaking use of psychoanalysis to study witchcraft in New England, see Demos, *Entertaining Satan*. Demos notes the importance of maternal themes in witchcraft material (pp. 181, 198–206) but then goes on to argue that since mothers are almost universally responsible for the care of children, the prevalence of witchcraft is best explained by general child-rearing practices among early New Englanders which resulted in a weak ego structure and a tendency to engage in a good deal of projective behaviour. He uses psychoanalysis, linked with attention to child-rearing practices, to construct a general pathology of New England society: I am using it rather to elucidate particular conflicts between people and illuminate psychic functioning in a manner which does not derive psychic meaning reductively from child-rearing practices. On psychic creativity, see Joyce McDougall, *Plea for a Measure of Abnormality; Theatres of the Body: A psychoanalytic approach to psychosomatic illness*, London 1989; and *Theatres of the Mind: Illusion and truth on the psychoanalytic stage*, New York 1985. A similar emphasis on projective identification is to be found in Evelyn Heinemann, *Hexen und Hexenangst. Eine psychoanalytische Studie über den Hexenwahn der frühen Neuzeit*, Frankfurt am Main 1986.

10 Oedipus and the Devil

In 1670, Regina Bartholome confessed that she had lived with the Devil as man and wife. Aged 21 when she was interrogated by the Augsburg Council, she had met the Devil five years before. She recalled that the Devil was clad in silken hose with boots and spurs and that he looked like a nobleman. They enjoyed trysts twice weekly at a tavern-bakery in Pfersee, a nearby village where Jews lived. The Devil ordered lung sausage, roast pork and beer for her and the two ate with relish alone in the inn parlour. He promised her money, but she had received barely 6 Kreuzer from him, and even that had turned out to be bad coin. In return for this meagre reward, Regina had signed a pact with the Devil for the term of seven years. She had forsworn God and the Trinity, and she had taken the Devil – her lover – as her father in God's stead.

This story, dramatic in its simplicity, begins to make more sense when related to the life-story which she also provided. Regina's father, a poor man, worked for the council as a day-labourer.[1] Around the time Regina first encountered the Devil, and having just reached puberty, she had embarked on her first sexual liaison with a man some years her senior, Michael Reidler, who worked as a prison overseer. At about the same period, her mother had initiated an adulterous affair with a young man, Regina's cousin, who boarded in the house. Mother and cousin had also travelled to the village of Pfersee, where her mother pawned the occasional item with the Jews. Regina's mother's affair ended in disaster: Regina's mother was publicly exhibited in the stocks and humiliated, she was banished forever from the city and her young lover fled the town and died 'of drink' not many years after. Regina, left alone with her father, cooked and kept house for him: 'when he came home from his hard work there was no one else who could cook him something warm so that he could restore himself'[2] as her father put it in a petition to the council on her behalf. So far as practical matters were concerned, Regina had taken her mother's place.

Bartholome took in another lodger, this time a young man named Jacob Schwenreiter who was engaged to be married and who worked, like him, as a day-labourer: the two men, Schwenreiter and Bartholome, shared the marital bed. Regina, now parted from her first lover, fell passionately in love with this new male presence, bringing him brandy, bread, cheese, soups and sitting on his bed. She told him she knew a ruse to get money from the Jews at Pfersee, and promised him a share in the proceeds. But her feelings were not returned. Schwenreiter soon brought his bride to the house, fondling her for hours, so Regina believed. Meanwhile, Regina's plot to swindle the Jew at Pfersee and thereby win the young man's affections had misfired: she had accused a Jew of having sex with her (a relationship which would have offended against the taboo on intercourse between Jews and Christians) but her target was a man of unimpeachable character and her accusations failed to stick. She was lucky to escape with a mere censure and brief imprisonment for perjury. She lost her young man Schwenreiter forever when he married, and about this time, so Regina claimed, another young man, a furrier, sought to gain her affections by plying her with a love potion.

The ensuing quarrels in the Bartholome's house finally brought the whole household, including the newly-weds, before the council's disciplinary officer, the mayoralty. Once there, Regina's publicly-uttered threat to kill the new bride was enough to guarantee her incarceration, and thus began the process of criminal interrogation which was to lead both to her confessions of involvement with the Devil and the revelation of her own history which I have provided here in brief.[3]

I

How can we explain the fantasy of Regina Bartholome, the woman who came to believe herself to be the Devil's lover, daughter and wife? What is the relation between the different narratives she supplied, diabolic and – in our terms – realistic? In this chapter, I shall argue that the fantasy of witch-hood is created in a project of collaboration between questioner and accused, and that the dynamic by which it progressed can indeed be usefully explained psychoanalytically. My claim is not only that, despite what seems at first acquaintance their exotic mental landscape, early modern people have recognizable subjectivities, evincing patterns with which we are familiar. I shall attempt to show that the logic of the interrogations and the process of constructing a full-blown witch fantasy can be illuminated by considering them in psychoanalytic terms.[4]

This may seem a perverse procedure for a historian to adopt. After all, in reaction to some bold early attempts to apply psychoanalytic interpretation to historical characters, historians of early modern Europe have mostly advocated caution. They have insisted upon the radical psychic difference between early modern people and ourselves, pointing to the historical embeddedness of such concepts as family, individual and subjectivity. As Natalie Zemon Davis has reminded us, early modern people characteristically presented their subjectivity in relation to others – family, guild, town.[5] Honour, so many historians have urged, was the substance through which early modern people conceptualized their own identity – and honour is an intrinsically social notion. In an honour society, people derive their sense of self-worth from that of the group to which they belong: the dishonour of one member imperils not the individual alone but the whole.[6] David Sabean has suggested that conscience, which psychoanalysis would see as an inherent part of superego formation, was actually a late child of seventeenth-century Protestantism.[7] Stephen Greenblatt has argued that psychoanalysis depends on a notion of the self which was itself only in the process of creation in the early modern period: consequently, we cannot apply psychoanalytic theory to people who conceived of the subject in a radically different fashion.[8] Early modern people are held to lack that conviction of individuality we take to be central to self-understanding: modernity consists in the chasm which separates us from them. Though psychoanalytic notions may yet flavour the textual interpretation we offer, a commitment to the historical seems to entail that psychoanalysis cannot be adopted by historians as a serious interpretative theory.[9]

While it is certainly true that early modern people thought differently about the relationship between mind and body,[10] held that dreams could aid diagnosis of physical, rather than mental disturbance,[11] believed that the Devil was active in the world and classed as 'real' phenomena which we would reckon to the world of fantasy, such arguments push caution too far. It is striking that it is the distinctive nature of early modern people to which historians point when ruling psychoanalysis out of court, so that what is modern is defined by a change in the notion of the self; a radical imputation of otherness which, however, is parasitic on our own determination to historicize subjectivity by providing a strong narrative of the birth of the self. Yet at the same time, historical interpretation as we undertake it day by day nearly always depends at base on the assumption of a measure of resemblance: how else can we make sense of historical actors? It does not, I think, endanger the status of the historical to recognize that some of its features are enduring: the importance of fantasy, the unconscious, the centrality of parental figures to psychic life, the way in which symbols or objects invested with deep psychic significance seep into more than one sphere of an individual's life. As psychoanalysis insists, identity is tenuous and is formed in part through identification with – and separation from – others, a feature which does not set the early modern period apart. Honour, it seems to me, was not the only or even primary way in which early modern people made sense of their predicaments: their rage at being dishonoured, their defence of reputation against insult, their fear of shame gave expression to what was felt as an attack on them in which the psychic and the bodily were indistinguishable – after all, a woman's honour was to do with her body. We would do better, I think, to relate honour to other features of the psychic and emotional lives of early modern people than to seek to explain their behaviour in terms of a reified notion of honour. A phenomenon such as witchcraft in which mental and emotional events have physical effects, in which the individual agency of both the witch and her victims is of the essence, in which we are confronted with the gripping nature of the lurid phantasms of the witch-craze, demands explanation not only in sociological but in psychological terms. When historians are drawn to apply psychoanalysis to the study of the witch-craze, they generally use it to derive conclusions about an entire society: here, however, I intend to draw on psychoanalytic ideas in order to reconstruct the mental life of an individual.[12]

Regina Bartholome was not generally reputed to be a witch. No one accused her of witchcraft, although people concurred that she was 'strange'. The history of witchcraft has often taken women to be victims, scapegoats for the anxieties of a society. Yet one of the troubling features of a case such as this is the witch's own self-destructive capacity. Regina precipitated her own imprisonment. She first embarked on the highly risky strategy of accusing a Jew of having an adulterous relationship with her, an imputation which she could not prove, and which threatened her own reputation as it undermined his. It also embroiled her in a dangerous criminal investigation from which she was lucky to escape with a short term of imprisonment.[13] Her history is littered with false accusations. She accused the young bride of Jacob Schwenreiter (the young man who was the object of her affections) of stealing something from her – as indeed she had; but it was her bridegroom, not her 'tin pan, bedstead and half a measure of corn' that she had stolen.[14] When Regina cited her before the authorities and then, in the chancellery itself, threatened to kill her, she secured her own imprisonment.[15]

The momentum of Regina's trial derived in part from her own drive to accuse herself, to punish herself and to uncover the truth of a crime she felt herself to have committed. Under interrogation the witch faced two council representatives and ultimately the torturer, who would be her executioner. It is easy to see their exercise of power over their victim: they stood for the power of the council, and they were armed with the instruments of torture. It is less easy, and less comforting for the historian, to see the witch's own manipulation, however unsuccessful, of the situation or to discern the ways in which the sadism of the questioning process may have gratified the needs of the witch.

But how do we interpret what she confessed? The content of witch fantasy is difficult territory for historians, trained as we are to look for verification or to construct social meaning. How can social meanings be derived from material which seems to us both patently unreal and recalcitrantly personal? The most illuminating interpretations have examined witch confessions as a collective psychosis, whose features are best outlined in terms of historical development. The historian's task is to trace the gradual appearance of such motifs as the witch's dance, the pact with the Devil, the satanic mass. These are explained as the production, in the mouths of the persecuted, of the fantasies gradually elaborated by their interrogators.[16] Looking from the other end of the telescope, Carlo Ginzburg has viewed these fantasies as the creation of the people, not of their élite interrogators, interpreting their features as the eruption of older, pagan patterns of belief.[17] He uncovers their mythic structures, tracing their elements back to their folkloric avatars. This is a process in which the fantasies of particular witches play little part: witches themselves, less significant than the culture they inhabit, are not Ginzburg's primary subject of concern.[18]

Both these approaches, however, concur in locating the source of fantasy outside the witch herself. She is merely a conduit either of the traces of a vanished primitive religion, or of the witch beliefs of her interrogators. But a witch fantasy had to persuade its hearers of its truth. Indeed, the interrogation was a lengthy process because the authorities had constantly to assure themselves of the witch's veracity, summoning witnesses to confirm details and checking punctiliously for inconsistencies in her account.[19] The fantasy had to be created by an individual witch out of the elements of fantasy available to her, from what her culture knew of the Devil and his ways, and what she selected had a logic.[20] In Regina Bartholome's account, there was no clutter of diabolic characters to distract from the central focus of the tale, the relationship between Regina and the Devil. There were no sister witches, no accomplices, no apprentice witches whom Regina had seduced, no nocturnal gatherings. Instead, this pared-down form of testimony allowed the themes of her own psychology to emerge more clearly.

II

How did the witch fantasy emerge? The summary of Regina Bartholome's relations with the Devil with which I began this chapter was not a free initial admission. It emerged, with considerable resistance, over the course of eight sessions of interrogation both with and without torture and its threat. During these she provided four different accounts of her relations with the Devil, each time moving the moment of her initial encounter with him further back into the past, and each time attaching the moment of his initial appearance to a different love relationship in her own short life.

First she told how the Devil appeared after she was given a love potion by the young furrier who she believed was trying to force her into marriage.[21] This was an extraordinary, voluntary admission, not a response to a question. It was Regina herself who brought the Devil into the story, explaining how he had visited her in her cell when she had first been imprisoned by the council: diabolic interpretation was not the consequence of the council's own determination to construct her story in this way. Once introduced, however, the Devil's role became a joint concern as her interrogators sought to make sense of her behaviour. Regina's first account soon gave way to the story that the Devil had appeared to her some months earlier, when she was involved in bringing the accusations against the Jew of Pfersee, at the time when she was hoping to persuade the young day-labourer Jacob Schwenreiter to be her lover. In a later interrogation, Regina confessed she had known the Devil long before, and dated the time of her diabolic seduction to the period when her mother began the adulterous affair which was to end in her banishment. And finally, in a last burst of revenge, she made this period more precise, associating it with her very first affair with Michael Reidler, the prison overseer. Why was he not punished as she had been, she demanded? This man, her first seducer, 'may well have been the Devil himself'.[22] As Regina well knew, this was an accusation which, if the council had believed her, would surely have led to his being incarcerated and tortured just as she was.[23]

Each new version of the story elicited in response to the council's questions thus progressively traced back the moment of her own departure from the Christian community to a prior period in Regina's own psychological history, stopping only when she reached puberty. We might note in passing that it parallels the explanatory logic of psychoanalysis, where the patient is encouraged to explore themes from his or her early life in order to understand subsequent conflicts and relations; and it was a logic of explanation shared by both council and witch.[24] As with the life narratives offered in psychoanalysis, it is not, however, a 'realistic' narrative which can be abstracted from the diabolic narrative, but a whole story which offers meaning. Along the way, Regina introduces us to the characters who populated her own life history. But there is something odd about this seemingly real 'life'. All the stories, apart from the first love potion story, reveal the same theme of love and rejection. Even the first story is an inversion of this pattern, for this time it is Regina who plays the part of the rejector, a role which, we might observe, she is also attempting to play (by means of the interrogation) in relation to the Devil, freeing herself from his power and attempting to rejoin the Christian community. And we might notice that the retelling of her stories in interrogation allows Regina to take revenge, to retaliate against those who rejected her, a dynamic which reaches its culmination in her accusation that her first seducer was the Devil himself.

Here we might make use of Joyce McDougall's helpful image of the 'theatres of the mind' which she employs to describe the use individuals make of other people to play the split parts of the person's own inner world, so that it is the individual's inner conflicts which are projected into fantasy and acted out in relations with others. Because these conflicts are intolerable and unresolved, they are constantly repeated and re-enacted.[25] Interrogation for witchcraft, we might say, offered the accused a theatrical opportunity to recount and restage these linked conflicts – and what better audience than the rapt ears of the council's representatives and the executioner?

But what are the themes of these dramas? The images which Regina chose and the narratives which she offered are littered with Oedipal themes. At its most basic, the logic of her account apparently suggests that she felt herself to have succeeded in gaining her father's love and stealing her mother's position – by cooking and keeping house for her father. It was as if, by a terrible retribution of fantasy, her forbidden Oedipal desires seemed to have been fulfilled.[26] No wonder she felt herself to be worthy of punishment. It is important, here, to note that these transactions occurred at the level of fantasy: there is no evidence that we are dealing with a case of incest, an observation which does not, however, diminish the importance of the theme. Oedipal themes also recurred in the relations she recounted with others. Her first lover appeared just as her mother took a new lover, deserting her father. Regina herself was aged only 12 at the time. This was in seventeenth-century eyes a precocious sexual affair with a man her social superior, senior to her in age. Ominously enough, Reidler seems to have worked as a prison overseer. If her first lover evinced some paternal characteristics, older than she, and a *Landsmann* of her father's, the second man with whom she fell in love, Jacob Schwenreiter, was yet more closely associated with her actual father. He shared not only her father's trade but even his bed. His inaccessibility and the cruel manner in which he flaunted his new wife only served to underline Regina's failure to establish an independent love-relationship: indeed, he allowed her to repeat the Oedipal drama, this time against a mother-figure who refused to be dislodged. And when Regina attempted to blackmail the Jew at Pfersee for engaging in sexual relations with her, her revenge displayed a similar retaliatory logic. He, too, was an older, married man. She had pawned goods with him just as her mother had pawned goods with the Jews at Pfersee, yet he had given her neither more money nor had he returned her goods. He had right and the law on his side: her revenge therefore had to take the form of an extreme and dishonest assault on his sexual reputation. In the kind of symbolic repetition that typifies Regina's story, she accused him of breaking a taboo akin to the taboo on incest, the taboo on sexual relations between Jew and Christian. Pfersee was, of course, the setting of the idyll between her mother and her nephew. And in a 'return to the scene of the crime' so characteristic of Regina's interrogations at every turn, it transpired in the end that Pfersee was the locale of her own seduction by the Devil. In the very same tavern, she finally claimed, the Devil and she regularly stole away to a side room where she did his will – a scenario, incidentally, which neither the bemused keeper of the inn, his wife nor his servant could bring themselves to substantiate.

There is no mileage, I think, in the usual historical strategy of teasing out the 'real' from the fantastic elements in this account. We cannot isolate the point at which events which we know to be 'real' – her mother's affair, her relationship with the prison overseer[27] – end, and where the fantastic begins. Indeed, discarding the fantastic would be an inappropriate strategy because what is important are the elements which Regina chose to make sense of her life. Her narration of one set of events, whether real or fantastic, does not so much indicate the cause of the events which occurred later as display the same pattern of meaning: in this case, multiple incest. This is not, of course, to claim that trauma does not leave its mark upon the psyche. But we cannot simply 'read off' the real event from the page of the interrogation. It is important first to uncover the psychic logic of her tale, a story which interweaves diabolic with sexual themes, before we can guess at its meaning.

So far, the patterns I have described are rather like the patterns which might be expected to be evoked by a kind of free association. But interrogations were not conducted as analytic discussions. The threat of torture, even when it was neither threatened nor carried out, was implicit in the interrogation and when there were specific points on which the council was not content with its subject's answers it would, after consultation, authorize the exhibition and then use of the instruments of torture. In Regina's case, actual torture was resorted to only once, after the sixth interrogation, when she was suspended from the rack with empty weights for two sessions. The application of torture, however – comparatively mild in this case – does not in itself explain what the witch confessed, why she provided the particular narrative she did or how she persuaded the council of its truth – the council knew that pain sometimes led people to false confessions.[28]

And there is another salient feature of difference in seventeenth-century witch narratives: the role of the Devil. To us, the fantasies which surround him seem clearly part of the realm of the imaginary, more definitively unreal than the material I have been describing. But to them he was part of the real world. In talking about the Devil, therefore, Regina was not engaged in an activity different in kind from the rest of the confession she gave. This observation is helpful in considering how we ought to interpret diabolic material. Diabolic fantasy as it appears in interrogation is not, I would argue, to be equated with some kind of hallucinatory activity or treated as any more part of the world of the imagination than the rest of her confession.[29] Instead, I think it should be interpreted as part of the whole narrative that the witch offered. In the figure of the Devil, the witch had available to her a character who could dramatize psychic conflicts with extraordinary clarity.

There were good reasons why, in seventeeth-century Germany, confessing oneself to be a witch might involve supplying both a life history and a story about the Devil. The Devil whom witches encountered was not an abstract force or a symbolic figure of evil. Though he appeared in different guises he was, first and foremost, on each occasion a character with whom one had a relationship. Regina, for instance, discovered he shared her taste for lung sausage and beer. His dashing clothes placed him as a nobleman in contrast to her drab workaday world. His appearance, his gestures and his attire always had to be specifically described by the witch, even while she drew from a possible repertoire of familiar elements with which to describe him. Becoming a witch meant engaging in an intimate relationship, usually sexual, with the Devil as a character, and consequently, its discovery entailed the analysis of the well-springs of the witch's own personality, motives and emotions. Interrogation therefore aimed at the construction of an account of the individual's own history and his or her relations with others which could explain how someone could come to sever human attachments, choosing instead to cleave to the Devil in a kind of perversion of the soul.

The diabolic elements of Regina's interrogation thus echoed the themes of the life history with precision. As the formula of renunciation of Christ which Regina provided had it, she had forsworn God and taken the Devil as her father. He, too, was her lover. She even imagined the possibility of giving him children: whether these were sired by him or by her other lovers, the Devil had told her she must surrender them to him. In this way, we might say, the story of the Devil allowed her to develop the Oedipal narrative yet further so that she might in imagination provide her father with the phallic compensation of children; but so powerful and persecuting was this father-figure that she was not even to be allowed to keep these children.[30] Of course no seventeenth-century court would have interpreted her story in this way. But her seventeenth-century hearers would have invested the diabolic narrative with a similar epistemological importance. For them, the diabolic narrative helped explain the life history, and the life history, the relationship with the Devil. It was because Regina listened to the Devil that she had acted as she had; it was because she wanted money and because she was lascivious that the Devil was able to seduce her.[31]

III

The Oedipal elements were not, however, restricted to the motifs of the narrative Regina provided. Her narrative was the product of a conversation. If we look at the interaction in the interrogation, we notice that much of it dramatizes relations between fathers and daughters.[32] Regina began her interrogation by appealing to her interrogators to be allowed 'to return to her father', and throughout the course of the interrogation, she made this appeal again and again: 'She pleads for God's mercy, that my lords should send her out again soon, so that she should return to her father.'[33] 'Oh you poor father, shall your child never come to you again? If they were to do anything to her, they would be killing her and her father.'[34] Return to her own place becomes equated with return to her father, an image she expresses in the compound word 'fatherland', as she begs with ominous prescience: 'My lords should let her die in her fatherland, so that she could only return to her father again';[35] 'if she were to be exiled they would be killing her, let them allow her to die in her fatherland'.[36] At the end of her very last interrogation she stated, half begging, half ruefully remarking 'if for God's sake one had only granted her life, for her old father's sake'.[37] Claiming to love her father and desiring to return to him, her pleas implicitly contrast him with the powerful, cruel council and show the council to be another powerful father-figure: 'She begs that my lords should behave to her as fathers, and should not drive her out of her fatherland.'[38] Repeatedly she rails against the council, castigating it for its lack of mercy, crying that 'she could not sense that there was a gracious authority here, because they were trying to drive her out into misery'.[39] Here she is rejecting the council's own claim to be a benevolent paternal authority, the vision of itself which it so tirelessly repeated in its steady stream of ordinances and public pronouncements. Behind the council, sanctifying its power, loomed another paternal authority: God. For Regina, he, too, was a father who failed her, and in his stead she said she had adopted the Devil as her father. As she put it in her rendition of her blasphemy against God, she admitted that 'she said because God was no longer her father, she would take the Devil as her father, he should be her father'.[40]

Regina's rage against paternal figures is uncontainable: against the council, whom she blames for her mother's exile, against God, who will not hear her. Her anger is expressed in her constant threats of suicide, the blame for which she lays at the council's door: 'if my lords were to shame her and to banish her then she would throw herself in the water. They had sent her mother away in the same way, let it rest on their consciences';[41] 'my lords should not drive her out into misery, for otherwise she would drown herself or hang herself, and then my lords would be responsible'.[42] Seventeenth-century people, who viewed suicide as a crime and a sin, had perhaps a livelier awareness than we do of the aggressive logic of killing oneself.[43] This rage is also expressed through the vehicle of a fear of *Spot*, of public mockery. Public humiliation, her mother's fate, was the outcome she claims constantly to fear; and yet her own behaviour precipitated her interrogation and ultimately the

most lurid, public form of shaming imaginable, a public account of her
sexual exploits with the Devil, read out for all to hear at the moment
of her execution.

It is evident that Regina's world is populated with good and bad
fathers. We might say, following Melanie Klein, that by splitting her
mental universe up into 'good' fathers, who offered protection and love,
and 'bad' fathers, who did not care for her, Regina was able to contain
a 'good' image of her own father while projecting the 'bad' father on
to other figures.[44] This was an assignment of values which was highly
unstable: the Devil, the 'good' father who offered her sausage, money
and love, proved unreliable and maltreated her, giving her false coin,
failing to prevent her imprisonment and beating her in her cell.[45] The
cost of Regina's perverse reassignment of moral values was immense.
Her pact with the Devil excluded her from Christian society, and made
her unable to recite the Lord's Prayer. It left her suffering from a rage
and anger against others which made it impossible for her to live
peaceably with her neighbours. Paradoxically, the interrogation thus
offered her the chance of reconciliation and reintegration with the community of Christians in the town, with the council, in acceptance of its
just power and in submission to its decrees about her fate, with God,
in conversion before her execution. By the fourth interrogation, after
about six weeks of being unable to recite an Our Father, she found she
was once more able to pray.

Regina's perverse reversal of moral values had protected her image
of her father as good and protective and kept her anger alive. When
this mental organization began to crumble, so too her unacknowledged
hatred of her father – whose inability to prevent the affair or prevent
her banishment had after all, in a sense, caused her mother's downfall
– began to emerge. In the sixth interrogation she began to distance
herself yet further from the Devil, saying, in response to the council's
question about whether the Devil was not comforting her, 'Yes, he
comforted her, but the comforting was no use. He was letting her stick
in it. It would have been better if she had called to God, God would
have helped her overcome.'[46] This was eventually to lead, under torture,
to her own terrible admission, later in the same interrogation, that she
had bought a little yellow powder from the apothecary with which to
poison her father. But in the very next interrogation she explained how
she had mixed the powder in with broth she made for him, a revelation she at once attempted to modify, saying the Devil had only told
her to give it to her father, and denying that she knew the powder was
poison – thereby informing the council, of course, that it was. Until the
sixth interrogation, Regina had not confessed to any acts of malefice
and her crime had concerned her pact with the Devil, not any use of
sorcery to harm man, woman or beast. But now she confessed to
attempting to set two houses on fire, to having attempted to poison the

bride of the young man with whom she was in love, to having 'ridden the beasts' naked at Göggingen, causing them to sicken, and to having tried to commit parricide, a transgression against natural affection and social order.

Witnesses were called to cross-check these latest admissions. The supposed victims of arson rejected all talk of sorcery out of hand; the shepherds at Göggingen could find nothing amiss with their herds. The young bride had noticed no ill effects but did express fear of Regina. But when Regina's father, Hans Bartholome, was interrogated, he faltered. He explained that he had no idea that his daughter had attempted such a thing. Seeking to defend himself from the imputation of fatherly irresponsibility, he stated that 'He could not say that on a single day of his life he had ever sensed that the Evil One came to her, as he only now heard, she was supposed to have had dealings with him [the evil one] at Pfersensteg.'[47] He explained that his daughter had been 'aggressive in the head' (*leppisch im kopf*) since her youth, but was not able to supply a forthright denial of the possibility that his daughter was a witch, or even to deny that she might have felt hatred for him. Regina ended her final confession beseeching the council to let her return to her father: tragically, he was in the end unable to protect his daughter. Like his wife before her, he was compelled to deliver Regina to the council's justice.

IV

To this point, we have explored the dynamic of Regina Bartholome's confession. But why should the council have believed that she was a witch? The answer to this question is not as straightforward as one might expect. For the council did have available to it an alternative explanation of Regina's behaviour: namely, that she was of unsound mind. Indeed, when she was at first tried for her accusation against the Jew of Pfersee, the council agreed with the assessment of her neighbours that she was simply 'a bit touched', and sent her on her way recommending that good care be taken of her. In the second trial, the council took care to have its own medical experts examine Regina to see whether she was mentally imbalanced: they determined that she was of sound mind and that her melancholic tendencies were to be explained, as she herself did, by the conditions of her incarceration.

Just twenty years later, two other supposed witches' lurid confessions of involvement with the Devil did not faze the council: in each case, it concurred with its own medical advisers that the woman was suffering from melancholy, and freed her.[48] And about the time that Regina met with execution for her whoredom with the Devil, Regina Schiller was failing to convince authorities in Augsburg and all over southern Germany that she was indeed, as she claimed, bound to the Devil by a diabolic pact written in blood. Regina Schiller's diabolic confessions were more elaborate and more riveting than those of Regina Bartholome: she could even produce the scrap of paper on which she had signed her baptismal birthright away in blood. Why then did the council suddenly change its mind about Regina Bartholome and embark on a trial for witchcraft?[49]

These disquiets led me back to the role of the interrogators: of the council, who formulated the questions and who voted on guilt; of the questioners, the council's representatives who interrogated Regina over eight sessions and who coaxed her answers from her; and the executioner. Their role as questioners was to tie in the threads of Regina's narratives, discarding what they took to be false or irrelevant. Their questions supplied a logic of motive for her admissions: why did she make a pact with the Devil? To whom did she feel hatred and envy? What had the Devil whispered to her? Some motives they held to be not further analysable, and greed was foremost among these: when Regina several times claimed she summoned the Devil 'for the sake of filthy money' they adopted this as a primary explanation of her sin in the final condemnation.[50] Similarly, they elicited material about paternal relations and not about maternal ones because women's relations with men fitted their own explanatory paradigm of witchcraft, women's seduction by the Devil.[51] Of course, we face particular difficulties here because we are dealing with a collective character, the council, not with a discrete individual. It is hard, moreover, to do more than guess at the psychic investments which underlay their interest. Of necessity our information must be indirect, derived from the question structure itself, its turns of phrase and its dynamic: interrogators put questions, and are not subject to them. None the less, asking questions is never an innocent activity, and questions shape narratives. That the councillors were able to elicit this material seems likely to have been in part because of their own unconscious investments in the elements of her tale.

Regina posed no real threat to the power of the council, but her extreme behaviour gave voice to an insubordination towards authority, secular and divine, which her audience of councillors found at once appalling and compelling. At her very first interrogation in the second trial her questioners demanded to know 'whether she did not have to realize and admit how kind the authority had been in punishing her so graciously', proceeding to ask her how she dared to claim the council was acting unjustly;[52] in the fifth interrogation they again asked, as Regina repeated her complaints, 'what she had to complain about, that one treated her too severely, since she had well deserved this many times before';[53] and in the sixth interrogation they once more asked her why she had said in the previous questioning session that she had an ungracious government (*Obrigkeit*), trying, with the following question, to bring her to confess that they were generous rulers.[54]

In part for this reason, the question script compiled on behalf of the council focused at first upon the pact Regina made with the Devil. It was not only that belief in the pact characterized élite beliefs in witchcraft, though this was clearly important as the council strove to make sense of the confrontation of its own demonological beliefs with the plethora of fantastical empirical evidence which Regina supplied. The pact was so significant because it gave documentary form to the transgression the council perceived to lie at the root of witchcraft: the rejection of the good, just and paternal authority and its replacement with its inverse, the Devil. By her eighth and final interrogation, Regina had surrendered herself utterly to the council's authority:

she had not been able to pray, but now she could pray; She asked my lords for God's sake, that one might yet grant her life if it could be . . . . If they should want to take her life, so let it be in God's name; if she were to be pardoned, she would have God and her government to thank.[55]

Witchcraft exposed the yawning possibility that an individual might attack paternal authority and, with it, society, the community of Christians which the city constituted. But it also made evident the fact that reintegration into the community was sanctioned, in the last analysis, by force: it secured Regina's acceptance of its 'gracious' authority by the relentless questioning and threats of torture of which she complained. This violence at the heart of the benign paternal relations of authority offered an arresting allegory of the psychic dimensions of the councillors' own power as fathers.

So concerned was the council that the witch should be brought again to true daughterly repentance that, as it usually did, it paid for a *Trostknecht* to accompany her in her cell and teach her to pray to Our Father.[56] The processes of imprisonment, prayer and repeated interrogation thus allowed the council to restage – through its representatives, the interrogators, scribes and hangman – the drama of the disobedient daughter. She complied with a riveting performance. Spitting at the council representatives while they hung her suspended from the rack, refusing to answer their questions, screaming and cursing them for their mercilessness, she called on the Devil to help her from the rack when Jesus, Mary and her interrogators failed to release her: 'come Devil and take me away, let thunder and hail strike all those to the ground who are here'.[57] Her disturbing fantasies of Oedipal union with the Devil may unconsciously have touched the raw nerves of their own Oedipal conflicts, played and replayed through early adulthood: sixteenth- and seventeenth-century society devoted much of its patriarchal disciplining skills to containing the exuberant aggression of its young men.[58] Here one might speculate that the councillors bore the double load of the traces of their own Oedipal organization and of their experiences as fathers, both real and ideal, in their turn. They thus formed perfect partners for Regina's self-dramatization.[59]

Witchcraft interrogations involve two parties, the witch and her interrogators. Both are required for the production of fantasy. It was her interrogator's relentless questioning and ruthless eye for detail which encouraged the fantasy from the witch, and supplied the connections to motive and guilt. Both had psychic investments in its content. At times, as the process of interrogation continued, the collaborative drive between witch and interrogator could become so intense that the questioners elaborated on the script of questions they had been given: it was her interrogators who suggested to Regina that she must have lived with the Devil as man and wife, a formulation which made deep psychological sense, and which she was willing to adopt as a description of her own behaviour.[60]

V

Historians have long puzzled why so many more women than men were the targets of witchcraft accusations. I have argued elsewhere that the prevalence of women among witches cannot be explained in terms of the sociological characteristics of women as a group: only a tiny proportion of women were interrogated for witchcraft, and they were often accused by members of their own sex.[61] But it can, I think, be related to dilemmas surrounding the psychic identity of womanhood. Elements in the interaction between the witch and her persecutors allowed the fantasy of witchcraft to unfold. The psychic conflicts attendant on the feminine position – whether Oedipal or related to motherhood – provided the substance of the psychic drama of the witchcraft interrogation, and supplied the material on which their interrogators could work in fascinated horror, developing in turn their own fantasies about femininity, about fatherhood and about diabolic activity. Most women, of course, managed the psychic conflicts of femininity without falling prey to morbid diabolic temptation. Not every case of witchcraft furnished interrogations displaying an emotional engagement with the Devil, nor did all witches produce witch fantasies. But in those few cases of women witches who did, the possibilities present in a culture obsessed with the power of the Devil, of fathers and of women, enabled a combustion of interests to occur, flaring up into interrogations under torture and the production of those sadistic, masochistic stories which so whetted their contemporaries' appetite for tales of the relation between women and the Devil.

There remains, however, something deeply troubling about the analysis I have offered. It would be possible to view Regina's interrogation as an attempt at self-cure – or, as the council might have thought, at readmission into the community of Christians; what Regina might have put as return to her father. Through her expiation of her sin at the executioner's block she won the hope of entering the heavenly kingdom. And on earth she entered the chronicles of the city as a witch whose death had purified the town.[62]

Yet deeply as we all crave happy endings, this cheerful functionalism will not do. For Regina, the result of the long sessions of interrogation and incarceration was an utter loss of will, fluctuating with a futile desire for revenge. She concluded without even pleading for her own life, relinquishing power over it to the council: 'If they should want to take her life, so let it be in God's name; if she were to be pardoned, she would have God and her government to thank.'[63] In relation to the Devil, the father she chose, Regina's submission to paternal authority did not bring the compensation of her own potent creativity, for in her peculiar brand of the diabolic bargain, she had to surrender any children to the Devil. The diabolic figure who urged her, from her first moment of imprisonment, to commit suicide, or the punitive father-figures who ultimately exacted death for her crimes, were persecutory presences of such severity that they in the end brooked nothing but her immolation. Regina's internal world, with its unstable assignments of moral values and veering absolutes, fell apart. This was a scenario in which the council, despite some misgivings among its members, was ultimately to collude: it played its part of punishing patriarch to the end, superintending her execution and the burning of her body.[64] We can construct interpretations of Regina's behaviour, we can locate it in its historical context, but it belongs to psychology as well as to history to recreate the bleakness of the individual psychic landscape from which it sprang.

NOTES

1 He paid the lowest rate of tax, the *Habenichts* rate, for those who had no taxable property or income, and he rented and did not own his lodging. In the taxbook, he is described as a *Nachtarbeiter*. The household lived in the Jakobervorstadt, a craft-dominated quarter and the poorest in the city – incidentally, the area where Bernd Roeck has argued that most witches came from (Bernd Roeck, 'Hexen "im ganzen Haus". Zur Sozialgeschichte von Hexen und Magie in der frühneuzeitlichen Stadt', lecture, Groupe de Travail International d'Histoire Urbaine de la Maison des sciences de l'homme, Paris, 12–14 March 1992). Hans Bartholome had lived in one house for three and a half to four years but had moved house six months before the case to another residence in the same quarter a few streets away. See Stadtarchiv Augsburg (hereafter cited as StadtAA), Steuerbücher, 1667, fo. 31 c; 1668, fo. 31 b; 1669, fo. 31 a; 1670, fo. 44 d; and witness statements 26 June 1670, StadtAA, Urgichtensammlung (hereafter cited as Urg.), Regina Bartholome, 1670. Gottlieb Spitzel, fascinated by witchcraft and possession, and a cleric at St Jakob's, the local church, also lived in the same tiny tax-district as the Bartholomes up until the move. He became involved in the contemporaneous case of the supposedly possessed woman Regina Schiller and failed to exorcize her. Gottlieb Spitzel, *Die Gebrochne Macht der Finsternüss/ der Zerstörte*

Teuflische Bunds- vnd Buhl-Freundschafft mit den Menschen . . . , Augsburg 1687; Staats-und Stadtbibliothek Augsburg, 2o Cod Augs. 288, Regina Schiller; Dietrich Blaufuss, *Reichsstaadt und Pietismus – Philipp Jacob Spener und Gottlieb Spizel aus Augsburg* (Einzelarbeiten aus der Kirchengeschichte Bayerns 53), Neustadt a. d. Aisch 1977. On the social history of Augsburg in the seventeenth century see Bernd Roeck, *Eine Stadt in Krieg und Frieden. Studien zur Geschichte der Reichsstadt Augsburg zwischen Kalenderstreit und Parität* (Schriftenreihe der Historischen Kommission bei der Bayerischen Akademie der Wissenschaften 37), 2 vols, Munich 1989; and Etienne François, *Die unsichtbare Grenze. Protestanten und Katholiken in Augsburg 1648–1806*, Sigmaringen 1991.

2 'Wann Jch Von meiner harten Arbeith anheimbs komme, so mir etwann Wass Warmbes kochen kann, darmit ich mich Widerumben erlabe, nicht habe': StadtAA, Urg., 1670, Regina Bartholome, petition of 12 Aug. 1670.

3 StadtAA, Urg., 1670, 23 June 1670, Regina Bartholome.

4 For the indispensable study of witch-hunting in the region, see Wolfgang Behringer, *Hexenverfolgung in Bayern. Volksmagie, Glaubenseifer und Staatsräson in der Frühen Neuzeit*, Munich 1987.

5 Natalie Zemon Davis, 'Boundaries and the Sense of Self in Sixteenth-Century France', in Thomas C. Heller, Morton Sosna and David E. Wellbery (eds), *Reconstructing Individualism. Autonomy, individuality, and the self in western thought*, Stanford, Calif. 1986.

6 For some excellent elaborations of the concept of honour in the early modern period, see Lucia Ferrante, 'Honor Regained: Women in the Casa del Soccorso di San Paolo in sixteenth-century Bologna', and Sandra Cavallo and Simona Cerutti, 'Female Honor and the Social Control of Reproduction in Piedmont between 1600 and 1800', both in Edward Muir and Guido Ruggiero (eds), *Sex and Gender in Historical Perspective* (Selections from Quaderni Storici), Baltimore, MD and London 1990; Martin Dinges, 'Die Ehre als Thema der Stadtgeschichte. Eine Semantik am Übergang vom Ancien Regime zur Moderne', *Zeitschrift für historische Forschung*, 16, 1989, Heft 1/4, pp. 409–40; Susanna Burghartz, 'Disziplinierung oder Konfliktregelung? Zur Funktion städtischer Gerichte im Spätmittelalter: Das Zürcher Ratsgericht', *Zeitschrift für historische Forschung*, 16, 1989, Heft 1/4, pp. 385–408; Susanna Burghartz, 'Rechte Jungfrauen oder unverschämte Töchter? Zur weiblichen Ehre im 16. Jahrhundert', in Heide Wunder and Karin Hausen (eds), *Frauengeschichte-Geschlechtergeschichte*, Frankfurt am Main 1992.

7 David Sabean, *Power in the Blood*, Cambridge 1984, see esp. p. 171.

8 Stephen Greenblatt, 'Psychoanalysis and Renaissance Culture', in *idem*, *Learning to Curse. Essays in early modern culture*, New York and London 1990; and see Charles Taylor, *Sources of the Self. The making of modern identity*, Cambridge 1989.

9 For an excellent recent biographical study which makes good use of psychoanalysis see Elizabeth Marvick, *Louis XIII: The making of a king*, London 1986; for its application to the political symbolism of a society, Lynn Hunt, *The Family Romance of the French Revolution*, London 1992; and the pioneering article by Sally Alexander, 'Women, Class and Sexual Differences in the 1830s and 1840s. Some reflections on the writing of a feminist history', *History Workshop Journal*, 17, 1984, pp. 125–49; and also Sally Alexander, 'Feminist History and Psychoanalysis', *History Workshop Journal*, 32, 1991, pp. 128–33; and for further examples of its use, Geoffrey Cocks and Travis Crosby, *Psycho/History. Readings in the method of psychology, psychoanalysis and history*, Yale, Conn. 1987; Psychoanalytischer Seminar Zürich, *Die Gesellschaft auf der Couch. Psychoanalyse als sozialwissenschaftliche Methode*, Frankfurt am Main

1989; for a subtle meditation on Freud's own essay on the possessed painter Christoph Haitzmann, see Michel de Certeau, 'What Freud Makes of History: "A seventeenth-century demonological neurosis" ', in *idem., The Writing of History*, trans. Tom Conley, New York 1988; and Freud's essay, 'Eine Teufelsneurose im Siebzehnten Jahrhundert (1923), in Alexander Mitscherlich *et al.* (eds), *Freud. Studienausgabe*, Frankfurt am Main 1989, vol. 7, pp. 287–322; for the use of psychoanalytic ideas in exploring the witch-craze, John Demos, *Entertaining Satan. Witchcraft and the culture of early New England*, Oxford 1982; and for an interesting application of Kleinian ideas to the study of the witch-craze which, however, is not satisfactorily worked out in historical terms, Evelyn Heinemann, *Hexen und Hexenangst. Eine psychoanalytische Studie über den Hexenwahn der frühen Neuzeit*, Frankfurt am Main 1989; for a theory of the self, Christopher Bollas, *Forces of Destiny. Psychoanalysis and human idiom*, London 1989.

10 See, for example, the *böse Blick* and other magical techniques: Eva Labouvie, *Verbotene Künste. Volksmagie und ländlicher Aberglaube in den Dorfgemeinden des Saarraumes (16.–19. Jahrhundert)*, St Ingbert 1992; Eva Labouvie, *Zauberei und Hexenwerk. Ländlicher Hexenglaube in der frühen Neuzeit*, Frankfurt am Main 1991; Ruth Martin, *Witchcraft and the Inquisition in Venice, 1550–1600*, Oxford 1989.

11 See Richard L. Kagan, *Lucrecia's Dreams. Politics and prophecy in sixteenth-century Spain*, Berkeley, Calif. 1990.

12 Compare by contrast, for example, John Demos, *Entertaining Satan*, who applies psychoanalytic ideas to the society of New England as a whole, considering child-rearing practices.

13 StadtAA, Urg., 1670, 23 June 1670, Regina Bartholome: she revoked the allegations on 27 June 1670. Her first criminal interrogation on the second set of charges took place just a month later, on 29 July 1670.

14 Jacob Schwenreiter married Maria Weikhart from Augsburg, widow: see StadtAA, Hochzeitsprotokolle, 1667–73, pp. 271–2, 26 May 1670: in the marriage protocols, Schwenreiter described himself as the more socially prestigious carter (*Karrer*), though in the witness statements in the *Urgichtensammlung* he is described as a *Tagwerker*. Interestingly, Bartholome did not act as one of the three guarantors (required by marriage legislation in the city) that the couple would leave the city if *Beisitz*, residence rights, were not granted. Since Schwenreiter was not from Augsburg, he needed to marry an Augsburg woman if he were to acquire residence rights, a fact which may have encouraged Regina Bartholome to imagine that Schwenreiter might consider her as a possible bride.

15 This took place on 22 July 1670. Here it is worth noting the corresponding investments of Regina's accusers in the fantasy of witchcraft, a theme I have explored in greater detail in 'Angst und Aggression. Hexenbeschuldigungen und Mutterschaft in frühneuzeitlichen Augsburg', *Sowi. Sozialwissenschaftliche Informationen*, 2, June 1992, pp. 68–76: just four years later, Maria Schwenreiter was among the witnesses against Anna Brühler and her husband in another case of accusations of sorcery. This time, she claimed that Brühlerin's husband had told her that Brühlerin had caused Schwenreiter, her husband, to lose his 'manhood', condemning her to a childless marriage (StadtAA, Urg., 6 Oct.–10 Nov. 1674, Anna Brühler, testimony Maria Schwenreiter, 20 Oct. 1674). Maria Schwenreiter thus not only saw Regina Bartholome executed, but Anna Brühler exiled for ever from the town: she, too, was caught up in a repetitive cycle of witchcraft accusation, tending to identify the sources of her misfortune in others.

16 See, for excellent explorations of fantasy in witchcraft, Richard van Dülmen,

'Imaginationen des Teuflischen. Nächtliche Zusammenkünfte, Hexentänze, Teufelssabbate', and Eva Labouvie, 'Hexenspuk und Hexenabwehr. Volksmagie und volkstümlicher Hexenglaube', both in Richard van Dülmen (ed.), *Hexenwelten. Magie und Imagination vom 16.–20. Jahrhundert*, Frankfurt am Main 1987; Robert Rowland, ' "Fantasticall and Devilishe Persons": European witch-beliefs in comparative perspective', in Bengt Ankarloo and Gustav Henningsen (eds), *Early Modern European Witchcraft. Centres and peripheries*, Oxford 1989; and Christina Larner, *Enemies of God. The witch-hunt in Scotland*, London 1981, pp. 134–56.

17 Carlo Ginzburg, *Ecstasies. Deciphering the witches' sabbath*, London 1990.

18 Ginzburg discusses the limits of the use of psychoanalysis in witchcraft studies and prefigures his own later preoccupation with mythical structures in 'Freud, the Wolf-Man, and the Werewolves', in *idem, Myths, Emblems, Clues*, trans. John and Anne Tedeschi, London 1990. He also considers (discussing Jung somewhat dismissively) the possibilities of analytic exploration of archetypes in thinking about the witch-craze.

19 This procedure had reached a level of extreme bureaucratic efficiency in Augsburg. So, for instance, witness statements were collected on 1 August 1670 in connection with her initial admissions of 29 July; on 2 September from Pfersee in relation to admissions Regina had made on 28 August; on 10 and 11 September in relation to her confession of 9 September. By the last years of the century, the questions throughout all the interrogation sessions were being through-numbered, so that rapid cross-reference could be made; and even witnesses' accounts were scrupulously ordered, dealing with precision with numbered points in the witch's confession and cross-referring to previous statements. This highly methodical organization and control of information is in marked contrast with the looser, more dynamic procedures adopted in earlier trials. It suggests, I think, not a routinization of witch-trials or of confessions, but an attempt to 'fix' with precision the lurid detail of the witches' accounts, using the technology of bureaucracy to arrive at the 'truth'.

20 For a highly sensitive reconstruction of the social and imaginative lives of the victims of the Salzburg Zauberjackl-Prozess, integrating social history and fantasy, see Norbert Schindler, 'Die Entstehung der Unbarmherzigkeit. Zur Kultur und Lebensweise der Salzburger Bettler am Ende des 17. Jahrunderts', in *idem, Widerspenstige Leute. Studien zur Volksultur in der frühen Neuzeit*, Frankfurt am Main 1992. Schindler points to the importance of fantasies of revenge and of compensatory potency: the *geisteschwacher* Elias Finck from Radstadt stated that the Zauberer-Jackl had taught him 'Lesen, Schreiben und Schiessen', the skills for which he longed (ibid., p. 301).

21 StadtAA, Urg., 23 June 1670, Regina Bartholome, interrogation (1) of 29 July 1670. The love potion consisted of *Haarbandperlen* which were dropped into the drink, an interesting conjunction since pearls may represent tears – hence lovers do not give them to each other and brides do not wear them (H. Bächtold-Stäubli, *Handwörterbuch des deutschen Aberglaubens*, 10 vols, Berlin and Leipzig 1927–42, vol. 6, p. 1498); while the *Haarband* may be used as a love token (Jacob and Wilhelm Grimm, *Deutsches Wörterbuch*, Leipzig 1854–1983, Bd 4 Teil 2, s. 24, source Johannes Rist). On love potions, see David Lederer, 'The Elixir of Love: Madness and sexuality in early modern Germany', forthcoming.

22 'Er möge wol selbs der Teuffel gewesen sein', StadtAA, Urg., 1670, Regina Bartholome, (7) 20 Sept. 1670.

23 Here her interrogation snakes back to a self-accusation: she admits she would

have 'given him something' if God had not prevented it, because (continuing her angry tirade against him)

> he seduced her in her twelfth year, and took her virginity from her, he was a thief and remains a thief, the thief will get his deserts one day, she wanted to hit him once, and she would have got him if it had happened

('Weilen Er sie im Zwelfften Jahr verführt, vnd Jhr die Jngfrauschafft genommen, Er seie ein dieb vnd bleib ein, dieb werde nach schon seinen lohn empfahen, sein leib habs Auch Einmal schlagen wollen, sie wurdts aber gewiss auch troffen haben wan es beschehen were'), StadtAA, Urg., 1670, Regina Bartholome, (7) 20 Sept. 1670.

24 As Carlo Ginzburg has pointed out, this parallel did not escape Freud himself: 'Freud, The Wolf-Man, and the Were-Wolves', pp. 150–1. Ginzburg cites Freud's letters to Wilhelm Fliess of 17 and 24 Jan. 1897: 'Warum sind die Geständnisse auf der Folter so ähnlich die Mitteilungen meiner Patienten in der psychischen Behandlung?' (Jeffrey Moussaieff Masson (ed.), *Sigmund Freud. Briefe an Wilhelm Fliess 1887–1904*, German edition revised and expanded by Michael Schröter, Frankfurt am Main 1986, p. 237). (Why are [the witches'] confessions under torture so like the communications made by my patients in psychic treatment?) And, with some unease, Freud goes on to conclude, after some fascinating associations on the fantastic elements of the witch-craze: 'Ich träume also von einer urälteste Teufelsreligion, deren Ritus sich im geheimen fortsetzt, und begreife die strenge Therapie der Hexenrichter. Die Beziehungen wimmeln' (p. 240). See also Carlo Ginzburg, 'The Inquisitor as Anthropologist', in *idem, Myths, Emblems, Clues*, where Ginzburg considers a similarly painful parallel.

25 Joyce McDougall, *Theatres of the Mind: Illusion and truth on the psychoanalytic stage*, New York 1985.

26 See Joan Riviere, 'Womanliness as a Masquerade' (1929), reprinted in Victor Burgin, James Donald and Cora Kaplan (eds), *Formations of Fantasy*, London and New York 1986.

27 For her mother's case see StadtAA, Urg., 2 July 1665, Georg Baur and 6 July 1665, Barbara Niess; Michael Reidler, ex-*Stockmeister* admitted to the affair with Regina in his witness statement of 12 Sept. 1670.

28 See Carlo Ginzburg, 'Witchcraft and Popular Piety', in *idem, Myths, Emblems, Clues*, on torture, the questioning process and the collaboration between witch and interrogator. However, Ginzburg still wishes to maintain that the witch does not 'succumb entirely to the inquisitor's will' (ibid., pp. 15–16), and that it is possible to extract the genuine popular notions from the confession: I would wish to stress the dynamic of emotional collaboration between the two as the fantasy is developed through the course of the trial itself.

29 For this reason, attempts to 'explain' the phenomenon of witch fantasy physiologically, by appeal to the effects of grain fungus, mushrooms, etc. seem to me unhelpful, because they do not explain why the specific fantasies developed in the way they did, why they employed particular elements, nor why they were of interest to the authorities. See, however, G.R. Quaife, *Godly Zeal and Furious Rage: The witch in early modern Europe*, London 1987; Piero Camporesi, *Bread of Dreams: Food and fantasy in early modern Europe*, trans. David Gentilcore, Cambridge 1989.

30 See Julia Kristeva:

> The discourse of analysis proves that the *desire* for motherhood is without fail a desire to bear a child of the father (a child of her own father) who,

as a result, is often assimilated to the baby itself and thus returned to its place as *devalorized man*, summoned only to accomplish his function, which is to originate and justify reproductive desire.

(*Desire in Language. A semiotic approach to literature and art*, trans. Thomas Gora, Alice Jardine and Leon S. Roudiez, ed. Leon S. Roudiez, London 1980, p. 238)

I think this helps us to see the full measure of what Regina's psychic bargain with the Devil meant: the loss of her own potency.

31 The final and eighth interrogation thus rehearsed the outlines of the confessions she had already given, structuring and tidying them to supply the material for her condemnation. This narrative, read out publicly at her execution, was recorded in the Council's Punishment Book: StadtAA, Strafbuch des Rats, 25 Oct. 1670, pp. 353ff.

32 For a collection of recent Jungian analytic writing on the role of the father, a subject on which there is something of a dearth, see Andrew Samuels (ed.), *The Father. Contemporary Jungian perspectives*, London 1985; and see also, Bollas, *Forces of Destiny*; Joyce McDougall, *Theatres of the Body. A psychoanalytic approach to psychosomatic illness*, London 1989.

33 'Sie bitte vmb gottes barmherzigkeit, meine herrn solen ihr bald aussschaffen dass sie wider zu ihrem vatter keme', StadtAA, Urg., 1670, Regina Bartholome, (3) 14 Aug. 1670.

34 'schreit immerzu nur O du Armer Vatter, soll dein Kind nimmer zu dir komen!', StadtAA, Urg., 1670, Regina Bartholome, (4) 23 Aug. 1670.

35 'Meine herrn wollen sie doch in ihrem Vatterland absterben lassen, dass sie nur wider zu ihrem vatter keme', StadtAA, Urg., 1670, Regina Bartholome, (2) 9 Aug. 1670.

36 'wan sies ausschaffen, dan sie brechtens vmbs leben. sie wollen sie doch in ihrem Vatterland absterben lassen', StadtAA, Urg., 1670, Regina Bartholome, (1) 29 July 1670.

37 'Ach ihres Armen Vatters, soll sie nicht Mehr zu ihm kommen!', interrogation of 9 Aug. 1670; 'vnd bittet in fine vmb gottes willen ob man Ihr doch dz leben geschenkt hette, vmb Ihres alten Vatters willen', her final words under interrogation, StadtAA, Urg., 1670, Regina Bartholome, 23 Oct. 1670.

38 'Sie bitte Meine herrn woll doch an ihr thuen als Vatter, vnd sie nicht aus dem Vatterland treiben', StadtAA, Urg., 1670, Regina Bartholome, (1) 29 July 1670.

39 'sie spure niht dass es Ein gnedige Obrigkeit alhier habe, weiln man sie also ins Ellend hinaus zutreiben begehre', StadtAA, Urg., 1670, Regina Bartholome, (4) 23 Aug. 1670.

40 'Sie habe gesagt, weiln Gott nicht Mehr Jhr Vatter, so wolle sie den Teuffel zu ihrem Vatter annemen, der soll Jhr vatter sein', StadtAA, Urg., 1670, Regina Bartholome, (3) 14 Aug. 1670.

41 'Wan Jhr Meine herrn Ein schmach anthun vnd sie ausschaffen werden, so sturze sie sich in ein wasser. Sie haben ihre Muetter auch also hinaus gebracht, sie gebs ihnen auf Jhr gewissen', StadtAA, Urg., 1670, Regina Bartholome, (3) 14 Aug. 1670.

42 'dass Meine herrn sie nicht hinaus ins Ellend treiben, sonst muese sie sich ertrencken oder erhencken, vnd sage Es frey heraus sie wolle alsdan auff Meine herren sterben', StadtAA, Urg., 1670, Regina Bartholome, (2) 9 Aug. 1670.

43 See Michael MacDonald, *Mystical Bedlam. Madness, anxiety and healing in seventeenth century England*, Cambridge 1981, pp. 132ff; idem, *Sleepless Souls. Suicide in early modern England*, Oxford 1990, pp. 16–76; H. Schär, *Seelennöte*

der Unterlanen: Selbstmord, Melancholie und Religion im Alten Zürich 1500–1800, Zurich 1985.

44 See Melanie Klein, *Love, Guilt and Reparation and Other Works 1921–45*, new edn, London 1988; *idem, Envy and Gratitude and Other Works 1949–63*, new edn, London 1988; *idem, Narrative of a Child Analysis*, new edn, London 1989; *idem, The Psychoanalysis of Children*, London 1989.

45 Interestingly enough, he also changed colour, appearing first dressed in white, then in black, as if reflecting his moral fluctuation.

46 'Er habs Ja vertröst, aber dass ihr dz trösten nichts thue, Er lasse sie iezo . . . stecken. Were besser gewesen sie hette Gott im himmel zugeruffen. Gott wolle Jhr helffen überwenden', StadtAA, Urg., 1670, Regina Bartholome, 9 Sept. 1670.

47 'Er kenne nicht sagen dass Er die Tag seines lebens gespührt habe, dass der böse zu ihr kommen, allein wie Er Jezo höre so solle sie beym Pfersensteg mit ihm zuthuen gehabt haben', StadtAA, Urg., 1670, Regina Bartholome, 11 Sept. 1670.

48 StadtAA, Strafbuch des Rats, 1654–99, 13 Oct. 1696, p. 682, Anna Bohm found to be not 'integra mentis', although she did evince all sorts of evil (*bosheit*); pp. 714–15, 14 July 1699, Anna Scheifelhut was found to be suffering from *melancholica* and her tendency to curse and blaspheme was held to be aggravated by loneliness. Her relatives were admonished not to leave her alone. We seem here to have practical examples of the way in which currency of the views of witch sceptics like Johannes Weyer or Reginald Scot that witch fantasies might be the melancholy productions of old women could co-exist with the belief that there were none the less real witches. cf. MacDonald, *Mystical Bedlam*, p. 155 on melancholy and diabolic delusion.

49 On the increasingly sophisticated medical understanding of melancholy and its relation to theological understandings of witchcraft, see H.C. Erik Midelfort, 'Sin, Melancholy, Obsession: Insanity and culture in 16th century Germany', in S.L. Kaplan (ed.), *Understanding Popular Culture*, Berlin 1984. However, one theory does not rule out the other; and in this case, the medical doctors who inspected Regina decided that she was sane. On religion and melancholy see Edith Saurer, 'Religiöse Praxis und Sinnesverwirrung. Kommentare zur religiösen Melancholiediskussion', in Richard van Dülmen (ed.), *Dynamik der Tradition. Studien zur historischen Kulturforschung*, vol. 4, Frankfurt am Main 1992; on the fashion for melancholy in the sixteenth century and its relation to gentility, MacDonald, *Mystical Bedlam*, pp. 133ff., 150–60; Wolfgang Weber, 'Im Kampf mit Saturn. Zur Bedeutung der Melancholie im anthropologischen Modernisierungsprozess des 16. und 17. Jahrhunderts', *Zeitschrift für historische Forschung*, 17, 1990, pp. 155–92.

50 'vmb des schnöden gelts willen', StadtAA, Strafbuch des Rats, 1654–99, 25 Oct. 1670, p. 354.

51 I have followed the evident themes of the interrogation in concentrating on paternal themes in my exposition of the case. However, Regina also called to Mary, the Mother of God, and accused the council of having punished her mother unfairly. She does not apparently evince the same splitting processes in relation to female figures, although this may be implicit in her appeal to Mary: splitting itself is most likely to be rooted in the maternal relationship and the frustrations which lead the infant to split off the bad, unsatisfying breast from the good breast.

52 'Ob sye nit erkhennen vnd bekhennen müsse, dz lobl. gedachte Obrigkeit Jres Jungst verübten verbrechens halber, oneracht sye desswegen wol ein mehrers, vnd gahr eine offentliche bestraffung verdienth hete, darnach gegen

Jr genad eingewendet... ?', 'nit recht procedirn vnd verfahren thette', StadtAA, Urg., 1670, Regina Bartholome, (1) 29 July 1670.

53 'Woher verhaffte... abnemme, dz sye kheine gnedige obrigkheith alhier habe, vnnd in weme sye sich das zubeklagen, dz man mit Jr bisshero zu streng oder scharpff verfahren, wie sye es schon hieuor mehrmahlen wol verdienth hette?', StadtAA, Urg., 1670, Regina Bartholome, (5) 28 Aug. 1670.

54 StadtAA, Urg., 1670, Regina Bartholome, (6) 9 Sept. 1670, qu. 8.

55 'habe nicht beten kennen, aber Jezo kenne sie betten, Sie bitte Meine herrn vmb gottes willen, dass man ihr doch möchte dz leben schencken wans sein kenne': but if not, she went on to plead that the *Stockmeister* should be punished too. 'Wa man Jhr dz leben nemmen wolle, so seie es in gottes Namen, wo sie aber möchte begnedigt werden so hebe sie gott darumb vnd Jhrer Obrigkeit zu dancken', StadtAA, Urg., 1670, Regina Bartholome, (8) 23 Oct. 1670.

56 On *Trostknechte* in Augsburg, see StadtAA, Reichstadt Akten, 1082, Stadtbedienstete. Baumeisteramt. Eisenmeister (Eisenväter), Eisenknechte, Trostknechte 1540–1710: the office still existed in 1802. Payment in the late seventeenth century was 10 fl. per quarter: StadtAA, Baumeisterbücher, 1669, fo. 104 a for Johannes Miller and Ciriacus Nestelin.

57 'kom Teüffel vnd hole mich hinweg, Schlag donner vnd hagel alle die zu boden, die da sein', StadtAA, Urg., 1670, Regina Bartholome, (6) 9 Sept. 1670.

58 See Chapter 5.

59 Interestingly, the council minutes include a sketch picture of her execution: StadtAA, Ratsbuch, 1667–70, p. 838.

60 This admission dates from 9 September 1670, and it was reconfirmed in the final interrogation and included in her condemnation.

61 See Stuart Clark, chapter on witchcraft and misogyny in his study of the intellectual context of the witchcraft debate: *Witchcraft in Early Modern Thought*, Oxford forthcoming 1994; and his 'The "Gendering" of Witchcraft in French Demonology: Misogyny or polarity?', *French History*, 5, 1991, pp. 426–37; and Robin Briggs, 'Women as Victims? Witches, judges and the community', *French History*, 5, 1991, pp. 438–50.

62 See, for example, Staatsbibliothek München, Handschriftenabteilung, Res. 4o Crim. 124, Samuel Valentin, *End-Urthel und Verruf... Aller derjenigen Manns- vnd Weibs-Persohnen so von Einem Hoch-Edlen und Hochweisen Rath, des HR. Reichs Freyen Stadtt Augspurg von Anno 1649 bis Anno 1759 vom Leben zum Tod condemniret...*, Augsburg, p. 11; SBM (Staatsbibliothek München) Cgm 2026, fo. 63 r; StadtAA, Malefizbuch Johann Bausch (Caminkehrer), 1755, p. 222; StadtAA, Chroniken, 27, under 25 Oct. 1670: this chronicle also mentions that her mother was held to be a witch.

63 See n. 55 above.

64 Although the council seemed agreed that Regina merited the death penalty, a vote was taken in the council as to whether her body was to be burnt or granted a burial at the gallows, and there is evidence of some debate as to whether she ought to be termed a witch. StadtAA, Urg., 1670, Regina Bartholome, slips of paper, 9 and 25 Oct. 1670.

Index